CLASSICAL PRESENCES

General Editors

Lorna Hardwick   James I. Porter

CLASSICAL PRESENCES

The texts, ideas, images, and material culture of ancient Greece and Rome have always been crucial to attempts to appropriate the past in order to authenticate the present. They underlie the mapping of change and the assertion and challenging of values and identities, old and new. Classical Presences brings the latest scholarship to bear on the contexts, theory, and practice of such use, and abuse, of the classical past.

Classics and Comics

EDITED BY

George Kovacs and C. W. Marshall

OXFORD

UNIVERSITY PRESS

2011

OXFORD
UNIVERSITY PRESS

Oxford University Press, Inc., publishes works that further
Oxford University's objective of excellence
in research, scholarship, and education.

Oxford   New York
Auckland   Cape Town   Dar es Salaam   Hong Kong   Karachi
Kuala Lumpur   Madrid   Melbourne   Mexico City   Nairobi
New Delhi   Shanghai   Taipei   Toronto

With offices in
Argentina   Austria   Brazil   Chile   Czech Republic   France   Greece
Guatemala   Hungary   Italy   Japan   Poland   Portugal   Singapore
South Korea   Switzerland   Thailand   Turkey   Ukraine   Vietnam

Published by Oxford University Press, Inc.
198 Madison Avenue, New York, New York 10016

www.oup.com

Oxford is a registered trademark of Oxford University Press

Library of Congress Cataloging-in-Publication Data
Classics and comics / edited by George Kovacs and C. W. Marshall.
p.   cm. — (Classical presences)
Includes bibliographical references and index.
ISBN 978-0-19-973418-4; 978-0-19-973419-1 (pbk.)
1. Comic books, strips, etc.—United States—History and criticism. 2. Classical literature—Influence.
I. Kovacs, George. II. Marshall, C. W., 1968–
PN6725.C57   2009
741.5'3142—dc22   2009053931

1 3 5 7 9 8 6 4 2

Printed in the United States of America
on acid-free paper

Contents

Introduction

C. W. MARSHALL AND GEORGE KOVACS

The helmeted gladiator swings his blade across the comic book cover, forcing Daredevil, "The Man Without Fear," to dive beneath the arc carved by the sword (figure 0.1). The contrasting trajectories in David Mazuchelli's image suggest opposite movements: The *gladius* overlaps the title logo and seems to leap out at the viewer; the blind hero, Daredevil, is about to enter into a shoulder roll and seems clearly outclassed by his foe. The simplicity of this cover and its evocation of Roman themes stand out. The story, "Warriors" (*Daredevil* 226, January 1986) was cowritten by Frank Miller and Denny O'Neill, both important names in American comics. Miller was to revolutionize American comics in 1986 by focusing on more adult-oriented themes, and O'Neill had introduced important mature themes to *Green Lantern/Green Arrow* and *Batman* in the 1970s. The Daredevil story should have been better than it was, then, and part of the disappointment for the aspiring classicist was that the Gladiator was not an ancient Roman at all but was Melvin Potter, a villain who owned a costume shop in New York City (and who had in fact been introduced twenty years before, in *Daredevil* 18, July 1966). A popular classical model was being used to sell a superhero comic, and even though the connection was not quite as integrated as we might have wanted, here was an intersection of the ancient world and modern comics.

Classics and comics: In this volume, we document many of the ways that the two have intersected. Like cinema, comics are a medium that developed and flourished in the twentieth century. Unlike cinema, however, comics have always languished in pejorative associations of low culture, categorized with or as pulp fiction. These implications of para- or sub-literary value stem from the medium's origins in American newspapers, where comics were printed to increase circulation among European immigrants with limited literacy in the English language. Later associations with juvenile delinquency in the popular psychiatry of the 1940s and 1950s galvanized comics' low position in public esteem. Labels such as "graphic novel" or "sequential art" have been applied in recent decades by creators and fans alike to connote a more mature medium, and yet no concrete distinction—whether in content or in form—can be made between these terms and the more traditional label, "comics." For our purposes, the popular appeal of comics, so disturbing to critics of high culture, presents an opportunity. In terms of the history of the reception of the ancient world, comics represent an important and underexplored corpus

FIGURE 0.1   Daredevil battles the Gladiator. *Daredevil* 226 (Marvel, Jan. 1986): "Warriors."
Cover art by David Mazzucchelli.

of material that reflects popular conceptions of antiquity. In four colors stamped on newsprint (with higher production values outside North America), comics present countless new worlds to the reader.

In the last three decades in particular, conscious literary sophistication has improved the quality of comics' narratives overall. Simultaneously, practitioners began developing theoretical approaches to comics that provided writers and artists—and their fans—with the critical vocabulary to better explain their own creative instincts. Comics also found a greater role in the public awareness as they began crossing into other media more regularly. This had always happened to some extent—Superman was on the radio in the 1940s, and Batman on television in the 1960s—but since the late 1980s Hollywood has discovered that considerable financial rewards are to be harvested from introducing comics-generated superheroes to other media.

All of this is very far from the academic study of Greece and Rome, of course. Classics is a discipline that embodies, even in its name, the high-culture associations and aspirations of Western culture. The discipline of Classics has also changed in recent decades, however, expanding its purview to include academic discussion of the uses to which antiquity has been put in more recent times. The reception of Classics (itself a refiguring of a concern for "the Classical tradition") looks at the place of Greece and Rome and at times at the idea of Greece and Rome in later cultures. However, it also recognizes that any audience for a text is a legitimate one and that our interpretation of an ancient source is itself mediated by those receptions and interpretations that have accumulated over the centuries. If any reading is an interpretation (and therefore a reinterpretation), our understanding of an ancient source will be enriched by looking at how that moment has been understood and read by others. Sometimes those readings will be poorly or mistakenly informed. That does not make them illegitimate, however. Plenty of operas and theatrical adaptations (to take examples from so-called high-culture appropriations) are undertaken without an interest in understanding how the source text originally created its meaning.

What matters is the decision to use the past to make sense of the present. Sometimes these rereadings can point to something that lies dormant in the text that has not yet been isolated. A dozen years after "Warriors," Frank Miller wrote and drew *300*, his five-part comics vision of the battle of Thermopylae. While mainstream appraisals of the story were generally positive, some Classicists balked at what were perceived to be historical inaccuracies. These certainly existed, but they matter less than the impact of a mass media presentation of this crucial event for Western history, an impact that was expanded when it became a film in 2007. Actual Spartans may not have fought with as few clothes as Miller depicts, but the resonances created with (the modern understanding of) heroic nudity, familiar from Greek (Athenian) vase painting, help create a valorization of the central events that would have been familiar to a fifth-century Greek.

Comics narratives can be articulated in terms of smaller units: panels on a page, pages in an issue, issues in a series. The serial format was especially important in the development of American comics: Readers were constantly encouraged to purchase the next issue through narrative techniques well known in other episodic media such as television dramas or eighteenth-century serialized novels. Cliffhangers, promised crossovers in which favorite characters guest-star in other titles, and macronarratives spanning multiple issues and titles are all designed to sell the next issue but also have important consequences on how readers are trained to interpret and reconstruct the narratives.

The space that exists between panels ("the gutter," as Scott McCloud has termed it) is a crucial means of creating narrative momentum. These are the grammatical units of a comics narrative, the sentences and paragraphs that articulate the overall structure. One convention in comics equates a single panel with a whole page—a splash page—to arrest the reader's progress and show something momentous. Sometimes these occur at the beginning or the end of an issue, and sometimes they even extend over two pages. The reader of *300* is struck by the frequent use of large panels that push the bounds of the page. Some of these are splash pages, some merely oversized or irregular. Speech bubbles (and thought balloons) exist within panels but sometimes escape as a line of dialogue leads the reader from one panel to another, bridging the gutter.

Reading *300* as an example of an individual artist's understanding of a defining moment of Western culture, one can see that Miller has attempted to impart an epic scope to his storytelling. Every double page in the series includes at least one panel that crosses the issue's center staplefold. Miller suggests that his story cannot be contained within the constraints of the standard comic-book size: The panels must somehow be larger than the medium itself. This particular aspect of the storytelling is lost in the collected edition of *300*, which presents each double-page spread in a long, landscape format. Collected, *300* no longer looks like a comic, and something is lost of the experience of having the fold interrupt at least one panel every time a page is turned. We're not saying that you should fold your own copy of *300* down the middle. However, it does add to the experience of reading the story to realize how Miller has experimented and innovated with the medium in order to lend a grandeur to his narrative. Nor is this the only way that reading *300* has changed. Since the war in Iraq (which began after the comic but before the film), the story of a militarily superior force invading an underarmed country with superior numbers and military technology finds resonances that overshadow the simple East-vs.-West binary that the mainstream media presented in the story after 9/11.

Even the history of comics as a medium is often articulated in terms inspired by the Classics. Fans talk of the Golden Age of comic books or of the Silver Age: periods that define in Hesiodic terms the development of the comics medium and point to key moments of its history. The Golden Age lasts from the 1930s to the 1940s. Some tie it to the debut of Superman in *Action Comics* 1 in 1938 or even earlier to the first comic books in 1933, which use the familiar shape and format still current today. Following World War II, for a variety of reasons, social pressures in the United States led to the cancellation of many superhero comics. Some historians recognize an interregnum of "Atomic Age" comics, but a new landmark is heralded with the publication of *Showcase* 4 in 1956, which introduced a new secret identity for the Flash. When Barry Allen became the Flash, assuming the mantle previously worn by Jay Garrick in the Golden Age until the title was canceled in 1949, superheroes were shown to be greater than the specific narratives that contained them. They could be universalized, rewritten, mythologized: The scope of what was possible became universal. Subsequent ages are sometimes articulated, though historians disagree about where the boundaries lie. Generally speaking, the Bronze Age includes comics in the 1970s until the work of Miller and Alan Moore in 1985–1986. This period is then followed by the Modern Age, which among other things has bestowed upon the industry a general cultural acceptance of comics in North America through the marketing of trade paperbacks (lagging behind Europe and Japan, where comics had not been so stigmatized).

Like the Hesiodic ages (*Works and Days* 109–201), the nomenclature is cluttered, and interlopers disturb patterns. Hesiod's Heroic Age (which falls between Bronze and Iron) corresponds to the time most frequently described in Greek myth. The idea that things are devolving, however, gradually getting worse, is interrupted by the Heroic Age, which improves on what has gone before, leaving the present Iron Age a crucible in which human action can determine the future. Later versions of these ages (e.g., Ovid, *Metamorphoses* 1.89–150) do not have such breaks in the metallic periodization, and this perhaps points to an earlier understanding that happens to be attested only late in the literary record. For Ovid, though, the ages are all in the past, removed from our experience of the world. In a similar way, the periodization of comics history can be done only in retrospect, and the precision of the dividing line matters less than the overall movement, which is progress despite the metallic debasement in the terminology. The outer-space and time-travel fantasies of the Silver Age have given way to careful examination of social problems that have relevance for readers of any age. And always, to some small extent, Classical antiquity is part of that conversation.

The chapters in this volume represent only the beginnings of what can be said about the interaction between the medium of comics and the Classical world. Even so, they consider a very disparate reading list. It will be a rare reader who comes to this volume having read all of the comics discussed here. It is our hope that even readers with less experience with comics will find much of value, just as comics fans will discover new levels on which to appreciate their favorites. Especially for those readers new to comics, at the end of this volume we provide a reading list of those that we feel are important points of contact with the ancient world. We also include several key works in scholarship on comics and a list of significant superhero comics, the genre that receives the most attention here. Kovacs's initial survey provides both an overview of many examples and categories that help us think about the ways comics can use Greece and Rome.

We have divided these chapters into four sections. In the first, "Seeing the Past through Sequential Art," the contributors outline some of the parameters of this intersection. At times an understanding of comics can enable a better understanding of antiquity, reversing the expected directionality of the reception process. Nisbet and Johnson demonstrate how the techniques of reading comics can be applied to ancient texts, as they provide new understandings of a papyrus fragment and a key passage in the *Iliad*. Theisen considers the nature of literary allusion and discusses how much the reader brings to the analysis of a text as he examines the Japanese manga *Apollo's Song*. Rogers shows that the techniques used by Classicists to understand how myth works are equally applicable to comics narrative, as he considers a crucial story arc in Spider-Man comics.

The remaining three sections each offer a test case for the nature of the intersection between Classics and comics. The second section, "Gods and Superheroes," continues the emphasis on superheroes, who for some readers help define the overall medium. Marshall examines how the Furies are represented in *Wonder Woman* and *The Sandman*, both comics published by DC (which with Marvel is one of the two largest publishing houses for comics in North America). Likewise, Dethloff traces the representation of Greek gods in comics from the 1930s to the 1970s. Simms then examines a 2006 vision of Ares in Marvel Comics. The section concludes with Stevens's examination of biblical imagery in the 1996 series *Kingdom Come*.

The third section, "Drawing (on) History," looks to the past. Tomasso and Fairey consider Frank Miller's use of Thermopylae in *Sin City* and *300*. Roman history is featured in the next two chapters: Strong considers the presentation of a well-known crux of Augustan biography in a single issue of *Sandman,* while Dinter surveys representations of Rome in European comics.

The final section, "The Desires of Troy," examines the centrality of the Trojan War in comics, which corresponds to the centrality it held in the popular imagination of Greece and Rome. Shanower has produced an original comic for this volume that details his process as he writes and draws his monumental re-visioning of the Trojan War, *Age of Bronze.* This is complemented by Sulprizio's examination of love and sex in *Age of Bronze.* In the final chapter Jenkins considers two European versions of the *Odyssey.*

All of these chapters make claims for the meaningful connection between comics and Classics. In offering a variety of theoretical models touching a range of texts, we risk appearing selective. In no way does this represent all that comics have to say about the ancient world. But it is a start. Our hope is that this volume will encourage other considerations of comics in the overall project of Classical Reception and that it will provide a foundation for further work. Moreover, in turn, we hope that an understanding of comics will enhance our appreciation and understanding of Greece and Rome.

A Note on References

The nature of the comics industry is such that many stories are frequently reprinted, recycled, or repackaged. The stories discussed in this volume are cited according to the first printed issue in which they appeared. Comics issues are listed in footnotes, not in the bibliography. Citations list writer (w.) and artist (a.), which usually means the penciler who drew the images but may also refer to the inker or colorist. The dates given are the cover dates: Comics issues frequently appear months ahead of these dates. Specific citations refer to page and (if applicable) to panel. Thus, "Neil Gaiman (w.) and Sam Keith (a.), *The Sandman* 2 (Vertigo, Feb. 1989) 18.3" refers to the third panel on page eighteen of the second issue of *The Sandman.* Later reprints (such as trade paperbacks, which collect multiple issues for resale) may have different page numbers. Efforts have been made to contact copyright holders. Several publishers have acknowledged that the use of a single page or panel as an academic citation constitutes fair use.

About Our Cover

Comics fans will recognize in our cover image an homage to *Action Comics* 1 (June 1938), the first appearance of Superman. This issue not only inaugurated the superhero genre, with which many of the papers in this volume are engaged, but also established the comic book, distinct from the comic strip, as a popular medium. In the original image, Superman destroys a car while several men flee. One must open the comic book to discover whether the caped man is friend or foe; his status as hero is initially ambiguous. In our image, Superman has been replaced by Heracles, one of the figures who inspired Superman's creators. Like Superman raising the car, Heracles is an ambiguous hero by both ancient and modern standards: He rids the world of threatening monsters but is himself monstrous. He sacks cities to seize pretty girls, and is victim to fits of heaven-sent madness.

The artist is George O'Connor, whose series *Olympians* began to appear after the chapters in this volume were completed (First Second Books; see the series website olympiansrule.com).

Each 80-page volume in *Olympians* is dedicated to a different Olympian god; as of this writing, the Zeus and Athena volumes have been released. We are grateful to O'Connor for our cover, which was done especially for this volume, and are pleased to be able to incorporate his vivid and dynamic artistic style in this way.

Acknowledgments

We would like to thank Mary-Kay Gamel, Barbara Gold, and Judy Hallett for their exceptional support and encouragement in the early stages of this project and particularly for supporting an Outreach panel on Classics and Comics at the 2008 American Philological Association meetings. At OUP, we are grateful to James Porter and Lorna Hardwick, series editors of Classical Presences, and to Stefan Vranka and Deirdre Brady and the anonymous reviewers, whose comments have improved many of the chapters. Our contributors have proven passionate about their subjects, yet were always willing to accept our (occasionally obsessive) suggestions. We have learned a good deal from them and have appreciated the support given by many others who were not able to contribute to this volume. Andrew McClellan proofread drafts and helped with indexing. We would also like to acknowledge the research funding offered by the H.S.S. Large Grants Program at the University of British Columbia and the Social Sciences and Humanities Research Council of Canada.

Classics and Comics

1

Comics and Classics

Establishing a Critical Frame

George Kovacs

In 1939, the adventuring caveman Alley Oop showed us that the best way to experience the ancient world is to use a time machine. In April of that year Oop, along with his girlfriend, Ooola, and Dr. Elbert Wonmug (an Einstein caricature), used a time machine to travel back to the time of the Trojan War. The writer of the long-running comic strip *Alley Oop*, V. T. Hamlin, introduced the time machine as a device to allow his characters a greater range of possible adventures, and the first place they went was Troy. Hamlin's send-up of the world of the *Iliad*, the *Odyssey*, and the *Aeneid* is clearly a loving tribute, and his work "presupposes a newspaper-reading public that is knowledgeable about Troy."[1] In subsequent decades, most of the major superheroes of American comics were making regular sojourns to ancient Rome, Pompeii, or Egypt.[2] Sometimes the ancient world would visit them.[3] In the modern academy, we do not have time machines. This is perhaps what most differentiates the classical scholar from the superhero. We also do not wear capes—most of the time.

In May of 1969 Superman was stunned to see his girlfriend, Lois Lane, gallop away, transformed into a centaur, apparently forever (figure 1.1).[4] Despite the claims of the cover image, Lois makes it out okay: Comics covers of the day were frequently and deliberately misleading in their attempt to sell comics. The cover image actually references the second story (of two) in this issue,

---

1. *Alley Oop* seems to be the first comic strip to portray the ancient world; see Levine (1994, 365–86). Levine's article on *Alley Oop* is, appropriately, one of the first studies of classics and comics. Bound volumes of *Alley Oop* are available though a number of publishers. Of interest are two volumes collected by Dragon Lady Press, *Alley Oop No. 2: Enter the Time Machine* (1987; includes Oop's *Iliad* adventures) and *No. 3: Oop vs. Hercules: Is This Homer's Odyssey?* (1988), as well as Kitchen Sink Press, *Alley Oop*, vol. 2: *The Mystery of the Sphinx* (1991).

2. An exhaustive search for stories of this type is difficult, even with electronic databases. Nevertheless, searching for famous figures from antiquity (such as Julius Caesar and Cleopatra) reveals that Superman (in both the *Superman* and *Superboy* titles), Batman, Iron Man, Dr. Strange, and the Human Torch all made such trips to the past.

3. A personal favorite is a one-page Captain America story that appeared in a number of Marvel titles in 1978, "Captain America and the Time Warp!" an advertisement sponsored by Hostess (writer and artist unknown). Captain America investigates a disturbance in Central Park to discover (presumably Julius) Caesar and his troops eating Hostess Twinkies after wandering into a time warp. As Captain America also enjoys delicious Twinkies, the two warriors are able to part friends. The earliest appearance of the ad seems to be in *Marvel Team-Up* 77 (July 1978).

4. Leo Dorfman (w.) and Curt Swan (a.), *Superman's Girl Friend, Lois Lane* 92 (May 1969).

FIGURE 1.1   Lois Lane horses around. *Superman's Girl Friend, Lois Lane* 92 (DC, May 1969): "The Unbreakable Spell!" Cover art by Curt Swan.

"The Chestnut Mare Ain't What She Used to Be!" in which Lois is turned into a superhorse by the evil wizard, Maldor, when she rebuffs his romantic advances. Lois is in fact a centaur for only a single panel as she transforms into the horse and then one more as she changes back. The story is balanced with the issue's lead tale, "The Unbreakable Spell!" in which Lois encounters Comet the Super-Horse (Supergirl's flying pet horse, making a guest appearance). In this story, Comet is briefly transformed into a human and tells Lois his own origin tale. He was himself a centaur named Biron until he fell in love with the witch Circe, a regular antagonist of Wonder Woman, who, like her model in the *Odyssey*, specializes in the transformation of humans and animals. In attempting to grant Biron a fully human form, she transforms him into a horse. Circe is unable to reverse the change and, as compensation, grants the new horse superpowers.[5] The story is hardly atypical: Images from Greco-Roman mythology and history permeate the comics medium. Sometimes the connection is casual, as with Lois Lane's new body: Centaurs, male and female, are a popular image in the Western world.[6] Sometimes the connection requires further effort on the part of the reader: Young readers may not immediately understand DC comic book sorceress Circe's connection to the *Odyssey*. These readers may appreciate her only for her magic skills (and scanty clothing), but there is nevertheless a classical paradigm functioning. Understanding that connection enriches our appreciation of the comic book. It also tells us something about the place of centaurs and Homeric witches in modern popular culture. However, deeper and more meaningful levels of engagement between the classical world and comics exist, and it is with these that this volume is concerned.

Though it is our hope that *Classics and Comics* will appeal to a range of audiences, our target demographic is the capeless classical scholar. Our engagement with comics, and that of our contributors, is specifically informed by—and seeks to develop—traditions of classical scholarship. Our intent is to help situate the modern medium of comics as literature within existing genres of world art and fiction. Our contributors bring to bear established methodologies of philology, historiography, philosophy, and archeology in order to understand comics and classics in new and meaningful ways.

With this approach, we are positioning ourselves within the rapidly increasing field of Reception studies. Scholars have opened up many new avenues of exploration as they begin tracing ways in which modern culture engages with the ancient world. Such reception-oriented scholarship has been around for a long time but until recently existed only in occasional case studies.[7] In recent years, however, studies in Reception have flourished and consolidated, with Hardwick's *Reception Studies* (2003), which serves as something of a watershed, defining and codifying this new subdiscipline. In the first decade of this millennium, works on Reception have appeared with increasing frequency and sophistication.[8] In addition to

---

5. The story is first told by Leo Dorfman (w.) and Jim Mooney (a.) "The Secret Origins of Supergirl's Super-Horse!" *Action Comics* 293 (Oct. 1962), reprinted in *Action Comics* 347 (March 1967).

6. Female centaurs were rare in ancient art and literature and likely unknown in the Archaic period but are attested by the fourth century BCE; see Gantz (1993, 146).

7. The earliest consideration of Classics and modern media that I know of is an editor's letter by B. L. Ullman for *Classical Weekly* in 1918 on the drawing power of cinema: "Moving pictures are an excellent means of showing that the Classics are not dead"; see Winkler (2001, 5–6), who quotes Ullman further.

8. In addition to Hardwick, the works of Martindale and Thomas (2006), Kallendorf (2007), and Hardwick and Stray (2008), to say nothing of the countless articles in recent years, have resulted in the coalescence of Reception studies into a recognizable and respectable (if often difficult to define) field of study.

these, studies focused on specific genres and authors have become very popular. Homer and Greek theatre have dominated the field most recently, although Virgil and Ovid are also popular subjects.[9]

The appeal of these reception-oriented studies is obvious. There is satisfaction in seeing that ancient myths, texts, history, and artifacts still have power to move contemporary audiences. There is also the chance, ordinarily unavailable to the classicist, to engage with a wide—sometimes daunting—range of contemporary responses to the works under study: background information on productions, comments by participants, responses, reviews, and commentaries (Gamel and Blondell 2005, 111–126). Of modern media, the cinema was the logical first focus for Classicists interested in popular reception. It is performance based, far reaching (often global in its scope), and diverse in its approaches, and it has long been recognized as a legitimate medium by which serious intellectual engagement with high culture can be transmitted and explored. Starting in the early 1990s,[10] much has been written on the subject, exploring, by and large, either the use of Greek myth or Roman history.[11] Comics are another natural step in this ever-increasing field.

It is our hope that other readers will find value in these studies as well. Comic book fans are more than welcome. We are pleased to acknowledge a growing overlap between these two sets of readers, a congruence that is hardly surprising. The comics fan is typically obsessive about a specific corpus of material, closely and frequently rereading it, and situating it within an ever-expanding, multimedia megatext. Classicists see where this joke is going: They, too, obsess about a comparatively small and static corpus of material, constantly rereading and reinterpreting their artifacts according to new and evolving methodologies. Among both groups, the degree of enthusiasm is frequently equated with the success or status of the fan or scholar.[12] As literature, comics frequently recall the task of classical mythographers and historians who pore over book fragments, papyrus scraps, and inscriptions in an attempt to reconstruct a consistent narrative (or at least establish the variant traditions). Dedicated readers of comics spend vast amounts of energy attempting to reconcile contradictory versions, retconned (revised) histories, and changes required by transference from one medium to another (e.g., film adaptations). See Stevens and Marshall in this volume for examples of how comics can engage with their own intertext, as well as with intertexts external to their own medium. As artwork, the interaction

9. The bibliography for these is large and particularly multilingual. On Homer, Burgess (2008) is a useful meditation. Revermann (2008) does the same for Greek drama. For bibliographies on the reception of Virgil and Ovid, see Ziolkowski and Putnam (2008) and Kennedy (2002).

10. Two notable pioneers are McDonald (1983) and MacKinnon (1986), both of whom feature the films of Michael Cacoyannis as key elements of their studies.

11. The literature is growing quickly. Some highlights include Solomon (2001), Wyke (1997), Cyrino (2005), and the series of film-specific volumes published by Blackwell on *Gladiator* (2005), *Spartacus* (2006), and *Troy* (2007), all edited by Winkler, and *Whither Quo Vadis?* (2008), by Scodel and Bettenworth.

12. The obsession of the comics fan has resulted in something of a hierarchy within comics culture, parodied most succinctly by Comic Book Guy, owner and operator of the Android's Dungeon and Baseball Card Shop on the television show *The Simpsons* (Fox Broadcasting Company, 1989–present). For a study of these power dynamics and how they have evolved, see Pustz (1999, 66–109): "The variety in this popular culture audience is important, helping to make comic book culture an important site for the study of audiences and the cultures they create around themselves and their favored texts" (66).

between text and visual element in comics is not unlike that of Greek and Roman visual art, notably vase paintings.[13]

We anticipate this volume will attract the attention of students early in their academic careers—whether or not they continue to pursue classical studies (which of course they should). Instructors have been using popular culture, particularly film, to help generate interest in the field for some time now. I have already noted the scholarly interest in the interaction of film and the Classics, and serious attention has been paid to how film might enhance the classroom experience (Clauss 1996; McDonald 2002). By their very nature, mass media provide the most widespread and effective means of disseminating knowledge and culture. Whether or not these media are having a detrimental effect on society has long been a subject of debate (renewed by the swift growth of the Internet). For good or ill, however, we must acknowledge that students are most likely to have had their first exposure to the ancient world through some expression of current media.

For both editors of this volume, early exposure to the ancient world was occasioned by viewings of *The Mighty Hercules*, the Canadian animated series that, from 1963 to 1966 (and thereafter in syndication), told of the adventures of the son of Zeus. Hercules naturally gained superpowers by donning the magic ring given to him by his father (the token of power is a device common to comics and other popular media), and he traveled the land with his companions, Newton the centaur and the verbally challenged Tewt the satyr. He fought classically inspired villains and monsters (including Daedalus, though he, like the others, often deviated greatly from his classical model), saving ancient Greece repeatedly in five-minute episodes.[14] This initial mode of exposure to the Classics has become almost guaranteed with the recent spate of Hollywood blockbusters based loosely on classical material (however derivative). Numerous comics have been developed with specifically pedagogic agenda, from short public-service announcements to more sustained attempts at introducing elements of high culture to young audiences; some of these are discussed later.

Furthermore, the mass media have become a crucial element in the development of our ability to make sense of the world about us, and this development extends to our ability to understand history and literature. Students take not only their narratives from popular culture but also their understanding of how those narratives are constructed and how they operate. Children who read comic books, for example, are well trained in postmodern techniques of constructing narratives from nonlinear fragments. They swap individual issues with each other, reading them out of sequence, allowing for chronological and interpretive gaps, and are happy to accept narrative continuities that extend from one title to another, as characters are given cameos and guest spots in other titles to boost overall sales. Character typologies are also imported directly from the traditions of Hollywood and comics. As any instructor of an introductory mythology course knows, many students enter the classroom with preconceived

---

13. Marshall (2001, 59–64) examines two vases depicting the mysterious "Goose Play" using principles unique to comics (text and image, relationship of images between "panels," condensation of time in a single image) as outlined in Eisner (1985) and McCloud (1993). A shorter but equally effective use of McCloud's ideas with a more traditional classical subject can be found in Marshall (1999, 189).

14. Johnny Nash's theme song sets the tone: "Hercules! People are safe when near him! / Hercules! Only the evil fear him! / Softness in his eyes, / Iron in his thighs, / Virtue in his heart, / Fire in every part, / Of the Mighty Hercules!"

notions of the hero, which must be dismantled before true understanding of Greco-Roman myth can begin. Hercules, for example, is not Batman and does not follow his mantras: He is not concerned with righting wrongs, he has no compunctions against killing, and he is driven by his own desires and needs rather than an internalized moral compass (see Rogers in this volume, who applies to comics means of analysis typically applied to classical sources).

The reader of *Classics and Comics*, regardless of academic or literary background, will find here new integrations of methodologies and media. Because of space constraints, we have limited this volume to comic books (excluding even the closely related comic strip) and have received much encouragement from colleagues. Nonetheless, we have already received suggestions on how other modern media might be profitably analyzed against classical models and subjects. Among these are animated children's cartoons, Japanese anime, and political cartoons. These we have reserved for future volumes: *Son of Classics and Comics* and *CC*^{3}: *Gutters of Dikê*.

For those who are not yet "true believers" (Stan Lee's address to comics fans), this must be said: Comics is a medium, not a genre. This medium is defined by its formal artistic elements (the combination of words and image), not by its print format. These artistic elements must be evaluated in combination, not separately, as manifestations of either text or visual art. For many, the term *comics* invokes the comic strip found in the funny pages of the newspaper or the comic book, approximately twenty-two pages (in its popular American format) of brightly colored newsprint. It is true that most of the chapters in this volume are concerned with manifestations of the latter format, in particular focusing on Western or American comic books that present elements of antiquity. However, some of the chapters are more free ranging, looking to non-American comics or engaging comics-generated theory.

Content is another red herring, one by which comics have frequently been (mis)understood. Comics, as both art and literature, have often been derided as childish, catering to (and sometimes allegedly perverting) the desires of adolescent boys. There is certainly plenty of evidence to support this perception, but there are also many counterexamples. Wonder Woman may wear a skimpy costume, but Tintin dresses quite neatly and is generally a well-behaved boy. It was this pejorative understanding of comics that very nearly allowed psychiatrist Frederic Wertham's famous *Seduction of the Innocent* to obliterate the medium in the 1950s. Wertham convinced officials that comics constituted a fundamentally subversive medium, one that was corrupting American youth.[15] He provided selected examples of covers of horror comics, popular in postwar America (admittedly racy for young boys but still only a fraction of the available material), comics panels without context, and images of naked women he alleged the artists had hidden in order to reach readers subliminally, to demonstrate comics' "destructive influence" on the morals of America. However ill founded, the attack was pervasive and effective, and the stigma on the medium persists. The immediate result of Wertham's testimony was the Comics Code Authority (CCA), a system of self-censorship within the industry not unlike the so-called Hays Code in American cinema twenty years earlier.[16]

15. In 1953, Wertham was a star witness for the U.S. Senate Subcommittee on Juvenile Delinquency (Hajdu 2008, especially 245–73).

16. The Motion Picture Production Code was more popularly known for its creator, Will Hays. There is a long and healthy bibliography on film censorship. Doherty (2007) provides a thorough discussion keyed to the role of Joseph Breen, the first administrator responsible for enforcing the Hays Code.

The CCA forbade all but the most innocent content.[17] While certain genres suffered under the CCA, others flourished, particularly superhero and fantasy titles. Protagonists of these comics tended to favor a more innocent worldview, while their villains turned from the sinister to the absurd.[18] The creators of these new superheroes brought almost unbridled creativity to their narratives. Wertham and the CCA indirectly ushered in a new age of imaginative literature: the so-called Silver Age of comic books. A very different, long-range effect was the development of underground "comix," in which independent creators, starting in the 1960s, began producing provocative, countercultural material, often with deliberately lower production standards. A subgenre of these comix was the "autobiographical" comic (though liberties in accuracy were a standard of the genre; Hatfield 2005, 108–127), well-known decedents of which include Art Spiegelman's *Maus* and Marjane Satrapi's *Persepolis*. The influence of the CCA began to wane in the 1970s, as even the major publishing houses began engaging with more serious themes and social issues.[19] Today, only Archie Comics and DC continue to submit select titles for approval.

However, just as the written word is found in the smuttiest romance novel and the loftiest epic poem, the sequential combinations of art and text are capable of detailing any subject. Content in comics, as with most modern art forms, defines not medium but genre. To use some very broad brushstrokes, the traditional American (and British) genres are those of the superhero (usually in comic *books*) and the funnies (usually in comic *strips*), but Westerns, as well as horror and romance stories, have all enjoyed popularity at various times. In Europe and Japan, comics have evolved differently, not only employing different styles of art and production but also foregrounding different genres of comics. An album format was often favored, with greater page counts and larger print size than the American issue format. Titles ranged from the light-hearted and humorous (the best known in America are *Tintin* and *Astérix*; see later discussion on the latter) to the more adult (such as *Métal Hurlant* or *Heavy Metal*).

The medium of comics is usually seen and understood as a hybrid: It is not art since it contains text, nor can it be literature since it contains illustrations. Neither is strictly necessary to the medium, but most comics (including all those featured in this volume) are a combination of art and text.[20] Several working definitions of the medium exist, but we are little concerned

17. Virtually every book on the history of comics and comics culture mentions Wertham and the CCA, a testament to the trauma felt by the industry at the time. Hajdu (2008) provides an analysis with further bibliography. Though the CCA was an American phenomenon, Lent (1999) examines the global ramifications of Wertham's campaign.

18. Though not a comic book, the 1960s' television series *Batman*, with Adam West and Burt Ward, characterizes this era of comics: often campy plots with buffoon villains meant only for the very young. Both this series and the era of comics it emulates retain huge fan followings.

19. Two notable examples from the major publishing houses include a Spider-Man story in which Harry Osborn, the son of Spider-Man's archrival, Green Goblin, is revealed to be addicted to drugs (Stan Lee [w.] and Gil Kane [a.], *Amazing Spider-Man* 96–98 (May-July 1971), "And Now the Goblin!" "In the Grip of the Goblin!" and "The Goblin's Last Gasp!"). Later the same year, Green Arrow discovers that his ward, Roy Harper (who was also his superhero sidekick, Speedy), was addicted to heroin (Denny O'Neil [w.] and Neal Adams [a.], *Green Lantern* 85–86 (Sept., Nov. 1971), "Snowbirds Don't Fly" and "They Say It'll Kill Me . . . but They Won't Say When").

20. Popular experiments exist. *Dinosaur Comics* by Ryan North (http://www.qwantz.com), a daily online strip, uses the same six-panel images derived from clipart every day, with only the text changing. After six years, the strip remains funny. Narrative continuities develop even within the formal limits North himself sets.

with challenging the limits of the form itself. McCloud provides a full definition: "Juxtaposed pictorial and other images in deliberate sequence, intended to convey information and/or to produce an aesthetic response in the viewer" (McCloud 1993, 13). This definition deliberately omits reference to content, production means, literary schools, and artistic styles.[21] McCloud himself admits that this definition is too clunky for everyday use, but it gets the job done. Throughout this volume, we generally refer simply to "comics."[22]

The specification of sequence in the preceding definition is crucial. Comics are meant to be understood as the reader internally reassembles specific elements (images and text) in a specific order intended by the creator. Even comics without words work in this sequential way. This is to say that one *reads* a comic usually from left to right, top to bottom (though creators regularly experiment with this arrangement). Creators in the comics industry have refined a variety of symbols and images that convey specific ideas as a sort of shorthand: The comics medium has its own (iconographic) language. Straight, horizontal lines can indicate that a character is moving quickly, while wavy, vertical lines mean the character is stinky. Again, ancient vase painters provide a useful parallel. These painters developed several iconographic traditions that freed up space on the vase and allowed the painters to establish a scene or mood more economically. An altar, for example, might be enough to suggest a ritual context—no need to paint the entire temple. A low stage might synecdochically represent an entire theater production and a single *omphalos* stone might locate a scene in Delphi.

Since the inception of the comic book in the 1930s, financial concerns have driven the mainstream comics industry at least as much as the creators' talents.[23] In the early decades, creators typically did not have control over their creations—property rights were owned by the publishers.[24] The names of writers and artists were often excluded, material was frequently repacked and resold, and the works of the few recognized talents were commonly ghostwritten or farmed out to art workshops. Stories were written and recycled to accommodate the perceived public demand. Publishing houses frequently folded or rebranded for a variety of legal and financial reasons, and creative rights were sold or transferred. The inevitable result is that the early American comics industry is a labyrinth of conflicting storylines whose points of origin are difficult to trace. In recent decades, many writers and artists have taken a keen interest in this turbulent past. Roy Thomas and Kurt Busiek, for example, plunder these conflicting stories, writing against an infinitely complex intertext, often resolving contradictions by over-writing them with their own narratives: a process known in the industry as "retconning," a verb built from an abbreviation of "retroactive continuity." The major publishers now regularly produce housewide events to reboot and realign overly complicated macronarratives. Comics creators

---

21. Variant criteria exist. Kern (2006, 11, 52) emphasizes mass production as a defining characteristic, for example.

22. The terms *graphic novel* and *sequential art* are also common designations that are representative of a conscious attempt to make comics appear more serious and to divorce them more thoroughly from their perceived content (the funny pages of newspapers).

23. Hence, the cheap newsprint and four-color printing process many continue to associate with comics. Kaveny (2008, 47–49) presents a clear account of the conflicting interests in the early comics industry. A warning, however: Kaveny does not hold back and includes needless spoilers for most of the comics discussed.

24. Again, this was the American standard. In European comics, creators—especially artists—were better recognized and respected.

have also worked to reassert control over their creations. Publishing houses have developed that allow their writers and artists greater creative control or offer distribution to independent creators. Even the larger publishers, which still maintain copyright over their characters, have recognized the marketability of known talents.

The masses have always been consumers of myth, though the mode of delivery changes frequently. No philologist needs to be told of the oral culture of Homer and his fellow *aoidoi* or of how, in the fifth and fourth centuries, theater was able to reach larger and larger audiences in ever-grander venues and thus slowly supplanted epic and elegy as the primary mode by which people learned their myths in classical Athens (at least).[25] In the Roman era, Virgil and Ovid, reasserting the primacy of epic, turned myth into a literary pursuit, and their efforts have preserved Greco-Roman myth for centuries.

Subsequently, the impact of the printing press cannot be underestimated, a crucial first step toward mass literacy and mass media. By the beginning of the twentieth century, technology and education had progressed to the point that mass media truly became possible. Information could now reach very large audiences without geographical constraints. What is more, that widespread audience could read and write: Literacy was at an all-time high. Comics and film are two specifically modern mass media—neither the technology to produce them nor the audience to receive them existed before the Industrial Revolution.

Over the course of the twentieth century, comics evolved in three geographically distinct regions—the United States (and Britain), continental Europe, and Japan—with broad idiosyncratic differences in compositional techniques. Japanese comics, enormously popular in their own country, developed with very little influence from the outside world.[26] Now popularly known as manga, these comics, among which are many genres targeted at audiences of specific demographics, developed with conventions radically different from those in the other two regions (which saw creative cross-fertilization much earlier). Motion, for example, is portrayed very differently: In American comics, straight lines stream behind a character in motion, and a particularly fast subject is blurred, while in Japanese comics, the custom is to blur the background while the subject remains in focus (McCloud 1993, 112–114). The visual logic of Japanese manga is heavily influenced by the tradition of reading from right to left, and this is often mirror-reversed for English translations (Kern 2006, 253).

Manga has become increasingly popular in the West, influencing American styles and often outselling popular American titles. The influence goes both ways, and Japanese writers have been known to mine Western themes and narratives, including the ancient Mediterranean, often with startling results. One very striking example is New York–based writer Jai Sen's *The Golden Vine* (2003).[27] In one sense, this comic is a standard piece of historical fiction, hinging on a single speculation: What if Alexander the Great's army had not rebelled at the Hyphasis River? *The Golden Vine* is also a beautiful work of art, illustrated in the Japanese style with special golden ink adding an extra dimension of visual appeal. Moreover, since Alexander

---

25. This is not to say, of course, that the epic was forgotten or became unpopular, just that theater became bigger business.

26. In Japan, manga represent more than 35 percent of all published material and account for more than a quarter of all sales (Fusanosuke 2003, 3).

27. Japanese artists Seijuro Mizu, Umeka Asayuki, and Shino Yotsumoto each illustrate one of the book's three chapters.

FIGURE 1.2   A typical day for Astérix and Obélix. *Asterix the Gaul* 13.3. (Dargaud, 1961).
Art by Albert Uderzo.

eventually reaches Japan, *The Golden Vine* becomes a work of historical nonfiction within its own speculative universe. The book is, sadly, out of print, but the website for Shoto Press promises a planned trilogy, so another print run is possible.[28]

Continental Europe presents a different story. With greater respect for creators of comics than in North America, artists could be more leisurely in their creative process without being slavishly bound to a monthly schedule. Financial concerns did not so aggressively overwrite creative concerns, and comics were marketed to more mature audiences and thus generally coincided with increased production values. This is most immediately noticeable in the use of color. In the 1950s, 1960s, and 1970s, while North American comics still preferred the cheaper four-color (CMYK: cyan, magenta, yellow, key/black) printing process, European comics like Hergé's *Tintin* and Goscinny and Uderzo's *Astérix* were using much fuller color palates (McCloud 1993, 190). A more adult audience meant greater audience competence, enabling more sophisticated storytelling and broader use of language. It was in this environment that adult comics such as the monthly science-fiction/erotica magazine *Métal Hurlant* developed. Known to British and North American readers as *Heavy Metal*, this imprint gave rise to two unique adaptations of the *Odyssey*.

This is also the context in which Goscinny and Uderzo created the long-running *Astérix*, foremost among comics that draw (on) the ancient world (figure 1.2). The comic depicts the adventures of the inhabitants of a small village in Roman Gaul in 50 BC, shortly after the conquests of Julius Caesar. These Gauls are famously able to maintain their independence in the face of the Roman conquerors, thanks to a magic potion brewed by their local Druid, Panoramix (known in English as Getafix). The series, which began as a weekly feature for *Pilote* in 1959, has become one of the best-known comics in the world, thanks in part to translation into

28. The website for Shoto Press (http://www.shotopress.com) is very detailed, with notes on research and production.

many major modern languages—more than one hundred languages and dialects, including Latin and Ancient Greek. The series also blends slapstick humor and social satire, with the result that *Astérix* has a widespread appeal for both children and adults. While creators Goscinny and Uderzo (Uderzo took over writing duties after Goscinny's death in 1977) avoided serious social commentary, they frequently satirized social institutions and mapped modern national stereotypes onto the various peoples encountered by Astérix and his friends. The formulaic stories, usually sending Astérix and Obélix off to a foreign land on a quest, facilitate these encounters with distant peoples both in and out of continental Europe.[29]

As a national icon, Astérix himself can be understood as a manifestation of Vercingetorix, the chieftain who organized the Gallic resistance to Julius Caesar.[30] In the early twentieth century, Vercingetorix was adopted as a national symbol of resistance in France even though, or perhaps because, he eventually fell to Caesar. After fighting three wars against a foreign aggressor (Germany, in the Franco-Prussian War and World War I and II), France found itself in need of such symbolism (King 2001, 113). Astérix, however, is an improvement over the defeated Vercingetorix, reconfigured into a more positive and optimistic model of French resistance. Astérix and his fellow villagers successfully defying an occupying Roman force surely recalled Nazi Germany (where neoclassicism borrowed heavily from Roman imagery) among readers in post–World War II France.[31] Despite its underpinnings of national trauma, however, *Astérix* never loses its lighthearted tone. Indeed, the series' writers freely distort and even invert the imagery of occupation. King cites the climactic battle of *Astérix chez les Belges* (*Asterix in Belgium* [1979]), which, through its location at modern-day Waterloo and verbal echoes of the poetry of Hugo, re-creates the fall of Napoleon—with Caesar taking the role of Napoleon, reversing Napoleon's own self-equation with the Roman conqueror (King 2001, 113).

Disruption of the classical setting of *Astérix* is a frequent source of humor as modern-day situations, images, and figures impose themselves. However, the humor is even farther ranging, employing frequent sight gags, verbal puns, and situation comedy.[32] Egyptian language, for example, is rendered in speech balloons as hieroglyphics, often as pictorial rebuses that pun on the translation. Those who cannot properly speak Egyptian have speech balloons with poorly drawn hieroglyphics.

Astérix has outlived its status as a national icon of resistance—it is now being read by generations who understand World War II only in historical terms. As World War II passes from living memory, the experience becomes depersonalized for the descendants of those who

29. Readers of the English translations can consult http://www.asterix.openscroll.org/. This website includes panel-specific annotations for all thirty-three volumes, along with detailed notes on the geography and history of the period. The series' official site (http://www.asterix.com/) has much of value. Also useful is Kessler (1995).

30. The opening sequence of the first volume, *Astérix le Gaulois* (*Asterix the Gaul* [1961]), makes the connection explicit: In the second panel Vercingetorix is seen dropping his armor at Caesar's feet.

31. The assimilation of Roman society and Nazi Germany is a phenomenon also seen in postwar cinema, in which many Hollywood epics depict militaristic Roman aggressors suppressing a humble Christian population. See Wyke (1997) and Cyrino (2005).

32. These, of course, are the greatest danger for any literary work being read in translation. Anthea Bell and Derek Hockridge deserve a great deal of credit for their English translations, preserving the jokes where possible and inventing analogous ones where not. Bell produced a short but rich essay detailing the difficulties of translating *Astérix* for the British Council (date unknown): http://www.literarytranslation.com/workshops/asterix/.

endured it. Nevertheless, after five decades, *Astérix* remains in print in many languages and continues to introduce the ancient world to new readers (as it did in the childhoods of both volume editors). Dinter's chapter in this volume offers further instantiations of Romans in French comics.

It is the American tradition and particularly the primary American genre, the superhero comic, however, with which most of the chapters in this volume are concerned. The genre was effectively created in 1938, with the publication of *Action Comics* 1, which featured the first appearance of Superman. The history of this period of comics, dominated by Jewish immigrants against the backdrop of World War II, is now well documented (Fingeroth 2007; Kaplan 2006, 2008; Weinstein 2006). In these early days, comics were indeed pulp literature, considered lowbrow and disposable. However, there were quality contributions even in the early days of American comics. Scholars have had no difficulty finding merit in, say, the surrealist art of *Little Nemo* by Winsor McKay (Heer 2006) or Will Eisner's innovative narrative and visual techniques in *The Spirit*. Fans have been collecting their favorite issues and series for decades for reasons beyond the purely nostalgic: It is not without cause that the iconic heroes of the Justice League (for example) remain popular after so many decades. In addition, movements within the industry, such as the countercultural comix movement of the 1960s, have always ensured that comics would find new audiences and new applications. In spite of all this, for decades the perception of comics as a cheap and pulpy subliterary entertainment, limited in appeal to the adolescent male, prevailed.

The mainstream perception of comics has changed dramatically. For the past two decades in particular, the medium of comics has begun to acquire recognition as a legitimate artistic and literary form capable of producing work of merit. This process of legitimization is the direct result of two interrelated trends that began within the industry but have since gone beyond it, as this volume shows.

The first front is found in the comics themselves: Writers simply started writing more serious and more intelligent stories to appeal to a wider audience. The year 1986 was a watershed (as described in the introduction to this volume). Alan Moore's *Watchmen* and Frank Miller's *The Dark Knight Returns* were published in that year and brought the concept of the "graphic novel" to the public consciousness, though both were initially published in serial format. The phrase had already been in use but was popularized within the comics industry when it appeared on the front of the softcover edition of Will Eisner's *A Contract with God* (1978). The first collected volume of Art Spiegelman's *Maus*, the first (and currently only) comic to receive a Pulitzer Prize, was also published in 1986. *Watchmen* and *The Dark Knight Returns* are both superhero comics, and both demonstrate an awareness of their literary and artistic heritage. The superhero was "dissected, analyzed and debunked, his irrationalities held up to the light to show them for the unworkable Rube Goldberg machines they are" (Busiek 1996, 9). The commercial and critical success of these "revisionary superhero narratives" (Klock 2006, 25) rejuvenated the comics industry and brought new, mature readers seeking intelligent fare. Of the many quality comics that came out of the late eighties and early nineties, Neil Gaiman's *Sandman*, which ran as a monthly title from 1989 to 1996, is of special note both for the industry (the collection *Endless Nights* eventually made the *New York Times* bestseller list in 2003) and for this volume. *Sandman* draws heavily on the myth of various cultures, especially Greek and Norse, not only for its characters but also for its narrative patterns. Marshall's chapter in this volume analyzes Gaiman's ability to employ the intertexts of classics and comics to create new myths. Likewise, Strong, in her chapter, demonstrates how Gaiman is able to produce a new reading of a well-known crux in Roman history and biography. Moore and Miller have also been known to engage classical paradigms. Miller, in 1998–1999, wrote his account of the battle of Thermopylae, *300*, a work now well known through its movie version, which draws heavily on modern adaptations and comic-book tropes (see Fairey in this volume). Miller's interest in Thermopylae is foreshadowed in his earlier work, notably *Sin City* (see Tomasso in this volume). Moore, Miller, and Gaiman remain influential in the medium.

Concurrent to these exciting developments in comics themselves, practitioners of the art were beginning to cast a more critical eye over exactly what it was they were producing. In particular, Will Eisner, with *Comics and Sequential Art* (1985; see also Eisner 1996), and Scott McCloud, with *Understanding Comics* in 1993 (and later volumes in 2000 and 2005), dissected their medium to find out not only what makes it unique but also how it is created and how the reader interprets the material of a comic. These were far more than "how to" manuals: Eisner and McCloud explored the ways we visualize, read, and understand abstract concepts like sound and time when they are put on a printed page, as well as how text and image are synthesized into a cohesive whole. As a result, their work has repercussions far beyond the medium of comics. Both Eisner and McCloud work from within the medium, using comics not only as examples but also as part of the narrative in their argument. Scholars are now slowly beginning to come to the field from the outside, producing lengthy and often complex treatises on how comics work. These include David Carrier's *The Aesthetics of Comics* (2000) and especially Thierry Groensteen's *Système de la bande dessinée* (1999, translated as *The System of Comics* in 2007). Groensteen's work, dense and theoretical, is typical of the European tradition of scholarship on comics, which is far more academic than its American counterparts and sometimes seemingly disengaged from its subject. Nevertheless, Groensteen's contribution to our understanding of how comics operate is significant, and Johnson in this volume applies his theories of panel-to-panel interaction to a well-known classical crux: the ekphrasis of the Shield of Achilles in *Iliad* 18. Nisbet also applies comics-generated theory of the interaction of text and image to produce a new reading of a unique papyrus fragment.

The ancient world manifests in the comics medium in a wide variety of ways, and in what remains of this chapter I briefly survey three of these. I find it helpful to distinguish between (1) passing references and cosmetic borrowings; (2) appropriations and reconfigurations in which classical models are displaced from their original context; and (3) direct representations of the classical world. I do not wish this list to be prescriptive, nor do I suggest that these categories are unique to comics; they can be found in any artistic medium to varying degrees. Even the order (which is not meant to suggest a ranking of importance) could be challenged: Is a comic that creatively adapts the *Odyssey* into a new time more or less engaged with its model than one that purports to supply a more historically grounded presentation?

Most instances of classical material in comics happen at a purely cosmetic level, in which elements of classical models (for instance, names or appearances) are applied to provide some depth or added meaning to a given narrative. Lois Lane's centaur body and Captain America's encounter with Caesar represent a deployment of classically inspired motifs that make few demands on the reader—it takes little knowledge of the ancient world to know what a centaur is, and Caesar could be swapped for any number of recognizable historical figures. This practice was particularly common in the industry's infancy, when comics were intended primarily for younger audiences and still regarded as a pulp literature without artistic merit. Nevertheless, this cosmetic use of classical imagery can have greater, sustained meaning. When William Moulton Marston (as Charles Moulton) created Wonder Woman in 1940, intending a powerful and independent female hero figure, the Amazon legends of ancient Greece provided a convenient shorthand (see Dethloff in this volume for this and similar instances in early superhero comics).[33] Later writers, such as George Pérez in the 1980s and Greg Rucka in 2002, have explored Wonder Woman's Amazonian heritage more carefully and turned it into a serious, even defining, component of Wonder Woman's psychological profile.

This cosmetic use is developed further in the frequent displacement of classical models (or "transplanting"; Hardwick 2003, 9–10), in which popular story motifs, settings, and characters are appropriated to new and improbable environments (my second category). This can bring about varied results. In the 1980s, for instance, Marvel released two four-part miniseries in which Hercules, banished from Olympus by his father, Zeus, traveled among the stars.[34] Hercules' space travels contribute little to our understanding of the ancient hero (though the character remained in the Marvel Universe), and the series clearly capitalized on popular trends and opportunities. The success of *Star Wars* had audiences desperate for space adventures, and publishers scrambled to supply them. Hercules took to the stars on screen as well in 1983 (with no apparent connection to the comics).[35] As a ready-made super-powered being with no licensing fees, Hercules holds obvious appeal for a publisher. Hercules has featured as a regular character in the universes of both major comics publishers, Marvel and DC, often with more *gravitas* than he is given in these miniseries.[36] Other gods of Greco-Roman mythology have followed similar patterns. Recently Michael Avon Oeming has given thoughtful treatment to the position of Ares, often treated as a villain, in the Marvel Universe (see Simms in this volume).

For another example, the years 1948 to 1952 saw one of the oddest appropriations of a classical figure in *Venus* (Atlas Comics), a nineteen-issue series that featured the goddess of love herself (figure 1.3). In it, Venus has come to Earth in the guise of career girl Vicki Starr, working as an editor of the fictitious *Beauty* magazine. At first the comic focused on the love triangle between Venus, her besotted publisher, Whitney, and rival love interest and office mate, Della. After a few issues, however, the series takes a sharp turn into action-adventure and another turn to nearly surreal science fiction and finally, for two issues, to a horror title. By that time Venus

33. Since George Pérez in the 1980s, writers have developed this heritage more meaningfully. Stanley (2005, 143–60) traces the development of this character and the comics' engagement with her Amazonian origins.

34. *Hercules, Prince of Power* (Sept.–Dec. 1982 and March–June 1984). Both series were written and drawn by Bob Layton.

35. The film starred Lou Ferrigno, best known for playing the Incredible Hulk in the television series, which ran from 1978 to 1982. Similar influence by *Star Wars* can be seen in the 1981 Ray Harryhausen vehicle, *Clash of the Titans* (directed by Desmond Davis), where Perseus' robotic pet owl, Bubo, has the color of C-3P0 and the vocabulary of R2-D2. In *Hercules, Prince of Power*, Hercules was accompanied by a robot known as the Recorder, a comic relief sidekick in the mold of C-3P0.

36. Hercules had his own title in the DC Universe as well. *Hercules Unbound* ran for twelve bimonthly issues (Oct. 1975–Sept. 1977; various writers/artists) and featured the Greek hero on Earth in 1986 after a nuclear war. Ares stood in as the villain, and the series was integrated with DC continuity—the writers even used the series to tie up narrative loose ends from other titles.

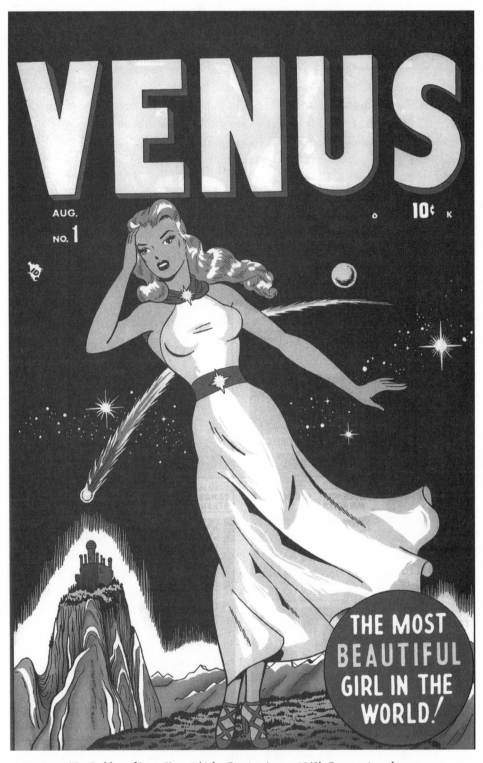

FIGURE 1.3 The Goddess of Love. *Venus* 1 (Atlas Comics, August 1948). Cover artist unknown.

had devolved into the standard plucky and useless-though-vocal-in-the-face-of-real-danger heroine (she had previously enjoyed the numerous powers one might assume an Olympian goddess to possess), and with nothing to distinguish—or sell—the magazine, the title was canceled. Atlas Comics evolved into Marvel Comics, and twenty years later Venus was integrated into the Marvel Universe when she was discovered to have become a humanities professor at UCLA.[37] She was even reunited with Whitney Hammond.[38] An iteration of the character also fights with the Agents of Atlas, though Venus has been revealed to be an impostor.[39]

Perhaps the most creative title in this vein is Eddie Campbell's *Bacchus* (figure 1.4). This was not really a series per se but rather a collection of miniseries and features that appeared in other collections and magazines. *Bacchus* made its debut in 1987 as a feature in Campbell's comic *Deadface*, published by Harrier Comics. *Deadface* was short lived (only eight issues), and the publisher folded soon after printing it, though not before publishing two dedicated *Bacchus* issues. Following the collapse of Harrier, Campbell sold *Bacchus* stories to other publishers, and a few miniseries were the result. In 1995 Campbell wrote his last *Bacchus* tale, which he self-published, and then collected the disparate *Bacchus* material into a single title. All told, Campbell produced sixty issues of *Bacchus*, which have been published in trade paperbacks, and the whole series is set to be released in two large volumes in 2011.[40]

As the title suggests, the main character is Bacchus, god of wine, but several other characters feature in their own narrative arcs as well. These include the now immortal Theseus (known as Joe Theseus) and the Eyeball Kid, grandson of Argus, the hundred-eyed monster of Greek myth. Numerous lesser and obscure deities from Greek literature skulk about in the shadows, which are plentiful in Campbell's grim tales. The story is set in the present day, when most of the gods of Olympus have perished. Those that remain, although still possessing some supernatural power, are generally older and weaker, having suffered from centuries without proper worship from humans. Bacchus himself is an old man, has only one eye, and wears a cap over the small horns on his forehead. Campbell's artwork, black ink in thin, scratchy lines, gives *Bacchus* a gritty feel (Campbell is perhaps better known as the co-creator, with writer Alan Moore, of *From Hell*, which has a similar visual style). *Bacchus* is not alone in the world, as a few of his kind survive, but he is a wreck, a shadow of his former glorious self, a decline he accepts with equanimity. Many stories, particularly shorter ones that first appeared as features in other comics, consist of Bacchus' telling his companions mythological yarns, invariably over a glass of wine. These stories are derived from Greek myth but colored with Bacchus' own insight into the motives of the gods or monsters involved. Like his counterpart in Greek mythology, Bacchus is generally affable, always prepared to share a drink, but violence is never very far away. Bacchus himself is reluctant to engage in violence, but bad things do happen to those who cross or disrespect him. Other stories involve descendants of the myths of Greece (and other cultures) jockeying for the power once held by Zeus and the Olympians.

37. Bill Everett (w./a.), *Sub-Mariner* 57 (Jan. 1973).

38. This took place after defeating Goom, emissary from Planet X. Frank Strom (w.) and Dan DeCarlo (a.), *The Marvel Valentine Special* (April 1997).

39. Apparently she was a siren, known for luring ships to their doom. It is unclear whether this is the same Venus as in earlier appearances. See Tomm Coker (w./a.), *Agents of Atlas* 1–6 (Oct. 2006–March 2007).

40. See Top Shelf Productions, http://www.topshelfcomix.com.

FIGURE 1.4 Eddie Campbell's Bacchus spins a yarn. *Bacchus: Doing the Islands with Bacchus*, "That Crafty Bastard Sisyphus," (Eddie Campbell Comics, 1997) 2.

It is not only the characters of myth and history who are appropriated to the comics medium, of course. Allusion, metaphor, and imagery allow writers to borrow narrative patterns and motifs from the ancient world, regardless of whether their texts explicitly acknowledge this engagement. We must be careful, however, not to create such comparative approaches when they do not exist and have nothing meaningful to teach us: This is a common methodological pitfall of modern comparative studies. Comics creators, however, tend to be heavy handed with allusions outside of the medium (a holdover from the perceived adolescence of the audience) and frequently signal the works against which their comics might be read. In Osamu Tezuka's manga *Apollo's Song*, for instance, the title and references to Apollo and Athena in the narrative suggest that the reader will find new meaning in the comic by reading against Greco-Roman myths and literature, even if this is not necessary for an understanding of the comic. Though not every Japanese reader will recognize them, some will perceive themes and images from the *Oresteia* permeating the story (as Thiesen argues in this volume).

This process of appropriation can be applied to entire narratives as well. The *Odyssey* is particularly susceptible to this kind of reconfiguration. Since the composition of the Homeric epics (and perhaps earlier), the *Odyssey* has consistently demonstrated that it is far more adaptable to other genres, cultures, and media in its millennia of reception.[41] The travel narrative and fantasy adventure genre, of which the *Odyssey* is the first Western example, have consistently enjoyed popular appeal, and this remains true in modern comics. Two comics by the publisher *Métal Hurlant* illustrate my point. Produced about a decade apart, and both with clear eroticism and psychedelic imagery, these two adaptations of the *Odyssey* are each examples of the Zeitgeist of their times.[42] Jenkins foregrounds these two works and their position in the reception history of Homer's epic in his chapter. The earlier adaptation, *Ulysses* (1968), converts the story into a science-fiction adventure in the style of *Barbarella*. The later *Odyssey* (1983), though taking artistic liberties, belongs to my next category since it is set in antiquity (albeit a stylistic version thereof).

One other comic worth mentioning here is the ongoing (at the time of this writing) miniseries *The Infinite Horizon*.[43] Modeled on the *Odyssey*, this comic tells a story set in the near future, in which an American army captain is stranded in the Middle East after an unrelated military incident in Taiwan destroys all communications satellites in orbit around Earth. Anarchy grips the world, and the unnamed Captain must navigate his way home to his wife in the American Catskills. Popular motifs are mapped onto this speculative future world, and the Captain encounters modern analogues of the Cyclops and other antagonists, while his wife struggles to protect the family's homestead against local thugs seeking not marriage but water, now a precious commodity. As with *Apollo's Song*, a classical exemplar is effectively reconfigured to the comics medium. The analogy is preserved but never slavishly so, and Phil Noto's beautiful artwork renders a bleak world through which the Captain travels.

Finally, there are those comics that are set in antiquity either by transcribing ancient sources into the comics medium or by using the ancient Greco-Roman world as a backdrop for

41. Hall (2008) demonstrates the global appeal of this Homeric epic.

42. George Pichard (w.) and Jacques Lob (a.), *Ulysses* (1968); Franco Navarro (w.) and José María Martín Sauri (a.), *The Odyssey* (1983).

43. Gerry Dugan (w.) and Phil Noto (a.), *The Infinite Horizon* (Dec. 2007–).

new creative fictions. To the latter category I ascribe the aforementioned story arcs of *Alley Oop*, as well as all of *The Golden Vine* and *Astérix*, which all tell tales that do not purport to convey any specific historical or literary moment but instead create new narratives within popular constructs of antiquity. Among the earliest instances of those works that adapt ancient sources are the *Classics Illustrated* versions of the *Iliad* and *Odyssey* of 1950 and 1951.[44] *Classic Comics* was begun in 1941 by Albert Kanter, a Russian immigrant to the United States, and underwent a title change to the more familiar *Classics Illustrated* in 1947. Kanter felt that comic books were drawing children away from what he considered to be serious literature. He was also aware of the financial opportunities represented by the rising popularity in comic books. Thus, the *Classics Illustrated* project was begun with two fundamentally competing goals: to make money from comics and to lure children away from them (Jones 2002, 7). Kanter began hiring writers and illustrators to produce comic book adaptations of the "classics" of world literature, starting with *The Three Musketeers*. Each volume finished with an afterword that provided further information and an incentive to visit the local library. Kanter's disdain for the comics medium led to several deviations from the standard comics format of the day: The comics were much longer than the regular superhero fare, cost more, and eventually featured painted covers to make them more closely resemble published novels. The title change, from *Classic Comics* to *Classics Illustrated*, was a deliberate attempt to distance the series from other comic books (Sawyer 1987, 5). The focus was on the literary element, with the art subordinate. Scripts were ghostwritten, with writing credit attributed to the original authors; the house style demanded realistic art with little variation in panel arrangement (Versaci 2007, 187). The result was a comic book not without merits but relatively bland in the final presentation. The ancient Mediterranean did not make an appearance until issue 35 and even then not from a classical source but as an adaptation of Bulwer-Lytton's *Last Days of Pompeii*.[45] Nonetheless, *Classics Illustrated* went on to produce, in addition to the Homeric epics, comics adaptations of Shakespeare's *Julius Caesar*, Caesar's own memoirs, and a biography of Cleopatra.[46] The series has changed ownership several times over the decades, and these comics have frequently been repackaged and reprinted.

In a similar vein are versions of the Homeric epics by Marvel Comics, who produced the *Iliad* and the *Odyssey* in 2008–2009, and just before this volume went to press, a summary of the Epic Cycle in five issues. Though pedagogical claims may be employed to sell these comics (they are marketed under the new *Marvel Illustrated* imprint, an obvious reference to the lofty goals of *Classics Illustrated*), there is little of real worth inasmuch as the epic narratives are carelessly grafted onto the tropes (and physiques) of superhero comics. The writing, by comics veteran Roy Thomas, is slavish to the original, and the pacing required for an eight-issue run

44. Homer (w.) and Alex Blum (a.), *Classics Illustrated* 77 (Nov. 1950), "The Iliad," and Homer (w.) and Harley Griffiths (a.), *Classics Illustrated* 81 (March 1951), "The Odyssey." On its cover, issue 77 promises a biography of the author: the Homeric question answered at last.

45. Edward Bulwer-Lytton (w.) and Jack Kirby (a.), *Classics Illustrated* 35 (March 1947), "The Last Days of Pompeii."

46. William Shakespeare (w.) and Harry Adler (a.), *Classics Illustrated* 68 (Feb. 1950), "Julius Caesar"; Julius Caesar (w.) and Joe Orlando (a.), *Classics Illustrated* 130 (Jan. 1956), "Caesar's Conquests"; Sir Henry Rider Haggard (w.) and Norman Nodel (a.), *Classics Illustrated* 161 (March 1961), "Cleopatra." In 2007 Jack Lake Productions released a new volume, Virgil (w.) and Reed Crandall (a.), *Classics Illustrated* 170, "The Aeneid."

means transitions are rarely properly signaled. Thomas's use of pseudo-Shakespearean English will also alienate some readers.

Of more merit is Shanower's *Age of Bronze*, begun in 1998. Expected to take many years, Shanower's project, published independently through Image, ambitiously seeks to retell the entire story of the Trojan War, reconciling variant traditions of classical material. *Age of Bronze* draws on ancient and modern material and aspires to historical and literary accuracy whenever possible. Shanower's work is more than compilation, and it has a clear interpretive agenda, marked most obviously in the rationalization of the supernatural. Though originally published in issue format, the series is available in trade paperbacks, which include thorough bibliographies and genealogies, giving *Age of Bronze* a strong didactic value. Shanower himself is a contributor to this volume and provides a creator's perspective on adapting antiquity. Also in this volume, Sulprizio comments on specific concerns of Shanower's narrative, notably his foregrounding of erotic subplots to generate a tale beyond the fighting, which would normally dominate the comics format.

Also in a didactic mode is Larry Gonick's *Cartoon History of the Universe*. This is a wide-ranging and humorous survey of human history (only the first issue is truly dedicated to the history of the universe).[47] Gonick dedicates individual issues to the ancient Greeks and Romans. Issue 5 presents Bronze Age and Archaic Greek myth and legend; issue 6 covers the Persian Wars; and issue 7 features classical Athens from the end of the Persian Wars to the campaign of Alexander the Great. Issues 11–13 present, respectively, the foundation of Rome to the creation of the Roman Empire, the rise of Christianity, and the fall of the Roman Empire. The series began in the 1970s, and Gonick produced nineteen oversized issues at fifty pages each. Gonick continues to produce cartoon manuals and histories under the *Cartoon History* title.[48] His work is well researched, if a bit fast paced, and there is much in these pages to engage new readers. The story is narrated by an Einstein-like history professor with a time machine, ostensibly Gonick's own authorial voice. The professor is clear about his sources, both primary and secondary, includes amusing and/or gory historical anecdotes to liven up the story, and humorously caricatures major historical figures.

Action Philosophers! by Fred Van Lente (writer) and Ryan Dunlavey (artist), was released in nine issues from 2005–2007 and takes a similar pedagogical approach. This comic presents the philosophies and theories of influential thinkers in human history, from the pre-Socratics to Joseph Campbell. Rather than take a chronological approach, each of the nine issues in this series groups together, somewhat esoterically, three philosophers. To each is dedicated about a third of the issue, forming pamphlet-style accounts. Plato is the first feature of issue 1, along with Bodhidharma and Nietzsche. Van Lente and Dunlavey, taking their cue from Diogenes Laertius' anecdote (*Lives of the Philosophers* 3.4) that Plato was named for his broad shoulders and wrestling prowess, present the philosopher in the mask of a Mexican *luchador* (wrestler). Van Lente's writing presents the philosophies of these thinkers in a clear and understandable

47. The nineteen issues of *The Cartoon History of the Universe* are available in trade paperbacks, comprising three volumes with full bibliographies. These are available as Larry Gonick, *The Cartoon History of the Universe: From the Big Bang to Alexander the Great*, vols. 1–7 (New York: Broadway Books, 1990), *From the Springtime of China to the Fall of Rome*, vols. 8–13 (1994), and *From the Rise of Arabia to the Renaissance*, vols. 14–19 (2001).

48. Gonick now alters the title to reflect content more accurately (e.g., *The Cartoon History of the Modern World*; *The Cartoon Guide to Physics*).

FIGURE 1.5 **Hera inhabits Io's cow body in** *Epicurus the Sage* **"The Many Loves of Zeus" (Piranha Press, 1991) and gives new meaning to her Homeric epithet. Art by Sam Keith.**

style and is juxtaposed against Dunlavey's playful art style, which often employs modern images to complement the text. As Van Lente explains the analogy of Plato's cave, for instance, Dunlavey depicts teenagers in a modern cinema. The ancient world is not the primary concern of *Action Philosophers!*, but it is well represented. In addition to Plato, Augustine appears in the second issue, while the seventh issue is dedicated to Greek philosophy, featuring the pre-Socratics, Aristotle, and Epictetus. Diogenes the Cynic also makes an appearance in issue 9's "lightning round."

Action Philosophers! was not the first comics series to engage the ancient philosophers in such a humorous way. In 1989 and 1991 William Messner-Loebs (writer) and Sam Keith (artist) released two oversized volumes (each forty-eight pages) titled *Epicurus the Sage*, an anachronistic mash-up of the philosophy, mythology, and politics of ancient Greece. Unlike *The Cartoon History* or *Action Philosophers! Epicurus the Sage* does not have a didactic agenda but makes greater demands on its audience, rewarding the informed reader. Epicurus is presented as one of the few sane and decent philosophers of the ancient world—most of the philosophers portrayed in the comic deserve the series' catch phrase, "Gawdamm Philosophers!" The comic relates the adventures of Epicurus, his best friend Plato, and a young Alexander III (after his tutor, Aristotle, abandons him). In the first issue, the trio is forced to investigate the mysterious disappearance of Persephone. In the second, Hera complains to our hero about the loves of Zeus, appearing in a form that gives new meaning to her Homeric "cow-eyed" epithet (figure 1.5). Along the way, Epicurus encounters a *Who's Who* of ancient philosophical and political thought, meeting Hesiod, Aesop, Alcibiades, Socrates, and many others. The two volumes were later bound together, along with a short black-and-white story that had originally appeared as the lead feature in *Fast Forward* 3 (1993, Piranha Press), in which Homer tells our heroes the story of Phaethon, as well as a new story for the collected edition, in which the heroes stumble into a very surreal account of the Trojan War.

However, whether a comic employs cosmetic borrowings to augment a narrative, appropriates a classical model to a different time or place, or realizes the ancient world as a setting for its story, the examples surveyed in this chapter all have certain things in common. They are all fun to read, for one thing. All depend, to some extent, on the audience's ability to recall and imagine antiquity or some small piece of it even as they redefine how that process of recollection and imagination works. Analyzing these demands on the reader tells us something about the place of antiquity in the popular consciousness of our own cultural contexts. At their best, comics supply a new way of understanding the Greco-Roman culture and history that classicists have been engaged with for centuries. Reception studies are growing rapidly as a subdiscipline of Classics right now, and these comics, both text and art, show the reason for their popular appeal. Comics can bring the Classics to life even if they sometimes do it on cheap newsprint in black and white. We classicists may not have capes or time machines, but the imaginative literature of the comics medium and the unique creative processes by which that imagination is realized supply us with new critical tools that are almost as powerful.[49]

49. I would like to acknowledge the help of my coeditor, C. W. Marshall, whose insights into both Classics and comics helped me articulate many of the ideas in this chapter. My debt to him is incalculable.

PART ONE

Seeing the Past through Sequential Art

2

An Ancient Greek Graphic Novel

P.Oxy. XXII 2331

Gideon Nisbet

Would we even know what irony is if it were not for comic books?
Scott Bukatman, *Matters of Gravity*

The "Heracles papyrus," *P.Oxy.* XXII 2331, is an isolated fragment of an ancient Greek book-roll, 23.5 cm (9.25 inches) wide by 10.6 cm (4.17 inches) tall—roughly the size of a man's hand. Excavated in the last years of the nineteenth century by Bernard Grenfell and Arthur Hunt from the trash piles of the ancient city of Oxyrhynchus in Greco-Roman Egypt, it was first published in 1954 in the series *Oxyrhynchus Papyri*. The style of handwriting suggests that this particular copy was produced in the mid-third century CE. In theory the original narrative could have been composed at any time prior to this, but the appearance of some highly unusual bilingual features may suggest a date in the Roman era.

The surviving text consists of one complete and two partial columns of verse in the characteristically Hellenistic meter of Phalaecians, better known by their Roman name, hendecasyllables. The text takes the form of a dialogue: An unidentified interlocutor addresses the famous hero Heracles and persuades him to tell the story of his Labors. Heracles obliges, beginning with the slaying of the Nemean lion. Successive editors of the text have reasonably assumed that the lost work of which the Oxyrhynchus fragment is a part took the twelve Labors as its overall theme. Since the iconic Labor of the Nemean lion is traditionally the first of the twelve, the surviving fragment likely comes from very near the beginning of the lost work of which it is a part; the fragmentary line ends to the left might well be from the very first column of text.

The survival of a complete column along with its original upper margin confirms that this bookroll was unusually short in height, placing it within the rare category of find known as a "pocket roll." Accordingly, the surviving column and the partial column to its right are disproportionately wide for their height. Columns of text in a papyrus roll are typically tall and thin; these are short and wide.[1]

---

1. For a fairly close parallel, cf. the pocket roll *P.Oxy.* LIV 3723 (elegy on gods and their *eromenoi*).

By far the most striking feature of the papyrus, however, is its inclusion of *grulloi*: humorous cartoons, drawn in black ink and with fading traces of original coloration in green and two shades of yellow. In the verse text, the interlocutor explicitly states that he will respond critically to each of the Labors by means of "a mighty *grullos*." The way in which he takes the reader into his confidence is probably intended to remind the ancient reader of the beginning of a typical third-century BCE New Comedy—this is the kind of opening address to the audience that we would expect from one of the wily slaves of Plautus or Menander. The self-characterization of the first speaker as a scapegoat gives additional encouragement to read the text in comic terms, as does the choice of Phalaecians, a meter associated with nonserious verse, including fragments of the fifth-century BCE Old Comic poet Cratinus.

For the modern philologist, the interlocutor's comedic self-referentiality also conveniently clarifies the sense of a term previously known to us from ancient literary sources, including the art criticism of the Latin author Pliny.[2] In Greek, the term *grullos* carries semantic overtones of vulgarity, which fit well with Pliny's "humorous figures of risible appearance." Cognate forms are used, perhaps onomatopoetically, of the grunting of pigs, and *grullos* itself is a colloquial term for a pig, "porker." A *grullos* can also be the performer of a *grullismos*, a presumably derogatory Greek name for an unknown Egyptian dance.[3] As cartoons, Pliny tells us that *grulloi* were used to illustrate scenes from comedy. They were also meant to be funny to look at, in and of themselves: A Christian author describes them as laughter inducing, *katagelastoi*.[4]

It is very unusual to find illustrations of any type in the extant literary papyri, and *grulloi* in particular are extraordinarily rare—this is still in fact the only unambiguous instance.[5] When the Heracles papyrus was first published, only one remotely relevant parallel to its style of illustration was known: the "Paris Romance," an unedited fragment initially described as part of an ancient illustrated novel. This was also the only available parallel for the text-and-pictures format of the Heracles papyrus.[6] The inclusion of illustrations made *P.Oxy.* 2331 a significant find; it was immediately hailed as confirming existing theories about the ancient illustrated book.

A photograph of the papyrus is presented as figure 2.1. I present a provisional translation as a basis for discussion: This is based upon the revised text presented by Maas and does not attempt to render the traces of line ends, which are all that remain of column 1.[7]

2. Pliny, *NH* 35.114. On *grulloi*, see exhaustively Hammerstaedt (2000). The term is used in a modified sense by the scholarship on medieval book illustration. See, for example, Camille (1992).

3. Diana Spencer suggests to me the translation "sand-dance," a modern equivalent in Orientalizing caricature of Egyptian dance.

4. John Chrysostom, cited in Hammerstaedt (2000, 33).

5. On illustration on papyrus generally, see Whitehouse 2007. Indicative of the rarity value of the ancient illustrated book are the excitement and controversy surrounding the so-called Artemidorus papyrus; see the first edition by Gallazzi, Kramer, and Settis (2008) and, polemically, Canfora (2008).

6. *P.Köln* 179 (second-century CE) appears to contain *grulloi*, but the images and text are in poor condition. Byzantine *grulloi* are investigated by Hammerstaedt (2000). For an instance of a related representational idiom see the tiny fragment PSI XIII 1370, first published in *Papiri della Società Italiana* 13 (1953): 239–240, and revisited in *Papiri dell'Istituto Papirologico "G. Vitelli"* 1 (1988: 36–37).

7. See Maas (1958, 171–172).

FIGURE 2.1 P.Oxy. 2331, the "Heracles Papyrus."

Column 2

[interlocutor:]   ... disputing about the Labors by means of a mighty cartoon at every turn, me, the scapegoat,—But here he comes himself! Coming on down from on high! A man of blood but not one for words, a Superman but a yokel ... the thrice-moonèd one is (approaching) me! ... I'm not the sort of coward who runs away, oh no, I'll strike up a conversation: "Hey! Child of Olympian Zeus, speak to me! Tell me: Tell me what kind of Labor it was you did first!"

[Herakles:]   Yes, learn from me which Labor I did first:
[first picture]

Column 3

[Herakles]   First I (laid hold of?) the Lion of Nemea, killed it with these mighty hands of mine.
[second picture]
I caught this slippery customer, this lion, on the ground; I (effortlessly?) choked the life out of it and laid it out dead.
[third picture]

Publishing the Heracles Papyrus

In 1954 C. H. Roberts's *editio princeps* appeared in a volume of *Oxyrhynchus Papyri*, coedited with Edgar Lobel. Roberts presents an edition of the text and a short apparatus. This is a minimal publication by papyrological standards today, and the decision not to offer a translation was clearly a value judgment even at the time, but Roberts's brevity is in keeping with the brisk procedures of the series in its earlier phases.[8] One line of the text is missing, which in a text of thirteen lines is a significant error; it is impossible to say at what stage the information was lost, but evidently Lobel and Roberts failed to pick it up in proof.[9] The editors also included a tinted monochrome photograph of the papyrus among the handful of plates at the back of the volume.

Roberts was an expert papyrologist but had never seen anything like this. Accordingly, he sought advice from the recognized academic authority: Kurt Weitzmann was not a classicist, but his *Illustrations in Roll and Codex* (1947) was the first serious treatment of the ancient illustrated book. Doubtless to Roberts's relief, Weitzmann responded with a detailed letter, which

---

8. A modern *editio princeps* typically presents two texts in parallel: a diplomatic transcript (an accurate, noninterpretive record of the ink traces visible on the papyrus), and an edition interpreting those traces, supplementing them with surmises about missing letters and words, and adding spacing and punctuation. Detailed textual notes follow. If the text is not previously known, it is translated into English. My personal impression as a reader of the series is that contributors to *Oxyrhynchus Papyri* in the 1950s translated only new texts to which they attributed documentary or literary value. Roberts translates the papyrus preceding *P.Oxy.* XXII 2331, a rare find from Ctesias' *Persica* ("History of Persia"), but does not translate the papyrus following it, which is from a Greek version of the subliterary Oracle of the Potter.

9. A preface by Eric Turner acknowledges the "extra effort" of OUP staff to get the book out by year's end in order to meet the terms of a UNESCO grant; the error is probably attributable to the rush.

Roberts (presumably with his consent) reproduced verbatim as the lion's share of the *editio princeps*. Weitzmann's letter acclaims the Heracles papyrus as welcome proof of his own views on the role of illustration in the ancient book, immediately doubling his evidence base. The argument of *Illustrations in Roll and Codex* had rested solely on the Paris Romance—a very slender basis for a grand theory, especially as the text of the Paris papyrus had not yet been made available through publication (and remains unpublished to this day).

Weitzmann's views may be summarized as follows. In classical antiquity, book illustration was reserved for well-loved literary classics—popular canon texts such as the *Iliad*. The illustrated versions of these were run off in volume for something approaching a mass readership, much wider than the readership that classicists and ancient historians would normally associate with ancient literary texts.[10] The pictures in these books were illustrations pure and simple, "physically bound to the text" and inserted "whenever the text required a picture" to clarify the sense of difficult or ambiguous passages: They showed only what the text said, and the meaning of the immediately adjacent text determined every aspect of their content (Weitzmann 1959, 1). The text, then, was primary. The pictures explained it to children and other less informed readers and are in turn explained *by* it in the interpretation of the modern expert scholar.

There are basic and obvious objections to this theory of the ancient illustrated book. With the exception of the Paris Romance, all of the evidence available to Weitzmann for *Illustrations in Roll and Codex* was unambiguously postclassical. Weitzmann reproduced the Paris papyrus photographically as a plate in his book, but in the absence of a published edition he was in no position to make a definite statement about its text and thus about the relation of image to text. As the years went by and the catalogue of published papyri grew ever more massive, the almost complete absence of illustrated fragments from the ancient literary canon argued increasingly strongly (albeit from silence) against Weitzmann's model of quasi-industrial production lines churning out illuminated classics. His axiom that book illustrations reflect the taste and needs of an immature or unskilled readership was in any case prima facie unlikely in an ancient context. Prior to the introduction of lithography, illustrated books had always cost more in time, materials, labor, and expertise. Illustration was conspicuous consumption; it was a supplement, promising something *more* than the text alone in fair return for the expense incurred.

As a new fragment of an ancient illustrated book, then, the Heracles papyrus must have seemed both a potential threat to Weitzmann's theory—most obviously because it is not a popular canon text—and a golden opportunity to demonstrate it in action. In his letter to Roberts, he attempts to force the new find from Oxyrhynchus into compliance with his model—to prevent illustration from turning into supplement and keep it bound to the text as a mere visual gloss. By the end of his letter, he has succeeded to his own satisfaction.[11] Along the way, though, the individual illustrations have given him moments of concern.

The first *grullos* is immediately problematic. Heracles is clearly visible at the left of the image, but the subject to his right is harder to identify. This is partly because of damage to the papyrus: A band of fibers has been lost from across this part of the image, leaving an inconvenient horizontal gap. From its position in the text, Weitzmann reasonably expects the image to

---

10. Weitzmann (1977, 9), extrapolating wildly from a single ambiguous reference in Pliny (*NH* 35.2.11)—an obviously problematic view given the expense of ancient books and low rates of literacy (Harris 1989, 13–20, 225).

11. In his own words, "fully vindicated" (Weitzmann in Roberts 1954, 87).

depict a scene from Heracles' first canonical Labor, the killing of the Nemean lion—as, evidently, do the second and third *grulloi* in the next column. But the lion is nowhere to be seen:

> The first scene is more difficult to explain [than the others]. Since the preceding text mentions the πρῶτος ἄθλος [first Labor] we can rightly surmise that the nude figure is once more Heracles and that the object raised in his hands may therefore be the club, although it admittedly looks more like a staff.... If we are not mistaken, the right half of the first miniature consists essentially of a ragged ground line and—above the missing fibres—of what looks like two hillocks.... Both of our two best literary sources for the labours of Heracles stress the fact that the adventure with the Nemean lion took place in a mountainous region. According to Apollodorus (*Bibl.* iv II 3–4) the lion retreated into a cave, according to Diodorus Siculus (II V I) into a cleft... the Diodorus text would fit the situation better, as there seems to be, indeed, a cleft between two mountain peaks.[12]

The surrounding text may not require a picture—or certainly not *this* picture—but another text can be found that *might*. That is, if we allow that the picture shows "two hillocks" in the first place—the resemblance is at best slender, and neither of the other surviving *grulloi* has a background landscape. Weitzmann seems aware of how thin his credibility is stretched by this very first picture ("If we are not mistaken . . ."). Having based his major monograph on the claim that the text always determines the content of its illustrations, he now develops a fragile cumulative argument that undermines the related claim that illustrations are for idiots. The letter comes close to reevaluating them as advanced literary allusions, with a cartoon of "two hillocks" now summoning up by association the great names of Hellenistic scholarship. Earlier in the letter, he has tried another spoiling tactic to explain the lack of connection between the text and the first and third *grulloi*: There must be lost lines of text under the two pictures, which presently sit at the foot of their columns, and these lines would surely have described in words whatever it is that the pictures show. This claim, unnecessary if we allow for a complementary rather than a directly expository connection between text and images, is in fact disallowed by the material remains and the surviving text. The narrative flows smoothly from the foot of column 2 to the head of column 3, and the bottom margin is clearly intact.

The second *grullos* is initially more promising for Weitzmann's original plan; this time around, we clearly have a tawny-colored lion. Thus, "the second of the three scenes can be identified with absolute certainty." However, Weitzmann does not draw attention to an additional feature. The lion of the second *grullos* is not in contact with the ragged ground line of the image; instead, it stands on what looks like a rectilinear platform. I return to this later.

Regarding the third *grullos*, Weitzmann is not absolutely but almost certain of his identification. There is no difficulty in identifying Heracles, whose stance is identical to his pose in the second *grullos*, albeit drawn smaller to fit into the available space. (Following standard ancient practice, the copyist of the text has left gaps for the pictures to be inserted into later on, and this one needed to be a little bigger.[13]) The creature to his right occupies the same position

12. Weitzmann in Roberts (1954, 86), also the source for my citation of Weitzmann on the second and third *grulloi*.

13. The ancient technique of book illustration is usefully summarized by Kramer (2001, 116); her note 3 offers a full bibliography.

as the lion in the second *grullos*, but it is not lionlike in shape, and the color is wrong. Weitzmann interprets as follows:

> He holds in his hands what, in our opinion, is the lion skin. . . . The only disturbing point is that the object we take to be the skin is painted green; but since these drawings are very sketchy indeed, it may be presumed that the painter simply used the same colour he had rightly used for the ground line for the rest of his picture as well.

There is no lion skin in the text, so the relevant portion of the text must be missing; the lion skin is green, but that is just a painterly economy. It *must* be a lion skin *because the missing text says so.*[14] Roberts's unhappiness with this explanation is expressed implicitly in a dissenting footnote—plainly, there *is* no missing text below the first and third *grulloi*—but he generously gives Weitzmann the last word (literally so—Weitzmann's conclusion closes the discursive part of the publication: "[W]e can without exaggeration say that the Heracles papyrus is the most important illustrated literary papyrus found so far"[15]).

Unchallenged, Weitzmann goes on to reiterate this interpretation of *P.Oxy.* XXII 2331 in *Ancient Book Illumination* (1959) and, more than twenty years after his exchange with Roberts, in *Late Antique and Early Christian Book Illumination* (1977). The noncanonical illustrated text of the Heracles papyrus continues to stand as exhibit A for a rule it breaks, that is, that illustration was reserved for canon classics: "It seems mere chance that neither an illustrated *Odyssey* nor any of the other Greek epic poems has survived" (Weitzmann 1977, 13). Weitzmann ingeniously blames the loss of these books on Julius Caesar's apocryphal burning of the Library of Alexandria: Many of its seven hundred thousand scrolls "must have been illustrated, and the loss for literature and for illustration must be considered equally tragic" (Weitzmann 1977, 9). The imaginary illustrated canon goes up in smoke; the Heracles papyrus survives, not worth Caesar's time to destroy, and the discrepancies between its text and images are passed over in silence.

The ensuing scholarly discussion of the Heracles papyrus continues to gloss over the basic problems of Weitzmann's theory and to defer to his interpretative method, including most of the details of his reading of the Heracles papyrus.

After Roberts and Weitzmann

In the years following the *editio princeps*, two publications remedy its shortcomings from the point of view of the expert textual scholar. The first is a short article in *Classical Review* by Denys Page, Regius Chair of Greek at Cambridge. Page was a committed textual editor with a history of close collaboration with papyrologists, particularly through his work on early lyric.[16] Page finds no more merit in the textual content of the papyrus than did its first editor. "In style

14. "[T]he text underneath scenes 1 and 3 is lost, which surely would have cast some light on the identification" (Weitzmann in Roberts 1954, 86).

15. Roberts (1954, 86-87). Roberts implicitly undercuts Weitzmann's claim that the papyrus is genuinely literary by opting not to include a translation.

16. For a useful biographical sketch see Lloyd-Jones (1982, 295–304); on his *Medea* commentary for the Oxford Reds see the witty and incisive Henderson (2006).

and diction the lines are . . . crude," Roberts had written (Roberts 1954, 85); Page amplifies: "humdrum . . . [and] mediocre, no better than a superior nursery-rhyme." Nonetheless, he declares that his "business is with the text only" (Page 1957, 189). (As we will later see, this is not entirely accurate.)

Page's business with the text is brisk and productive. He reinstates the missing line, corrects several transcriptional errors, and offers learned comment on the "very rare" epithet τρισέληνος ("thrice-moonèd"). He also draws attention to three admittedly odd choices of adjective in the second line of column 2: κάρναρις ἄστομος . . . ἄγροικος ("a man of blood but not one for words . . . a yokel"). Building on an isolated comment by Roberts, Page asserts that all three indicate that the text as a whole is an inept translation of a Latin original. For ἄγροικος [yokel], for instance, "the writer had in mind Latin *agrestis*, which . . . may mean 'brutal,' 'savage.'" Part of this work (κάρναρις) is only tenuously attested as a Greek word and probably relates to the Latin *carnarius* [butcher]. Roberts has already suggested this connection, as well as a figurative reading—"man of blood"—based on a parallel in the Latin satirical novelist Petronius. In addition, the form of the word for "I"—a Latinesque ἐγὸ (*ego*) in place of the regular Greek ἐγώ—is certainly an extraordinary find, as Maas confirms.[17]

Page is pushing the text hard, though, and this takes him into tendentious territory, albeit from an angle rather different from Weitzmann's.[18] He emends κάρναρις into an otherwise unattested transliteration (κάρναλις) of a Latin adjective (*carnalis*, fleshly), which hardly fits the context in any case, and is hard put to explain ἄστομος [speechless] even by emendation— "I suspect a mistranslation from Latin into Greek, but cannot think of the right word, unless the writer meant ἄστομις, *effrenus* [unchecked, reckless]" (Page 1957, 190). We might speculate that, as a lifelong Hellenist, Page could well be strongly motivated to blame this "mediocre" text on half-barbaric Rome, and the presence of pictures underwrites his license to meddle. The text is already contaminated by the irruption of images, so why not assume that the Greek itself has been dirtied by an influx of Latin?

Page's account produces a convenient parallelism in which the illustrations are as "rough" as the text is "humdrum" (Page 1957, 189). Page is no art historian, but since the *grulloi* are not art, he will not be treading on anyone's toes by trying his hand at their interpretation (so much for "the text only"). Presenting his revised text, he interleaves descriptions that enshrine and amplify Weitzmann's readings. The difficult first *grullos* is now, beyond a doubt, "Heracles facing (right) a rocky or mountainous landscape"—Weitzmann's "two hillocks" have swollen into a whole mountain range. The second *grullos* is the lion, of course. In the third, the green mutant lion "looks much less comfortable; I suppose it is dead" (Page 1957, 191).

Paul Maas's textual note of the following year, explicitly responding to Page, again plies the route of the dedicated textualist tarrying with a mediocre text. Once more, the work in question lacks all literary value—"that strange document"—except as a pretext for showcasing what can be achieved with unpromising material. Maas in fact moves the game on significantly.

---

17. Page (1957, 190); Roberts (1954, 88). Maas (1958, 173): "[W]ere it not a fact I should have declared it incredible."

18. Compare the fun he has as editor-*cum*-inventor of numerical puzzles in Greek isopsephic epigram; see Page (1981, s.v. "Leonides").

He establishes that the narrative is in dialogue form (a point not drawn out explicitly by previous editors), and his identification of a previously unnoticed visual play on words uncovers a previously unsuspected level of interaction between text and images. In the penultimate line Heracles boasts of having caught a "lion, on the ground." The Greek for this, including Maas's plausible supplement to fill a gap in the papyrus, is χα[μαι] λέοντα. Read aloud as one word, this gains a second sense: "chameleon" (we should bear in mind here that Greek texts on papyrus do not include spaces between individual words in any case; readers must decide as they go along where each word begins and ends). And a chameleon is surely what the picture shows:

> The colour of the animal in the drawing . . . is green . . . as is the colour of the ground on which the group stands. The painter, then, knew that the chameleon adapts its colour to its surroundings . . . (Maas 1958, 173)

This is a major breakthrough. Text and image are now seen as interacting: The picture draws out a latent second meaning in the text that would not be evident if the text were read in isolation, and vice versa. Maas has implicitly demonstrated that Weitzmann is wrong about how text and image interact—or at least that he is not always right. Nonetheless, Maas appears unwilling to recognize the huge potential significance of his own insight:

> It seems likely that in the eleven remaining Labours the Challenger [Maas's term for the unnamed interlocutor] proved his superiority by jokes of a similar [i.e., poor] quality. Will classical scholars wish fervently that some of them should come to light? I wonder. (Maas 1958, 173)

Despite this interpretative shift, in Maas's new reading, taken as a whole, the images *are* still bound to the text—and every bit as mechanically, albeit for a different reason. A *grullos* is now inserted wherever the text requires, not a picture per se but a visual indication of a change in speaker. A minority only, such as the chameleon, additionally activate puns in the text. These aside, Maas's theory offers no advance on Weitzmann's in accounting for the pictures and perhaps even makes less satisfactory sense. Why insert pictures *at all* by this account? Why does the author or copyist not just employ the *paragraphos*, the simple horizontal line used by ancient copyists to indicate a change of speaker in drama and dialogues?

The new theory also makes nonsense of the text on which the pictures are supposed to depend. The line before the first *grullos* ("Yes, learn from me which Labor I did first") and the final couplet of the third column ("I caught this slippery customer," etc.) are both now allocated to Maas's Challenger, and this cannot be right—these lines clearly must go to Heracles.

Page and Maas, then, share certain key assumptions with Weitzmann. Although the papyrus gets attention only because of the *grulloi*, the proper task of the classical scholar is to stick to the text, at least notionally. The pictures are approached primarily through art history as vehicles for a basic descriptive (or exegetic) textual gloss: Page's "mountain range" looks back to Weitzmann's description of "two hillocks," not to the image on papyrus. Even the chameleon, brought back to life by Maas's inspired textual supplement, is dismissed as a feeble visual pun dependent on the newly clarified text.

The *Grulloi* Revisited: Mixed-Media Narrative

It is time to look at the *grulloi* with fresh eyes. I present a reading here that integrates the images as active agents in critical dialogue with the text.[19] This is precisely and explicitly the role assigned to them by the comic interlocutor, who sets about "disputing about the Labors by means of a mighty cartoon at every turn." Early editors strenuously resisted this straightforward and literal reading of the papyrus text (Page: "I can do nothing with these lines"). The hardcore philologist's sudden inability to construe some rather basic Greek reflects a conviction, shared with Weitzmann, that images are always subservient to the text they "illustrate"; that they might take a syntactic and semiotic lead is unthinkable.[20]

The first *grullos* interrupts Heracles as he starts to narrate his first Labor. Immediately after the picture, he picks up and continues with the same story. Through repetition, the hero emphasizes that his is the authoritative version—this famous and much-illustrated Labor was the first fight of his professional career as a world-saving hero ("Yes, learn from me which Labor I did first," "First I (laid hold of?) the Lion of Nemea"). However, in the meantime we have been shown something else entirely. We have not seen a lion or the hillocks-*cum*-mountains in which it might be hiding if we had studied our Diodorus. Instead we—and Heracles—have been confronted by a large, ungainly bird (figure 2.2).

Heracles and the bird face each other; the line of its neck, long and curved like a swan's, continues below the blank band of missing horizontal papyrus fibers. To the right of the image are the raised wings, with short ink strokes indicative of feathers. Iconographic parallels from vase illustrations strongly support an identification of this unexpected creature as the subject of one of Heracles' more obscure and inglorious Labors: the killing of the flesh-eating birds of Lake Stymphalus.[21] In the usual version, Heracles shoots them; the object he is holding here cannot be a bow, but Weitzmann was right to feel uneasy in identifying it as Heracles' iconic club. From the way it is held, it most resembles a fishing rod.

I suggest we read this first *grullos* as contradicting Heracles' own self-publicizing verbal narrative. Beginnings are important, and Heracles opens with a crowd-pleaser, one of his most famous and photogenic Labors. The *grullos*, though, shows us the hero's inglorious Secret Origin—a minor Labor and (with the addition of the fishing rod) an accidental one at that. Both parties appear equally surprised by the encounter: Heracles' mouth is wide open, and the bird's wings are raised in alarm.

My hypothesis, then, is that the *grulloi* function as a satirical narrative strand, in active and mutually illuminating dialogue with its partner text. The illustrations demystify Heracles' career as a hero, cutting him down to size by showing the distinctly unheroic reality behind his boasts. This fits very well with the interlocutor's comedic manifesto of "disputing about the Labors by means of a mighty cartoon at every turn."

---

19. For an initial version of this interpretation aimed at an art-historical readership see Nisbet (2002).

20. σ]θεναρ[ῳ] πάντοτε γρύλλῳ | π]ε[ρὶ] ἄθλων ἐρίσας. Maas (1958, 172) adopts E. A. Barber's conjecture of π]ε[ρὶ]. The ink traces in the preceding line suggest σ]θεναρ[ῷ], 'mighty,' as noted by Maas (1958, 172). The fit is so compelling that I can only imagine Roberts and Page discounted it as nonsensical when applied to an illustration. As a qualifying adjective it is of course peripheral to the syntax that so puzzled Page (1957, 189).

21. *LIMC* s.v. "Hercules."

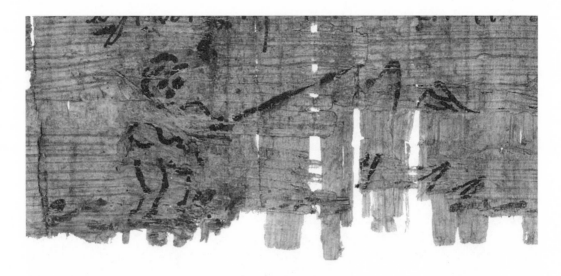

FIGURE 2.2   P.Oxy. 2331, close-up of *grullos* 1: Heracles with his fishing rod?

This hypothesis was, based on the evidence, unthinkable to the early editors and scholars. They were not looking for a bird; they knew that this picture must represent the start of the Nemean lion story *because that is what the immediately adjacent text is describing*. This knowledge determined what they allowed themselves to see, just as it prevented them from construing the Greek in its syntactically obvious sense. The model of book illustration they shared makes it unthinkable that even an explicitly comic image can "dispute" with its text.

By way of contrast, the identification of the right-hand subject as a bird strikes many nonacademic readers today as fairly obvious (at the very least, it appears much more plausible than calling it a line of hills). In particular, a comics-literate readership will recognize the deconstructive interplay between image and text as a familiar phenomenon.[22]

Ancient readers, too, might well have been predisposed to expect a humorous exposé of Heracles even without the explicit tip-off that they receive at the start of the fragment. Old and New Comedy had repeatedly satirized him as loud, self-aggrandizing, and slow witted. Here, perhaps, he blurs into the New Comedy stereotype of the *miles gloriosus*—the braggart soldier, addicted to his own tall tales of past glories.

The second *grullos* can certainly be read as supporting this interpretation. This is the only illustration that unambiguously shows Heracles wrestling a lion, just as he says he did in the immediately adjacent text. "First I (laid hold of?) the Lion of Nemea, killed it with these mighty hands of mine" (figure 2.3). The two parallel lines below the lion are a disturbing anomaly, though—the text does not suggest that it should stand on "another, higher . . . ground line" and still less on a neat stack of *two* (Weitzmann in Roberts 1954, 86). Nor is there any prospect of convenient "lost" lines of text below the *grullos*, which is in the center of the column. Anton

22. My grounds for this claim are essentially anecdotal. I solicited the views of comics creators by presenting a paper on the Heracles papyrus at two small-press conventions; I also sampled a nonspecialist audience by showing the image to miscellaneous fellow train passengers in the early 2000s.

FIGURE 2.3   P.Oxy. 2331, close-up of *grullos* 2: Heracles wrestles the "lion."

FIGURE 2.4   P.Oxy. 2331, close-up of *grullos* 3: The lion slain.

Bitel has suggested to me a reading I find very persuasive: The lion is not standing on a ground line but on a stepped base of cut stone. In other words, this is *not* a real lion—it is a statue of one, and the interlocutor has caught Heracles in the act of faking his most famous Labor.

Heracles may not be hero enough to wrestle a lion, but, as Maas observed, he can take on a punning substitute. "I caught this slippery customer, this lion, on the ground; I (effortlessly?) choked the life out of it and laid it out dead." The creature in the *grullos* (figure 2.4) closely matches descriptions of the chameleon in ancient literary sources: It is lizardlike, with a long tail, and it can change its color to match its surroundings. Here, as Maas observes, both the creature and the ground line are green. What Weitzmann took for the colorist's laziness or parsimony is in fact the clue that sends us back to the text with a more critical eye, ready to find the hidden second meaning of χα[μαι] λέοντα. The identity of Heracles' new opponent does not cast him in a heroic light: The chameleon is "harmless" and as slow moving as a tortoise.[23]

We can go even further: Heracles cannot even successfully strangle the chameleon. Aristotle tells us that the chameleon changes color by inflating itself with air—and if Heracles is really "choking the life out of it," this cannot be happening. Aristotle also tells us that when a chameleon dies, it turns yellow (Aristotle, *HA* 303a15)—the color the cartoonist chooses *not* to use in this one instance. So Heracles is not choking and has not choked his chameleon; he is just holding it. This, then, is another posed shot, just like the second *grullos*; no great monster-killing Labor is in the cards.

The Heracles Papyrus in Its Cultural Context

Is this too subtle a reading? Any answer will depend on the cultural competence we attribute to the intended readership of the Heracles papyrus. Expecting a "superior nursery-rhyme" for children or sub-literate adults, the first editors missed the chameleon entirely—it was too clever to exist in their version of the Heracles narrative. The mere fact of illustration was proof of inferiority and thereby excluded complex literary or textual effects. This version has staying power: The standard catalogue of ancient manuscripts calls the text "barbarous verses . . . (for school use?)" (Pack 1965, 1931). A 2001 account of ancient education finds in the Heracles papyrus a school primer "geared to instruct and entertain an inexperienced reader"—an "elementary text" illustrated by "simple sketches that represent different moments of the Labor," just as Weitzmann said.[24] As we have seen, however, sophisticated readings emerge if we let them—that is, if we permit ourselves to posit an élite adult readership with an advanced literary education.

The material realities of the papyrus strongly argue for just such a readership. Literary texts from Oxyrhynchus (including canon texts) are typically found on the reverse side of the roll; their copyists reused the backs of redundant documents to produce homemade books on the cheap.[25] The Heracles narrative uses expensive new papyrus cut to a special format. The text has been professionally copied in a clear and attractive book hand.

This book must also have been inordinately time consuming to manufacture. First the copyist reproduced the text, leaving appropriately sized gaps in all the right places; then the cartoonist went through, drawing in the outline figures. Each of these stages introduced many opportunities for mistakes; leaving a gap in the wrong place or inserting the wrong picture would have meant giving up and starting over with a fresh roll.[26] Clearly it was necessary to hire

---

23. For physical and behavioral descriptions see in particular Aristotle *HA* 303a15. The "harmless" chameleon: Pliny *NH* 8.122.

24. Cribiore (2001, 138), echoing Page (1957, 189) practically word for word.

25. Each roll has a definite front and back; the older terms *recto* and *verso* are still sometimes used. On the front the fibers run from left to right, guiding the pen; on the back they run from top to bottom, making it harder to write smoothly.

26. This is the origin assumed, perhaps hastily, by the editors of the Artemidorus papyrus.

a good copyist. The cartoonist was probably a skilled specialist as well: Despite the rarity of *grulloi*, a compound verb, *grullographein* [to cartoon], is attested.[27] This expertise cannot have come cheaply. Finally, the cartoonist or a second specialist added the color washes either all at once or one at a time. Three were used in this short fragment alone, and there might have been additional colors elsewhere—a single papyrus image of a leaf, recently published, contains four.[28]

This gives us a range of three and five expert processes—at a minimum—as opposed to the single and potentially do-it-yourself process of copying a nonillustrated text. Each time, the roll had to be rewound to its start before being passed on to the next specialist. The book would have taken much longer to manufacture than a nonillustrated text. Specialist materials were also required; color is relatively rare on papyrus. The economics of ancient book production are notoriously hazy, but these material concerns indicate that illustrated books of any kind must have had a core market that was willing to pay a premium.

Conclusion

> [Image and text] serve to extend, complicate, negate and consolidate each other . . .
> [Each] element can operate to undercut or question the claims of the other. Every
> message [combining text and image] sets itself up for subversion. It requires a cer-
> tain act of will to avoid it.
>
>   BLANSHARD, *"The Problems with Honouring Samos"*

What does the Oxyrhynchus Heracles papyrus tell us about ancient mixed-media narratives? Its status as an isolated instance within the collection at least indicates that this kind of book must have been relatively rare. A century's worth of literary and miscellaneous texts awaits publication in *Oxyrhynchus Papyri*, but the complete archive of crated fragments was roughly sorted by type in the early days, so it is unlikely that we will see more from that source. The Heracles papyrus ends up telling us more about modern scholarly preconceptions than ancient cartooning practices or the economics of the ancient book. The only known parallel to its illustration style is the aforementioned Paris Romance; recent examination suggests that the accompanying text is a martyrology, so the *grulloi* there are probably not offering a satirical commentary. Then again, perhaps they are; we will not know until someone publishes an edition of the text.

We cannot be confident that we know what the rest of the roll contained. Scholars have reasonably presumed that the Heracles narrative filled the book, but it need not have. Perhaps the author and illustrator moved on to other heroes, other topics; we will never know. Similarly, we can do no more than speculate on the narrative system of the Heracles narrative in its totality.

Images in adjacent columns clearly had the potential for meaningful interplay as the reader scrolled through the roll; Groensteen's remarks on the double page are of interest here,

---

27. Known from a fragment of Philodemus' *On Rhetoric* on carbonized papyrus from Herculaneum; for discussion see Hammerstaedt (2000, 35).

28. *P.Oxy.* LXXI 4839, discussed by Whitehouse (2007, 302–303).

in a format where every column makes "doubles" with those to its left and right.[29] The same scholar's model of restricted or restrained arthrology is clearly applicable. As we read the first column we glance ahead to the second; the appearance of a lion in the second *grullos* accentuates and problematizes its absence in the first. As we continue into the next column, the juxtaposition of the lion and chameleon *grulloi*, separated by a thin "gutter" of text, directs our attention to the pointed similarity of composition. This puts the two images in dialogue, with the results we have seen; in addition, the identity of Heracles' stance in these later scenes and in the first *grullos* forces us to read the spread as (part of) a dynamic semiotic system. However, the general arthrology ("braiding") of the larger narrative is lost beyond recall—if it ever existed in the first place. We can never know how these three images interacted (if at all) with images elsewhere in the roll or what importance (if any) was attached to their position within a column.

We can enjoy the Heracles papyrus as (something like) a well-crafted, double-page spread, but we can never recover the experience of reading it as part of its lost totality. Clearly, though, this type of mixed-media narrative delivered a unique experience. Its consumers may have read the text aloud (a reading practice that was at least frequent in antiquity) but simultaneously enjoyed a silent reading, personal to them alone; no wonder the interlocutor calls his images "mighty."[30]

29. Groensteen (2007, 35–39). For definitions of the terms in what follows, see Groensteen (2007, 21–22).

30. I thank the editors, the volume's anonymous reader, and Dr. Diana Spencer for their helpful criticisms and suggestions.

3

Sequential Narrative in the Shield of Achilles

Kyle P. Johnson

This chapter proposes that comics and verbal description share some fundamental principles in how they tell stories. Comics, defined by Will Eisner, are "the arrangement of pictures or images and words to narrate a story or dramatize an idea" (Eisner 1990, 5). Likewise, Murray Krieger finds sequence in ekphrasis, understood as literary description of a work of art:

> Every tendency in the verbal sequence to freeze itself into a shape . . . is inevitably accompanied by a counter-tendency for that sequence to free itself from the limited enclosure of the frozen, sensible image into an unbounded temporal flow. (Krieger 1992, 10)

Comics and ekphrasis are both pictures in sequence. This chapter explores what theoretical studies of these two means of description may offer one another. Taking Homer's Shield of Achilles (*Iliad* 18.483–608) as a test case, it offers a novel perspective on the famous ekphrasis.[1] First, the Shield is demonstrated to be constituted of many discrete and fragmentary images. In that the Shield has discrete visual segments that form narratival relationships with one another, it resembles the comics medium's primary method of organizing images in panels for storytelling purposes. Next, to further refine the analogy, Thierry Groensteen's *System of Comics* (2007) is introduced. Groensteen offers a methodology for a more precise understanding of the relationships of images to narrative in sequential art. Though most of the Shield's images are static fragments, when approached diachronically in the reading process, they create an impression of narrative action. The rest of the chapter exhibits how the three major thematic sections of the ekphrasis (the cosmology, cities, and rustic episodes) have distinctly different organizations of sequential images.

---

1. Standard works on ekphrasis include Hamon (1981), Fowler (1991), and Krieger (1992). For an accessible overview of ekphrasis in the discipline of classics, see Goldhill (2007b). Good introductions to the concerns of comics scholars are D'Angelo and Cantoni (2006) and Groensteen (2007, 12–20). The bibliography on the Shield is staggering. The most important works, in English, include Muellner (1976), Atchity (1978), Hardie (1985, 11–31), Edwards (1991, 200–232), Westbrook (1992), and Becker (1995). See Edwards (1991, 200–211) for a succinct overview of scholarship. Becker (1992) and Becker (1995, 9–22) have good summaries of the Shield's reception in, respectively, antiquity and the 18th century.

The Shield occupies the last third of book 18 of the *Iliad*, when Achilles, waiting for Hephaestus to forge new arms, is on the verge of returning to battle. This ekphrasis describes at length the god's embellishment of Achilles' shield. The narrator articulates its imagery by introducing nine sections with the adverb ἐν [in] and a verb of fabrication, such as ἔτευξ' or ποίησε [he made]. There are four thematic sections: the cosmology (483–489), cities at peace and war (490–540), rustic scenes (541–606), and Ocean (607–608). For a complete translation of the Shield's description, see the appendix to this chapter.

Significant debate arose during the 18th century concerning how the Shield conveys narrative.[2] Interpretations often boil down to two related questions: the number of images the Shield contains and how these work in relation to narrative time. To the former question, Jean Boivin de Villeneuve, in the essay "Le bouclier d'Achille, divisé par cercles et par tableaux" (Boivin de Villeneuve 1715, 262–280), imagines the Shield to contain numerous small pictures that depict fixed moments in time.[3] For example, Boivin de Villeneuve divides the city at war into three separate paintings. Gotthold Ephraim Lessing devotes the nineteenth chapter of his *Laocoon* to refuting Boivin de Villeneuve's position and writes that the Shield has only nine images in total (Lessing 1766/1853, 133–134). Moreover, Lessing holds, these images need not represent fixed moments in time or even be at all representable in the visual arts (Lessing 1766/1853, 132).[4] For an idea of how some have conceived of the Shield, see the drawings accompanying Alexander Pope's translation of the *Iliad* (1715–1720; Pope follows Boivin de Villeneuve), John Flaxman's early-nineteenth-century bronze sculpture, and figure 3.1 for a simple schematic from Willcock (1976, 210). This chapter's analogy to the comics medium shares Boivin de Villeneuve's and Lessing's interest in the number of images in the ekphrasis, in locating temporality, and in how images and temporality interact to create stories.

This chapter identifies as many discrete images as possible, arranges them in an outline, and observes how these images, like panels in a comic strip, work to form a narrative. Discrete images are determined, as explained later, according to meter, adverbs, syntax, sense, and visuality. Then each item is arranged in a tabular outline. An image lies in parataxis if it describes a scene or an object equal in status to what comes before or in hypotaxis (nested one tab) if the fragment elaborates on an antecedent object.[5] Observe this operation applied to the cosmology:

2. Some contemporary scholarship has also sought to unravel the relationship between image and narrative in the Shield. Becker (1992, 1995) and Byre (1992) argue that the narrator moves between levels of representation while describing the ostensible object. Becker holds that the narrator variously refers to his own reaction to the imagined object, the material images on the shield, Hephaestus in the act of creating, and, by dramatizing what is seen, the shield's actual referents (1995, 41–50). Byre observes a dynamic relationship between narration and description in the Shield, writing that the narrator at times describes static objects and at other times "narrates their development through time" (1992, 37). That is, some descriptions remain close to the object's images, while others drift so far from these that they become narrativized stories.

3. Alexander Pope would later follow Boivin de Villeneuve in his "Observations of the Shield of Achilles," 1715–1720, vol. 5, 104–125.

4. For more on Boivin de Villeneuve and the Shield in 18th-century France, see Moore (2000).

5. Hamon (1981) notes that rhetoricians have observed something like this breakdown. "The stylistician," he writes, "does not move from detail to detail, but rather from the particular to the general, and from the general to the particular" (11). For more on decomposition and rearrangement of text, see Barthes (1972b).

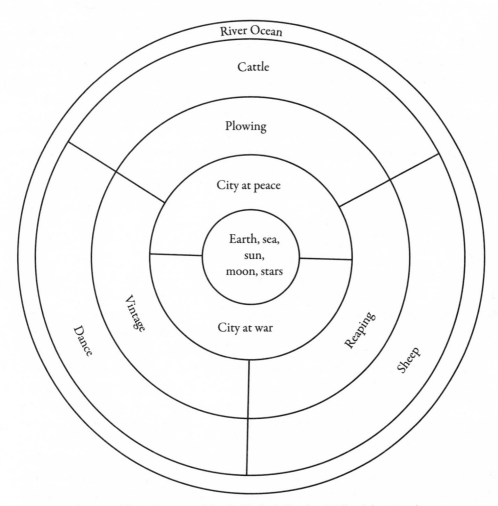

FIGURE 3.1 One possible configuration of the Shield of Achilles, from Willcock (1976, 210).

I.   (483) ἐν μὲν γαῖαν ἔτευξ᾽ |
II. ἐν δ᾽ οὐρανόν,
III. ἐν δὲ θάλασσαν, ‖
    A. (484) ἠέλιόν τ᾽ ἀκάμαντα |
    B. σελήνην τε πλήθουσαν, ‖
    C. (485) ἐν δὲ τὰ τείρεα πάντα, |
        1. τά τ᾽ οὐρανὸς ἐστεφάνωται, ‖
        2. (486) Πληϊάδας θ᾽
        3. Ὑάδας τε |
        4. τό τε σθένος Ὠρίωνος ‖
        5. (487) Ἄρκτόν θ᾽
            a. ἣν καὶ Ἄμαξαν | ἐπίκλησιν καλέουσιν, ‖
            b. (488) ἥ τ᾽ αὐτοῦ στρέφεται |

c.   καί τ' Ὠρίωνα δοκεύει, ‖

d.   (489) οἴη δ' ἄμμορός ἐστι | λοετρῶν Ὠκεανοῖο. ‖[6]

I.   (483) On it he made the earth

II.   and on it the sky

III.   and on it the sea, ‖

    A.   (484) and the untiring sun

    B.   and the full moon ‖

    C.   (485) and on it all the constellations,

        1.   and the sky is crowned by these, ‖

        2.   (486) and the Pleiades

        3.   and the Hyades

        4.   and the might of Orion ‖

        5.   (487) and Ursa Major,

            a.   which they also call by the name "Wagon," ‖

            b.   (488) and it revolves in the same place

            c.   and watches Orion ‖

            d.   (489) and she alone has no share in the baths of the Ocean. ‖

Four nested units result, being all of creation (I.–III.), objects in the sky (III.A–C.), constellations in the sky (III.C.1.–5.), and Ursa Major (or "Bear," III.C.5.a.–d.). One inconsistency must be noted, that the description of the sky follows III., the sea, and not II. This is the only instance of such irregularity in the entire Shield. Particles and meter play a central role in the description's division into discrete segments. As elsewhere in Homer, μέν [indeed] (though here untranslatable, 483) introduces a new episode, thought, or idea.[7] Correlative τε . . . τε [both . . . and] join words and phrases that are syntactically parallel and "mutually dependent."[8] Meter also works hand in hand with segmentation. Twelve of the fifteen fragments end with caesura or a line-end. In addition to particles and meter dividing the description into discrete units, segmentation corresponds to discrete visual units.

Each segment, except for the narrator's verbal comment at III.C.5.a., is itself a succinct visual image, such as of the earth, Pleiades, or Ursa Major. In the cosmology, these segments are the smallest meaningful units in terms of visuality. That is, they cannot be broken down into smaller segments and still communicate visual meaning. The segments are meaningful in and of themselves and also with respect to those that precede and follow. For example, when the Pleiades are mentioned at III.C.2., one thinks of the constellation. The Pleiades, though, are part of a list elaborating constellations in general (III.C.). When considered together, linguistic and

---

6. | marks caesura and ‖ line ending. Text from Allen (1931). All translations are my own.

7. On μέν establishing discourse in Homer, see Bakker (1997, 80–85), Denniston (1959, 359–64, §I. A. [1]–[9]), Cooper (2002, 3039, §2.29.44.4 [A]), and Monro (1891, 313–315, §345).

8. Monro (1891, 301, §331). See also Cooper (2002, 3101–3102, §2.29.70.1[A]). In Homer, τε . . . τε connects words or phrases, rarely clauses; see Denniston (1959, 503, §I.[2]), while at III.A.–C. (484–485) and III.C.5.b.–d. (488–489) we find τε . . . τε . . . δέ, which operates the same as τε . . . τε . . . τε (Cooper 2002, 3101–3103, §2.69.70.1[D]). Denniston (1959, 513, §I.[6]) differs, explaining δέ as adding contrast. For a general critique of this latter view of δέ as a particle of contrast in Homer, see Bakker (1997, 62–71). Here (and in the description of Ursa Major, lines 487–489) τε . . . τε . . . δέ mark mutually dependent image fragments.

metrical segmentation clearly work in unison for the creation of discrete visual segments. This outline and brief analysis of the cosmology reveal three things: First, the cosmology comprises visual segments; second, these segments are discrete and meaningful in and of themselves; third, they lie in relation to one another. Discrete visual units, from which the Shield is constructed, are remarkably similar to comics panels, for comics panels, too, are discrete and relational and form narrative through sequentiality.

Turning, therefore, to comics is only natural for insights into how to come to terms with segmentation in the Shield. Groensteen's *System of Comics* (2007) develops an interpretive framework for understanding narrative in comics and is rooted in several principles. First, the smallest significant unit, thinking semiotically, is the panel and not individual elements of the drawing within (Groensteen 2007, 3–7). Second, he argues that comics are in essence a visual (not verbal) medium (7–12). Third, narrative meaning arises from the relationships of panels to one another (21–23). From this latter principle in particular, *The System of Comics* becomes a study of "joints" between panels. Groensteen terms the study of such joints "arthrology" (Greek: *arthron* = "joint of a limb").[9]

Groensteen posits three conceptual levels to comics. First is the "spatio-topical system," which accounts for things like the physical shape of the page, the shape and size of frames, and the organization of frames on a page. For the purposes of this chapter, the most pertinent aspects of the spatio-topical system are the six functions of the frame, which explain how frames inform the meaning of their contents (Groensteen 2007, 37–57).[10]

The *function of closure* contains an image, enclosing "a fragment of space-time belonging to the diegesis, to signify the coherence" of a drawing (Groensteen 2007, 40). The *separative function* accounts for how a self-contained image is distinct and independent. The frame's *rhythmic function* advances narrative but also delays it. The *structuring function* pertains to how a frame "is a determinant element of the composition of the image" (46). A frame's *expressive function* conveys information about the meaning of an image inside a panel. Last is the *readerly function*, which calls one to look at the image. These six functions structure the composition of comics, as well as readers' interpretation.

The other two levels of Groensteen's system are devoted to understanding how panels interact with each other locally and globally, restrained arthrology and general arthrology, respectively.[11] Restrained arthrology determines and explains temporal connections between panels (Groensteen 2007, 103–143). After a reader has interpreted a panel in and of itself

---

9. It goes without saying that there are significant difficulties in applying *The System of Comics* to literature. Chief among them is the status of space in the two media, for mise en page is irrelevant to the printed text of Homer; in comics, an artist painstakingly crafts the space of panels for a page of particular dimensions. The same applies to the form of comics panels. The size of comics panels and their situation to others inform the way in which readers interpret individual fragments and create narrative. Descriptive fragments in literature do not operate in this visual manner, though their length (the closest equivalent of text to space) is relevant to a reader's production of meaning. While the *Iliad* is obviously not composed in a visual medium, it does construct visuality in an important way. See Bakker (1993) and (1997, 54–85) on how the poet's narratological stance is essentially "a verbalization of things seen" (Bakker 1997, 55). Narratology is an example of another semiotic approach that has enjoyed widespread success in the study of Homer since the publication of de Jong (1987).

10. See also Eisner (1990, 38–99) for an artist's discussion of comics panels.

11. Groensteen's terms are *arthrologie restreinte*, perhaps better translated as "restricted arthrology," and *arthrologie générale*.

according to the functions of the frame, one then places the panel in relation to that which immediately precedes and follows.[12]

General arthrology studies the joints (e.g., thematic, iconic, diegetic) between disparate panels beyond those of linear temporal sequence (Groensteen 2007, 144–158). This final level of Groensteen's system accounts for the larger leaps that a reader makes when reading a comic in its entirety.[13] In its dissection of the fundamentals of narrative in the comics medium, *The System of Comics* is a comprehensive yet flexible apparatus for discussing comics in all their diversity.

Groensteen's system offers also a framework for understanding discrete units in descriptive and narrative text. In the outline of the cosmology provided, each fragment may be considered analogous to a comics panel.[14] In this outline, as in comics, narrative meaning is constructed arthrologically—from one fragment to the next.[15]

Looking back to the breakdown and recomposition of the cosmology, the framing of the cosmology's images hinders narrative within them, as their brevity prevents storytelling. For example, the first two functions, that of closure and of separation, can be seen in each verbal fragment's clear distinction from others. For example, all three fragments describing the sky at III.A.–C.5.A.–D. end with caesura or line ending, and connectives clearly divide them. The rhythmic function here makes for a rather fast description whose complexity is not marked by ornamentation but by an abundance of parallel individual units. The structuring function (how the frame limits representation) and the expressive function (how the frame influences interpretation of its contents) affect narrative. As to the former, the short clausulae allow only for brief, clipped combinations like the subject-noun pairs of III.A.–C. (484–485). As to the latter, the brevity of these fragments contributes to the finitude and discreteness of the objects of description. The readerly function indicates how a frame leads one to consider its contents.

---

12. The term for the organization of temporal coordinates is *breakdown*, which explains how any given narrative or discourse is transformed into comics form (117–121). For a more hands-on approach to breakdown in comics, see Harvey (1996, 9 and passim). See also Carrier (2000) on sequence. Readers of *Understanding Comics* will call to mind Scott McCloud's analysis of panel transitions (1993, 60–93), where the gutter is the primary interpretive site for comics readers "to connect moments and mentally construct a continuous, unified reality" (67). Groensteen finds fault with this emphasis on the gutter (2007, 112–115).

13. In the way that breakdown governs the sequential distribution of images into panels, "braiding" (tressage) joins sequentially and nonsequentially related panels; see Groensteen (2007, 22, 145–147, 156–158).

14. A fascinating area of inquiry would be sequentiality in Archaic and early Classical metopes. Though ancient art falls outside the scope of this chapter, it offers valuable evidence of Greek ideas of events in time and space. See Hanfmann (1957) on the Parthenon and the deeds of Theseus at the Athenian Treasury at Delphi, as well as Hurwit (1977) on how metopes frame images.

15. There have been some noteworthy approaches to segmentation in narrative and descriptive text. See Iser (1978, 111) on the sentence, which prefigures a horizon of expectation, yet also introduces indeterminacies. Fowler (1995) writes about segmentation as a concept central to Lucretius' poetics in the *De rerum natura*. For further reading on discontinuity and fragmentation, see Henry (1994), an edited volume that builds on Barthes (1964, 1972a). Scholars have approached Homer with numerous ideas of segmentation. Auerbach (1968) writes that in Homer "the separate elements of a phenomenon are most clearly placed in relation to one another." These elements define persons and things, yet with these elements, claims Auerbach, Homer fashions "a continuous rhythmic procession of phenomena" (6). Kahane (1994, 17–42) looks at the correspondence of sense units with metrical units. See Bakker (1997, 54–85) on the role of connective particles in the temporal progression of narrative and Minchin (2001, 100–131) on brief descriptive segments.

The most important result of the cosmology's brief segments is that narrative within the fragments is highly limited, save for a modicum of movement in ἥ τ᾽ αὐτοῦ στρέφεται [and revolves in the same place] (III.C.5.b., 488).[16] These small frames prevent action from occurring inside them. As will be seen, this preponderance of small descriptive fragments in the cosmology is unique in the Shield.

Looking at III.C.5.c. (488), there is more suppression of narrative. Ursa Major watches Orion (Ὠρίωνα δοκεύει) but does not actively flee from him. Flight, though, was common in ancient descriptions of constellations, such as the Pleiades' fleeing Orion in Hesiod's *Works and Days* 619–620.[17] Further, δοκεύειν [to keep a good lookout for] is usually applied to an aggressor, not a victim.[18] Thus, the viewing relationship is the inverse of what is expected, as one would instead expect Orion to look aggressively at Ursa Major. Further, even in places where Homer's audience might expect action, it is remarkably absent. The sum of these frames is a very compartmental and orderly representation, which seems to reflect an idea of the heavens as themselves having these qualities.

Restrained arthrology, unlike the spatio-topical system, produces an impression of narrative due to the order of the described items. For while there is little or no development of actors from panel to panel, a requirement for narrative as conventionally construed, the order in which objects are narrated nevertheless offers an impression of a story by virtue of being similar to expected narratives.[19] For example, the order in which Earth, sky, and sea are mentioned recalls Hesiod's *Theogony* 126–132, where Gaia [Earth] begets Ouranos [Sky] and then Pontos [Sea]. In part due to similarity to Hesiod's cosmogony, the general arthrology of the first three segments in the Shield gives the impression of this, too, being a creation of the universe. If this order of creation was conventional and considered unchangeable by the poet, then the slightly off subordination between II. and III. may be explained. Philippe Hamon, explaining Lessing on Homer, elaborates this sort of implied narrative as "a movement of characters" that "takes charge of them in a 'natural' successivity of a motivated prescription" (Hamon 1981, 17). Another example of implied narrative is in the interaction between Orion and Ursa Major (486–489). First Orion is mentioned, then Ursa Major, then Orion. Since flight of constellations is a common motif in Archaic Greek poetry, a logical inference is that there will be a pursuit by the aggressive Orion. There is none, however. When the segments are approached diachronically, though, Ursa Major's watching appears to be a reaction to Orion.[20] Reading from panel to panel, the fabrication of narrative is possible, if not probable, even in the stillness of the cosmology.

The cities at peace and war (490–540) differ from the cosmology in descriptive style. The frames of the segments vary in length, some short, as in the cosmology, others long, allowing for more storytelling potential. These frames' restrained arthrology strongly implies narrative. The

---

16. See Becker (1995, 101n184, 145–148) on the difference between movement and action.

17. See Edwards (1991, 212) and West (1978, 314), who lists numerous instances of constellations' flights from one another.

18. See Heubeck, West, and Hainsworth (1988, 278) on *Odyssey* 5.273–275, identical to *Iliad* 18.487–489.

19. McCloud (1994, 99–106) illustrates rich narrative possibilities in not following convention regarding comics panels' successive development of actors.

20. Leaf and Bayfield (1962).

complicated parataxis and hypotaxis of segments in the outline reflect the subject of the passage. That is, a busy city cannot be illustrated with only one paradigmatic example, as in the cosmology, but with multiple smaller ones. In the second episode in the city at peace, the trial in the agora (497–508) is organized in outline form as follows:

I.   (490) ἐν δὲ δύω ποίησε | πόλεις μερόπων ἀνθρώπων ‖ (491) καλάς.
    A.   ἐν τῇ μέν ῥα |
        1.   γάμοι τ' ἔσαν εἰλαπίναι τε,
           a.   . . .
        2.   (497) λαοὶ δ' εἰν ἀγορῇ ἔσαν ἀθρόοι· |
           a.   ἔνθα δὲ νεῖκος ‖ (498) ὠρώρει,
           b.   δύο δ' ἄνδρες | ἐνείκεον εἵνεκα ποινῆς ‖ (499) ἀνδρὸς ἀποφθιμένου· |
               (1)   ὃ μὲν εὔχετο πάντ' ἀποδοῦναι ‖ (500) δήμῳ πιφαύσκων, |
               (2)   ὃ δ' ἀναίνετο μηδὲν ἑλέσθαι· ‖
               (3)   (501) ἄμφω δ' ἱέσθην | ἐπὶ ἴστορι πεῖραρ ἑλέσθαι. ‖
           c.   (502) λαοὶ δ' ἀμφοτέροισιν | ἐπήπυον ἀμφὶς ἀρωγοί· ‖
           d.   (503) κήρυκες δ' ἄρα λαὸν ἐρήτυον· |
           e.   οἳ δὲ γέροντες ‖ (504) εἵατ' ἐπὶ ξεστοῖσι λίθοις ἱερῷ ἐνὶ κύκλῳ, ‖
               (1)   (505) σκῆπτρα δὲ κηρύκων | ἐν χέρσ' ἔχον ἠεροφώνων· ‖
               (2)   (506) τοῖσιν ἔπειτ' ἤισσον, |
               (3)   ἀμοιβηδὶς δὲ δίκαζον. ‖
               (4)   (507) κεῖτο δ' ἄρ' ἐν μέσσοισι | δύω χρυσοῖο τάλαντα, ‖
               (5)   (508) τῷ δόμεν ὃς μετὰ τοῖσι | δίκην ἰθύντατα εἴποι. ‖
    B.   (509) τὴν δ' ἑτέρην πόλιν ἀμφὶ |
        1.   . . .

I.   (490) And on it he made two cities of mortal men—(491) beautiful.
    A.   And in one
        1.   there were both weddings and nuptial feasts
           a.   . . .
        2.   (497) And people were crowded into the agora.
           a.   And there a quarrel (498) had arisen,
           b.   and two men were quarreling on account of the blood price (499) of a dead man.
               (1)   One man was asserting that he had paid all the ransom, (500) addressing the people,
               (2)   but the other man was refusing to take anything.
               (3)   (501) And both were eager for a judge to make a decision.
            c.   (502) And the people, advocates to both, were applauding on either side.
           d.   (503) And heralds were restraining the people.
           e.   And elders (504) were sitting on smooth stones in an august circle,
               (1)   (505) and they were holding the scepters of clear-voiced heralds in their hands.

(2) (506) they then were leaping up with these <scepters>,

(3) and in turns they were giving judgments,

(4) (507) and in the middle were lying two talents of gold

(5) (508) to be given to him who among them should speak the best judgment.

B. (509) And around the other city

   1. . . .

As may be seen in the appendix, the rest of the cities show similar organization. The segments are less numerous (on average roughly one fragment per line) than in the cosmology (roughly two fragments per line). Here they also show greater variety in length, the panels having from three to ten words. For connective particles, the agora scene relies mostly on δέ [and]. Meter tends to coincide with panel segmentation; however, caesurae and line endings occur frequently here within segments, as in I.A.2.: δύο δ' ἄνδρες | ἐνείκεον εἵνεκα ποινῆς ‖ ἀνδρὸς ἀποφθιμένου [and two men were quarreling on account of the blood price ‖ of a dead man] (498–499). Two instances of dissonance occur between meter and segmented images at I.A.2.a. and I.A.2.b. (497–498), where the image ends in enjambment.

The longer, though variable, panels evoke the sense of a disorderly subject. Consider the structuring and expressive functions at I.A.2.e.: οἱ δὲ γέροντες ‖ εἵατ' ἐπὶ ξεστοῖσι λίθοις ἱερῷ ἐνὶ κύκλῳ [and the elders ‖ were sitting on smooth stones in an august circle] (503–504). This discrete unit holds far more descriptive information—of people, what they are doing, and how they are arranged—than a smaller one could. According to the structuring function, the longer frames allow for greater detail within this fragment. The longer frame, through the expressive function, also conveys meaning about its image, perhaps that fragment I.A.2.e. is more important than others around it, especially since it introduces the next five images. Smaller frames are of presumably less importance. The agora scene, like the rest of the cities at peace and war, varies the descriptive units in a play of the rhythmic function. For example, the reader rushes through the brevity of some descriptive units, as at I.A.2.e.(2)–I.A.2.e.(3), then lingers over longer ones, such as I.A.2.e.(4)–I.A.2.e.(5). In the way that the text moves in and out of detail, the description is at moments advanced, at others delayed. The panels function to manipulate and perhaps destabilize one's sense of space and action in the cities.

Descriptive units move in and out of subordination in contrast to the increasing detail of the cosmology. Several times this selection moves into subordination on as many as five levels, as at I.A.2.b.(1)–(3) and I.A.2.e.(1)–(5). The effect of this is best understood in contrast to the cosmology. For while the cosmos can be exemplified by one example, Ursa Major, the cities cannot. Instead, the city at peace has two examples, the festivities and the agora scene. Further, descriptions of each unit have subordinated parts. The form of the cities' description seems to correspond to their subject matter—human beings. The activities of numerous people cannot be generalized but must be described with many small examples.

As in the cosmology, obvious sequentiality is limited, though the breakdown in this scene creates the impression of narrative. Judging by temporal adverbs, the episode appears to happen mostly at the same moment. Only two joints clearly advance the narrative: I.A.2.e.(1)–I.A.2.e.(2) and I.A.2.e.(2)–I.A.2.e.(3). In the former, the elders, who at line 503 are sitting, dart up: τοῖσιν ἔπειτ᾽ ἤϊσσον [they then were leaping up with these <scepters>] (506).[21] The brevity of this segment and the unexpected shift of time in ἔπειτ᾽ [then] give a sense of urgency to the administration of justice. Action occurs between this and the next segment with ἀμοιβηδὶς [in turns]: ἀμοιβηδὶς δὲ δίκαζον [and in turns they were giving judgments] (506). Aside from these two adverbs, there is nothing that clearly communicates temporal development.

The impression of narrative, on the other hand, might reasonably be found in the arrangement of actors and events, for they are introduced in an expected order: a quarrel arises, one man speaks, the other refuses, and judges deliberate. Principally, narrative lies in a reader's diachronic movement through descriptive segments. To various degrees, segments individually lend themselves to narrative, but primarily narrative emerges from their juxtaposition. It is precisely this ability to be read both ways—as static and narratival—that allows for the poet's pretension that a fixed object is being described. Byre is correct in writing that the trial scene has "a high degree of narrativity" (Byre 1992, 39), though this has very little to do with straightforward sequentiality in the story. Likewise, Becker's statement that the Shield is a "description of a . . . complex *experience* of images" (Becker 1990, 140) may be refined. There are, instead, at least three different sorts of narrative: that within discrete panels (as coordinated by the spatio-topical system), that clearly marked by adverbs and movement of actors, and that created in the reading process through restrained arthrology.

A series of scenes from the countryside make up the third major section of the Shield (541–606; see appendix, sections 3 through 8). These episodes show strong similarity to each other in thematics and their creation of narrative. Further, these six sections show a spatio-topical system and arthrology distinctly different from the cosmology and cities. The rustic scenes consistently have rather long fragments, nearly all of which lie in parataxis. A representative example is the reaping episode (550–560).

I.   (550) ἐν δ᾽ ἐτίθει τέμενος βασιλήϊον· |
    A.   ἔνθα δ᾽ ἔριθοι ‖ (551) ἤμων ὀξείας δρεπάνας | ἐν χερσὶν ἔχοντες. ‖
        1.   (552) δράγματα δ᾽ ἄλλα μετ᾽ ὄγμον | ἐπήτριμα πῖπτον ἔραζε, ‖
        2.   (553) ἄλλα δ᾽ ἀμαλλοδετῆρες | ἐν ἐλλεδανοῖσι δέοντο. ‖
        3.   (554) τρεῖς δ᾽ ἄρ᾽ ἀμαλλοδετῆρες ἐφέστασαν· |
        4.   αὐτὰρ ὄπισθε ‖ (555) παῖδες δραγμεύοντες | ἐν ἀγκαλίδεσσι φέροντες ‖
            (556) ἀσπερχὲς πάρεχον· |
        5.   βασιλεὺς δ᾽ ἐν τοῖσι σιωπῇ ‖ (557) σκῆπτρον ἔχων ἑστήκει | ἐπ᾽ ὄγμου
            γηθόσυνος κῆρ. ‖
    B.   (558) κήρυκες δ᾽ ἀπάνευθεν | ὑπὸ δρυΐ δαῖτα πένοντο, ‖
        1.   (559) βοῦν δ᾽ ἱερεύσαντες μέγαν ἀμφέπον· |
        2.   αἳ δὲ γυναῖκες ‖ (560) δεῖπνον ἐρίθοισιν | λεύκ᾽ ἄλφιτα πολλὰ πάλυνον. ‖

---

21. Leaf and Bayfield (1962, 458) interpret γέροντες as the subject of ἤϊσσον. The subject of the first half of 506 might be the litigants; see Edwards (1991, 217). Looking at how the breakdown of images tends to work in the cities at peace and war, Edwards's solution creates a relation between fragments that is unparalleled in the Shield, for nowhere else do the subjects of the panels change with such rapidity.

I. (550) And on it he made a king's estate:

    A. and there reapers, ‖ (551) holding sharp sickles in their hands, were reaping. ‖

        1. (552) And some thick handfuls they were making fall to the ground along the furrow, ‖

        2. (553) and other <handfuls> binders were binding with straw bands. ‖

        3. (554) And three binders stood by;

        4. but behind <the reapers> ‖ (555) boys, gathering the handfuls, carrying them in their arms, ‖ (556) were tirelessly at hand;

        5. and a king, among them, in silence, ‖ (557) holding a scepter, stood among them at the furrow, rejoicing in his heart. ‖

    B. (558) And apart <from them> heralds under an oak were preparing a feast, ‖

        1. (559) and, having slain a great ox, were busying about.

        2. And women ‖ (560) were sprinkling the food for the reapers with much white barley.

The separative function is at its strongest in the rustic scenes since δέ [and] introduces nearly every fragment.[22] Lacking particles that introduce complex series—like correlative τε . . . τε [both . . . and] or discourse-establishing μέν [indeed]—these lines are straightforward and paratactic. Compared to the previous two examples, segmentation and meter here are most in coincidence since a line ending or a caesura separates every fragment. Furthermore, while this breakdown is very paratactic, like the other rustic scenes, several subordinating segments introduce it. Here, the narrator first declares the subject to be "a king's estate" (I.), next refines it to a scene of reapers on the estate (I.A.), and then describes their labor in detail (I.A.1.–I.A.5). The embedding of fragments achieves a different end than in the previous two examples, here putting the reapers' actions on equal representational footing.

The segments are uniformly of a medium length. In the harvesting episode there are ten panels for eleven lines (roughly one per line). While the city at peace has the same average of fragments per line, there is discrepancy between short and long. As noticed in the city at peace, longer panels allow for greater narrative within the panel than shorter ones. In their medium length, these panels accommodate (according to the structuring function) simple human action and one additional piece of information, such as setting or an accompanying object. For example, I.B. has people doing a simple action (preparing a feast) in a setting (under an oak tree): κήρυκες δ' ἀπάνευθεν ὑπὸ δρυΐ δαῖτα πένοντο [and apart <from them> heralds under an oak were preparing a feast] (558). The absence of small frames prevents this description from turning into a series of lists, as in the cosmology. Thinking of the expressive function, these uniform fragments might reinforce an idea of the regularity and repetition of the rustic people's activities.

These long frames lie in consistent parataxis, not moving in and out of detail (as in the cities) or resorting to high levels of specificity (as in the cosmology). Events in the country, it seems, are neither so complex that they call for subordinated description nor so generalizable that they can be summed up by one example.

22. μὲν introduces fragment I.H. (line 585) in the herd scene (573–586). The dance (590–606) shows somewhat more variation in segment-introducing particles: τῷ I.A. (591), μὲν 585 I.H. (593); καί I.B.3. (597); and ὡς I.C.1. (600).

Restrained arthrology creates a clear and uncomplicated narrative of laborers harvesting and preparing a feast. There are no temporal linguistic markers, making for a piece that may be understood as static. Like the previous two examples, however, images are narrated in a specific order such that their juxtaposition creates a sense of action. The reapers follow the steps necessary to harvesting: They hold sickles, cut down the crop, bind it, and pass it along. After their labor, the workers will partake in the feast meant for them (I.B.–I.B.2.). When seen from this perspective, Becker's observation that the scene lacks narrative because "the same figure does not perform consecutive actions" (Becker 1995, 132) is in error. Implied sequentiality here (and in fact in most of the rustic scenes) is especially strong.

Groensteen's system of comics allows for a controlled discussion of the smallest meaningful units from which the *Iliad*'s famous ekphrasis is built. The Shield satisfies the oppositional demands of representing static images and narrativized referents with a careful use of spatio-topical and arthrologic principles. Even this brief overview of comics theory has demonstrated the Shield's undernoticed (if not unnoticed) coordination of meter, particles, conjunctions, images, narrative, and thematics. Still unconsidered is Groensteen's third major element of comics—general arthrology, narrative fashioned by readers connecting panels outside of the linear reading processes. Such an analysis is called for, certainly, though space (for this author space in the form of a word count) is coming to an end.[23]

Appendix: The Shield of Achilles, *Iliad* 18.483–608

This appendix presents *Iliad* 18.483–608, the ekphrasis describing the shield forged for Achilles by Hephaestus, articulating the unit breaks employed in this chapter (due to its compression, the city at war [509–540] is uniquely difficult to organize). Line numbers are presented in a column on the right. Since the arthrological segments do not always correspond with line ends, line numbers here indicate where a line begins. The ‖ symbol connotes a line ending.

1. **The Cosmology**		**483–489**
I. On it he made the earth	·	483
II. and on it the sky		
III. and on it the sea, ‖		
A. and the untiring sun		484
B. and the full moon ‖		
C. and on it all the constellations,		485
1. and the sky is crowned by these, ‖		
2. and the Pleiades		486
3. and the Hyades		
4. and the might of Orion ‖		
5. and Ursa Major,		487

23. Gratitude goes to Ann Bergren and Joy Connolly, in whose classes these ideas were first developed. I also give thanks to this volume's editors, to the members of the IFA–GSAS Forum on Forms of Seeing at New York University, and to readers of earlier drafts: Joel Christensen, Michèle Lowrie, Rose B. MacLean, Jessie Owens, Benjamin Sammons, Amit Shilo, and Christos Tsagalis.

	a.	which they also call by the name "Wagon," ‖		
	b.	and it revolves in the same place		488
	c.	and watches Orion ‖		
	d.	and she alone has no share in the baths of the Ocean. ‖		489

2. The Cities at Peace and War   490–540

I. And on it he made two cities of mortal men ‖—beautiful.   490–91

    A.   And in one

        1.   there were both weddings and nuptial feasts, ‖

            a. and from bridal chambers under blazing torches ‖   492

                 they were leading maidens through the city,   493

            b. and a great wedding song arose; ‖

            c. and dancing youths were spinning,   494

                (1) and among them flutes ‖

                (2) and lyres were making a cry;   495

            d. and women, ‖ each standing in her doorway, were admiring; ‖   496

        2.   And people were crowded into the agora.   497

            a. And there a quarrel ‖ had arisen,   498

            b. and two men were quarreling on account of the blood price ‖

               of a dead man.   499

                (1) One man was asserting that he had paid all the ransom, ‖

                     addressing the people,   500

                (2) but the other man was refusing to take anything. ‖

                (3) And both were eager for a judge to make a decision. ‖   501

            c. And the people, advocates to both, were applauding on either side. ‖   502

            d. And heralds were restraining the people.   503

            e. And elders ‖ were sitting on smooth stones in an august circle, ‖   504

                (1) and they were holding the scepters of clear-voiced ‖   505

                     heralds in their hands.

                (2) they then were leaping up with these <scepters>,   506

                (3) and in turns they were giving judgments, ‖

                (4) and in the middle were lying two talents of gold ‖   507

                (5) to be given to him who among them   508

                     should speak the best judgment. ‖

    B.   And around the other city   509

        1.   two armies of men were sitting around ‖ shining in arms;   510

            a. and they [the besiegers] were divided between two plans, ‖

               whether to sack the city or to divide apart all, ‖   511

               however much property the lovely city held within; ‖   512

        2.   but the besieged were not yet persuaded,   513

            a. and they were secretly arming themselves for an ambush; ‖

            b. dear wives and young children, at the wall ‖   514

               standing, were keeping guard;   515

            c. and with them men whom old age held; ‖

3. and they went out;　516
    a. and Ares and Pallas Athena were leading them, ‖ both gold,　517
    b. and they wore golden clothes, ‖
    c. both beautiful and great with their arms,　518
    d. and as fit for gods ‖ both were conspicuous;　519
    e. and the people were smaller in scale. ‖
4. And when they arrived there it was opportune to lie in wait ‖　520
    on a river,　521
    a. and where there was a watering place for all beasts, ‖
    b. there they were sitting, wrapped in shining bronze. ‖　522
5. And then apart from them two scouts of the　523
    <besieged> people were sitting, ‖
    ooking for whenever they might see sheep and curved-horn oxen. ‖　524
    a. And soon these came,　525
    b. and two herdsmen were accompanying, ‖ delighting in the syrinx;　526
        (1) and they did not foresee the trick at all. ‖
    c. They [the scouts], catching sight of these, ran upon them,　527
    d. and then swiftly ‖ they were cutting the herds of oxen and fat flocks ‖　528
        of white sheep,　529
    e. and they were killing the shepherds. ‖
6. And as they [the besiegers] now heard a great clash among the cattle, ‖　530
    [the besiegers] sitting in front of their place of assembly,　531
    a. right away their swift horses ‖ mounting, they followed after,　532
    b. and on a sudden they arrived. ‖
7. And making a stand they were doing battle along the
    banks of the river, ‖　533
    a. and they were throwing bronze spears at one another. ‖　534
    b. and amid [them] Strife and Confusion and　535
        destructive Death were in the throng, ‖
        (1) [Death] who holds one man recently wounded,　536
        (2) another unwounded, ‖
        (3) another, dead, she drags by the feet through the din of battle; ‖　537
        (4) and the garment about her shoulders was dark　538
             with the blood of men. ‖
        (5) and like living mortals they were joining in and fighting, ‖　539
        (6) and they were dragging the dead corpses of one another. ‖　540

3. **Plowing Scene**　**541–549**
I. And on it he made a soft field, rich earth, ‖ broad, thrice plowed;　541–42
    A. and many plowmen in it, ‖
        whirling the yokes of beasts, were driving here and there; ‖　543
    B. and when, having turned, they came to the end of the field, ‖　544
        and then to each in their hands cups of honey-sweet wine ‖　545
        a man pouring was giving;　546

C. and they were turning back to the furrow, ‖

pressing themselves to come to the end of the deep field. ‖ 547

D. And it was black behind each, and it resembled a plowed field, ‖ 548

though being gold; 549

E. he had fabricated a marvelous sight. ‖

4. Reaping Scene **550–560**

I. And on it he made a king's estate: 550

A. and there reapers, ‖ holding sharp sickles in their hands, were reaping. ‖ 551

1. And some thick handfuls they were making fall 552

to the ground along the furrow, ‖

2. and other <handfuls> binders were binding with straw bands. ‖ 553

3. And three binders stood by; 554

4. but behind <the reapers>, ‖

boys, gathering the handfuls, carrying them in their arms, ‖ 555

were tirelessly at hand; 556

5. and a king, among them, in silence, ‖

holding a scepter, stood among them at the furrow, 557

rejoicing in his heart. ‖

B. And apart <from them> heralds under an oak were preparing a feast, ‖ 558

1. and, having slain a great ox, were busying about. 559

2. And women ‖ were sprinkling the food 560

for the reapers with much white barley.

5. The Vintage **561–572**

I. And on it he made a vineyard, very heavy with bunches of grapes, ‖ 561

of beautiful gold; 562

A. and the grapes were black, ‖

B. and it stood up on silver poles throughout; ‖ 563

C. and around there was a ditch of dark blue, 564

D. and about he drove a fence ‖ of tin; 565

E. and there was only one path to it, ‖

by which the carriers went when they would reap. ‖ 566

F. And maidens and young men, bearing the tender fruit, ‖ 567

in plaited baskets they were bearing the honey-sweet fruit. ‖ 568

G. And in the middle of them a boy with a clear-voiced lyre ‖ 569

was playing lovely, and was singing of beautiful Linus ‖ 570

in a delicate voice; 571

H. and beating the ground together, ‖

skipping with their feet, they were accompanying with dance and shouting. ‖ 572

6. The Herd **573–586**

I. And on it he made a herd of straight-horned cattle ‖ 573

A. and the cattle were made of gold and tin ‖ 574

    B.   and with a bellowing from the cow-yard   575
          they were hastening toward the pasture ‖
          alongside a sounding river, alongside a swaying thicket of reeds. ‖   576
    C.   And golden herders were marching with cattle—‖ four [cattle],   577–78
    D.   and nine swift-footed dogs were following them. ‖
    E.   And two fearsome lions among the foremost cattle ‖   579
          were holding a bellowing bull;   580
    F.   and it, bellowing for a long time, ‖ was being dragged away;   581
    G.   and now the dogs and vigorous youths were pursuing it. ‖
    H.   The two <lions>, having burst open the hide of the great cow, ‖   582
          were swallowing the entrails and black blood;   583
    I.   and the herders ‖ in vain tried to set on the dogs. ‖   584
    J.   and <the dogs> shrank from biting the lions, ‖   585
    K.   and they, standing very near, were barking and were fleeing. ‖   586

7. **The Valley**   **587–589**

I.   And on it the famous one of crooked legs made a great pasturage, ‖   587
   in a beautiful valley, of white sheep, ‖   588
   and farms and huts and covered pens.   589

8. **The Dance**   **590–606**

I.   And on it the famous one of crooked legs embellished a place for dancing, ‖   590
    A.   similar to that which on wide Knossos ‖   591
          Daidalos made for Ariadne of beautiful locks. ‖   592
    B.   There young men and oxen-bringing maidens ‖   593
          were dancing, holding their hands on the wrists of one another. ‖   594
        1.   And the maidens had smooth linen,   595
        2.   and the young men ‖wore well-spun tunics, glistening slightly with oil; ‖   596
        3.   and the maidens had beautiful crowns,   597
        4.   and the young men daggers, ‖ golden, hanging from silver straps. ‖   598
    C.   And at one time they ran with skilled feet ‖ very lightly,   599–600
        1.   as when a seated potter tries ‖
           a wheel fitted to his palms, whether it will run; ‖   601
    D.   and at another time they ran back in rows facing each other. ‖   602
    E.   And a great crowd was standing around the lovely dance, ‖   603
          delighting;   604–05
    F.   and two tumblers about them ‖
          were spinning through the middle, taking the lead in the dance. ‖   606

9. **Ocean**   **607–608**

I.   And on it he strongly made the great might of the river Ocean ‖   607
   along the outermost rim of the firm shield. ‖   608

4

Declassicizing the Classical in Japanese Comics

Osamu Tezuka's *Apollo's Song*

Nicholas A. Theisen

To ask the question "how are the classics treated in manga?" seems an unnecessary one. There are numerous adaptations of the *Tale of Genji* (*Genji monogatari*), of the *Tale of the Woodcutter* (*Taketori monogatari*), or, more broadly speaking, the legend of Kaguya-hime (the so-called Shining Princess), of the *Chronicles of Japan* (*Nihon shoki*), and even of Chinese classics like the *Journey into the West* (*Saiyūki* in Japanese, *Xiyouji* in Chinese), which serves as the source material for, arguably, one of the most recognizable manga both within and without Japan, namely Toriyama Akira's *Dragonball* (*Doragonbōru*). However, when and if we in the West ask this question, we do not mean "how is *koten* treated in manga" but how the literary, philosophical, and historical (that is, altogether, cultural) output of the ancient Mediterranean, with particular regard to that of ancient Greece and Rome, is treated. I do not mean to imply there is anything untoward in asking about "classics" in manga but to say that asking such a question in a culture with its own history of classicism and a complicated relationship to the classics of another neighboring culture, namely greater China, might yield a response that is wholly unexpected. Ironically, that wholly unexpected response is the only one that is capable of appropriately elucidating the fundamental problem in the initial question: that the "classics" in manga and likewise in Japanese culture are precisely not classical. They are not the foundation of an intellectual/literary history whose reception of Greco-Roman ideas, stories, and whatnot informs in various ways how that history has developed and are therefore not afforded a somewhat privileged status by the educational institutions that teach and perpetuate the intellectual history of the West.

Most of this goes without saying, but it is important as a reminder that the phenomenon I address here, manga, has both clear Western and Eastern influences and that the two are often difficult to disentangle. I also do not wish to historicize notions of the "classical" but rather to be clear that in order to understand the meaning of "classics"—in the context of this chapter, myth especially—when such works appear in manga. Knowledge of their reception in the West and of their proper context may as often be misleading as informative because manga and Japanese literature are marked much more by a lack of engagement with Greco-Roman classical materials than by an obvious and concerted reception thereof.

If one assumes a Japanese reader to have no necessary knowledge of Greek myth, then the work of Osamu Tezuka (1928–1989) poses an intriguing difficulty, particularly in the long graphic novel *Apollo's Song* (*Aporo no uta*, 1970), to be considered here in detail. His knowledge of Greek myth cannot reasonably be disputed. The obvious allusions to Apollo and Daphne in this work, to the god Hephaestus (as Vulcan) in *Phoenix* (*Hi no tori*, 1967–1988), and to the god of the west wind in *Zephyrus* (*Zefirusu*, 1971) make it clear that Tezuka had at least some familiarity with Greek myth. However, the problem with identifying an allusion to Aeschylus' *Oresteia* in *Apollo's Song*, as I do here, is a readerly one precisely because what allusion there may be is not obviously identified. From this perspective, one has to wonder whether a Western reader is primed to see in Tezuka's manga something that may in fact be merely coincidental and easily explained by a narrative pattern more familiar to the Japanese.

By 1970, Tezuka's graphic style, despite his being the so-called "god of manga" (*manga no kami-sama*), was rather dated. His Disneyesque characters (visually, not literarily speaking), after the advent of the more realism-oriented and overtly political *gekiga* ("dramatic pictures" as opposed to "whimsical pictures," the literal meaning of the word *manga*) artists of the 1950s and 1960s, seemed a throwback to the early influence of American comics in the 1940s, when one might genuinely claim that manga was specifically marketed to young boys and girls and as such roughly synonymous with an older (and often derogatory) notion of comics and cartoons, except that, even though Tezuka's visual style had not changed much, the content had. No longer was he merely the author of beloved children's manga such as *New Treasure Island* (*Shin-takarajima*, 1947) or *Astro Boy* (*Tetsuwan Atomu*, 1951). He was also the director of the sexually explicit *Cleopatra* (*Kureopatora*, 1970)[1] and writer of gritty, human dramas like *Ode to Kirihito* (*Kirihito sanka*, 1970–1971).

Even the question of manga itself needs consideration: what it is and whether in historical and cultural terms it is perfectly commensurate with comics or Eisner's somewhat looser concept of "sequential art." The word *manga* originally refers to quick sketches, often comical, of daily life collected into handsewn books. One of the best examples of this early manga is the *Hokusai Manga* (1814)—the same Hokusai perhaps better known for his prints *The Great Wave of Kanagawa* and the *Thirty-Six Views of Mount Fuji*—a collection of sketches of landscapes, of vegetation, of city life, and of mythological creatures with none of the narrative sequencing we commonly associate with comics and with contemporary manga.[2] Because these early manga have little in common, seemingly, with contemporary comics and contemporary manga, for that matter, some critics, like Kinsella, have emphasized the transformation it underwent in the postwar period especially as a result of the influence of American comics and animation during the U.S. occupation (Kinsella 2000, 28–29). That the *Encyclopedia of Contemporary Manga* (published in 2006) begins in 1945 is testament to the significance of that transformation. However, other critics prefer to emphasize the continuity between

---

1. Tezuka is as well known for his animated films and series as he is for his manga. Much of what I have to say here about *Apollo's Song* applies as well to *Cleopatra*. The film drastically rewrites the history of Caesar's and Cleopatra's relationship and is well worth greater consideration than I can give it here.

2. Though the *Hokusai Manga* is indicative of the earliest usage of the word *manga*, Kern (2006), in his extensive study *Manga from the Floating World*, has noted the similarities in terms of print form to the *kibyōshi* picture books of the late 18th century.

contemporary and earlier popular art forms, if not manga, particularly *emaki* (scroll paintings) and *nishiki-e* (multicolored woodblock prints),[3] as a means of showing manga to be a syncretic art form merging native and foreign artistic traditions into one.

This argument of continuity is implicit in compilations like *One Thousand Years of Manga*, where examples of the traditional styles of ink painting and printmaking are set side by side with examples of contemporary manga to show the "clear" influence of one on the other. Admittedly, scroll paintings in particular have a kind of narrative flow from one end to the other, but the question as to whether they are to be "read" in the same way as comics is as much a question as whether, as Scott McCloud asserts, something like the Bayeux Tapestry can be read as sequential art in the manner of comics (McCloud 1993, 12–13).[4] None of the continuity arguments deal well with Kinsella's objection, though, that the change in postwar manga is as much a sociocultural shift as it is a stylistic one:

> The opposition to the manga and animation industries by conservative elements in post-war society has encouraged the defenders of manga, namely professional manga critics, to emphasize or even invent stylistic origins for manga in ancient Japanese history. Its critics have hoped that if they could prove manga is, somehow, a part of *traditional* Japan, then it cannot possibly be uprooted and repressed by the government. This defensive argument has drawn attention away from the fact that manga is a strikingly *contemporary* phenomenon. (Kinsella 2000, 19)

Kinsella's point that the continuity argument fails to account for the subversive nature of much postwar manga, particularly the gritty social realism of the *gekiga* artists, buttresses an important problem I see with regard to the compatibility of manga and comics in terms of their respective recent histories.

Stylistic similarities and differences alone cannot account for how much more ubiquitous manga is in Japanese society and how it covers a wide range from children's entertainment to adult themes of murder, sex, history, and, frequently, corporate life and culture. Kinsella has this to say:

> One of the most common synonyms used to describe manga is "air," something that has permeated every crevice of the contemporary environment. Manga can be purchased from train platform kiosks, in book shops near railway stations and on shopping malls and streets, as well as in art book shops and luxury department stores; it can be bought from any 24-hour convenience store, a snack bar in a car park at a tourist resort, at a grocery store serving the needs of a remote village, or from a vending machine chained to the corner of a street. It can also be bought from second-hand manga superstores and

---

3. For the argument for continuity with earlier Japanese art forms see especially Ito (2008).

4. *Emaki* are "read" or, perhaps more appropriately, viewed by unrolling the scroll in the left hand and rolling it back up in the right in a manner roughly analogous to how the Torah is manipulated as it is read. This has the effect of moving the observed portion of the scroll from left to right, and as what is framed changes, so, too, does the narrative the scroll depicts. However, simply because these paintings occasionally have a narrative does not mean that they are narratologically similar to manga and comics, whose stories tend to be fragmented into panels, nor were they part of the print culture of the late Edo period as *kibyōshi*, *ukiyoe*, and early *manga* were.

specialist bookshops, or from homeless men vending already discarded manga, arranged
on blankets in underground pedestrian passes. It can be discovered left behind on seats
in trains or borrowed from collections made available for browsing in love hotel
bedrooms, manga cafes or diners. (Kinsella 2000, 4)

Manga is, in Japan, more properly a medium than a genre, or perhaps it is even the constellation
of particular genres with which American comics have become associated as a result of the rise
of the superhero with the prominence of large publishers like Marvel and DC and as a result of
the suppression of more "mature" subject matter with the institution of the comics code in the
1950s.[5] Manga never underwent any of these developments and came to be defined much more
by the weekly magazines and serial anthologies that organized them according to age appropri-
ateness and social status: *shōnen* for young boys, *shōjo* for young girls, *seishun* for adolescent
males, manga for salarymen, manga for housewives, manga for students, and so on.

When a given manga makes use of Greco-Roman mythological or historical material, it
has more to do with genre or the individual whims of the artist than its significance in or relevance to a larger history of reception. One rarely sees a strict retelling of a myth or some story
with either historical or mythological significance retold for its own sake. The material is nearly
always adapted to some other purpose for which there is often little concern over the degree to
which it may distort or rewrite the "original." Of course, anyone familiar with Greek literature
is aware that even in, say, Athenian tragedy the variations on mythological stories are not consistent with each other, but when one sees a mythological reference in manga, it needs to be
clear that its story is not being told. It is the narratological equivalent of a stock photo: Its
graphic and literal elements may be in play, but its narrative elements are not. This use of mythological material is very much unlike an allusion in that knowledge of the source or reference
not only may not add complexity to the story being told, ironic or otherwise, but also may end
up confusing the reader.

At the extreme, in Kurumada Masami's *Saint Seiya* (*Seinto seiya*, 1986–1990) are all the
trappings of a kind of Greekness; the vast majority of characters are named after mythological
figures, but they only vaguely resemble their namesakes. A team of so-called saints, a group of
powerful cosmic warriors, is led by a beautiful, young woman named Athena (reincarnated in
the manga as Kido Saori), who is sent by the Olympian gods every 250 years to combat whatever evil threatens to take over the Earth. Her base of operations, Sanctuary, is modeled on the
temple of Athena Parthenos on the Acropolis, and the individual members of the three classes
of her saints are all named after constellations. Rather than be strictly or even loosely adapted
from an actual Greek myth (or contain any obvious reference thereto), *Saint Seiya* follows quite
closely the conventions of *sentai* or "team" manga, in which a group of warriors, who often
believe themselves to be ordinary humans but come to an awareness of their powers in adolescence
(an equivalent of the superhero/secret identity duality), comes together under the guidance of
an aloof yet powerful being to defend the Earth, galaxy, universe, and so forth against the threat

---

5. I realize this is something of a gross generalization, but the vast majority of popular comics and graphic novels
to this day in the United States are limited to roughly superhero and sci-fi/fantasy genres. The more "underground"
works of, say, Daniel Clowes or Robert Crumb are not as immediately recognizable as the established superhero
titles of Marvel and DC, nor are they in the popular imagination as synonymous with comics as the superhero and
fantasy genres are.

of a series of increasingly powerful villains. This trope of *sentai* is so common in *shōnen* manga that Kōji Aihara and Kentarō Takekuma parody it at length in their *Even a Monkey Can Draw Manga* (*Saru de mo kakeru manga kyōshitsu*, 2002). To a Japanese reader this would clearly be the driving force behind the development of the narrative and not the relatively superficial sense of mythology that lends the characters their names, be they protagonist or antagonist.

However, in Riyoko Ikeda's *Window of Orpheus* (*Orufeusu no mado*, 1975–1981) one finds what appears to be more straightforwardly an allusion, specifically to the love story of Orpheus and Eurydice and its tragic end. *Window of Orpheus* tells the story of three young men—Isaac, Klaus, and Julius (though Julius is, in fact, a woman disguised as a man)—at a music conservatory in Regensburg in 1903, where there is a window, so the legend in the manga goes, that, should a man look upon a woman through it, he will fall in love with her, and their affair will be as passionate and as tragic as that of Orpheus and Eurydice. The story has many of the most common elements of *shōjo* manga: The story takes place (initially) in a relatively clois- tered academy, there is a love triangle (both Klaus and Isaac see Julius through the window), a young woman's identity is concealed as a man, and so on.[6] However, while *Window of Orpheus* adheres to (or perhaps creates) the conventions of its genre, unlike *Saint Seiya*, the "classical" material it refers to maps more obviously onto the story being told. At the very beginning of the first volume Ikeda tells a version of the Orpheus myth complete with snakebite, descent into Hades, and dismemberment by Maenads, so that the classical reference is clear from the story's inception. The narrative does develop away from the major characters' "school days" and as such away from the allusion, but this matters very little as this is not a retelling or reimagining of the Orpheus and Eurydice myth. The one peculiarity, though, in the myth that Ikeda does tell is the claim that Orpheus is not, in fact, Thracian but rather the son of a French king. Why she chooses to alter the myth in this way is unclear, but in her lack of concern for total consistency of the myth with a known version and in her anachronistic choice to make Orpheus specifically "French" the tension between variance and invariance in myth making is made plain.

Doubt is important for myth. For example, even though what Odysseus recalls of Oedi- pus in his brief encounter with Jocasta at *Odyssey* 11.271–280 does not fit perfectly with what transpires in *Oedipus the King*, some knowledge of Oedipus' origins and some expectation that things turn out badly for him are necessary for understanding how he unwittingly curses him- self at the beginning of the play. Perhaps Orpheus' being French changes a great deal, and per- haps it changes very little, but our collective unfamiliarity with this "fact" breeds suspicion as to precisely what is going on in the greater narrative and in the myth as retold. This is why I assert the only truly useful perspective to have on the presence of the classical in manga is doubt: doubt as to whether mythological material is anything but purely nominal (as in *Saint Seiya*); doubt as to whether—even when largely consistent with a properly ancient version—the myth as told is merely the figment of an individual author's imagination remolded to suit solely her purposes (as with *Window of Orpheus*); and doubt as to whether a classical allusion can

---

6. It is worth noting that many of what today would be considered "tropes" of *shōjo* manga have largely to due with the popularity and influence of Ikeda's earlier manga *Rose of Versailles* (*Berusaiyu no bara*, 1972–1973) on the art- ists who followed her. Her work has much in common with the subgenre of *shōnen-ai* or "boy love," in which ado- lescent boys engage in homoromantic relationships and which flourished only until the late 1980s, even though arguably it has its continuation in the *yaoi* subgenre of *dōjinshi* amateur manga and even though elements of its visual style, based on the all-female Takarazuka theater troupe, can be seen to this day.

properly be said to exist at all when both the condition of the text and our own predispositions as readers conspire to make an intertextual connection that may have never been intended. This latter doubt is precisely what is at issue in the work of Osamu Tezuka.

Apollo's Song is divided into five chapters and a prologue spanning three volumes in the Japanese at least; the recent translation by Camellia Nieh was published in a single volume. Citations are, for the most part, from the three-volume edition of *Apollo's Song* in Tezuka's collected works (*Tezuka Osamu manga zenshū*) though I note the corresponding pages in Nieh's translation in brackets. In addition, significant differences between the Japanese and English editions are in some cases merely noted (see the appendix to this chapter), but others, such as the "necessary" page mirroring of the text, are discussed in greater detail at the end of this chapter.

Apollo's Song begins with a massive crowd of sperm/men in what appears to be a tunnel rushing toward "the queen," that is, the egg with whom they will join to form an embryo. Then it suddenly cuts to a young man, Chikaishi Shōgo, being admitted to a psychiatric hospital under the care of Dr. Enoki. Shōgo's recent violent behavior has the local authorities quite worried, and his nonchalance convinces Dr. Enoki to begin immediate electroshock therapy. It is during this procedure that Shōgo hallucinates, one supposes, a vision of a goddess who looks remarkably similar to Athena but is never identified as such. The goddess forces Shōgo to reexperience his childhood memories of his lascivious mother, whose lovers she would present to Shōgo as his father. His disdain for amorous relationships and his violent reactions to them, as made evident by an adolescent episode with a snake and two birds (discussed later), is judged to be unacceptable. His punishment is to suffer for eternity loving one woman, tragically, again and again over the course of several "lives" that play out in the manga.

When Dr. Enoki first attempts to treat Shōgo using electroshock therapy, he hallucinates, one supposes, a vision of the goddess Athena—or rather more specifically the statue of Athena Parthenos—who interrogates him telepathically as to the origin of his distaste for love, to which the answer is a series of flashbacks. They follow a roughly psychoanalytic pattern: Shōgo's mother "rejects" him by refusing to breast-feed him and further alienates her son by imposing her lovers upon him. He thus lashes out at animals and inanimate objects, effectively rechanneling onto them his anger toward his mother.

The last of these vignettes finds Shōgo huddled beneath a tree watching as a snake is about to attack a male and female bird in their nest. He encourages the snake, telling it to "gobble up the eggs" the female bird is keeping watch over, effectively murdering her offspring.[7] Most of the panels on the five pages over which the flashback is recounted are taken up with the cinematic fight between the snake and the male bird trying to protect his mate's nest, during which the snake is killed when the male bird penetrates its skull with his beak, and the bird is critically injured when the snake coils about his body, crushing him as it dies. The bird limps back to his mate, who licks his wounds. Shōgo, unsatisfied with the result, crushes the two birds and their eggs with a massive rock. The last the reader sees of the adolescent boy is his uncontrolled sobbing over the crushed nest.

7. Tezuka (1977, vol. 1, 37 [37]).

This tale from Shōgo's childhood serves as a theme for the variations that play out in the diverse lives he leads either as a result of the goddess's explicit command[8] or the various events that render him unconscious; it is never entirely clear who or what is responsible. In the first variation, Shōgo is a German officer in World War II guarding a train that is transporting Jewish prisoners, when suddenly the train is attacked by an American bomber, and both the prisoners and the guards are forced to flee for their lives. Shōgo notices and immediately becomes enamored with a young Jewish woman named Elise, whom he saves from being raped by two German officers despite the fact she has just shot him several times with a machine gun. Elise is wounded, though, and she lies down next to Shōgo in a disheveled haystack, where they die during the night. The next day, a platoon of German soldiers looking for the missing men Shōgo has killed find his and Elise's dead bodies in the pile of hay: His body is left to rot where it is, but the commander orders his men to take her body back with them, as her "hair will become stuffing for a mattress."[9]

In this first "life" Shōgo and Elise are analogous to the two birds in his adolescent experience—their nest is the pile of hay in which they collapse—the two soldiers who try to rape Elise correspond to the snake, and the platoon that arrives after all of the events seem analogous to Shōgo and his rock. All of these analogies are well and good, except the actual narrative of Shōgo's first "life" does not match well with that of the snake and the two birds: It is Elise, not the soldiers/snake, who ultimately kills Shōgo; the soldiers who cart off Elise's body don't weep over what they do as Shōgo does over the crushed nest; and, most important, Shōgo himself has completely changed roles. No longer is he the murderer but the murdered, and the love the two birds demonstrate for each is no longer the object of his ire but is now what he himself feels. This first reversal is important. Each successive "life" or hallucination Shōgo experiences may include all of the various elements of his adolescence and waking life, but the narrative has changed. This serves a literary purpose: It is through being different each time that Shōgo's steady and painful transformation is revealed. The text requires multiple, sometimes contradictory, perspectives on the narrative, and which perspective is in play at any one time is wholly dependent upon the action at that moment: No one character is ever fixed in relation to a particular image.

Both the manner in which the symbolic imagery seems to recompose itself throughout the narrative of *Apollo's Song* and the fact that the individual images have no fixed relationship to particular characters are remarkably similar to the shifting patterns of symbols in Aeschylus' *Oresteia*, especially *Libation Bearers*. However, first a word of caution: Everything I have to say in what follows can only be provisional, for to posit an actual relationship between the *Oresteia* and *Apollo's Song* would require evidence beyond the coincidental that does not exist and would mean that at least some of Tezuka's readers would be expected to have a literary/cultural background that they most likely do not possess. If the narrative patterns of Aeschylus' trilogy are, in fact, a model for Tezuka, they may not be necessary for understanding *Apollo's Song* because of the cultural milieu from which it originates. All of this seems to fly in the face of similarities that are themselves quite apt. Orestes, like Shōgo, has what could be called a rather strained

8. Ibid., 41 [41].

9. Ibid., 78 [78].

relationship with his mother, Clytemnestra, a lascivious woman herself, who in a dream imagines she gives birth to a snake, whose bite draws both blood and milk from her breast:

Chorus: I do know, my child, because I was there. That godless woman sent these drink-
          offerings because she was shaken by dreams and wandering terrors of the night.
Orestes: Did you learn what the dream was, so as to be able to tell it accurately?
Chorus: As she herself says, she imagined she gave birth to a snake—
Orestes: That vision is not likely to have come for nothing!
Chorus: —and nestled it in swaddling clothes, like a baby.
Orestes: What food did it want, this deadly new-born creature?
Chorus: In her dream, she herself offered her breast to it.
Orestes: Then surely her teat was wounded by the loathsome beast?
Chorus: So that in her milk it drew off a clot of blood.

                                             (*Libation Bearers*, 523–533)[10]

Orestes and Shōgo "turn snake," the former by assuming the role of murdering his mother in
accordance with the dream:

> Orestes: Well, I pray to the Earth beneath us and to my father's tomb that this dream be
> fulfilled in me. See, I shall interpret it so that it fits exactly. If the snake came out of the
> same place as I did, and found a welcoming home in my swaddling-clothes, and opened
> its mouth around the breast that nurtured me, and made a clot of blood mingle with the
> loving milk, and she screamed out in fear at the experience—then, you see, as she nursed
> this monstrous portent, so she is destined to die by violence. I become the serpent and
> kill her: so this dream declares. (540–550)

The latter, Shōgo, assumes the snake's role by crushing with a stone what it could not destroy of
its own power. In so doing both young men begin a cycle of reversal that finds them initially the
aggressor and eventually the victim. For both, the snake is the singular sign by which this reversal is made evident: Orestes goes from assuming the identity of the snake in Clytemnestra's
dream (so as to kill her) to suffering the antagonism of the snake-haired Furies:

> Orestes: Ah, ah! I see these hideous women looking like Gorgons—clad in dark-grey
> tunics and thickly wreathed with serpents! I can't stay here! (1048–1050)

Likewise, Shōgo goes from egging on and supplanting the snake in his childhood to being the
victim of the animals of the remote island he and a young photographer inhabit in his second
"life."
       After Shōgo recovers from the electroshock therapy, he is sent back to his room. Shortly
thereafter Dr. Enoki arrives to try hypnosis instead, and Shōgo imagines he is a pilot transporting a young female photographer. When he and the photographer find themselves stranded on

10. The translations are Alan Sommerstein's from the 2008 Loeb edition of the *Oresteia*.

a deserted island, his first order of business is to capture a rabbit, kill it, and eat it to survive. In retaliation, the animal inhabitants of the island kidnap the young woman during the night, maul her within an inch of her life, and leave her nearly lifeless body beside his campfire. Shōgo is then put in the position of nursing her back to health in a very real nest he builds high in a tree in order to keep himself and the young woman safe from the danger posed by the animals that surround them. As if the nest were not explicit enough, Shōgo has to, at one point, chew a clump of berries and spit them into the woman's mouth because she is unable to do so herself, feeding her as a mother bird would her chicks.

With this second transformation of Shōgo's symbolic identity, he has gone from snake to male bird to female bird nursing/comforting his beleaguered companion in a manner analogous to the mother bird in the flashback to his adolescence. His new metaphorical identity has put him in the position of his mother (though, admittedly, with differences) in much the same way as Orestes, when being hounded by the Furies causes him to suffer the way Clytemnestra does in the *Libation Bearers*: afraid of the ominous presence of snakes.[11] The correspondences between the *Oresteia* and *Apollo's Song* are too many to enumerate in detail, but some follow. In the parodos (the first ode performed by the chorus) of the *Agamemnon*, Calchas reports that Artemis bears a grudge against Zeus (and incidentally against the whole expedition to Troy) for the pregnant hare slaughtered by the two eagles (134–137). He recognizes in the twin eagles the two sons of Atreus, Agamemnon and Menelaus, and Artemis as the cause of the strong wind that keeps their ships at bay (148–156). Similarly, one recognizes the paired birds (like the twin eagles who appear to stand for Agamemnon and Menelaus) of Shōgo's adolescence in him and the photographer. So when he kills a rabbit for sustenance, the animal's revenge appears to be analogous to Artemis'. Orestes is raised and nursed by a woman other than his mother;[12] Shōgo's mother refuses to breast-feed him.[13] Shōgo's mother figuratively murders his father by concealing his identity from Shōgo; Clytemnestra literally murders Agamemnon, and so forth.

However, a Japanese reader could not reasonably be expected to make this implicit connection between Shōgo and Orestes, and the cycles of reversals Shōgo undergoes could just as readily be understood as a Buddhist parable of desire and reincarnation in which the goddess, whom a Western reader might quickly identify as Athena, would be Kannon (or Guanyin, the Japanese and Chinese names respectively for the bodhisattva Avalokiteśvara). After all, it is Kannon/Guanyin who punishes Son Gokū, the so-called Monkey King, at the beginning of the *Journey into the West* by enslaving him to a mendicant monk. So, her role here as judge in Shōgo's successive reincarnations is explained just as well by Buddhist theology and an Eastern classical tradition as by a Greek one. Furthermore given the fact that the character I earlier recognized as Athena is never identified as such—she is referred to only as goddess (*megami*)—to read her as Kannon would not be entirely implausible. She looks like Athena but acts like

---

11. At *Libation Bearers* 523–525, the chorus claims that Clytemnestra has left offerings at Agamemnon's grave only because of her dreams and night terrors, especially the dream in which she imagines she has given birth to a snake.

12. See in particular the nurse's speech at *Libation Bearers* 749–762.

13. Tezuka (w./a.) (1977, vol. 1, 27 [27]).

Kannon, so perhaps she is both. Perhaps . . . but this doubt as to the goddess's identity (or rather her allusive identity) is the crux of the matter. With the possible allusion in *Apollo's Song* to the *Oresteia*, the best we as readers can do sometimes is doubt because the shifting patterns of reference in the imagery could just as readily be used to justify an allusion to the *Oresteia* as to deny it.

Moreover, none of the aforementioned transformations or correspondences explain in an obvious way what *Apollo's Song* has to do with Apollo. He is mentioned by name for the first time only halfway through the second volume (in chapter 3), when Shōgo, having escaped from a juvenile home in what we suppose is still his "real life," chases a woman named Hiromi, a marathon runner (and, as we learn later, a psychiatrist), in a scene that appears to allude to Apollo's chasing of Daphne. Shōgo, exhausted by the futility of the chase and the heat of the sun, collapses onto the sand and sighs a single word, "Apollo."[14] I say "appears to allude" because even though the similarity is easy to spot, I wonder how this scene reads to a hypothetical Japanese reader. In addition, I can only wonder, as my own cultural and educational history is not well suited to reading Shōgo's chasing Hiromi in relative ignorance. My suspicion is that a Japanese reader's ignorance of the myth of Apollo and Daphne is analogous to Hiromi's when Dr. Enoki tells her the story in the third volume,[15] so that it is important to note that the explicit retelling of the myth comes after the scene to which it seemingly alludes. For a Japanese reader, Shōgo's running after Hiromi may only be analogous to Apollo and Daphne in hindsight, meaning a "Japanese" perspective on the chase would be doubled: Read it first as a manifestation of Shōgo's internal, psychosexual conflicts and then later as a mythical allusion to Apollo and Daphne. However, even when Dr. Enoki recounts the myth, Shōgo's chase does not necessarily have to become an allusion to it because the immediate context is sufficient for explaining why the story is being told. Hiromi wants both to avoid Shōgo's sexual advances and to keep him interested, so Dr. Enoki suggests that she "should become a laurel tree,"[16] which, though oddly out of the blue, is a kind of solution to her problem. This seeming relation/ nonrelation is emblematic of the difficulty inherent in identifying allusion not merely outside its "proper" cultural context but within it as well. The same could be said of the connections I have already made between *Apollo's Song* and the *Oresteia*, that no matter how apt they may be, they only serve to prove a potential allusive relationship, one that a reader primed by knowledge of Greek tragedy may be possibly inventing and not merely discovering. So, in the absence of any clear documentary evidence, it seems best to hold back from definitively identifying Shōgo with Orestes and *Apollo's Song* with the *Oresteia*.

Yet, is this late revelation of Apollo not precisely how the *Oresteia* develops in terms of its narrative? Are not *Apollo's Song* and the *Oresteia* both about the son of Leto in much the same way? He is, after all, but one of several gods invoked in the first chorus of the *Agamemnon*, then the specific but absent object of Orestes' oath to kill Clytemnestra in the *Libation Bearers*, and finally a real personage in the trial of Orestes in the *Eumenides*. The same could be said of

14. Ibid., vol. 2, 73 [239].

15. Ibid., vol. 3, 113–123 [482–491].

16. Ibid., 113 [482].

Apollo's Song: The snake in volume 1 could be an allusion to the animal with which Apollo is most commonly identified; he is invoked by name in volume 2; and in the third volume he acquires a real presence in the form of the story Dr. Enoki tells. The connection between these two stories—ancient and modern, Greek and Japanese—is easy to make, and the points of comparison seem obvious.

Apollo's Song is a mirror in which we might see ourselves and not necessarily the culture whence it comes. It is a mirror, and the text a mirror image, particularly in translation. Manga are read the same way any other Japanese text is, generally from right to left,[17] and in the process of translation most Western publishing companies reverse all of the images so that the comic[18] will read from right to left, though some publishers do leave the images as is and note how they are meant to be read. This is clear in Vertical's 2007 translation,[19] where the statue of Athena Parthenos on pages 23 and 41 is obviously reversed, with the smaller statue of Nike, in the English translation, in Athena's left rather than her right hand. As originally drawn, Nike is in Athena's right hand. Normally, this mirroring of images would be puzzling at best, but it has the potential to create problems of interpretation specific to the translation.

The most obvious of these occurs in the story Shōgo tells the queen of the Synthians, in the last of his imagined "lives," of a robot designed to be a housekeeper who falls in love with her/its master. The robot observes human behavior and tries to imitate it for his own benefit. One day, she/it sees him embracing a woman outside the house and, when he comes back inside, embraces him so tightly that she/it crushes his bones and kills him. In the translation, the full-page image of the robot embracing her/its master[20] is remarkably similar to Jean-Léon Gérôme's painting of Pygmalion and Galatea, a visual "fact" that led me to make the connection between the robot housekeeper and Galatea in the first place. From that "fact" I superimposed a necessary correlative (the "master" was also the creator) and an ironical relationship between Tezuka's text and the Pygmalion myth (in the process of coming to love her/its master, the creation destroys the master, ironic because in the Pygmalion myth Galatea's coming to life in essence destroys the work of art). It made perfect sense, as Galatea's name means something like "milky" or "milk white," and the Synthian race is classified as "Homo lacteus" (Nieh's translation of Tezuka's "Homo gyunyus"),[21] so it makes sense that Shōgo would tell such a tale to their queen. However, in the Japanese the image is reversed and consequently does not evoke Gérôme's painting as clearly, leaving little to indicate that the robot's master is also her/its creator.

17. There is no standard orientation of Japanese text. It can be read from top to bottom, left to right (as in English) or from right to left, top to bottom. However, of these, the more common is the first, starting on the right-hand page and progressing to the left. All I mean to say is that manga is read from what we might consider the back of the book.

18. I use the word *comic* here to emphasize that the translation of manga involves more than simply converting the text in terms of the language used. To some translators, it demands an acclimation to our habitual reading practices as well.

19. Tezuka (w./a.). *Apollo's Song*, trans. Camellia Nieh (New York: Vertical, 2007).

20. Ibid., 367.

21. Ibid., 292.

The Japanese text is a hybrid in which the "Western" and "Japanese" elements are sometimes easy to distinguish and sometimes not. The scientific name Tezuka uses for the Synthians, Homo gyunyus,[22] combines both the Japanese word for milk (*gyū'nyū*) with a Latin masculine singular ending (*-us*). And like the allusion to Apollo and Daphne in the second volume, the classical elements we find are as much a reflection of a real textual intimation as of our expectation of finding them there. I suggest that manga—and this one in particular—requires a doubled perspective in which we recognize how we interpret a text and hold in abeyance those intertextual connections that may as easily originate in the reader as they do in the text under consideration.

Appendix: Mirror Images

The differences in the graphic and structural natures of the Japanese text and its only English translation are important because much of what is said here is dependent upon visual similarities between the individual panels of Tezuka's manga and certain works of art. The most significant difference is the orientation of the images. Because Japanese text reads, typically, from top to bottom, and the lines progress from right to left, the standard for reading the progression of panels is different from what one would expect in Western comics. Where the panels of an American comic would go from left to right and then down the page, the panels of a manga proceed from right to left, and one reads from what might seem to be the back of the book. This means that often in translation, in order for the manga to read in a manner more in accordance with the expectations of a Western reader, the individual pages are mirror-reversed. This preserves the narrative sequence of the original Japanese text while rendering it something more akin to how Western books and comics in particular are read. This works well enough in practice but has the unfortunate potential of creating a visual similarity where there may not be one and obscuring similarities that are in fact present. One can correct for this somewhat when reading the English translation by either imagining it in reverse or perhaps even holding the text up to a mirror.

While the structural differences may not be as significant for the argument here, they are worth noting. The Japanese text, as it appears in Tezuka's collected works, is in three volumes that roughly correspond to the three embedded narratives that relate Shōgo's alternative "lives." However, the length and size of each volume is standard, a format commonly used to collect sections of a larger text published serially in the weekly/monthly manga anthologies like *Shōnen Jump* or *Margaret*, so any correspondence between the narrative and the three volumes may be purely coincidental. The English translation published by Vertical prints *Apollo's Song* in one large volume, so the obvious structure to attend to there would be the five chapters and prologue. However, even the chapter divisions have been altered. The first example is the beginning of chapter 2, whose title Tezuka has in the panel where Shōgo and the photographer wash up on the beach of a deserted island (95 in vol. 1 of the Japanese [also 95 in the English]), but Nieh's translation places this scene several pages earlier (81), when Dr. Enoki returns to Shōgo's

---

22. Tezuka (w./a.) (1977 vol. 1, 127 [292]).

cell. Even more egregious is the shift of the beginning of chapter 3 from vol. 2, page 62, of the Japanese (English 28), where Hiromi is swimming in the lake, to English page 172, when Shōgo comes to from hypnosis. This is easy enough to see in the translation: The large blank space at the top of page 228 is where the title should be. Be aware that in going a long way to accommodate its assumed reader, the translation obscures much of how the original appears and reads. My references are generally to the Japanese text, so readers of the English translation should keep in mind that what I say may not obviously correspond to the text before them.

5

Heroes UnLimited

The Theory of the Hero's Journey and the Limitation of the Superhero Myth

Brett M. Rogers

At the dawn of the 21st century, heroes run free in Western narrative. To be sure, Greek *hêrôes*—brave and powerful demigods—have led cattle raids and adventures overseas since Homer's *Iliad* and *Odyssey* (c. 750 BCE). In the last century, however, a new breed of superheroes has emerged, costumed crime fighters who fight for truth, justice, and the American way.[1] During the present decade a legion of superheroes has splashed across comic book panels, televisions, and silver screens: Superman, Batman, Wonder Woman, Spider-Man, the X-Men, the Fantastic Four, the Incredible Hulk, and Iron Man (to name but a few). Like their Greek ancestors, these superheroes explore and exceed the limits of morality, humanity, and imagination. They have found free rein in our imaginations because, as Peter Coogan (2005) has suggested, "superheroes stand as metaphors for freedom—the freedom to act without consequences and the freedom from the restrictions of gravity, the law, families, and romantic relationships" (14).[2]

But are superheroes really free? While they may seem to leap and bound with freedom, superheroes in fact move within a limited range of actions and narrative patterns. Writers of superhero narratives exist in our world and have been conditioned by age-old storytelling traditions and specific ideas about how these traditions work. Superman, the "archetypal superhero," embodies this contradiction in what I call the *superintelligence fallacy*.[3] Writers occasionally attribute to Superman the power of superhuman intelligence; Superman solves

---

1. Several artists and critics view superheroes in terms of classical heroes. O'Neil (2005, 24) relates that Superman creator Jerry Siegel conceived of the hero as "Samson, Hercules, and all the strong men I ever heard of rolled into one—*only more so*"; cf. Coogan (2006, 116–17). In an interview in the *Comics Journal* 69, Gerry Conway compares superheroes to the heroes of Greek drama, although he stresses that comic book heroes are not direct descendants; see Spurgeon (2006, 247–48). Eco (1972, 15) connects superheroes to the traditional heroes of classical and Nordic mythology but argues for a "fundamental difference" in the narrative structures of their stories.

2. Cf. Eco (1972), who discusses strategies used by early comics writers (e.g., failure to acknowledge previous narratives, production of "imaginary" or "untold tales") to "remove Superman from the law that leads from life to death through time" (17) and thus to free him from consequences.

3. I owe this observation to my brother, Scott Rogers. The term *superintelligence fallacy* is my own.

difficult problems by virtue of his advanced Kryptonian brain. (A clear but exaggerated depiction of this power appears in "The Amazing Story of Superman-Red and Superman-Blue" in *Superman* 162.[4]) Superintelligence, however, is a subtly false ability—even more so than the patently fictional powers of flight or heat vision—because any "superhuman" solution that Superman devises has necessarily been devised by a human writer in the first place. Superman's superintelligence is limited a priori by human intelligence.

The microproblem of the superintelligence fallacy mirrors a problem in superhero narratives. Writers for comics, film, and television learn their craft through fandom and years of studying hero tales, other narratives, technical writers' manuals, and so on. However, three generations of writers have been influenced by one especially popular account of hero narratives, Joseph Campbell's theory of the Hero's Journey. Campbell first offered this theory in *The Hero with a Thousand Faces* (hereafter *HTF*), published in 1949. Campbell's theory gained popularity with *The Power of Myth*, both a book and a television documentary, produced for the Public Broadcasting Service (PBS) in 1988 and recorded in part at Skywalker Ranch, the home of *Star Wars* creator George Lucas. Due to the PBS series and Lucas's support,[5] the Hero's Journey is treated in the popular consciousness not as a theory but as a cross-cultural given. Writers and critics familiar with Campbell's theory consequently produce hero narratives and critical readings that reproduce the theory. Thus, Campbell's theory indirectly shapes and delimits the expectations of audiences, critics, and storytellers. As in the case of the superintelligence fallacy, superheroes that seem to exceed the boundaries of human imagination in fact act according to the limitations of Campbell's theory.

How has the theory of the hero's journey come to limit the way we view superhero myths? In what follows, I first examine the origin of the hero's journey in the fields of formalism, anthropology, and psychology. Second, I describe how Campbell's theory has influenced writers of hero narratives, considering technical manuals and other discussions of the production of comic books, film, and video games. As evidence of Campbell's pervasive influence, I offer a reading of one recent incarnation of the Spider-Man mythos, the first story arc of *Ultimate Spider-Man*.[6] In the final section I contrast this reading with the original Spider-Man/Green Goblin stories published between July 1964 and July 1973. (I choose the Green Goblin since he is the first villain who appears when Spider-Man narratives are translated into a new series or medium, thus offering a stable point of comparison.) I argue that the application of the hero's journey to the Spider-Man/Green Goblin mythos "flattens" the narrative by failing to grasp the meanings, importance, and influence of these original stories. This reading, I hope, will encourage storytellers and audiences not only to avoid using the theory of the hero's journey as a prescriptive template but also to examine other strategies for the interpretation and construction of superhero narratives.

4. Leo Dorfman (w.) and Curt Douglas Swan (a.), *Superman* 162 (DC, July 1963). For a discussion of Superman's superintelligence, see Bowermaster and Gordon (2007).

5. For discussion of Joseph Campbell's influence on George Lucas and the *Star Wars* films, see the 1997 interviews conducted by Seabrook (1999, 205) and Weinraub (1999, 219), as well as the documentary *The Mythology of Star Wars with George Lucas and Bill Moyers* (1999), a sequel to *The Power of Myth*.

6. Brian Michael Bendis and Bill Jemas (w.) and Mark Bagley (a.), *Ultimate Spider-Man* 1–7 (Marvel, Oct. 2000–May 2001), collected as a trade paperback, *Power and Responsibility* (Marvel, 2001).

The Hero's Journey in the 19th and 20th Centuries

The Hero's Journey, or "monomyth" (as Campbell calls it), posits that hero adventures follow a three-tiered story pattern: "a separation from the world, a penetration to some source of power, and a life-enhancing return" (*HTF*, 35). Campbell further breaks each tier into subcategories and offers a composite picture of the story elements that can make up a hero's adventure (table 5.1). For Campbell, there is "astonishingly little variation in the morphology of the adventure, the character roles involved, [and] the victories gained" in storytelling traditions across time and cultures, from Greece, Rome, the biblical world, medieval Europe, and the Orient (38). This pattern, Campbell argues, reveals not only the meaning of heroes as "images for contemporary life, but also the singleness of the human spirit in its aspirations, powers, vicissitudes, and wisdom" (36). The Hero's Journey makes accessible "the world's symbolic carriers of the destiny of Everyman" and, in Campbell's view, offers wisdom to all possible audiences, regardless of sex, culture, or creed (36).

Campbell draws upon a variety of stories to demonstrate the ubiquity of the Hero's Journey, but the theoretical basis for the monomyth derives from three distinct theories about how myths work. The shape of the monomyth indicates the influence of formalism, the oldest of these theories. Formalists since Aristotle have studied the form of narratives and devoted attention to the essential components of a given story type. In the fourth century BCE, Aristotle examined the elements of Greek epic and drama, positing in the *Poetics* that every story should both prioritize action (i.e., the arrangement of incidents) over character (1450a15–b4) and contain a three-act structure: a beginning, a middle, and an end (1450b21–34). In the late-nineteenth and early-twentieth centuries, scholars such as Johann Georg van Hahn, Edward Tylor, Otto Rank, Vladimir Propp, and Lord Raglan sought to uncover and clarify the constituent elements common to hero myths in particular.[7] Although Campbell does not explicitly refer to the school of formalism in *HTF*, his aim to delineate the "morphology of the adventure"—that is, both the shape of and the rules for the sequence of actions in hero myths—places him firmly in this tradition.

The formalism of the Hero's Journey, however, is modified by a development from the field of anthropology. In 1909 Arnold van Gennep published *Les rites de passage*, in which he examines ceremonies surrounding life transitions such as pregnancy, birth, marriage, and death. To describe these transitional ceremonies, van Gennep coined the phrase "rites of passage." Every culture possesses rites of passage, although they vary in their details by culture. Campbell

TABLE 5.1   **Summary of the Hero's Journey, based on Campbell (1949)**

1. Separation/Departure	2. Initiation	3. Return
a. Call to Adventure	a. Road of Trials	a. Refusal of the Return
b. Refusal of the Call	b. Meeting of the Goddess	b. Magic Flight
c. Supernatural Aid	c. Woman as the Temptress	c. Rescue from Without
d. Crossing of the Threshold	d. Atonement with the Father	d. Crossing of the Return Threshold
e. Belly of the Whale	e. Apotheosis	e. Master of the Two Worlds
	f. Ultimate Boon	f. Freedom to Live

7. See Segal (1987, 1–2) and Csapo (2005, 190–211).

understands the purpose of these rites of passage "to conduct people across those difficult thresholds of transformation that demand a change in the patterns not only of conscious but also of unconscious life" (*HTF*, 10). Moreover, van Gennep identified three distinct stages in the *rites de passage*: separation, initiation, and return. For Campbell, these three stages, which "might be named the nuclear unit of the monomyth," are the three acts upon which the narrative of the Hero's Journey is constructed (30).

Note that Campbell sees rites of passage as conducive to "a change in the patterns not only of conscious *but also of unconscious life*" (my emphasis). Campbell's emphasis on the unconscious indicates the third and perhaps most important influence on the Hero's Journey—namely, psychoanalysis as articulated in Sigmund Freud's theories about dreams and the unconscious, as well as Carl Jung's notions of the collective unconscious and the archetype. While formalism and van Gennep's rites of passage explain how the Hero's Journey works, providing its skeletal framework, psychoanalysis provides an explanation for why the Hero's Journey works cross-culturally. Campbell argues that myth is a form of dreaming shared by the collective human psyche, "the secret opening through which the inexhaustible energies of the cosmos pour into human cultural manifestation" (*HTF*, 3). For Campbell, myths look the same cross-culturally because, like dreams, they provide universal symbols that tap into the consciousness of all human beings at every stage of life.

The Hero's Journey in Practice (and *Spider-Man*) in the 21st Century

Comics authors and critics readily accept certain components of the Hero's Journey. Most comics writers are formalists by necessity, as comic books are produced on a monthly basis with strict deadlines. Some writers work on multiple titles at the same time; in the sixties Stan Lee simultaneously wrote "fourteen superhero titles, some westerns, some humor books, and occasional odd projects that don't categorize easily" (O'Neil 2001, 24–25), while Brian Michael Bendis has in this decade written as many as five separate titles at once. Consequently, comics writers use guidelines for writing scripts quickly, often based on the sequence of actions in the narrative. In the *DC Comics Guide to Writing Comics* (2001), Dennis O'Neil recommends a three-act story structure: the hook/inciting incident and establishment of situation and conflict (act I); development and complication of the situation (act II); and climax/denouement (act III).[8] This same three-tiered structure appears in influential film manuals, such as Syd Field's *Screenplay: The Foundations of Screenwriting*.[9] Of course, not all writers follow the three-tier template. In *Understanding Comics* (1993) and *Making Comics* (2006), Scott McCloud combines formalist analysis with other theoretical approaches, such as semiotics, in order to examine and produce narratives that range in length from two panels to graphic novels.

8. O'Neil (2001, 34–45). Abel and Madden (2008, 128–29) offer the same elements but in five stages: protagonist, spark, escalation, climax, and denouement. Cf. Gertler and Lieber (2004, 46), who identify superheroes as a distinct "genre" (40) containing both a situation and a complication. Elsewhere they offer a more amusing three-tiered story pattern: hero-meets-villain, hero-punches-villain, hero wins (40).

9. Field's paradigm of a screenplay is the three-act structure of Set-Up, Confrontation, and Resolution (1979, 7–13). Cf. Wolff and Cox (1988, 18–29), Field (1998, 26–34).

Comics writers and critics also generally accept Jung's notion of the archetype. In one of the earliest works of comics criticism, Umberto Eco proclaims that "the mythological character of comic strips finds himself in this singular situation: he must be an archetype, the totality of certain collective aspirations, and therefore he must necessarily become immobilized in an emblematic and fixed nature which renders him easily recognizable (this is what happens to Superman)" (Eco 1972, 15). O'Neil similarly calls the archetype "an inherited memory represented in the mind by a universal symbol and observed in dreams and myths . . . an image that's hard-wired into our mental computers" (2001, 23). However, O'Neil contests the "immobility" of the superhero's "emblematic and fixed nature." Although O'Neil agrees "that comic-book superheroes are modern incarnations of some of the archetypes the good Dr. Jung mentioned" (24), he argues for modifying Jung's theory to take into account changes in archetypes that occur as time passes, authors age, audiences change, and superheroes cross into different media. O'Neil suggests thinking in terms of what he calls the "meme-archetype," an archetype that changes and evolves from generation to generation (25–28).

Few writers, however, exhibit O'Neil's willingness to challenge and nuance models of narrative production, and many writers treat the Hero's Journey as a mere template. I have already alluded to Campbell's influence on George Lucas and *Star Wars*. Lucas's commercial success has ensured that college students read *HTF* in courses on anthropology, mythology, and screenwriting. Campbell's theory, however, gained further traction when Disney story consultant and lecturer Christopher Vogler produced a seven-page memo in the late eighties to serve as a practical guide to the Hero's Journey. The memo circulated widely throughout Hollywood, and Vogler turned it into an influential manual, *The Writer's Journey: Mythic Structure for Writers* (1992, third edition 2007). In the *Writer's Journey*, Vogler modifies Campbell's theory and explicitly affixes it to the three-act structure (as seen in table 5.2). Vogler's version of the Hero's Journey has drawn significant attention from writers in comics, video games, and film. O'Neil refers to Vogler for his definition of the hero (2001, 60). Troy Dunniway (2000) recommends Vogler's version of

TABLE 5.2   **Campbell's Hero's Journey and the modifications of Vogler (2007)**

	Campbell's Hero's Journey	**Vogler's modifications**
		Ordinary World
Act 1: Departure	Call to Adventure	Call to Adventure
	Refusal of the Call	Refusal of the Call
	Supernatural Aid	Meeting with the Mentor
	Crossing of the Threshold	Crossing the First Threshold
	Belly of the Whale	
Act 2: Initiation	Road of Trials	Test, Allies, Enemies
	Meeting with the Goddess	Approach to the Inmost Cave
	Woman as the Temptress	The Ordeal
	Atonement with the Father	
	Apotheosis	
	Ultimate Boon	
Act 3: Return	Refusal of the Return	Reward
	Magic Flight	Road Back
	Rescue from Without	The Resurrection
	Crossing of the Return Threshold	Return with the Elixir
	Master of the Two Worlds	
	Freedom to Live	

the Hero's Journey for its utility in developing stories quickly.[10] Stuart Voytilla (1999) uses Vogler's schema to explain the success of fifty Hollywood films, including *Citizen Kane*, *Annie Hall*, *Raiders of the Lost Ark*, and (in what amounts to a tautology) the *Star Wars* trilogy.

Many writers who use Vogler's summary of the Hero's Journey as a prescriptive model work in media that are not necessarily serialized—namely, film and video games. Since narratives in these media are generally conceived of and produced as stand-alone works, the Hero's Journey offers a template for the narrative from start to finish. In contrast, narratives in media such as comic books and television are more open ended: A typical comics series runs twelve issues per year; a typical television program consists of twenty-two episodes per season; both formats can last for years or decades. This is not to say that the Hero's Journey model cannot and has not influenced serial narratives. George Lucas uses the Hero's Journey in his *Star Wars* films, yet this series consists of six individual films produced over a period of thirty years.[11] Moreover, authors of serial narratives regularly derive inspiration and techniques from cinema. Brian Michael Bendis has claimed that, when he received the assignment to write *Ultimate Spider-Man* (hereafter *USM*), his goal was to "really flesh Spider-Man's origin out in a cinematic way—to use the most overused term in comics."[12] Even if authors of serial narratives do not consciously evoke the Hero's Journey, there is circumstantial evidence that they have absorbed the model from their congeners.

Bendis's work on *Ultimate Spider-Man* provides an example of the Hero's Journey in a serialized comic-book format. In 2000, Marvel Comics editors, in an effort to reach readers unfamiliar with four decades of narrative continuity, decided to relaunch several of their popular titles in the *Ultimate* Marvel line, including *Spider-Man*. When we first meet Peter Parker (*USM* 1, 5.1–3), he is studying in the Westwood Mall food court, Queens (in what Vogler, table 2, identifies as the ORDINARY WORLD). He is, as the issue title denotes, "powerless." This changes when a genetically modified spider bites Peter during a field trip to the laboratory of scientist (and future villain) Norman Osborn. Throughout the next two issues, Peter develops supernatural powers—the ability to stick to walls, spider sense, superstrength—and declares "I am Hercules!" (*USM* 2, 16.4). This new Hercules (like the Greek original) does not know how to control his powers, and he breaks the hand of school bully Flash Thompson in a fight (2.8). In order to help his Aunt May and Uncle Ben pay Flash's medical bills, Peter puts his powers to use in the professional wrestling ring, at which point he receives his costume and the

---

10. See also Waugh (2007).

11. Wasley (2005) argues that the *Star Wars* series really consists of one single "postmodern art film."

12. From an interview published in *Write Now!* 1 (Aug. 2002), reprinted in Fingeroth (2008, 13). Influence goes both ways, as filmmakers have derived inspiration from comic books since the 1940s. It is rumored that Orson Welles used lighting techniques and camera angles for *Citizen Kane* (1941) derived from early *Batman* comics and even contemplated making *Batman* films as early as 1946; see Ellis and Ellis (2008, 49). In his novel *The Amazing Adventures of Kavalier and Clay* (2000), Michael Chabon dramatizes the cross-fertilization of film and comics when his protagonists, comic-book creators Joe Kavalier and Sammy Clay, attend the premiere of *Citizen Kane*. The fictional Welles confesses that he doesn't "like to miss a word" (358) of the protagonists' comic, *The Escapist*. Kavalier marvels "that *Citizen Kane* represented, more than any other movie Joe had ever seen, the total blending of narration and image that was . . . the fundamental principle of comic book storytelling . . . *Citizen Kane* was like a comic book" (361–62). In the past two decades, writers such as Kevin Smith and Joss Whedon have started working in both film and comics. Robert Rodriguez, director of *Sin City* (2005), and Zak Snyder, director of *300* (2006) and *Watchmen* (2009), have both collaborated closely with comics author Frank Miller, who directed the film based on Will Eisner's comic, *The Spirit* (2008).

name "The Amazing Spider-Man" (*USM* 3, 18.5) (CALL TO ADVENTURE). However, after some money mysteriously disappears, the manager drives Peter out of the wrestling organization. In a funk, Peter refuses to prevent a robbery at a deli, begins to fail in his schoolwork, and runs away from home (REFUSAL OF THE CALL). Although Peter considers talking to a doctor, it is Uncle Ben who tracks Peter down and lectures him on the great responsibility that comes at this turning point in his life (*USM* 4, 17–19) (MEETING WITH THE MENTOR).[13] When Peter returns home, however, he finds the threshold blocked: The street is filled with police cars, while the front door is covered with police tape (*USM* 4, 22.3). Peter discovers that Uncle Ben has been murdered (*USM* 5, 3–5), shot by the same robber whom Peter failed to stop outside the deli. Peter leaves home to seek vengeance (*USM* 5, 6.6–7), this time as Spider-Man (CROSSING OF THE FIRST THRESHOLD). Thus, we find all five phases of DEPARTURE in succession in the first five issues.

In accordance with the second phase of the Hero's Journey (INITIATION), Peter enters into the life of a superhero in *Ultimate Spider-Man* 6–7. Readers are introduced to a potential ally, *Daily Bugle* editor in chief J. Jonah Jameson, who is the first to classify Spider-Man as "hero or villain" (*USM* 6, 3.5) and eventually becomes an enemy in the media. Norman Osborn becomes the Green Goblin (TEST, ALLIES, AND ENEMIES). The Green Goblin attacks Peter's high school, setting off a series of explosions that turn the school halls into a dark, cavernous space (figure 5.1). Here Spider-Man meets the Goblin (*USM* 6, 16–17; APPROACH TO THE INMOST CAVE), and the Goblin reveals that he knows Spider-Man's real identity. While Spidey's first quip to the Goblin—"Uh . . . you wouldn't happen to be the new Home Ec Teacher, would you?" (*USM* 6, 18.1)—seems innocuous enough, the joke reveals the stakes of the confrontation; in the very halls in which Peter Parker was once bullied and then found his strength, he now must confront a new challenge, one that has physically destroyed his life at school and has the potential to destroy his life at home (SUPREME ORDEAL).[14]

Bendis follows the first two stages of the Hero's Journey in *Ultimate Spider-Man* 1–7, but he does not complete the third stage of the journey (RETURN). Though Bendis initiates Spider-Man (and the reader) into a new world, he brings completion neither to Spider-Man's *rite de passage* nor to the serial narrative. (As of June 2010, Bendis still writes the series, though now under the title *Ultimate Comics: Spider-Man*.) Spider-Man's incomplete *rite de passage* hints that other forces (Bendis's livelihood, profit for Marvel Comics) work actively against narrative conclusion. The Hero's Journey, however, does find completion in other versions of the mythos, in film (such as Sam Raimi's 2002 film, *Spider-Man*) and other comic books. In 2004 the Gotham Entertainment Group published *Spider-Man India* 1–4, which tells the story of Pavitr Prabhakar and his confrontation with Nalin Oberoi/Rakshasa (an Indian version of Norman Osborn/the Green Goblin).[15] Dan O'Rourke and Pravin Rodrigues have shown that the series indeed follows

---

13. Peter's idea to consult a doctor evokes the view of medicine and psychoanalysis in Campbell (1949, 9): "The doctor is the modern master of the mythological realm, the knower of all the secret ways and words of potency. His role is precisely that of the Wise Old Man of the myths and fairy tales whose words assist the hero through the trials and terrors of weird adventure." The intervention of Uncle Ben might thus suggest that, despite Peter's advanced scientific knowledge, the power of mythic wisdom supersedes that of modern medicine.

14. The Green Goblin will nearly destroy Peter's home life when he almost kills Peter's girlfriend, Mary Jane Watson, in *USM* 25–26.

15. Sharad Devarajan (w.) and Jeevan J. Kang (w./a.), *Spider-Man: India* 1–4 (Gotham Comics: Nov. 2004–Feb. 2005).

FIGURE 5.1   Spider-Man first confronts the Green Goblin in *Ultimate Spider-Man* 6 (Marvel, April 2001)
18. Artist Mark Bagley uses one full page without words—filled with the Goblin's body, smoke, and water—
to create a sense of confined, cavernous space and to heighten the drama of this initial confrontation.

the Hero's Journey through all three stages. They argue that *Spider-Man India* is a "'transcreation' monomyth," a myth that, with some modification for an Indian audience, works across cultural boundaries and therefore demonstrates the validity of the Hero's Journey model (O'Rourke and Rodrigues 2007, esp. 112–114, 120–125). While *Spider-Man India* has enjoyed neither the success nor the longevity of its American counterpart—perhaps suggesting that the third stage of the Hero's Journey threatens to exhaust a serial narrative—*Spider-Man India* demonstrates that the Hero's Journey has become a template for writers and readers worldwide.

Reframing the Hero

While the Hero's Journey has been used globally, it has also generated debate and resistance. Victoria Schmidt includes the Hero's Journey among her eleven "master" plot structures in *Story Structure Architect*, but she concludes, "this Journey model became so popular at one point that many feel it has been overdone" (2005, 73). Bob Bates has asserted in the game-developer forum *Gamasutra* that "[w]e are continuously cautioned against using the Hero's Journey as a template.... Campbell's work is *descriptive* rather than *prescriptive*" (his emphasis; 2005). Tadhg Kelly (2005a) adds the following:

> The Hero's Journey is **just** a literary analysis tool.... It's a means of evaluating and criticising **existing** works based on [observations]. As with any other literary school, it is imperfect and there are works that don't sit well within it. This is true of Marxist theory, Feminist theory, Modernism, Postmodernism, Structuralism, and it is true of the Hero's Journey.[16]

Taken together, Schmidt, Bates, and Kelly not only indicate a widespread discomfort with the "overdone" Hero's Journey but also offer a fundamental revision to mainstream views of Campbell's work: The Hero's Journey is not a prescriptive template but a descriptive theory.

When we view the Hero's Journey as a descriptive theory with a particular pedigree, we gain insight into its "imperfection" or limitation. Consider the character development of a hero. Aristotle and subsequent formalist approaches emphasize the hero's actions rather than the hero's identity—the journey rather than the hero. Moreover, as Douglas Wolk observes, superhero narratives prioritize action over premise.[17] Thus, when writers use the Hero's Journey as a prescriptive template for superhero narratives—that is, when they apply a model that emphasizes action to a genre that prioritizes action—they risk creating flat superheroes bound to meaningless sequences of action: "[Y]ou always end up with a generic result" (Kelly 2005a). In contrast, Bates asserts that a story pattern must be shaped around the premise of the story, featuring heroes and villains who embody that premise. A hero's character must precede the hero's actions.[18]

16. Kelly's comments belong to a series of responses to Bates (2005); see Kelly 2005a, 2005b; Veugen (2005).

17. "What matters most in superhero comics is *what happens to whom* and *what it looks like*—the actual plot and dialogue, and the content of the images" (emphasis in original), as opposed to characterization, style, or other content (Wolk 2007, 110).

18. This lack of emphasis on character has been similarly noted by critics of the formalist Vladimir Propp; see Csapo (2005, 201–209, esp. 204–205).

Part of the early success of Marvel Comics was Stan Lee's focus on premise and character. Gerry Conway, who succeeded Lee as writer for *The Amazing Spider-Man* (*ASM*), has claimed, "There practically were no plots in Marvel books [in the sixties]. Stan was more interested in what the character was feeling, and how to express that, than setting up clever story puzzles for the hero to solve."[19] For example, consider how characters feel about money. Economic class is a category of analysis wholly ignored by Campbell's theory. In Bendis's *Ultimate Spider-Man*, class concerns are largely suppressed: While Peter's family worries about a potential lawsuit when Peter accidentally breaks Flash Thompson's hand, there is no greater sense that they face financial distress except the need to pay off this one medical bill. However, in the first *Amazing Spider-Man* issues featuring the Green Goblin, Spider-Man's financial anxieties play a prominent role, leading him to work as an actor in a phony film in New Mexico (14) and to attend a Spider-Man fan club meeting to win over fans (17).[20] While Peter's economic concerns are muted in subsequent issues (*ASM* 23, 26–27, 39–40)[21]—anxieties about keeping a science scholarship and earning money give way to repeated "fast-moving cops and robber stor[ies]" (*ASM* 23, 2.1)—economic desires remain central to the Green Goblin's motives. The Goblin attempts to control local crime rackets by hiring henchmen (14, 39) and fighting gangsters such as Lucky Lobo (23) and the Crime-Master (26–27) (figure 5.2). For both Spider-Man and the Green Goblin, then, these stories focus on their feelings about money: Peter's anxieties about supporting himself and his Aunt May; the Goblin's desire to control not New York but the city's criminal syndicates. Economic conflicts and desires drive the characters, and the characters drive each plot.[22]

When the Green Goblin reveals his identity (in *ASM* 39–40), we discover he has been driven not by a mere desire for wealth but by his own obsessive economic anxieties. Indeed, *Amazing Spider-Man* 40 consists of eleven continuous pages of exposition as Norman Osborn recounts his past; a single father, Norman has turned to a life of cutthroat business tactics and crime in order to give material comfort to his son, Harry (*ASM* 40, 3–6). A subsequent laboratory accident has left Norman with brain damage and an obsession with becoming "the greatest

19. DeFalco (2004, 43). In a twist on Campbell, Conway refers to the Marvel style of characterization in the sixties as "the Hero with the Fatal Flaw" in Spurgeon (2006, 247).

20. Stan Lee (w.) and Steve Ditko (a.), *Amazing Spider-Man* 14 (Marvel, July 1964) and *Amazing Spider-Man* 17 (Oct. 1964).

21. Lee (w.) and Ditko (a.) *Amazing Spider-Man* 23 (Apr. 1966), *Amazing Spider-Man* 26–27 (July–Aug. 1966); Lee (w.) and John Romita Sr. (a.), *Amazing Spider-Man* 39–40 (Aug.–Sept. 1967).

22. These economic anxieties seem to account for the original success of *ASM*. Spider-Man first captured national attention when *Esquire* magazine (Sept. 1965) featured an article on the "Heroes of the California Rebels," a list of twenty-eight individuals considered influential among college students at the time. The list includes several people indicative of the social and economic radicalism of the midsixties: John F. Kennedy, Bob Dylan, Vladimir Lenin, Malcolm X, and Fidel Castro (*inter alia*). Last on the list comes Spider-Man (another comic book figure, the Incredible Hulk, also made the list, just above Spider-Man, due to anxieties about nuclear energy). The article claims that students identified with Spider-Man because he is a "fink kid" fighting in "figurative fantasies" (97), suggesting that his status as a "kid" (a teenager in high school) provided the locus of identification for students. We see in this description why Spider-Man might fit into the mold of the hero's journey; Peter undergoes many *rites de passage* in his transition from "fink kid" to adult. However, Spider-Man's inclusion on this list also suggests something that cannot be identified within the parameters of the hero's journey—namely, that audiences considered Spider-Man, struggling with the need to pay for college and support his aunt, to be emblematic of the social and economic struggles that students were facing at the time. Indeed, an oft-repeated but false anecdote—that the *Esquire* list places Spider-Man alongside Che Guevara—reinforces this perception.

FIGURE 5.2 Early *Amazing Spider-Man* issues, such as *Amazing Spider-Man* 23 (Marvel, April 1965), treat the Green Goblin as either in league with or in competition against other gangsters. Cover art by Steve Ditko.

costumed criminal of all time" (*ASM* 40, 5.6). Norman's mental trauma is alleviated only when, in the ensuing battle, the Goblin suffers an electrical-chemical charge that results in amnesia (*ASM* 40, 16.4–17.5). All successive Green Goblin narratives (*Spectacular Spider-Man* 2, *ASM* 96–98, 121–122) revolve around episodes in which Norman becomes so overwhelmed by economic and familial stressors that the Green Goblin persona reemerges.[23]

It is significant that *Amazing Spider-Man* 39–40 shifts attention away from Spider-Man's character to his adversary's character and anxieties.[24] Unlike the early issues of *Ultimate Spider-Man*, many *Amazing Spider-Man* issues focus on the character of Spider-Man's opponents; sometimes Spider-Man is a foil for another character's journey. Such is the case in *Amazing Spider-Man* 96–98 (May–July 1971), in which Norman remembers that he is the Green Goblin, while Harry becomes addicted to drugs. From the perspective of the Hero's Journey, this story provides merely one small episode (TEST, ALLIES, AND ENEMIES) in the six-year Spider-Man/Green Goblin narrative arc, scarcely contributing to Spider-Man's "journey." From the perspective of the Green Goblin's character, the story rearticulates the conflict between Norman, the caring father, and the Goblin, obsessed with killing Spider-Man. Our web slinger defeats the Goblin by forcing him to acknowledge a hospitalized Harry, causing the Goblin to pass out and return to his identity as Norman Osborn (*ASM* 98, 3.17–18). These three issues do not advance any journey but emphasizes the internal conflict between father and villain in the same character.

Moreover, *Amazing Spider-Man* 96–98 were a crucial battleground for larger ideological forces at work in the comic-book industry. The U.S. Department of Health, Education, and Welfare asked Stan Lee to produce a comic "warning kids about the dangers of drug addiction" (Thomas and Sanderson 2007, 110), but this required Lee to publish the comics in violation of the Comics Code Authority, a self-imposed regulatory code that had been observed for almost two decades.[25] Lee convinced Marvel's publishers to release the three issues without the code's seal of approval. These issues received critical acclaim and ultimately led to a significant revision of the Comics Code Authority, expanding the breadth of characters and topics that were permitted to appear in comics. Thus, *Amazing Spider-Man* 96–98 demonstrate that the Hero's Journey fails not only to serve as an adequate descriptive theory to explain narrative composition—especially when the narrative focuses on the villain's complex psychological character—but also to take into account the extratextual pressures that shape the composition of narratives. The Hero's Journey demands action that can be iterated; this Spider-Man story responds to the demands of a specific historical moment.

23. Stan Lee (w.) and John Romita Sr. (a.), *Spectacular Spider-Man* 2 (Marvel, Nov. 1968); Stan Lee (w.) and Gil Kane (a.) *Amazing Spider-Man* 96–98 (May–July 1971); Gerry Conway (w.) and Gil Kane (a.), *Amazing Spider-Man* 121–22 (June–July 1973).

24. See O'Neil (2001, 74) on writing villains: "Everything that's true about creating heroes is equally true about creating villains. If you're going to be a slacker, be lazy about your hero and save the industriousness for your villain. . . . A hero is only as good as his antagonist."

25. Amid the panic of the McCarthy era, psychologist Fredric Wertham wrote *Seduction of the Innocent* (1954), in which he argues that comic books promote juvenile delinquency. The U.S. government consequently launched an investigation into the comic industry. Several publishers responded by forming the Comics Code Authority, which banned from comics depictions of excessive violence, sexual matters, drugs, and, of course, vampires.

FIGURE 5.3 The death (and quasi-crucifixion) of the Green Goblin in *Amazing Spider-Man* 122 (Marvel, July 1973) 18.5-7. Art by Gil Kane.

The final issues of the original Spider-Man/Green Goblin narrative arc (June–July 1973) similarly respond to extratextual pressure. Several series writers decided to make the unprecedented move of killing off one of the series' main characters (Conway 2006, 2–4). Norman Osborn, anxious about his dire financial straits and Harry's return to drug abuse, again becomes the Green Goblin. The Goblin kidnaps Peter's girlfriend, Gwen Stacy, and a fight ensues in which Gwen is knocked off the George Washington Bridge and killed.[26] Spider-Man tracks the Goblin to his lair, nearly murdering the Goblin in his anger. The Goblin attempts to impale Spider-Man using his jet glider but accidentally impales himself (figure 5.3). It is not the hero who symbolically dies and resurrects himself, as in Vogler's schema, but it is the Green Goblin who is "crucified, not on a cross of gold—but on a stake of humble tin" (*ASM* 122, 18.5–7). In death, the Goblin becomes both a symbol (along with Gwen Stacy) of the lost innocence of Silver Age comics readers and a martyr ushering in a new age of comic narrative in which no character is safe. Spider-Man the hero leaves the scene of the battle (*ASM* 122, 19.5–6) and returns home with no boon or elixir to bestow—just suffering and death.

Taken in their original contexts, the Green Goblin narratives confound the validity and utility of the Hero's Journey. If these stories offer wisdom to a broad audience, it is a wisdom specifically located in the criminal underbelly of New York, in characters struggling against economic hardships, in modern forms of psychological trauma, and in the idiosyncrasies of the comic book industry. While Bendis's "Campbellized" version of Spider-Man captures much of

26. Fans have long argued over who actually kills Gwen Stacy. Spider-Man claims that the Goblin has killed her; the Goblin claims, "a fall from that height would kill anyone—before they struck the ground" (*ASM* 121, 19.6). Kakalios (2005, 46–52) argues that Spider-Man accidentally snaps Gwen's neck when he catches her with his webbing. I thank Toph Marshall for this reference.

the charm of these stories, they also erase the possibility of their most powerful moments. We do not remember "The Night Gwen Stacy Died" (*ASM* 121) because Gwen's death reminds us of our own mortality, "the destiny of Everyman," but because the story exposes the fragility of each *Spider-Man* reader's fantasies. Even icons can die.

Superhero narratives and theories about them have changed dramatically since the "death" of the Green Goblin in 1973.[27] In *American Splendor*, Harvey Pekar exalts lower-class heroes who triumph over and succumb to the difficulties of daily life—not in journeys but in single panels and vignettes.[28] Alan Moore has challenged the moral basis of the hero's membership in the community in *Watchmen*.[29] Victoria Schmidt has criticized the Hero's Journey for depicting a model of experience that specifically excludes female protagonists (2005, 74–75), and she has offered feminine and masculine journeys as alternatives (76–80). This present study of Spider-Man and the Green Goblin perhaps suggests that we learn more about superhero narratives by articulating the Villain's rather than the Hero's Journey. Nevertheless, despite numerous claims that Campbell's theory suppresses cultural, social, economic, gender, and racial difference, the Hero's Journey continues to permeate comic books, film, and video games. It is our task, then, to accept the boon bestowed by the Spider-Man/Green Goblin narratives of the sixties and seventies. They show that the path to freedom from the Hero's Journey lies neither in the use of a descriptive theory as a prescriptive template nor in the guidelines of technical manuals but in engagement with the particular, with the experience and specificity of character in its historical moment.

27. A more appropriate term is "comic book death": More than two decades after Gerry Conway killed off the Green Goblin, writers chose to resurrect Norman Osborn during the second Clone Saga (1994–1996).

28. Harvey Pekar (w./a.), *American Splendor* 1–17 (Harvey Pekar Comics, 1976–1993); *American Splendor* 1–4 (Vertigo, Nov. 2006–Feb. 2007); plus several one-shots.

29. Alan Moore (w.) and Dave Gibbons (a.), *Watchmen* 1–12 (DC, Sept. 1986–Oct. 1987).

PART TWO

Gods and Superheroes

6

The Furies, Wonder Woman, and Dream

Mythmaking in DC Comics

C. W. Marshall

When Aeschylus presented the *Oresteia* in 458 BCE, among his many mythographical innovations was a new conception of the Erinyes: Where Homer had presented them as forces of natural law who, among other things, prevent horses from talking and have a special responsibility for oaths (*Iliad* 3.279, 19.409), in Aeschylus the Furies become a chthonic force for the avenging of blood guilt, and we specifically see Clytemnestra's Furies as the chorus of *Eumenides*, hounding the matricide Orestes and being equated with the *Semnai Theai* [august goddesses] in Athens (Pausanias 1.28.6). The physical appearance of the Erinyes in Aeschylus' *Oresteia* also reinvented their visual presentation for the Athenian mind. In the late 420s, Euripides could use the appearance of an Erinys as a symbol, when it is predicted that Hecuba will transform into one in the moments before her death.[1] While originally they were functionally limitless in number and were associated with an individual, by the time of Euripides' *Trojan Women* (produced 415 BCE) there were only three, and they were no longer host specific.[2] By the time of Virgil's *Aeneid*, the three Dirae had names: Allecto, Megaera, and Tisiphone.[3] It is this personalized conception that infuses later Latin literature, including Lucan, Statius, and Claudian's *In Rufinum*. Against this conception, the single Fury driving the shade of Tantalus in Seneca, *Thyestes* 1–121, seems to operate only in the underworld and is no longer tied to the living. With Dante, *Inferno* 8–9, the Virgilian Furies are appropriated into a Christian cosmology, which is also seen when John Webster recognized the tension between Aeschylean and Virgilian conceptions of the Furies in his play *The White Devil* (1612): "There's but three Furies

---

1. Euripides, *Hecuba* 1258–74, esp. 1265.

2. Diggle (1981, 62–63) discusses the issue with reference to *Trojan Women* 457. Even if the reference to three Erinyes here is part of a metaphorical application to three specific individuals (Cassandra, Clytemnestra, and Aegisthus), the number soon becomes canonical in nonmetaphorical contexts (e.g., *Orestes* 408 and 1650).

3. Mackie (1992, 354–56) emphasizes that while the names appear first in a literary context in Virgil, they are attested in vase painting from the fourth century and are established within the tradition. The three names are also found, for example, in the Scholiast to Lycophron, *Alexandra* 406.

found in spacious hell; But in a great man's breast three thousand dwell."[4] Mythographically, that is where the Furies remained until 1983, when a young woman, Hippolyta Trevor, disguised her identity and began fighting crime as the Fury.

Lyta Trevor was introduced in *Wonder Woman* 300[5] as the daughter of the Earth-Two Wonder Woman, and subsequent stories published by DC Comics had her appear as the Fury. My purpose in discussing some of these stories is threefold. First, the developments in the concept of the Furies in comics in the past twenty-five years are operating in the same way mythographically as did the innovations to their literary identity in antiquity: Authors adapt figures for their own narrative ends, are aware of what has gone before, and situate their creative work in an ever-evolving continuum. As an imaginative construct, the development of the Furies in comics is part of that ongoing process. Second, any mythological developments made in our hyperliterate age must meet the exacting expectations of cross-referencing and consistency demanded by a readership that ascribes value to recherché allusions not only within a series but also within the larger megatext of "the DC universe."[6] The contortions that are required to enable a consistent narrative to be told would make even the head of a Hellenistic librarian spin, but they are an integral part of the process of reading mainstream comics today. As will become clear, this is nowhere truer than in the work of Roy Thomas, creator of the Fury (among many other comics characters).[7] This narrative sophistication is characteristic of mainstream hero comics in North America and is central for understanding how they operate. Examining the Furies in the DC Universe becomes one small, localized test case in this process. Third, the Furies in whatever form continue to embody a relentless, indefatigable sense of purpose. As

4. This passage is quoted by the Corinthian in Neil Gaiman (w.) and Marc Hempel (a.), *The Sandman* 69 (July 1995) 4.8; about this series, see note 8 below. Jacobean drama is relevant to one of the story arcs in *The Sandman*, *The Kindly Ones* (= *The Sandman* 57–69 [Feb. 1994–Dec. 1995]); see Bender (1999, 192–93). In this light it is perhaps significant to note the prominence given to the near-contemporary Shakespeare's *Tempest* (c. 1611), which is the focus of Gaiman (w.) and Charles Vess (a.), *The Sandman* 75 (Mar. 1996), the series' final issue.

5. Roy Thomas and Danette Thomas (w.) and Gene Colan et al. (a.), *Wonder Woman* 300 (Feb. 1983), 14.4.

6. I take the idea of a megatext from Segal (1986, 48–74) (= "Greek myth as a Semiotic and Structural System and the Problem of Tragedy") because it recognizes the larger structures at work that help to unify a set of diverse texts, developed over time by multiple creators, with diverse agendas. Like Greek myth, the consistencies (and inconsistencies) that exist among texts produced by a single comics publisher ("the Marvel Universe" or "the DC Universe") create resonances that allow deeper understanding of a given work.

7. Since 1965, Thomas (b. 1940) has had a full career in comics, working for both Marvel (succeeding Stan Lee as editor in chief in 1972) and DC. His many writing credits betray several themes pertinent to this chapter. With Marvel, he created *What If?* (forty-seven issues, Feb. 1977–Oct. 1984), which explored alternate (comics) histories. Thomas has an interest in mythic themes and grand narratives: His run on *Thor*, issues 272–99 (June 1978–Sept. 1980), integrated the Eternals, aliens who in antiquity were revered as the Greek gods (created by Jack Kirby in 1976), into the Marvel continuity; "The Kree-Skrull War," in *The Avengers* 93–97 (Marvel, Nov. 1971–March 1972), presented a story arc with Earth caught between two warring interstellar powers. Thomas has also adapted for American comics many works from other media, including *Conan the Barbarian* 1–115 (Marvel, Oct. 1970–Oct. 1980; the series ran 275 issues until Dec. 1993, during which time he also wrote many annuals and spin-offs), *Star Wars* 1–10 (Marvel, July 1977–April 1978; the series ran 107 issues until July 1986), and *Marvel Illustrated: The Iliad* 1–8 (Marvel, Feb. 2008–Sept. 2008). In this light, it is worth noting that his first credited story published was the "The Second Trojan War" in the short-lived *Son of Vulcan* 50 (Charlton, Jan. 1966), which concerned a mysterious disaster at a film set at Hissarlik, with the director recounting the ancient story, from Helen's abduction to the Trojan horse, abridged (this was the second of only two issues of *Son of Vulcan*, the series numbering having been inherited from *Mysteries of Unexplored Worlds*).

such, they stand in tension with the postmodern reading strategies that episodic hero comics demand. The presence of the Furies serves a literary purpose in these narratives. They offer an absolute that challenges the new conception of storytelling, to which modern readers are now habituated.

It is precisely this sense of storytelling that infuses *The Sandman* by Neil Gaiman.[8] The penultimate story arc, *The Kindly Ones*,[9] presents the title character, Dream, the incarnation of storytelling and imagination, being pursued by the Furies. Gaiman's Furies are conceived in several respects within the Aeschylean tradition, but as their relentless pursuit of Dream is made personal, their inescapability becomes reinforced in the alternating visions of reality and madness the story provides. The Furies have been invoked by Hippolyta ("Lyta") Hall. While it is never stated explicitly in *The Sandman*, this is the same character that had appeared in *Wonder Woman* 300, inaugurating the modern hero figure of the Fury,[10] fighting crime in a red-and-gold costume with a distinct Amazonian flavor.[11] Lyta Hall fought as Fury in Roy Thomas's team comic, *Infinity, Inc.*[12] It was here that she met Hector Hall, the Silver Scarab, who died, leaving a pregnant Lyta grieving.

The commercial aspect of comics production and marketing means that most heroes never really die, and Hector Hall returned in *Infinity, Inc.* 49 as the Sandman, a hero who could leave his Dream Dimension for only one hour a day and who haunted his wife's nightmares. This was a short-lived reinvigoration of a Joe Simon and Jack Kirby comic, which appeared in seven issues from 1974 to 1982.[13] The Simon/Kirby Sandman was the actual supernatural being in charge of sleep and dreams and is therefore close to Gaiman's conception, which finds its classical roots in Somnus and Morpheus in Ovid's *Metamorphoses* 11 and Somnus in Statius, *Silvae* 5.4.[14] Nevertheless, later comics associated the Kirby figure more closely with a traditional

---

8. Neil Gaiman (w.), *The Sandman* 1–75 (DC, Jan. 1989–March 1996). Also part of the continuous story is *Sandman Special* 1 (DC, 1991), by Gaiman (w.) and Brian Talbot (a.), and there have been assorted smaller projects Gaiman has written involving the protagonist Dream and his siblings.

9. See note 4.

10. There are in fact a number of heroes who are called Fury: In addition to Lyta Hall, another is Helena Kosmatos, who first appeared in *Young All-Stars* 1 (Roy Thomas and Dann Thomas [w.] and Brian Murray et al. [a.], *Young All-Stars* 1 [DC, June 1987]). I leave aside the Female Furies, a superpowered elite squadron serving the supervillain Darkseid on the planet Apokalips, who first appeared in Jack Kirby (w./a.), *Mister Miracle* 6 (Feb. 1972), because there is no explicit attempt to connect any of them to the Greek Furies.

11. Some of the information in this and the next paragraph is drawn from Rozakis (2003).

12. Roy Thomas and Dann Thomas (w.) and Jerry Ordway et al. (a.), *Infinity, Inc.* 1–53 (DC, March 1984–June 1988).

13. An initial issue intended as a "one-shot" (Simon [w.], Kirby [a.]; Winter 1974) was followed by five further issues (numbered 2–6, April/May 1975–Dec./Jan. 1975–1976; Michael Fleisher [w.], Ernie Chua [a.] [2–3], Kirby [a.] [4–6]), whereupon the series was canceled. The final story, "The Seal-Men's War on Santa Claus," was intended for issue 7 (Fleicher [w.], Kirby [a.]) but was eventually published in *The Best of DC Blue Ribbon Digest* 22: *Christmas with the Super-Heroes* (March 1982).

14. There are other influences on Gaiman in the creation of his protagonist, such as the villain Nightmare, who first appeared in Stan Lee (w.) and Steve Ditko (a.), *Strange Tales* 110 (Marvel, Aug. 1963), as the inaugural opponent to Dr. Strange, who was also introduced in that issue. Though Nightmare was published by Marvel, similarities exist both in terms of concept (a being in charge of a dream dimension) and appearance (pale white skin). It is presumably a coincidence that Dr. Strange's origin was provided in *Strange Tales* 115 (Marvel, Dec. 1963), an issue that features another story, with Spider-Man fighting the Marvel version of the villain named the Sandman.

superhero: *Wonder Woman* 300 reveals that Sandman was Professor Garrett Sanford, and in *Infinity, Inc.* 50 (May 1988), less than a year before the début of *The Sandman*, we are told Sanford committed suicide within the Dream Dimension.

The process of introducing a retroactive continuity ("retconning"), that is, rationalizing different stories produced by different writers and artists into a homogenous and consistent narrative, is particularly associated with Thomas, who is believed to be the first to use the term retroactive continuity in print—in the letters column of *All-Star Squadron* 18 (Feb. 1983). In this case, the human alter ego of the Sandman is meant to be retrojected by the reader onto the earlier instantiations of the character. In *Wonder Woman* 300, there is even an acknowledgement, as Sanford admits, "Heck, I even christened myself the Sandman after . . . an old comic book hero" (29.1), for which some readers might imagine the Simon/Kirby Sandman is meant, though others will make the association with an even earlier Sandman, Wesley Dodds, a DC pulp hero who fought crime wearing a gas mask and a fedora.[15] This association of one comics character with a previous one may in itself be an allusion to the reimagining of the Flash, a hero who moves at superspeed, in *Showcase* 4.[16]

This is the situation Gaiman inherited and which he assimilated into his Dreamworld. Gaiman presents Hector and Lyta Hall living in the Dream Dome in *The Sandman* 11 and 12 (Dec. 1989–Jan. 1990). Lyta is still pregnant, sleepwalking through her existence, until Dream comes and lays claim to her child. Hector, the Sandman, is killed by Dream, the Sandman, leaving Lyta, the Fury, grieving the loss of her husband once again. In writing the series, Gaiman was under no obligation to draw upon the earlier DC Comics legacy: *The Sandman* could have operated independently of the larger continuity, as had happened with Jack Kirby's *Fourth World* saga (1970–1973), even though this was later incorporated into the larger DC continuity. Gaiman's script assumes many of the tenets established in earlier DC comics, including multiple Sandman identities, flights into madness and fantasy, recursive narratives, and a Fury from a parallel dimension.

Gaiman's story presents Dream and his siblings operating on a cosmic scale. Nevertheless, it is the repercussions of these events from *The Sandman* 11 and 12 that lead to the story arc of *The Kindly Ones*. Lyta, the Fury, invokes the Furies because of what Dream, the Sandman, has done to her son by Hector, the Sandman. And the Furies invoked are cosmic forces themselves. A leitmotiv of the series is the recurring presence of goddesses who are three in one. Over the course of *The Kindly Ones*, the three Furies are mapped onto and at times assimilated with the three Fates, the three Graeae, the three Gorgons, triform Hecate,[17] and the life stages of maiden, mother, and crone; I suspect we are also supposed to perceive echoes of the three witches from

15. This character was introduced in a six-page story by Gardiner Fox (w.) and Bert Christman (a.), "The Tarantula Strikes," *Adventure Comics* 40 (DC, July 1939).

16. *Showcase* 4 (DC, Oct. 1956) contained two Flash stories: Robert Kanigher (w.) and Carmine Infanto (a.), "Mystery of the Human Thunderbolt!," and John Broome (w.) and Infanto (a.), "The Man Who Broke the Time Barrier!" While there had been a Flash in comics in the 1940s, this Flash, Barry Allen, had a different costume and secret identity. When he discovers he has superspeed, Allen calls himself the Flash, remembering the comic books he had read as a young man. Flash was the first of many DC heroes to be revised in this way, and today *Showcase* 4 is generally considered the beginning of a new Silver Age of comic books (though this term itself has problems and has been questioned in some scholarly contexts).

17. Gaiman uses the term *Hecataeae* in Gaiman (w.) and Sam Keith (a.), *The Sandman* 2 (Feb. 1989), 18.3.

Macbeth in this slurry of syncretism. The single shadow that the Furies cast when they eventually confront Dream in *Kindly Ones*—"We are not Lyta Hall. . . . We are vengeance and hatred unending. We are your doom."—epitomizes this blurring of functions (see figure 6.1).[18] Seeing the Furies in shadow in this full-page panel reinforces their three-in-one nature, and the jagged red borders of their speech balloons separate their speech from that of other characters in the series (in the same way that gloomy Dream gets black balloons). In assimilating the Furies with other triform Greek goddesses, Gaiman's syncretism reinforces the extent of the Furies' power, privileging their connection with blood vengeance but linking it with fate and, by extension, with the end of stories.

Where Dream embodies the polyvalent possibilities of narrative, understood as broadly as possible, the Furies have a single purpose, which is to stop stories and, through the action of *The Kindly Ones*, to stop Dream, who is the principle of storytelling itself. Gaiman's Dream is more than a universal abstraction, however: He is also a sullen workaholic with a string of bad relationships and a history of poor family communication. The success of Gaiman's story depends on the reader accepting both perspectives simultaneously, and it is Dream as an individual, whose sense of duty motivates so many of his actions even when it comes at a personal cost, that invokes the reader's sympathies as the Furies pursue him. As she drifts in and out of madness, the Fury from *Infinity, Inc.* becomes Medusa, the mortal Gorgon, while she seeks her revenge at various figurative crossroads: "My hair. There are snakes in my hair," she announces, only to be told "Soon you'll be just like Medusa."[19] Significantly, in this sequence, we see only two of the Fury figures, explicitly named as the Gorgons Stheno and Euryale;[20] Lyta becomes (or has always been?) the mortal third.[21]

Lyta Hall believes that the Furies are her agents of revenge for her to control. She is working entirely within the Aeschylean model, though she does not understand all of its implications. When it emerges that elements of the Virgilian conception are at work, the Furies' power is seen to be much more indefatigable than was originally expected. It is rule bound and ancient and proves to be a chthonic force not for endings but for change. The scope of the *Sandman* narrative is such that both Dream and the Furies exist at a level of reality above other mythologies (the Norse gods and the fairies from *Midsummer Night's Dream* are also characters, and Christian, Muslim, Greco-Roman, Egyptian, Japanese, Romani, and prehistoric African belief systems are incorporated into the series). The reader is presented with a painfully real hero whose status as tragic victim seems to be avoidable, but, as with Orestes, this proves to be an inescapable result of the choices he makes.

My use of the word "tragic" here is deliberate: I think Gaiman has worked to script a tragedy in the Athenian sense, which unfolds in the seventy-five issues of the series (plus specials and other stories written after the series finished). Dream's position is such that his choices have a much wider effect than those of most of us—in Aristotle's terms, it is serious and complete and has magnitude (*Poetics* 6, 1449b 24–25)—but the fundamental conflict, a sense of

---

18. Gaiman (w.) and Teddy Kristiansen (a.), *The Sandman* 64 (Nov. 1994), 18.1.

19. Gaiman (w.) and Hempel (a.), *The Sandman* 61 (July 1994), 2.6 and 7; a snake is first seen in panel 5.

20. *The Sandman* 60 (June 1994), 16.7.

21. Ibid., 16–17; 61 (July 1994), 1–3.

FIGURE 6.1 The shadow of the Furies falls upon Dream. Art by Teddy Kristiansen. *The Sandman* 64 (DC/Vertigo Comics, Nov. 1994) 18.

devotion to one's job at the expense of other relationships, is one with which many Western readers can readily identify. Apparently harmless actions such as granting favors when asked as a royal prerogative have repercussions inasmuch as characters that Dream has honorably helped later return as dishonorable foes. At one level, it is the Furies who infect the situation: Lyta Hall's grief, whether or not it is justified, inexorably spirals into revenge and hate. Dream tries to act with mercy and forgiveness, but his help comes too late, and the repercussions exact a tragic cost. The reader pities Dream and recognizes that everything happens because he is true to himself. The only way to escape would be to act against his essential nature.

The language of tragedy is explicitly invoked at two points during *The Kindly Ones*. In *Sandman* 61, the Norse god Loki addresses a human friend of Lyta Hall:

> Do you know your tragedy, Carla? . . . It's that, for all your goodwill, for all your willingness to help, you never knew what any of this was all about. What was going on. You don't know how it ends. And you'll never get to find out.[22]

Loki's vision of tragedy residing in Carla's ignorance resonates with the theology he articulated on the previous page: "There's a theory that for a human to be killed by a god is the best thing that could possibly happen to the human under discussion. It eliminates all questions of belief, while manifestly placing a human life at the service of a higher power."[23] For Loki, tragedy is a necessary consequence of the human condition since none of us can know "how it ends."

But tragedy is not limited to humans. It can be found in any significant power imbalance, as the second allusion indicates. Even a Miltonesque Lucifer can attribute to himself a quality associated in most readers' minds with the tragic hero: "I had the hubris originally to regard myself as a collaborator, as a co-author. . . . Very rapidly I found myself reduced to the status of character, following something of a disagreement in the fundamental direction of the Creation."[24] The literary imagery is particularly important for the textual layering Gaiman imposes on the *Sandman* series generally, focalized in the (scripted) character of Dream as the principle of all storytelling. Lucifer's existence now is presented as prolonged inaction, his tragedy residing in an inability to act independently, which is a quality of all literary creations. In the following panel, Lucifer muses, "Now I sometimes feel I'm simply waiting around to see which of us was right, which was wrong. But even if it turns out that I was right, what good does it do me?" Gaiman's sense of tragedy is universalized from the specific case of Dream so as to embody all levels of existence and all literary creations. Tragedy resides in the end of things.

Gaiman's conception of the Furies, which motivate this tragic perspective, had appeal among comics readers, and as the critical response to *The Sandman* grew, various spin-offs emerged. One of these was a ninety-six-page story titled *The Sandman Presents: The Furies*.[25]

22. *The Sandman* 61 (July 1994), 24.2–3.

23. Ibid., 23.4.

24. Ibid., 69 (July 1995), 16.3. Though hubris is not mentioned in Aristotle's *Poetics*, its use in English today associates it as a paradigmatic example of Aristotelian *hamartia*.

25. Mike Carey (w.) and John Bolton (a.), *The Sandman Presents: The Furies* (DC/Vertigo Comics, 2002); hereafter *The Furies*.

Lyta Hall has been put through the wringer, and *The Furies* finds her perpetuating a cycle of grief at the loss of her child through despair, hiding herself in serial anonymous sex. However, her connection with the Furies persists, and since she was able to invoke them against Dream, she attracts the attention of the titan Cronus, who is working to restore his pre-Olympian influence. The story calls him the Changer, and as such he becomes a doppelgänger of Dream, a meta-Morpheus. Cronus is systematically eliminating all of the Olympian gods; as the story begins (set presumably in 2002, the year of its publication), the only god left is Hermes, whose speed has so far allowed him to stay one step ahead of his pursuer. Cronus is willing to kill without mercy: We see the trees Baucis and Philemon murdered in a conflagration, for example, evoking and concluding the central narrative in Ovid's *Metamorphoses*, in book 8. His grand plan in *The Furies* is to eliminate the Furies and to usurp their place as the universe's instrument of revenge. To do that, Cronus attacks Lyta, believing that her natural and mortal connection with the Furies makes them vulnerable. Lyta is simultaneously both an embodiment of the Furies (when she channels them, her speech balloons are given an irregular, blood-red frame, which they also had in *The Kindly Ones*), but she is also their quarry, due to Cronus' machinations.

One of the themes the story examines is vulnerability. Lyta has suffered severe emotional damage and becomes a Persephone figure, even experiencing a *katabasis* when she eats some pomegranate seeds. As in *The Kindly Ones*, Lyta in *The Furies* appropriates an outward appearance of Medusa when she becomes the avatar for the Furies (see figure 6.2),[26] but this change emphasizes the fact that she remains mortal. Nor is she the only symbol of vulnerability. Cronus thinks he has engineered a foolproof plan of self-advancement, but in doing so he exposes himself to his own presuppositions. Hermes is running for his life.

The realistic painterly style of the art stands in juxtaposition to the fantastic events the story presents, but at times the backdrop seems heavy handed: Cameos of *Sandman* characters seem unnecessary, and the small American theater troupe performing *The Oresteia* in Greece provides a gratuitous underlining of the mythical elements. Whatever interest the story provides (and both Hermes and Cronus are creative reconceptions of the mythical figures), Carey does not develop the Furies themselves in any interesting way: As was the case often with the post-Aeschylean Furies, they are more a tenet of the cosmology than the result of an engaged attempt to comprehend them as a collective individual. Much more successful in this respect is the presentation of the Furies in *The Hiketeia*, another ninety-six-page story from 2002, written by Greg Rucka.[27]

The Hiketeia presents the same intersection of mythical narrative and comics form as is found in *The Sandman*. In it, Wonder Woman—Princess Diana, who is an ambassador in Washington, D.C., for the Amazon island nation of Themiscyra—accepts the supplication of a young girl who is fleeing Batman. The story is written as a conflict between Wonder Woman and Batman, who are both presented as adhering to an absolute moral code. Between them is Danielle Wellys, a teenage girl who has hunted and killed the four men she holds responsible

---

26. The pages of the story are unnumbered but, given the volume size, may be conceived of as spanning [1]–[92]. Snakes are explicitly present in Lyta's hair on pages [84]–[86] and suggested in the art on pages [87]–[88].

27. Greg Rucka (w.) and J. G. Jones (a.), *Wonder Woman: The Hiketeia* (DC, 2002); hereafter *Hiketeia*.

I STARE
THEM
DOWN.

FIGURE 6.2   **Lyta Hall takes on the form of Medusa in** *The Furies*. **Art by John Bolton.** *The Sandman Presents: The Furies* (DC/Vertigo Comics, 2002).

for her sister's death. Danielle's guilt is not in question any more than it is for Orestes. The issue is not, however, the expected one, of the degree to which she should be held responsible for her actions. For Batman, his single-minded pursuit of justice (itself motivated by childhood trauma and the death of family) means that no mitigating circumstances are to be admitted: Though the victims are drug-dealing pornographers, they have still been murdered, and murderers must be punished. Batman adheres in essence to a post-Oresteian conception of justice, which requires the intervention of a (human) court of law and deliberately removes it from the realm of supernatural or divine justice.

For Wonder Woman, the obligation created by Danielle's supplication overrides any other obligations she might have—to the law, to her friend and Justice League ally, Batman, and to herself: "*Hiketeia* is law. *Hiketeia* is ritual. It is never to be ignored. Like all ritual, it has rules. . . . There is but a single power that [the supplicant] retains. Only he can end the obligation. He must leave on his own accord."[28] The rules of *hiketeia* are spelled out for the reader in the book's opening pages: Four full pages set in classical Athens show a suppliant being accepted and then rejected by his host, while Diana's voice articulates the rules (4–7). The next two pages (8–9), drawn with heavy shadow and without narrating text (and therefore

28. Ibid., 5–6.

suggesting that the consequences are not fully understood or known by Wonder Woman), show the Furies attacking and slaying the host. The visual layout of the sequence is careful and deliberate. Three mysterious cloaked figures first appear in the bottom right-hand corner of the opening two-page spread of the embedded narrative.[29] Their size, shape, position, and placement replicate that of the three shadow shapes outside the Themysciran embassy on the previous page,[30] which have been explicitly associated with the Furies: Though they have only been called "cruel sisters,"[31] the audience is shown bloodstained mouths and has hints of serpentine hair in panel 3; this is now a standard element in the DC iconography of the Furies. The reader has also been shown images that purport to depict the Furies on a red-figured vase in one of the books in Diana's library.[32]

The ritual of *hiketeia* as presented in *The Hiketeia* is not quite the same as that found in epic and tragedy or as is described in Gould's 1973 article: It is more structured, with specific words that need to be said as a binding formula. While many classical scholars have rejected the formalism of Gould's account, preferring a less rigorous explanation,[33] Rucka actually increases the ritual's formalism. Rucka adds another innovation in making supplication the responsibility not of Zeus (who has among his cult titles "Hikesios"[34]) but of the Furies. While *Choephori* 476–478 has the *makarês chthonioi* [blessed earth goddesses] being invoked to recognize suppliancy and *Odyssey* 17.475 makes the Furies protectors of *ptôchoi* [beggars], Rucka extends their classical responsibilities in a direction that is entirely credible both within the comics world and, I suggest, within that of Greek tragedy. The Furies become a fourth primary character, situated above the conflict between Batman and Wonder Woman and whose power resides in Danielle's successful supplication of Diana. For most of the story, it is only Diana who can see them, hooded with bloodied mouths and serpent hair, because it is only she whom they can affect: In receiving Danielle's supplication, cosmic forces are invoked not for revenge (so that they would be pursuing Danielle) but for social obligation, so that they wait, anticipating a violation, as a result of Diana's choice to protect the girl. The three panels on page 40 make this explicit as the layout replicates the cinematic effect of a camera pulling back, widening the shot (see figure 6.3). In the first, we see Diana on a street, confronting the Furies. In the second, wider frame that appears to lie underneath the panel above it, we see Diana standing alone on a street in the same pose, staring at the emptiness. In the third panel, the borders of which equate with the page itself, we are looking with Danielle through the embassy window down onto the street at Diana, standing alone. Danielle's hair overlaps with the second panel, reinforcing the continuity between the two, and the absence of speech balloons again focalizes the scene through Danielle's perspective—at a distance and behind glass. She sees only Diana and is unaware of the cosmological situation.

29. Ibid., 5.9.

30. Ibid., 3.5.

31. Ibid., 2.1.

32. Ibid., 2.4 and 3.1–4, though the details are clear only in panels 2 and 3. Tiny writing in panel 1 labels the (fictional) vase "Heketeia Krater" [*sic*] and attributes it to the (real) potter "Euxithe[os]" (Diana's hand covers the last letters of his name).

33. Gould (1973); compare, for example, Lynn-George (1988) and Crotty (1994).

34. This is found, for example, in Aeschylus, *Suppliant Women* 616, and Euripides, *Hecuba* 345.

FIGURE 6.3 In *The Hiketeia*, only Wonder Woman can see the Furies. Her supplicant Danielle is unable to see them. Art by J. G. Jones. *Wonder Woman: The Hiketeia* (DC, 2002) 40.

By tying *hiketeia* violations to the Furies' revenge, Rucka allows new insights into the enactment of supplication on the Greek stage. Danielle wants desperately to justify herself before Wonder Woman, but Diana is not interested in the reasons: She acts because she has to, because of the old laws, and not because she cares about Danielle as an individual. "You . . . you haven't asked," Danielle protests, "If you ask me I can't lie . . . you should ask me why, Princess."[35] Batman understands that Diana acts out of obligation and believes that his monomaniacal drive for justice is somehow worthier than hers. The conflict is played out first on the balcony of the embassy (48–58) and then at the edge of town (80–85). In his assessment of the strength of their relative drives, Batman is found to be wrong. He cynically tries to circumvent Diana's opposition by supplicating her himself (83–84). This act is rejected—the text explicitly associates the moment in *Iliad* 21 with Lykaon's supplication of Achilles: "I use [the ritual] as your ancestors did. I use it like Lykaon and Achilles," says Batman. "Then you don't know your *Iliad* as well as you should. Achilles refused Lykaon. Just as I now refuse you," Diana responds, kicking him away.[36]

Further, the classically informed reader may also tie Batman's manipulation of *hiketeia* with Odysseus' behavior in Euripides' *Hecuba*, hiding his hand in his cloak so that the ritual may not be completed effectually by Polyxena (*Hecuba* 342–345). For Odysseus, it is an interesting character point: Hecuba has conceivably supplicated him for up to sixty lines, and Odysseus has resisted despite the legitimacy of Hecuba's arguments;[37] nevertheless, he actively resists entering into any sense of obligation to Polyxena ("Odysseus has taken counter-measures"[38]). Odysseus behaves legalistically, uninterested in the divinely sanctioned bond the ritual creates and concerned only with adhering to (his interpretation of) the performative mechanics of the ritual. Similarly, Batman's weaseling is met with contempt: It was simply a combat tactic with no acknowledgement of its ritual significance ("I had to try," he says, casually excusing his attempt[39]). Consequently, the reader is left with the feeling that Wonder Woman's value system has more authority because it possesses greater moral integrity. This story provides a genuine mythological development of the Furies, one that inevitably, as when any myth develops, forces retrospective reassessment of previous versions.

In Homer and Euripides, the motions of *hiketeia* draw the participants into a relationship. The repeated rejection of supplication on the human level until the final book of the *Iliad*

---

35. *Hiketeia* 45.1, 6, 7; the moment is recapitulated on 62, with Danielle grasping at Wonder Woman's magic "lasso of truth," which leads to the backstory provided on pages 63–68. On 62.8 we see Danielle on her knees, the lasso draped over her wrists, leading us to believe that the inset narrative represents the truth (as she believes it). After her story, on 69.1, she is in the same position, and the lasso is at her side.

36. *Hiketeia* 84.5–6.

37. Stage directions can be inferred only from the text because none survive in the ancient manuscripts; consequently, the precise duration is unclear. Kovacs (1995, 423, 429) suggests that Hecuba's supplication lasts from line 273 to line 333. In contrast, Gould (1973, 84–85) argues that Hecuba's supplication is only figurative: "The full ritual act in this scene is constantly expected, constantly deferred and in the end does not take place, since Polyxena scorns to supplicate" (84n54).

38. Gould (1973, 84). Similarly, Agamemnon avoids Hecuba's grasp at *Hecuba* 812–13. Epic and tragedy do represent anxieties about cross-gender supplication, but nowhere is it suggested that it is inappropriate as a ritual for women.

39. *Hiketeia* 85.1.

represents a series of theological violations, showing that the characters' actions are increasingly at odds with Homer's moral universe. In Rucka's comic, the introduction of human choice as a required component for the completion of the ritual—the bond does not exist if it is not accepted—both authorizes the shift from the suppliant to the supplicated and establishes a tension concerning the invoked parallel with Lykaon. Rucka implies that Achilles' rejection of Lykaon was a morally neutral choice, not the significant ethical violation Homer depicts. Since for Rucka the bond established persists until it is discharged, Wonder Woman's rejection of Batman's supplication is not a morally questionable act, but his manipulation of a ritual is, as he invokes divinities he does not acknowledge or worship. While this may lead to an unintended irony ("you don't know your *Iliad* as well as you should"), it affirms a consistency in Wonder Woman's behavior crucial to the story being told.

"*Hiketeia* is never about the suppliant . . . but always about the supplicated," the Furies explain to Diana.[40] Such an articulation changes the emphasis found in Greek myth but proves not to be incompatible with it. The narrative motive for this conceptual development forms part of an examination of the place of the Furies today. An attempt to integrate the Furies into a modern perspective shows a popularization of classical concepts operating to a much greater extent in popular culture and with a much greater degree of sophistication than might be expected. Narrative developments in the mythological treatment of the Furies operate entirely within the spirit of classical mythography. In particular, the Furies consistently possess the Aeschylean quality of indefatigable pursuit when presented in the DC Universe. It creates an absolute that resonates at a deeper level even than Batman's quest for justice. The fact that all of the texts examined here emerged from a producer of mainstream superhero comics is perhaps surprising, but narrative and form intersect in the creation of a modern myth that Aeschylus would have understood.

40. *Hiketeia* 39.4–5.

7

Coming up to Code
Ancient Divinities Revisited

CRAIG DETHLOFF

When Jerry Siegel described the epiphany that produced Superman, he stated that he was "lying in bed counting sheep when all of a sudden it hits me. I conceive a character like Samson, Hercules, and all the strong men I have ever heard tell of rolled into one" (Fingeroth 2004, 13). Crediting his account, the origin of the first comic book hero has at least one of its roots firmly planted in the mythology of ancient Greece and Rome. Following the success of Superman and innumerable other superhuman characters with the reading public, the Greek and Roman divinities that inspired them reemerged as active players in fresh contemporary narratives. To accomplish this, the writers and artists who produced them had to choose, adapt, and ultimately defend them in a social and cultural environment that did not accept their reappearance without apprehension.

The world of comics and pulp magazines into which Superman emerged in 1938 was already full of fantastic action heroes such as Tarzan, Buck Rogers, Doc Savage, and the Spider. As might be imagined, the adventures of these protagonists left little room for intrusion by a Greek or Roman deity, and neither initially did those of Superman. In contemporary criticism, to emphasize the rift between comic books and more traditional reading material, Sterling North decried that "The old dime novels in which an occasional redskin bit the dust were classic literature compared to the sadistic drivel pouring from the presses today."[1]

Clearly there was a disjuncture between how gods and goddesses acted among human beings in the literature of the ancient past and how they could be portrayed as doing so now in a manner that would be acceptable to audiences. To literary critics for whom the medium was the message, this was a nearly impossible task, but readers who enjoyed and appreciated these stories could reasonably have expected certain facets to appear. The character would have to have power and use it responsibly to defend the weak against the strong. The readers might also anticipate a costume and a secret identity, as these had become regularly occurring facets of pulp and comic characters. However, most important, they might also possess some knowledge

---

1. From the article "A National Disgrace (and a Challenge to American Parents)," quoted in Hajdu (2008, 40).

of the divinity in advance, which comic creators would have to take into account to make their treatment a success.[2]

Other more subtle challenges presented themselves in adapting the role of divinities to the activities of superheroes. In his account, Siegel did not cite any feature of Hercules other than his strength when he conceived of Superman, but while most ancient gods obviously possessed power, not every one of them exercised it in a way that lent itself to the sort of action the comics required. Additionally, the mission of the superhero, to protect the innocent and uphold justice, seemed antithetical to the responsibilities of some divinities. And while the costume of an ancient god or goddess could easily serve as distinctive emblems of their identity in the performance of their heroic duties, the figuration of stable secret identities proved elusive. By 1940, however, comics featuring Superman were selling more than a million copies per month, and this provided creators with a strong incentive to return to the same well from which Siegel had drawn, and three different characters named Hercules made their appearance within months of one another (Horn 1999, 312–313).

The first, published by Timely (later to become Marvel) Comics, was a character akin to Doc Savage. Raised in Arctic solitude by his father, Dr. David, to be "the perfect physical and mental specimen," he was given the name Hercules when he was brought back to America by two unscrupulous circus managers.[3] His adventures were brief and disjointed and lasted only two issues. Three months later, MLJ Magazines published their own Hercules. In these stories, Zeus sends Hercules back to Earth to perform updated versions of his mythological twelve Labors. In the first story, for example, he had to defeat the gangster "Leo Nymia—Lion of the Underworld."[4] Subsequent episodes revealed a wry interpretation of the labors sometimes based on simple wordplay, but this series outlasted its rival by only two issues. The last Hercules to appear also proved to be the longest lived. Running for almost two years, Joe Hercules bore little resemblance to his namesake save for the super strength that he used to thwart his own coterie of gangsters and corrupt businessmen.[5]

What each of these Hercules reveals is the distance between the Greek and the Roman divinity and a model of the costumed superhero, which was rapidly becoming the norm. While they all possessed the name "Hercules," none of them concealed an alter ego like Clark Kent or Bruce Wayne. Nor did their costumes allow for that possibility; each regularly appeared only in trunks, Joe Hercules being somewhat exceptional in that he also wore a cape and boots. Translating ancient iconographical attributes such as a club or the skin of the lion of Nemea was attempted either not at all or only in a much-denuded fashion.[6] Only one of them claimed to

2. On a superficial level, this could account in part for the preference of the Latin over the Greek form of the names for certain divinities when they appear. In the works I have examined, Hercules, Mars, Venus, and Mercury are preferred to Heracles, Ares, Aphrodite, and Hermes; most of the former perhaps possess the advantage of being more recognizable by virtue of also being the names of planets.

3. Writer and artist unknown, "Hercules," *Mystic Comics* 3 (Timely Comics, Jan. 1940).

4. Joe Blair (w.) and Eli Wexler (a.), "Hercules: Modern Champion of Justice," *Blue Ribbon Comics* 4 (MLJ Magazines, June 1940).

5. Gregg Powers (w.) and Dan Zolnerowich (a.), "Hercules," *Hit Comics* 1 (Quality Comics, July 1940).

6. In the MLJ series, after defeating Leo Nymia, Hercules takes on his "skin," a blue business suit. He wore it for only two issues. Additionally, Zeus, the only other Olympian to appear in the series, is depicted as wearing a yellow cape, green gloves, and a red robe emblazoned with a sun. See Joe Blair (w.) and Eli Wexler (a.), "Hercules, Modern Champion of Justice," *Blue Ribbon Comics* 5 (MLJ Magazines, July 1940), 1.

be divine, while the other two were humans who owed their powers to superior physical conditioning or other reasons left unexplained. If the influence of Hercules on Superman proved an unqualified success, these kinds of instantiations of him proved decidedly less so.

In between the arrivals of the first and second Hercules as distinct characters, however, another hero emerged linked to the god in name and ability and who proved to be a much more viable product. Published by Fawcett Comics, Captain Marvel amalgamated the appeal of Superman with the mythological tradition of Greek and Roman divinities in a way that was both unique and contested. By saying the magic word "Shazam," as a shorthand invocation of Solomon, Hercules, Atlas, Zeus, Achilles, and Mercury, young Billy Batson became not just an adult but an adult possessed of the wisdom, strength, stamina, power, courage, and speed of each of these figures. As part of his mission, the wizard who granted Billy this ability set him the task of combating the "Seven Deadly Enemies of Mankind": Pride, Envy, Greed, Hatred, Laziness, Selfishness, and Injustice.

In his costuming, Marvel mimicked the key components of Superman's wardrobe with a cape, boots, tight pants, and prominent chest emblem.[7] Appealing especially to younger audiences, his alter ego was an orphan child. The relationship with ancient heroes and divinities he invoked was that of the recipient of the gift of their abilities, which they gave him each time he spoke his magic word. Initially they did not appear in person beside Captain Marvel but rather acted as removed and unseen benefactors lending their assistance to humankind through him. The motivations behind their participation on one side of a transcendent struggle against the Seven Deadly Enemies of Mankind were not explained, but Marvel worked against foes such as Dr. Sivana as their concrete agent in it. This relationship demonstrated itself to be extraordinarily popular with audiences and profitable for its publisher.[8]

Captain Marvel's creators had found a successful formula for integrating Greek and Roman deities into comics, which the different Hercules series had not. Rather than have the gods fight gangsters or criminals directly, this comic portrayed them as empowering an emissary whose character and appearance were more in tune with contemporary taste in superheroes. The involvement of the ancient deities served as a balance in the contest against the Seven Deadly Enemies, in which they did physically participate. By contrast, MLJ's Hercules was sent to fight gangsters and corrupt politicians directly just as Marvel was, for the cause of right and justice, but his struggles were set within the context of accomplishing the mythological labors rather than any larger, persistent threat. The difference in the two representations of the gods was soon reconciled, however, as the threat of the Second World War drew more Olympians, even those of Captain Marvel, down to earth.

Six months after the transformation of Billy Batson, August 1940 saw the second and last appearance of Timely's Hercules. That same month another divine character was introduced by Timely in the first issue of *Red Raven Comics*. This publication remains generally noteworthy for three features. It was the first comic Timely published named after its principal character. It

---

7. Captain Marvel's likeness to Superman in fact proved too close for Superman's publisher, Detective Comics, which sued Fawcett in 1941 for copyright infringement. The suit was eventually settled out of court in 1953, when Fawcett agreed to pay DC $400,000 and cease publishing the character (Steranko 1972, 21).

8. To give some indication of the popularity not only of Captain Marvel but also of comic books in general at the time: "Issue 51, January 1946, hit a record circulation sale of 1,384,000" (Steranko 1972, 17). In comparison, the top-selling comic book for September 2008, Marvel's *Secret Invasion* 6, sold a total of 240,750 copies (Doran 2008).

stands alone because no second issue ever appeared. Finally, it contains the first work for Timely by artist Jack Kirby in a story titled "Mercury in the 20th Century."[9] The story begins much like that of MLJ's Hercules. Zeus sends Mercury to earth in order to end a global war led by the god Pluto, who has disguised himself as Rudolf Hendler, dictator of Prussland. Directly confronting Pluto, Mercury leaps at him saying, "Foul demon! How I wish you were mortal so I could strangle you slowly . . . I can't kill you. But I can fight you, Pluto. I show man the way to peace as you did to war."[10] After Mercury steals certain critical war plans, the story ends with the war in a stalemate.

As it stands it is difficult to tell whether this story was intended to last beyond its first episode, yet it reflects a unique blending and advancement of the elements featured in earlier portrayals of the gods. Most notably, there is the appearance of the "bad" god. In the character of Pluto, the story takes a step beyond the conceit of superior influences that move humans to perform bad actions (as in Captain Marvel) when it actually shows Pluto exhorting his armies as Rudolf Hendler. Mercury still acts as an emissary of Zeus, as MLJ's Hercules did, but the physical and graphical opposition of the two makes the adversarial struggle of "good" versus "evil" in which they were involved more consistent and manifest.[11] The gains of "Mercury in the 20th Century" in terms of the balance between the two do not seem to have taken hold. However, it would not be the last opportunity for one of its creators, Jack Kirby, to explore the theme, and the new element of the "bad" god reemerged relatively soon after.

In November 1941, "Mars, God of War," appeared as a new feature among the lineup of science fiction stories regularly featured in the Fiction House serial *Planet Comics*. As a series, "Mars" presented a curious take on the usual superhero narrative. Instead of featuring a hero victoriously defeating assorted adversaries, it featured a villain suffering various defeats.

For its departure point, it began with a story very similar to "Mercury in the 20th Century," in which Mars takes possession of a number of "evil" individuals, including "Der Fuehrer," dictator of the "Axians," whom he uses to wage war on a futuristic America.[12] In contrast to his science fiction circumstances, when not possessing someone, Mars always appears wearing the helmet, breastplate, and greaves of a Roman general. His presence in the possessed is usually signaled by their eyes turning red. During subsequent episodes, characters who looked into these eyes would likewise fall under his spell.[13]

By consistently portraying Mars as the adversary and shifting the context toward science fiction, the series evaded the difficulties previously encountered in molding a divinity to the conventions of the superhero. No specific mention of his presence in Greek or Roman

9. M. A. Bursten (w.) and J. Kirby (a.), "Mercury in the 20th Century," *Red Raven Comics* 1 (Timely Comics, Aug. 1940). Reprinted in Kirby (2004, 6–14).

10. Kirby (2004, 10).

11. This is reinforced in "Mercury," when Pluto is referenced in the story as the "Prince of Darkness." Additionally, when he drops his Hendler disguise, he resembles the depiction of Mephisto in Murnau's *Faust*, replete with horns and red costume. By contrast, Mercury is recognizable by the prominent white wings on his boots and headband (ibid., 2004, 7).

12. Ross Gallun (w.) and Joe Doolin (a.), "Mars, God of War," *Planet Comics* 15 (Fiction House Magazines, Nov. 1941), 1–8.

13. Mars' possession, like that of "Mercury's" Pluto, is similarly cast in a Christian understanding. See, for example, Ross Gallun (w.) and Joe Doolin (a.), "Mars, God of War," *Planet Comics* 19 (Fiction House Magazines, July 1942), 5.

antiquity is referenced, and it is hinted that his origins are extraterrestrial.[14] In terms of simple longevity (it lasted until July 1945), "Mars" surpassed any previous story featuring a Greek or Roman character as its title character. This last episode ended when he was defeated and replaced by "Mysta of the Moon" but only after he had already destroyed Earth.[15]

Despite difficulties, the first appearances of Greek and Roman gods immediately prior to America's involvement in World War II had managed to convey their activities much in the manner that antiquity did. They acted independently while invisible to mortal eyes or sometimes with a sudden but brief epiphany. At other times, they assumed likenesses not their own, took possession of particular individuals, or lent to them a strength or resilience that they would not normally possess.

A trend had also developed where the gods were largely disinterested in the particulars of crime for profit, which they left to their superhero or villain proxies. Instead, their direct engagement was more concerned with much larger ambitions such as peace, war, or death, which they sought for their own sakes. Although seldom fitting into the superhero or costumed vigilante mold, their ranks had also become split into "good" and "evil" gods, a distinction buttressed by creators with the use of various Christian elements.

As the United States moved closer to a war that was already taking place on the pages of its comics, the gravity of that event was influencing the portrayal of the gods. Into the space between the roles of gods like Mercury as he appears in Captain Marvel in 1940 and as he appears in "Mercury in the 20th Century," an entire pantheon would soon come down to accompany the most popular heroine in comics history. And the story begins, most fittingly, with the plane crash of pilot Steve Trevor on Paradise Island, home of the Amazons, in December 1941.

Created for DC Comics by Harvard-educated psychologist Dr. William Moulton Marston (under the pseudonym Charles Moulton), Wonder Woman had not one but three origin stories in three years, each firmly rooted in ancient mythology.[16] In her first and later appearances there was much to echo the example previously set by Captain Marvel, where the gods were invoked as givers of gifts and Wonder Woman was described as follows: "As lovely as Aphrodite—as wise as Athena—with the speed of Mercury and the strength of Hercules."[17] However, even in the first story something has changed. When Queen Hippolyte is directly confronted by both Aphrodite and Athena, who appear "as through a mist," they reveal that they were the ones who caused Steve Trevor's plane crash in order "to help fight the forces of hate and oppression." As Athena bluntly states, "American liberty and

14. The introductory panel to his first appearance reads as follows: "Down through the ages, a foul spirit has infected the universe, a god of hate, creating strife through the infection of his personality into the bodies of evil, and now, leaving his planet in chaos, this invisible horror invades Earth . . . . Mars, God of War!" (ibid., 1941, 1).

15. Ibid., *Planet Comics* 35 (July 1945), 12–19.

16. As a foreshadowing of current examples of retconning, each of the three stories was designed to make new readers familiar with the story. They appeared in Charles Moulton (w.) and Harry Peter (a.), "Introducing Wonder Woman," All-Star Comics 8 (DC, Dec. 1941–Jan. 1942); Charles Moulton (w.) and Harry Peter (a.), "The Origin of Wonder Woman," Wonder Woman 1 (DC, Summer 1942); and in the newspaper strip for King Features Syndicate beginning on May 8, 1944 (Daniels 2000, 52–55).

17. Charles Moulton (w.) and Harry Peter (a.), "Introducing Wonder Woman," All-Star Comics 8 (DC, Dec. 1941–Jan. 1942), 1.1.

freedom must be preserved. . . . For America, the last citadel of democracy, and of equal rights for women, needs your help!"[18]

For comic book divinities, this marks a substantial shift in that for the first time they are marked as active forces in a world that, while fictional, is more realistic than that of "Mercury in the 20th Century." In that story, when Mercury sought to stop Rudolf Hendler, he did not fight for any particular country or even any precise political or ethical notion. Hendler, moreover, was only a mask used by another god simply to further "war" as a cause in itself. The gods and goddesses of *Wonder Woman* not only exist as real entities but also make their approval of contemporary political entities and support for specific values felt directly through their superhero standard bearer.

Thus, by the summer of 1942, it probably came as little surprise when she appeared on the cover of her own self-titled magazine not only in her familiar red, white, and blue costume but also leading a charge of Allied soldiers into the German lines astride a white horse. Between the covers was another iteration of her origin, which revealed that behind the current conflict was the antipathy of Ares and Aphrodite, who rule the world "as rival gods," the former seeking to "rule by the sword" by placing the whole world at war and the latter seeking to "conquer with love" "when America wins."[19] Moreover, Marston himself seems actually to have viewed the conflict largely in this way and altered the original story to emphasize the point.[20]

The depiction of the gods in *Wonder Woman* marked a turning point and signaled that they had successfully integrated themselves within the new medium of comic books as full characters. Their actions could be based on their mythological dispositions, but there was still room left to contemporize without simplifying them. More important for creators of comic books, however, this treatment of the gods demonstrated that audiences were receptive to this nuanced approach, thereby opening the way for further exploration. Soon even Captain Marvel would actually appear fighting physically beside the gods.[21] However, almost from the beginning the very existence of superhero stories themselves had been criticized for their depiction of sex, violence, and vigilantism, and this criticism inevitably redounded upon their divine counterparts. The critics of superhero comics seem never to have isolated the portrayals of ancient gods and goddesses in the medium as targets for their attacks but rather to have seen in superhero comics a perverted atavism that resurrected all of the sensationalism surrounding ancient myth and religion without any of the substance.

As early as 1938 Catholic groups such as the National Organization for Decent Literature (NODL) and the Catechetical Guild in particular had set to work to warn parents

---

18. Ibid., 15.1.

19. For the interconnection of gods and contemporary circumstance, it is telling that while Wonder Woman would not appear again that year challenging the Axis so directly, the cover of the second issue of Wonder Woman shows her toppling Ares from a parapet (see figure 7.1).

20. Referring to his reinterpretation of the story of the Amazons, which did not appear in the first version of Wonder Woman's origin, Marston remarked that "The Greeks put them in chains of the Hitler type, beat them, and made them work like horses in the fields. Aphrodite, goddess of love, finally freed these unhappy girls." From "Our Women Are Our Future," Olive Richard, *Family Circle* (Aug. 14, 1942).

21. See, for example, Dave Berg (w./a.), "The Lost Lightning," *America's Greatest Comics* 5 (Fawcett Comics, Dec. 16, 1942).

especially of the danger that these publications posed for young people.[22] Moreover, although it had taken the context of World War II to speed the gradual introduction and revival of the ancient gods in comic books and the superhero genre in particular, the terminus of this evolutionary reinterpretation was itself the subject of their attack.

If comic book authors and audiences initially found Greek and Roman gods hard to accept because of their differences from superheroes and the characters of the pulps, critics found those same characters objectionable precisely for their similarities. Therefore, it did not matter how many bund members, spies, and saboteurs Superman dispatched because the problem, as Catholic writer Thomas F. Doyle put it, was this:

> In a vulgar way this fantastic character seems to personify the primitive religion
> expounded by Nietzsche's *Zarathustra*. "Man alone is and must be our God," says
> Zarathustra, very much in the style of a Nazi pamphleteer. (Doyle 1943, 548–549)

Anachronism aside, what Doyle was objecting to was the depiction of Superman as being above any law, either social or divine, save his own. The fact that Superman ostensibly fought for truth and justice counted for little as he did so extrajudicially and without any assistance apart from his own personal interpretation of what those values meant. Or as Walter Ong put it: "In achieving its success, the Superman strip has patterned itself not only on the blind hero-worship motif developed by Hitler and Mussolini, but also on the pagan Hellenistic values so useful to a super state" (Ong 1945, 39).

During the war, Superman—for these critics, who were fearful of fascistic influence—was precisely what his name meant, the *Übermensch*, "an Apollo-like creature who jumps over skyscrapers" (Doyle 1943, 549–550). In addition, both he and Wonder Woman, with her devotion to Aphrodite, were tokens of a similar "Hitlerite paganism."[23] Absurdly using their powers only to thwart crime, the superheroes distracted youngsters not only from democratic ideals and tales of real heroism but also from higher literary fare.

This opposition to comics both as a distraction and a proponent of the fascist ideal would eventually wane as the war ended and the Allies emerged victorious. Instead, the threat they posed throughout the next decade and more was not subversion to the ideology of a foreign enemy but psychological damage and juvenile delinquency.

The closing months of World War II heralded a rapid decline in the popularity of the superhero genre of comics. Anxious to retain their markets, comic book publishers struggled to diversify their offerings with war, western, science fiction, romance, and, most sensationally, horror and crime comics. This last genre, whose origins lay again in pulp fiction, was to prove the focus of later efforts to censor the medium, yet it still did not offer much of a place for ancient divinities, whom the comic creators struggled to fit into as many of the other categories as they could with little success. Most characteristic of the shifting tastes of the period was *Venus*, one of Timely Comics' last forays into the mythological. Originally appearing in August 1948, the title character was both the goddess and ruler of the planet Venus. There she lived on

22. On the origins and activities of NODL in particular, see O'Connor (1995).

23. "Are Comics Fascist?" *Time Magazine* (Oct. 22, 1945).

Mount Lustre with the other gods until finding herself magically transported to Earth and the editor of a fashion magazine.

The story of the first issue, blending as it did elements of science fiction, romance, and adventure, would only be exaggerated in the course of the magazine's nineteen-issue run at the end, when it finally detoured into horror (Nolan 1996). By this time, however, under the looming threat of outside regulation, the comics industry had already adopted a provisory code of self-censorship as endorsed by the Association of Comic Magazine Publishers (ACMP). The measure was envisaged by some as acting much as the Hays Code of 1930 had for motion pictures. To a large degree the measure was ineffectual due to lack of enforcement, but calls for stricter measures did not diminish (Nyberg 1998, 104–106).

In 1954 the comic book industry faced its greatest challenge to date on this score in the form of hearings conducted by the U.S. Subcommittee on Investigating Juvenile Delinquency, chaired by Sen. Robert C. Hendrikson and Sen. Estes Kefauver. Established with the broad mandate to investigate the perceived rise in juvenile delinquency, this committee began with the intent of conducting a serious investigation into the realm of public entertainment (Hajdu 2008, 251). Here it became clear that the problem with crime comics, of which superhero comics were considered a part, was not solely the subversion of morality in favor of "paganized sexuality" (Doyle 1943, 549) or of political values by their purveyance of a fascistic "cult of force" (Ong 1945, 37). It was a question of mental health, and the doctor who had set out to cure it was Dr. Fredric Wertham.

A German-born psychiatrist who immigrated to the United States before World War II, Wertham was convinced of the ill effects comics produced in the form of juvenile delinquency. He published these views along with copious anecdotal evidence in his influential 1954 book, *Seduction of the Innocent*. In it he arrived at conclusions linking comics to the causes of juvenile delinquency among American youth by statements such as "the superman ideology is psychologically most unhygienic" (Wertham 1954, 97) and descriptions of Wonder Woman as "the cruel, 'phallic' woman" (Wertham 1954, 54).

As a whole, *Seduction of the Innocent* was perhaps the most comprehensive and influential treatment of the perceived flaws in the entire medium of its day. However, the breadth of its scope was mitigated by the Wertham's reductionism. In it, he conflated superhero and crime comics, and he drew no apparent distinction between mythology and folklore. To those who defended comics as an expression of psychological forces he countered, "I do not believe that comic books—any more than slums—come from the 'unconscious.' Both are kept alive by the same social forces" (Wertham 1954, 244). The work is filled with similar dichotomies: conscious/unconscious, visual/literate, solitary/collective, primitive/civilized, all constructed to deny the comics of any connection with "higher" literature:

> Comic books are not dreamlike and not symbolic. . . . "The comics may be said to offer the same type of mental catharsis to its readers that Aristotle claimed was an attribute of the drama," says one of the experts. But comic books have nothing to do with drama, with art or literature. To invoke Aristotle in their defense is like invoking Beethoven in defense of street noises. (Wertham 1954, 241)

Consequently, Doyle and Ong maintained that comic book superheroes were paradoxically both too close to classicism (and fascism) and completely divorced from it. The aim of the inquiry was to determine whether comics, without discriminating between genres such as crime or superhero comics, were harmful to youth generally and whether they were a contributing factor to juvenile delinquency specifically, but at its core the dispute essentially revolved around the issue of the impact of media on behavior, with the defenders of comics arguing that their product was positive or at the very least neutral in its effects. Their position, needless to say, did not win the day, and both the fallout from the commission and the negative public attention the inquiry brought to the comics culminated in the adoption of the Comics Magazine Association of America (CMAA) Comics Code of 1954.

When Greek and Roman gods were adapted by the creators of superhero comics, they were implicated by the expectations of the reading public in the moral struggle of good and evil. One of the principle criticisms of superheroes themselves, however, was that they did not actually participate in such a system at all but rather operated outside of it. If comic book superheroes, because of their violence or sexuality, were not really good or if, as vigilantes, they broke the law and were criminals, adherence to even the first standard of the Comics Code presented a substantial challenge:

1. Crimes shall never be presented in such a way as to create sympathy for the criminal, to promote distrust of the forces of law and justice, or to inspire others with a desire to imitate criminals.

    Even murkier could be the following:

2. In every instance good shall triumph over evil and the criminal [be] punished for his misdeeds.

Many of the Code's other provisions were more specific, restricting authors from describing crimes in too much detail and publishers from using the word *crime* on the cover. Artists were required to clothe and pose figures in an unsuggestive manner. In an effort to be comprehensive, the Code also contained sections on dialogue, religion, marriage, and sex, as well as a code for advertising matter. As a tool, however, it proved a blunt instrument. The tension and ambiguity between what and who was good and evil, just or criminal, for example, was an intimate part of tragedy, but by the definition of the code, it became increasingly difficult for such narratives to pass the censors.[24]

The result of the hearings and their negative impact on the public's perception of comics precipitated enormous losses for the industry. Although characters such as Mercury, Mars, or Venus either were never meant to last, or never gained a firm foothold with the reading public, even previously popular characters such as Captain Marvel were abandoned.[25] The original home of Wonder Woman, *All-Star Comics*, left its superheroes behind to become *All-Star Westerns* in 1951. *Sensation Comics*, which had launched its first issue with Wonder Woman on

---

24. See the story "The Whipping," which replicates Aristotelean tragic themes such as hubris, reversal, recognition, and pity, which Wertham used to criticize the depiction of racism in comics (Nyberg 1998, 64–72).

25. See note 9.

the cover as the featured story in 1942, likewise changed to a horror/thriller format in 1952 before ceasing publication altogether a year later. Many publishers went out of business, and the next ten years marked a period of relative staidness as companies tried to adhere to the standards of the CMAA.

In 1963, however, a new generation of readers was once again ready to embrace comics and in particular superhero comics. World War II was almost twenty years distant, and while the Cold War was very much active, the focus had long ago shifted from ferreting out potential threats within to engaging threats without. In this new atmosphere, from the company formerly known as Timely Comics, now renamed Marvel Comics, emerged a new group of heroes, including the Fantastic Four, Spider-Man, and the Incredible Hulk.

The hallmark of these new figures was a heightened realism. Apart from their superhuman abilities, the Fantastic Four seemed to constitute a "normal" family. Spider-Man was a vulnerable teenager, and Bruce Banner, the Hulk's alter ego, was a man trying to cope with his condition almost as one would with a chronic illness. The appearance of the Hulk seems to have been the catalyst for the emergence of the most prominent god-hero in comics, Thor. Believing that audiences were overly familiar with Greek and Roman divinities, Stan Lee, Larry Lieber, and Jack Kirby (the same artist who had drawn "Mercury") created Thor in 1940 (Lee and Mair 2002, 158).

On the basis of his initial success with audiences, for the first time an ancient divinity stood front and center in his own monthly title, where his creators endowed him with other features commonly assigned to superheroes, such as a secret identity and a distinctly modern costume. The exploits of Thor and his evil brother, Loki, demonstrated that an updating of ancient myths could again win readers and supplied precedent for the reintroduction of the god Hercules, along with the other Olympians in 1965.

The return of divinities to the mainstream of the superhero comic genre in this way was far more prominent and long-lasting than any previous representation in the comics medium had been. Comparing the creation accounts given by Siegel and Lee, Siegel crafted Superman out of "all the strong men I have ever heard tell of rolled into one." To arrive at Thor, Lee described his thought process as a reversal of the question. In his own account, he was wondering how to create a character stronger than the Hulk, when he hit upon the answer, "Don't make him human—make him a god" (Lee and Mair 2002, 157). Superman may have been a superhero born from stories about gods, but Thor was a god born from stories about superheroes.

Under the Code, superheroes reasserted their dominance over the medium (Nyberg 1998, 158), and their relationship with gods in their stories has grown ever closer. In 1971 Jack Kirby launched his series *The New Gods* for DC, and five years later he crafted a similar story for Marvel, called *The Eternals*, in which the old Mercury from 1940 was revealed to actually have been named Makkari, who came from a prehistoric race of humans genetically altered by an alien race of "space gods" known as the Celestials.[26] The background of this situation appears to have been the idea of Erich von Däniken that ancient gods were in fact alien visitors, and in the course of the series it was revealed that other Eternals, such as their leader, Zuras, as well as

---

26. Jack Kirby (w./a.), *The Eternals* 1 (Marvel, July 1976).

Thena and Ikaris, had alternately at other times either been mistaken for or consciously posed as Greek divinities.[27]

The original run of *The Eternals* lasted only two years. During that time, however, due to the existence of both the Asgardian and the Olympian pantheons as established fixtures in Marvel stories, a debate occurred both on the letters pages and also among the members of the company's editorial board about how to reconcile the existence of these new beings with their "real" counterparts. As one letter writer opined, "I find it difficult to believe that the Eternal called Zuras is the Zeus of Roman Mythology [*sic*], when I can see the red-beard popping up in every few issues of another magazine."[28] Yet another writer objected to the seriousness of this explanation of ancient theology with the "frivolity" of its treatment.[29] In response, two arguments appeared for the separation of the Eternals from ancient gods as presented in comics and elsewhere. The first, supported by Kirby himself and echoing previous defenses of the medium, insisted that these stories were purely for entertainment.[30] The second proposed that due to their content these stories should be held separate from "the Earth of Marvel Super-Heroes" to maintain "sufficient latitude in story-telling," as well as "continuity and verisimilitude."[31]

The central issue of both reactions was the question of how this particular hybrid of gods and heroes could appropriately fit within the new relationship of gods and superheroes. By the end of the run in 1978, enough significant steps had been taken to establish the Eternals within the existing world of Marvel superheroes, although this reconciliation would not be finalized for another two years.[32]

Thus, this intimate connection of superheroes and ancient "pagan" gods, which had proven neither obvious, stable, nor popular with reading audiences at the beginning of the new genre but which critics saw as menacingly patent, found itself enduringly cemented. The Comics Code, which arose from the concern of those critics, however, has undergone two revisions, once in 1971 and another in 1989, influenced by creators and publishers, changes in the distribution methods, and the shifting tastes of the reading audience. While the Code is currently still in force, many publishers have chosen to make available noncode comics for their different audiences (Nyberg 1998, 150–151).

Yet the Comics Code—and the rationale that went into producing and enforcing it—demonstrated the delicacy of the issue, which either equated comic superheroes with ancient gods when opposing fascist or pagan ethics or separated them as the worthy substantive

27. In two essays that appeared in the letters column "Eternal Utterings," Kirby does not mention von Däniken by name, but the cover of the second issue of *The Eternals* describes the story within as "More Fantastic than Chariots of the Gods!" J. Kirby (w./a.), *The Eternals* 2 (Marvel, Aug. 1976). Kirby's comments within the essays appear noncommittal about the veracity of these kinds of claims, but he acknowledges that "The compelling quality inherent in this type of theme has led me to project its mystifying questions into comic magazine storytelling." See "Eternal Utterings," J. Kirby (w./a.), *The Eternals* 1 (Marvel, July 1976), 19.

28. D. Mallonee, letter, *The Eternals* 12 (Marvel, June 1977), 19. For further background on the company's internal movements surrounding this question of continuity, see also Hatfield (2005, 182–85).

29. G. Potter, letter, *The Eternals* 6 (Marvel, Dec. 1976), 19.

30. J. Kirby (w./a.), *The Eternals* 2 (Marvel, Aug. 1976), 19.

31. R. Macchio, letter, *The Eternals* 3 (Marvel, Sept. 1976), 19.

32. See Roy Thomas (w.) and Keith Pollard (a.), *The Mighty Thor* 291 (Marvel, Jan. 1980).

creations of cultured and literate civilizations. At stake in both arguments was not so much the legacy of the past as that of the future. "Can you imagine," Wertham opined, "a future great writer looking for a figure like Prometheus, Helena or Dr. Faustus among the stock comic-book figures like Superman, Wonder Woman or Jo-Jo, the Congo King?" (Wertham 1954, 233).

Ironically, this vision of the relationship of the Greek or Roman god with the comic book superhero revolves around the evaluation of their "ruin value" and relies less on interpreting what these objects and concepts actually meant to their contemporaries than on their role in the future. Ancient divinities were to be admired in the present for the spirit of aesthetic elegance they conveyed through classical art and literature but rejected in their potential to compromise current political, religious, or moral standards. Comic superheroes, insofar as they could be argued to resemble these gods, could not evoke the aesthetic and might even compound the compromising elements, particularly in the younger generation.

In the end, however, code control of comics proved elusive and secured neither the production nor the interpretation of these figures either in the comics or elsewhere. Conversely, there has been a remarkable plasticity with which writers and artists have continued to engage this material in an effort to win audiences as the industry has adapted to changing times. Moreover, as superheroes and gods continue in new relationships despite the divergence of their historical origins, moving past the Code impels us to view them freely once again as subjects of more historical investigations, more valid comparisons, and more liberated imaginations.

8

The Burden of War

From Homer to Oeming

R. Clinton Simms

As the preeminent personification of war and martial violence, Ares makes an exceptional supervillain in the comic book universe. The ancient god has been steadily employed as an archnemesis of Wonder Woman, manipulating Axis powers during World War II, and as an occasional foe of the Avengers and the Champions, facilitating cold-war tensions and nuclear arms proliferation between U.S. and Soviet forces. In these instances, Ares' incarnations are generally limited to symbolic projects. He functions as an anthropomorphized synecdoche for the constancy of war and military aggression in the world.[1] As the sinister force and guiding intelligence behind war, Ares is a figure of blame; the fault for humankind's boundless propensity for war is shifted conveniently to a distant and imaginary other. This is evident as early as Homer, where at *Iliad* 5.888–898, Zeus curses Ares as the most hated of all the gods because he loves only war. In 2006, however, Marvel released Michael Oeming's *Ares: God of War*. This successful five-issue miniseries featured an entirely new and complex character. Oeming's Ares, disgusted with the haughtiness of the Olympians, simply quits being the god of war to live a quiet, semimortal, seminormal life as a construction worker and father. This retirement frees Ares from the constraints of his mythic personifications and, since military engagements persist in his absence, shifts the blame for war and atrocity back onto humanity. Unlike a symbol, which emphasizes permanence that transcends change, Oeming allegorically defines Ares through a conflicted ambivalence toward what he represents as the god of battles and slaughter.

Ares, Axis Aggression, and Nuclear Arms

When Charles Moulton published the first issue of *Wonder Woman* in the summer of 1942, the god of war figured prominently in the Man's world *mythos* as a personification of the total war *zeitgeist* that covered the globe. After Wonder Woman rescues Steve Trevor and returns him to

---

1. Coleridge remarks: "The Symbolical cannot, perhaps, be better defined in distinction from the Allegorical, than that it is always itself *a part of* that, of the whole of which it is the representative" (Raysor 1936, 99).

America, she drops an ancient parchment that chronicles Amazonian history.[2] Earth is ruled, as Dr. Hellas at the Smithsonian translates the Greek text, by rival gods: Ares, who threatens that "men will rule with the sword," and Aphrodite, who promises that "women shall conquer men with love."[3] The goddess of love shapes a race of women to be stronger than men, which enrages Ares. The god of war enlists Hercules to subdue the Amazon queen, Hippolyte. She cannot be defeated in combat but, to her regret, can be conquered through romance. Hercules seduces the queen and tricks her into allowing him to hold her girdle, the source of Amazonian power. Penitent and defeated, Queen Hippolyte prays to Aphrodite for forgiveness and the strength for Amazons to overcome their captors. Aphrodite agrees, but the Amazon women must forever wear their wristbands as a reminder of "the folly of submitting to men's domination."[4] The god of war declares that the world is at war and that he rules Earth, but Aphrodite promises that America will win and that she will send one of her Amazons to help.[5] The chronicles then relate Diana's deceit of her mother and her victory in the games that enable her to travel to man's world.

Moulton's opposition of Ares/Mars to Aphrodite maintains a basic dichotomy well established in Greece and Rome.[6] Ares typifies war and all its horror: a confrontational figure whose mythic nature is aggressive, eager for violence, and representative of the darkest and most horrible atrocity humanity can inflict on itself. In primeval history, according to Empedocles, before even the reign of Kronos, there was only love, represented by Aphrodite. Ares was unknown:[7]

> There was no god Ares, or Battle-god,
> No lord Zeus, or Kronos, or Poseidon,
> Only Love was queen.
>   (FR. 128.15–17)

Ares exists in opposition to love, but their union is often presented as necessary to an ordered universe (Lamberton 1986, 228). Lucretius' depiction of the god subdued by Venus in *De Rerum Natura* 1.29–40, which is influenced by Empedocles and Hellenistic elements,[8] suggests that peace can come only from love's conquest of war.[9] Moulton rearticulates the polarized mythology of Ares and Aphrodite. Instead of a union that establishes peace, the gods are antagonistic,

2. Charles Moulton (w.) and Harry G. Peter (a.), *Wonder Woman* 1 (DC, Summer 1942), 2.4.

3. Ibid., 2.7.

4. Ibid., 5.2–3.

5. Ibid., 8.7.

6. The distinctions between Ares and Mars that existed for Greeks and Romans do not appear to persist in comic-book presentations. Moulton seems simply to regard Mars as Ares with a Roman name. See *Wonder Woman* 1, 2.8.

7. See also Kirk and Raven (1957, 349).

8. See further Edmunds (2002), Furley (1970), and Cole (1998).

9. Notably, in the *Hymn to Ares* 16–17, the god of war takes on a related but often overlooked aspect as the guardian of peace: "Grant, Blessed one, that we remain in the laws of peace without harm and avoid battle, death, and violence from our enemies."

defined in strongly separate and gendered terms that reduce to a Freudian *Eros/Thanatos*: The Amazons embody the productive and generative power of women, which Wonder Woman naturally epitomizes, holds sway over a masculine power of war and destruction.

For Moulton, Ares (as Mars) is a guiding intelligence behind war in a world dominated by martial aggression and violence. In *Wonder Woman* 2 a scroll surrounded by peritextual figures and an emblematic depiction of Mars ensnared by Wonder Woman's magic lasso narrates an explanation of his role in the contemporary world: "Today the Spirit of War rules supreme over the entire earth. Whence does it come? Why do human beings every generation or so, since the beginning of history, feel an uncontrollable urge to fight and kill one another?" Moulton claims the Greeks believed there was an "invisible God of War who urged human beings to conquer their fellows and destroy every man and woman who resists." Perhaps, he suggests, scientists will someday prove his existence because "it is he who stirs up the spirit of war" and now rules Earth from Mars. Moulton also suggests a timelessness and an atemporality in the conflict between love and war in the claim that Mars and Aphrodite "have been rivals for control of this earth since life began."[10]

Moulton's Mars directs his minions—the Earl of Greed, Lord Conquest, and the Duke of Deception—to control the minds of Axis leaders. Greed convinces Japan that wealth is worth war with America and also persuades Hitler to invade Russia.[11] Indeed, Hitler is presented as a frustrated and paranoid leader. At one point, an aide stands too close to his desk. Convinced that this is an assassination attempt, Hitler draws his Luger. Privately, however, Hitler gives "way to a strange impulse which at times possesses him, [he] bites the rug. Then suddenly his weird brain receives the Martian radio message."[12] In this way, we are given to realize that Hitler is merely a puppet of a larger and more threatening force for war. In another instance, the Duke of Deception "persuaded the black-brained yellow shadows of the rising sun to make peace talk at Washington while they struck with deadly venom at Pearl Harbour [*sic*]."[13] Notably, the effects of Mars' minions are also felt in their absence. When Deception fails to capture Wonder Woman, he is thrown into a dungeon with Greed, who had earlier disappointed the god of war. Deception's incarceration briefly breaks his control over Hirohito. The emperor, currently in talks with Mussolini's ambassador, "abandons his method of treacherous deceit and talks frankly,"[14] though still with malign intentions. Thus, Ares and his subordinate abstractions effectively control the evil forces of World War II. Such symbolic personification persists into the age of nuclear arms proliferation.

In April of 1972, Hawkeye (then Goliath) is missing from the Kree-Skrull war. In an effort to locate him Captain America trolls the television networks and happens on a

10. Moulton (w.) and Peter (a.), *Wonder Woman* 2 (DC, Fall 1942).

11. Ibid. 2, 1.

12. Ibid. 2, 3.5.

13. Ibid. 2, 1. It is worth commenting, apropos the unbridled racism displayed in this quote, that 1942 (the year of Wonder Woman's release) was also the year in which the U.S. government issued a series of military directives that culminated in the civilian exclusion order that forced all citizens and noncitizens of Japanese descent in the United States to relocation centers.

14. *Wonder Woman* 2, 2. This scene in Wonder Woman is particularly interesting because it suggests that, despite being under Deception's influence, Hirohito is still evil, just not at this particular moment deceitful.

rousing evangelization for war from Mr. Tallon (aka Warhawk).[15] Tallon uses a kind of street-preacher-style rhetoric to win over the teeming crowd and swell his ranks of followers. Tallon's influential power, however, comes from a pair of hooded, monklike minstrels playing panpipes. These pipers are satyrs, whose "melodic trilling"[16] rouses all who hear them with violent lust for nuclear war. Captain America and Iron Man are under his influence soon after their arrival and quickly turn on their teammates. Thor recognizes Tallon as Ares and attempts to explain the war god's sinister, though obscure, motives: "For reasons we know not, he seeks to stir nation against nation—brother against brother—and he must be stopped, ere he sets the earth ablaze with nuclear torches!"[17] Here again, as a personification, Ares is a symbol of society's aggressive predisposition. He becomes a convenient representation for war and a target of blame for its ongoing presence and threat.

Ares' ability to rouse the world to nuclear war is a thread also taken up by Pérez in his efforts to update *Wonder Woman*. Hermes brings his daughter Diana (aka. Wonder Woman) to Man's world in order to "put an end to Ares' madness."[18] He gives her the talisman, mad Harmonia's necklace, which aids in solving Ares' plans to annihilate all humankind with nuclear weapons.[19] Pérez preserves Ares' power over generals and world leaders, mediated by his subordinates, who encourage Soviet forces to strike against the United States.[20] Wonder Woman combats Ares' cronies, Decay and his two sons, the oafish Phobos and Deimos, who, despite being the more intelligent of the two, eventually gets his head sliced off by the business end of her razor-edged tiara.[21] Renegade troops take command of a U.S. nuclear missile base, and while Steve Trevor combats the leader of an army of burning zombies, Wonder Woman is transported to Ares' realm. The god of war gloats over his influence in the world in a series of insets. He toys with Wonder Woman, yet once ensnared by her lasso, Ares comes to realize that if he annihilates the world, no one will remain to follow him, there will be no one to contend with, and his existence will be without purpose. Confronted with the logical terminus of his actions, Ares weeps.[22]

With the threat of global nuclear annihilation somewhat relaxed, recent storylines tend to address topical issues like the possible terrorist threat from characters with superpowers.[23]

---

15. Roy Thomas (w.) and Barry Windsor-Smith (a.), *Avengers* 98 (Marvel, April 1972), 3.3.

16. Ibid., 6.3.

17. Ibid., 17.3.

18. George Pérez (w./a.), *Wonder Woman* 3 (DC, April 1987), 2.4. The title was restarted, with fresh numbering, under Pérez in 1987.

19. For a poetic description of the origin and fashioning of the necklace, see Statius' *Thebaid* 2.269–305.

20. *Wonder Woman* 3, 17–18.

21. Pérez (w./a.) and Len Wein (w.), *Wonder Woman* 5 (DC, June 1987), 19.6.

22. Ibid. 5, 21.

23. In Brian Michael Bendis (w.) and Frank Cho (a.), *Mighty Avengers* 1 (Marvel, May 2007), 20–22, when Ares is called to join the Mighty Avengers, for instance, he is strong-armed by Iron Man under threat of deportation from America for failing to register with the U.S. government. Ares, currently working construction in New Jersey, is approached at his job site and slapped with an ultimatum: Come to work with the Avengers, or they will arrest him and have him sent back to Olympus. He agrees to join the team as long as they match his current pay of $44 an hour.

Rather than influence the world's military affairs, Ares pursues personal vendettas against his family, specifically Hercules.[24] In the aftermath of "World War Hulk," Ares dictates the terms of Hercules' amnesty for supporting Hulk with a new set of humiliating labors. Adding insult to injury, he tells his half-brother to sign the recruitment papers and then says, "Drop and give me twenty."[25] Hercules throws Ares through a wall, frees Amadeus Cho, and flees. Ares then brazenly manipulates the law to pursue his revenge. He convinces the Avengers that only bullets of frozen hydra blood will stop Hercules. Just as Wonder Man convinces Hercules that the Avengers have no intention of humiliating him, Ares steps in and declares: "Pursuant to article IV Section 106(c) S.H.I.E.L.D. rules of engagement, lethal force is authorized: suspect is threatening the life of my teammate." However, when Wonder Man protests, Ares fires the hydra-blood bullets into Hercules and claims: "I am sorry, teammate Wonder Man! I cannot hear you over returning fire!"[26] Rather than subduing Hercules, the infection sends him into a mindless rampage. Ares' plan, as Wonder Man realizes, was never to capture Hercules but to make him such a threat that the Avengers (and everyone else) would have to use extreme force to kill him. During the climactic brawl between Ares and Hercules, we again see an emphasis on the eternal and unchanging aspects of Ares' nature. He is frustrated and envious that people love Hercules but despise him even though "war turns nations into empires! Peasants into heroes! Men into gods!"[27] Ares identifies himself as a metaphysical and causal force of change but remains himself unaffected by change.[28] Hercules tosses him from a S.H.I.E.L.D. helipad, and Ares is hit with three missiles. In a panel of rolling explosive clouds and *KHOIPHOOM*, Ares in a small bubble simply says, "Ow," an understatement that implies that Hercules has not destroyed Ares but only that this particular confrontation is over.[29]

Oeming's *Ares: God of War*

The presentations of Ares discussed so far can be framed in de Man's terms as a symbolic project. As a personification of war, Ares stresses "endurance within a pattern of change, the assertion of a meta-temporal, stationary state beyond the apparent decay of a mutability that attacks certain outward aspects of nature but leaves the core intact" (de Man 1989, 197). This is emphasized by his guidance in mortal military matters and by his implicit and explicit suggestions that war is a constant in human affairs. In 2006 Oeming presented a miniseries in which Ares

24. Rivalry between the two goes way back in comic books. Although at one point Hercules was willing to work for Ares to capture the Amazons, those days are long over. After the Avengers briefly run Ares off of Earth in his failed efforts to rouse Americans to nuclear war as Tallon, Ares attempts to take control of Olympus but is thwarted by Thor and Hercules. Additionally, Hercules fights against Ares alongside the Champions when he supports a coup by Pluto to take over the UCLA campus.

25. Greg Pak and Fred van Lente (w.) and Khoi Pham (a.), *The Incredible Hulk/Hercules* 112 (Marvel, Dec. 2007), 14.4. The series underwent a title change to *The Incredible Hercules* when the Olympian hero took over the title. Issue 112 is on the cusp of that change, with conflicting titles on the cover and interior pages.

26. Pak and van Lente (w.) and Pham (a.), *The Incredible Hercules* 113 (Marvel, Jan. 2008), 16.2–4.

27. Ibid. 115 (Marvel, May 2008), 13.2.

28. See also ibid. 113, 18.3, where Ares tells Wonder Man: "The struggles of the gods are eternal. They will continue long after you, S.H.I.E.L.D. and everything Stark has built has turned to dust."

29. Ibid. 115, 15.4.

abandons his martial functions and lives on Earth raising his son, Alexander. His peaceful workaday world is destroyed by the machinations of his father, Zeus, who seeks to draw Ares into a conflict that the Olympians cannot win without him. Oeming's presentation of Ares emphasizes the gods' estrangement from the Olympians, his self-loathing as a force of war, and his difficult reconciliation with his own identity. Oeming deploys a number of strategies that make a rampantly one-dimensional character psychologically complex, most notably in his retirement from war and his paternal attachment to his son. These narrative elements shift from symbolic representations toward allegory, with a strong emphasis on mutability and temporality. Characterizing Ares in this way shifts the burden of blame as a governing intelligence in the world of war and martial aggression back onto humanity.[30]

Oeming's eponymous hero of the miniseries has an inner complexity that develops from the impossibility of reconciling what he can do as a force of war with an ordinary life removed from the battlefield. Foreman adeptly renders an unexpectedly troubled and introspective god of war on the cover of the first issue (figure 8.1), visually compressing his weariness and frustration. Ares stands in a freshly won battlefield under a turbulent red sky. The god is heavily armed, and the lion pauldrons at his shoulders are suggestive of his animal savagery. Ares' lack of a shield indicates that in this most recent clash he has given no thought to his own safety and protection; his preference for two weapons reveals an aggressive offense. His head is lowered in thoughtful brooding, and despite his pronounced musculature, he looks physically exhausted. A great axe rests on his shoulder; although his weapon is heavy, burdensome, and seemingly unwieldy, he does not appear ready to put it down. His other hand firmly grasps a sword that droops to the ground and rests on a low heap of corpses that are impassable unless Ares is willing to step on or around them. The corpses also provide a chronology of abject slaughter. At his feet lie freshly mutilated and decapitated remains, but just behind Ares are weather-worn skulls. A helmeted head in the peaceful sleep of death is set alongside a head that appears to have just recently stopped screaming. These juxtapositions suggest a place where there are often battles and always deaths. This most recent conflict appears finished, but a still-living hand reaches from among the corpses to grasp his sword and pull it down. This visual hypallage, which transposes the natural or expected relationship between hand and sword, along with the arrangement of corpses, anchors Ares to the battlefield. Despite his fatigue and any wish that he may have to depart, no convenient path is open to him; Ares is stuck.

The presentation of Ares as a force is central to Oeming's depiction of the god; however, his ability to become such a bloody and pitiless force leads to his alienation.[31] Ares

30. As De Man suggests: "Whereas the symbol postulates the possibility of an identity or identification, allegory designates primarily a distance in relation to its own origin, and, renouncing the nostalgia and the desire to coincide, it establishes its language in the void of this temporal distance" (De Man 1989, 207).

31. For Edgar Rice Burroughs, Mars is also an irresistible force of war and battle, one whose cosmic presence calls John Carter to his swashbuckling destiny on the red planet. Burroughs's Carter describes being called to the planet from the Arizona desert: "My attention was quickly riveted by a large red star close to the distant horizon. As I gazed upon it I felt a spell of overpowering fascination—it was Mars, the god of war, and for me, the fighting man, it had always held the power of irresistible enchantment. As I gazed at it on that far-gone night it seemed to call across the unthinkable void, to lure me to it, to draw me as the lodestone attracts a particle of iron" (Burroughs 1963, 20; originally published serially in *All-Story Magazine* in 1912). Mars is thus a cosmic force, an attraction that defies resistance.

FIGURE 8.1   On the cover of the first issue of the Marvel miniseries, Ares looks the part of the
traditional god of war. Cover art by Travel Foreman. *Ares: God of War* 1 (Marvel, March 2006).

FIGURE 8.2 **Ares tries to lead a normal life in the Marvel miniseries. Art by Travel Foreman.**
Ares: God of War 1 (Marvel, March 2006).

defines his savagery, claiming that he "evokes not just the power of war, but something more. The will to do the deeds that others cannot."[32] During the *concilium deorum* after the fall of Troy, however, he overhears contempt expressed against him. His willingness to become a force, to go beyond and "spill the brains and taste the blood" of Olympus' enemies also sets him apart from his family.[33] The Olympians reject him as incompatible with their higher attitudes. Unable to endure their haughtiness, he leaves the pantheon as an outcast, hating himself and anyone that reveres him. Many years later, we find Ares waiting for a parent-teacher conference with his son Alex's teacher (figure 8.2). He has turned his back on the gods and on a life of war to live as a mortal man on Earth, supporting himself and his son on pawned Greek antiquities and a job in construction, content that no one, including his son, knows his true identity.

Oeming's programmatic scene of expatriation turns the Homeric presentation of Ares on its head. In the *Iliad*, Homer sets Ares in opposition to Athena. The two antagonize each other, and as Otto suggests, this is likely to have more to do with their natures than their choice of sides in the Trojan War (Otto 1954, 46).[34] Athena represents wise council, and her

32. Michael Avon Oeming (w.) and Travel Foreman (a.), *Ares: God of War* 1 (Marvel, March 2006), 1, 3.4.

33. Ibid., 7.6.

34. See also Darmon (1991, 414–15). Deacy (2000, 285–98) convincingly argues that the distinctions between the two gods are not nearly so simple for the Greeks as we might suppose.

intercession often discourages heroes from the rash actions more often associated with Ares' behavior.[35] In their rivalry, Athena always defeats Ares.[36] This has interpretive value as the triumph of reason and wisdom over madness in combat.[37] After Diomedes wounds Ares, the god returns to Olympus and accuses his father of failing to check Athena and letting her get away with whatever she wants. After his protest, Zeus admonishes his son:

> Then looking sternly at him, cloud-gathering Zeus said: "Don't switch sides and then come here sniveling to me. You are the most detestable of all Olympians: strife, war, and battles are all you love. Your mother Hera is just as unruly and disregards my authority. I'm certain she had something to do with this mess of yours. Nevertheless, I won't let you suffer needlessly. You are my son and your mother's child. But if any other god had fathered such an evil as you, you would have found yourself further from Olympus than even the children of Uranus." (*Iliad* 5.888–98)

Here, Ares demonstrates a genuine relationship with a callous father who openly expresses contempt for his son and his sibling rivalry. He functions within the narrative as a character; however, his symbolic identity effectively relegates him to a position of contempt and scorn wherein Zeus' chiding, and, most important, his expression that Ares is the most hated of all the gods voices a nearly universal hatred for the bloody face of war. Oeming plays off this image of a contemptible god who is shunned by his family in order to make Ares a sympathetic outcast and an antihero. When Oeming quotes Zeus' words from the *Iliad*—that Ares is the most hated of all the gods—to begin the first issue, this proves to be a distorted echo of Homer. In the *Iliad*, Ares is a detestable constant among humankind who delights in the suffering he causes. Oeming's Ares, full of self-loathing and disgusted with Olympian snootiness, simply walks off the job in quiet protest.[38]

The germ of Ares' abandonment as a controlling force in mortal matters of war can be found in *Wonder Woman* 6; however, the narrative is most strongly patterned after Destruction's abandonment of his realm in the *Sandman* story arc "Brief Lives." After Wonder Woman forces Ares to realize the consequences of a nuclear holocaust and the god of war sobs, he renounces control over humankind's martial affairs. Ares declares that "man must decide his own destruction"[39] and entrusts to Wonder Woman the task of guiding and teaching them, but Pérez does not remove the threat of Ares' meddling entirely. If she should fail, Ares promises to return. Oeming's Ares takes positions similar to Gaiman's Destruction, most notably in the character's detachment from his cosmic function. War and Destruction persist, but only

---

35. Cf. *Iliad* 1.188–222. As Minerva she counsels and favors Tydeus at *Thebaid* 2.682–90.

36. See *Iliad* 5.824–64, 15.121–42, and 21.391–415.

37. See Clarke (1999, 269–72). See also (Doty 1993, 141).

38. It is unlikely that Statius' *Thebaid* influenced the development of Ares in the comic book universe; however, it is worth briefly mentioning that during the Theban conflict, Mars underperforms in his duties and fails to demonstrate an appreciable eagerness for sowing the seeds of war as Jupiter instructed him (*Thebaid* 7.27–32). Indeed, Mars appears most comfortable pursuing his own military triumphs in Hyrcania (*Thebaid* 7.69) or enjoying the battles as a spectator and canoodling with Venus (*Thebaid* 9.821–822).

39. Pérez (w./a.) and Wien (w.), *Wonder Woman* 6 (DC, July 1987), 21.

as empty and ungoverned motion. The power is displaced, and the characters are no longer coextensive with their attributes. As Sandman's older brother claims, "Destruction did not cease with my abandonment of my realm. . . . Perhaps it's more uncontrolled, wilder. Perhaps not. But it's no longer anyone's responsibility."[40] Destruction's decision to leave his realm is motivated by Sir Isaac Newton's speculation in 1704, "Are not light and gross bodies convertible into one another," a premise that will lead to "flames . . . the big bang. The loud explosions." Essentially, this will be Destruction's time, and he wants no part of it.[41] There are, however, significant differences in how Ares and Destruction spend their leisure time. Destruction writes bad poetry and has been an artist, a mercenary, a canal digger in Panama, and a prankster. Ares, however, spends his days in manual labor, raising his son and protecting him from the Olympians. The world continues to happen around them, so the power to shape events clearly rests with humanity.

While Ares is away from Olympus, the androgynous Amatsu Mikaboshi,[42] "the August Star of Heaven," gathers an army to encroach upon and destroy the divine pantheons of the world gods. Amatsu has already destroyed many of the Eastern gods, Asgard, and the Norse gods and now turns on Olympus. When Amatsu's forces overrun the Greek gods and heroes, they are unable to repel the attack. Losing the battle, Zeus calls for Ares. Hermes arrives at Ares' construction site and insists on Zeus' behalf that he return. Ares is disgusted with his father's fair-weather attitude. The god of war claims he will return to Olympus only to paint its walls with Olympian blood and then shoots Hermes in the foot with a nail gun.[43] To pull Ares into the conflict, Zeus kidnaps Alexander. Ares, as the most paternal of the Olympians,[44] is enraged by this maneuver, which forces him into the conflict for the sake of his son. His love for Alexander forces him to go for his guns and use fully his powers as the god of war.

Ares' reluctance to engage in conflict is apparent during his arming scene. He enters an arsenal, hidden behind a closet, and gathers his weapons. Even though Ares has retired, he has kept up with all the trends and advances in small-arms combat. Arming scenes have a long history, and Oeming centers his Ares within this tradition. When a character straps on his gear, we anticipate an eventful battle. After the Olympians kidnap Alex, Ares admits that he cannot escape what he is and that he was fooling himself to think he had retired.[45] Meanwhile, the local

40. Neil Gaiman (w.) and Jill Thompson (a.), *The Sandman* 49 (Vertigo, May 1993), 11.

41. Ibid. 46 (Vertigo, Feb. 1993), 20–22.

42. After the events of *Ares: God of War*, Mikaboshi is recruited to represent the East in Hercules' "godsquad." Hercules is far from thrilled about his presence on the team. See Pak and van Lente (w.) and Rafael Sandoval (a.), *The Incredible Hercules* 117 (Marvel, July 2008), 15–17.

43. *Ares: God of War* 1, 14.

44. Cf. *Iliad* 15.113–18. For a pop-psychology discussion of Ares as a symbol of paternity see Bolen (1989, 194–95, 198). Something of this paternal nature is also seen in Ares' relationship with Cassie Sandsmark (aka Wonder Girl), where he becomes a tutelary and directing, albeit suspicious, influence. See Geoff Johns (w.) and Mike McKone (a.), *Teen Titans* 2 (DC, Oct. 2003), 15.2, in which Ares calls ominously to her from the bay; *Teen Titans* 4, 13–15, in which Ares presents Wonder Girl with her own lasso; Johns (w.) and Tom Grummett (w.), *Teen Titans* 15 (Nov. 2004), in which she demands to know why he takes such an interest in her; and Geoff Johns and Marv Wolfman (w.) and Todd Nauck (a.), *Teen Titans* 33 (April 2006), 6–8, in which Ares explains that he only wants her familial love.

45. *Ares: God of War* 1, 20–21.

police, in their search for Alex in the mortal realm, have turned up inconsistencies in the identities of father and son and arrive to question Ares.

One interesting feature of Ares' arming scene is its contemporaneous handling of a stock heroic motif that conveys a cynical outlook on humankind's predilection for war. The panels in which Ares arms himself alternate with television footage of the Iraq War. The interspersing of his dramatic arming sequence with footage of a mass grave and an execution room suggests that, even though Ares had long since absented himself from human affairs in war and atrocity, they persist. This allegorical distance between the god of war and martial conflict emphasizes that something integral to human nature compels war; battles will be fought whether Ares is present or not, just as Destruction predicts of his own absence from the world.

In a foretaste of the violence Ares intends for his father, he promptly routs the mortal law-enforcement figures, which stresses Ares' marginal and antiauthoritarian position. As the detective knocks at his door, Ares shaves his head down to his former Mohawk, which he also sported as Tallon. His familiarity with a range of weapons is evident as he checks a rifle, some grenades, a sword, and a battle-ax. Law-enforcement agents (a detective, a uniformed officer, and a SWAT team) make an unsuccessful attempt to take Ares into custody. The ensuing "chaos is a sign the god of war has returned."[46] The violence into which he seems reluctantly forced is quickly embraced. Ares declares amid explosions and gunfire the tonic effects of his violence: "I'm doing this for Alex," and, after a big *Ka-Boom*, "and it feels good."[47] Thus, Ares rejoins, though initially with unwillingness and later with unsettling eagerness, the world of carnage and conflict. Unfortunately, when he arrives at Olympus, he learns that Amatsu has taken Alex. He enters into an uneasy alliance with the other Olympians not just to win the war but also to rescue his son.

The absence of his usual compatriots provides a sharper contrast to the love between Ares and his son. An interesting revision in characterizing Oeming's adaptation of Ares from his predecessors is the absence of his companions, who are often personifications of emotional states of violence and war.[48] Oeming's Ares is a loner. The absence of subordinates reinforces his marginalized and alienated position. Additionally, Ares' usual relationship with Aphrodite is left undeveloped. In the mythic tradition, their illicit tryst often signifies the power of love to still the power of war. This romantic association typically weakens an otherwise strong figure. Demodokos' song on the affair between Ares and Aphrodite and their capture in the golden net reveals the embarrassment of the god's indiscretion and makes him a source of laughter for the other gods.[49] No one laughs at Oeming's Ares. Lucretius' portrait of Mars in Venus' lap at *De Rerum Natura* 1.29–40 likewise diminishes his presentation as a powerful and destructive force. The image of Mars subdued by Venus peaks in

46. Ibid., 2, 6.9.

47. Ibid., 7.16–18.

48. In antiquity, Ares is frequently accompanied by his sons Deimos [Fear] and Phobos [Panic] (Hesiod *Theogony* 933–37) and his sister Eris [Strife]. See *Iliad* 4.440 and 15.119. In Statius' *Thebaid* Mars' cohort stand as sentries around his palace and accompany him into battle. His minions are Impetus, Nefas, Ira, Metus, Insidia, Discordia, tristissima Virtus, Furor, and Mors (7.47–53).

49. *Odyssey* 8.267–366.

Chaucer. When he develops their relationship, his madness and passion for Venus present him as completely conquered:

> For she forbad him jelosye at alle,
> And cruelte, and bost, and tirannye;
> She made him at hir lust so humble and talle,
> That when hir deyned caste on him hir yë,
> He took in pacience to live or dye;
> And thus she brydeleth him in hir manere,
> With no-thing but with scourging of hir chere.
> (Chaucer, *The Compleynt of Mars* 36–42)

His warrior nature is subdued, and he is so dominated by love that he takes on qualities that we do not easily associate with him: He is forbidden cruelty, boasting, and high-handed rule. Venus has made him humble and docile.[50] This sort of emasculating submissiveness and weakness is also demonstrated in *Champions* 3, when Ares stammers out an apology to Venus for his support in Pluto's attack on Olympus.[51]

The world in which Oeming's Ares moves is hypermasculine. Since depictions of an erotic relationship with Aphrodite tend to knock the edges off Ares, the absence of her softening presence enables him to dominate the narrative as the manliest of men: the strongest, most brutish and violent figure who succeeds in bloody battle where everyone else in his family fails. Alex has a mother, but when he asks his father about her at the end of the series, Ares evasively states: "It's complicated."[52] The lack of his usual accompaniment with either his underlings or Aphrodite enables a presentation of Ares as a lone alpha male who is committed exclusively to the task of raising his son. Whereas in Moulton's *Wonder Woman* the generative powers of love and production were distinct from the powers of destruction and violence, in Oeming's Ares we find this dichotomy collapsed and internalized. Indeed, as Ares' thoughts reflect during his parent-teacher conference with Mrs. Perrine, the absence of maternal influence is to be carefully avoided in his prescriptive pedagogy: "It's that kind of woman's touch that I don't want raising my son. Alex will never meet his mother and he'll never need to. A woman will make him soft. And in this world of Man, only the strong survive. Even in the third grade."[53] This method of characterizing Ares separates him from earlier, more symbolic presentations and becomes particularly important for the theme of succession developed throughout.

Where Ares plays the strongly paternal father, the absence of a mother allows Amatsu to step in and deceive the boy as a surrogate parent. During the initial conflict between Amatsu

50. Readers unfamiliar with Middle English should note that "talle" here means "docile."

51. Tony Isabella and Bill Mantlo (w.) and George Tuska (a.), *Champions* 3 (Marvel, Feb. 1976), 30.4.

52. *Ares: God of War* 5, 21.3. Bendis (w.) and Alex Maleev (a.), *Mighty Avengers* 13 (Marvel, July 2008), 7–8, reveals that Alex is actually the god Phobos. Given Ares' contempt for Deimos and Phobos (demonstrated at *Ares: God of War* 4.19–20), it is unlikely that Alexander was (in this particular spin of the narrative) Phobos. Nevertheless, being *polumuthon* [subject to multiple narratives] is as much a feature of comic book narrative as it is epic, and there is no reason to niggle over a lack of seamless consistency as some fans have.

53. *Ares: God of War* 1, 8.7–8.

and Olympus, Alex is spirited away to the lands of the Eastern dead, taken from the Olympians who originally kidnapped him. In true form Amatsu has amorphous hydra-like features with inky flailing tentacles. However, Amatsu takes on feminine features in front of Alex, is gentle and loving with him, and encourages him to drink a tea-like concoction that makes him suscep- tible to suggestions of killing his father and taking his own place as the true and noble god of war. Amatsu reveals the truth about Ares to Alex and the violence of the Olympian pantheon and encourages him to right the wrongs of murder and violence endemic to his father's and grandfather's history. To clear the way for Alex's succession, Amatsu disguises a "pet" as Alex and sends it to Zeus. The ancient god embraces the likeness as his grandson and is impaled through the back. The wound leaves him hovering between life and death. This near assassina- tion of Zeus leaves a power vacuum that Ares' presence quickly fills. For five years, war rages, and Amatsu fully indoctrinates Alex into his army, and the boy is prepared to kill his father. Through the deceit of Hermes and Inari, the remaining Eastern gods join the Olympians in a final assault on Amatsu's compound, which concludes the series.

Claiming power through violence is the appropriate order of succession among the Olympian gods. Oeming is considerably preoccupied with the theme of succession and power among the Greek immortals. The predictability of interfamilial violence gives Amatsu the advantage to play son against father in his expansion of empire. Of course, death is problematic for a group that is immortal; thus, binding and containing the god is the standard practice in Greek myth (Burton 2001, 46). Oeming's Olympians, however, can die. Amatsu's great strength lies in the secret knowledge of how to destroy gods. Zeus is astonished when he embraces what he thinks is his grandson, only to be run through with several hydralike tentacles.[54] However, Zeus' death should not come as a surprise. Oeming and Foreman present a withered god that falls far from the powerful Zeus of ancient epic. Though certainly strong, Zeus sometimes appears as though he has just too many years behind him, especially when he is depicted next to his young and vivacious wife, Hera. Compared to Ares and Hercules, he seems frail.[55] When Ares strikes him for kidnapping his son, the blow meets no resistance, and it is surprising that there is not any damage.[56] Zeus' physical weakness is further suggested by Hercules' haste to step in and defend his father from his violent half-brother. Even at this early stage, Ares seems the dominant figure despite Zeus' powerful blast of lightning, which breaks up the quarrel between his sons and restores order among the Olympians.

While Alexander is under the influence of Amatsu, he is being trained to defeat his father and to succeed him as the god of war. In the final battle at Amatsu Mikaboshi's compound, Ares attacks Mikaboshi but is swatted away. Amatsu claims: "You will fall, but from your scion's rage! It is the Greek way!"[57] Amatsu then reveals Alexander, who promises to continue the tradition of patricide, as the New God of War in the palm of his giant hand. Of course, this is both literally and metaphorically appropriate. Ares is forced into mortal combat with his own son. Alexander strikes at his father with a sword and draws blood. The two fight, though notably

54. Ibid. 3, 22; 4, 2–3. Hercules and Ares fight the evil god in a scene that recalls the mythic combat against the Lernaean hydra. See ibid. 4, 8–9.

55. See ibid. 1, 6–7; 2, 16; 3, 4, and 4, 11.

56. Ibid. 2, 17–18.

57. 5, 3.

Ares is unarmed, and Alexander eventually defeats Ares. Though Ares is overpowered by his son, it is unclear whether he is beaten because his love for his son prevents him from fully using his strengths or because Alexander, under Amatsu's tutelage, now surpasses his father in physical prowess. During their fight, there is a brief moment when, after Ares takes a swipe in the throat from his son's blade, he declares that the mythic tradition also includes fathers killing sons. He pins the boy to the ground and demands his surrender but cannot hold him. Alexander drives the sword through his father's back. As Ares lies dying in agony, Zeus uses "one last act of magic"[58] to uncloud his grandson's mind. Alex recalls his love for his father, turns the sword on Amatsu, and slays him. The combined forces of East and West then proceed to purify the compound with fire and water. Ares and Alexander recuperate on the mythic plains of Africa, where the boy shows tremendous enthusiasm for his newfound, albeit "dysfunctional," family.

War, it is generally agreed, dehumanizes, and Oeming's Zeus sagely acknowledges that a valiant and honorable fight at Troy produces only stalemate and that winning necessitates an ability to go beyond and smash the skulls and drink the blood of enemies, which is why he drew him into the conflict with Amatsu. As the god of war, Ares displays a cruel and unflinching eagerness to annihilate. However, as an allegory for war, Ares demonstrates an inability to come to terms with aggression. Oeming's character is endowed with all the martial power one would expect to find in the god of war, but this power is offset by a troubled reluctance to use it and later an unsettling delight. He is either on, or he is off.[59] There is considerable distance between this Ares, who clearly has trouble being what he is, and former, more symbolic, presentations, in which he is driven by a single-minded purpose and delight in war. This single-mindedness reaches its absolute limit in Pérez's depiction. Ares realizes that he can go no further and that he can never have total annihilation because he would no longer have a purpose. In Oeming's series, however, Ares' concerns are no longer self-serving, and his martial talents are applied for the safety and well-being of another. The innovation of Oeming's Ares is his ability to circumvent his proxy functions as a governing intelligence for war, seemingly for its own sake. Homer claimed that war and bloodshed are ever a delight to the god of war, and this is why Zeus calls him the most hated of all the Olympians. In order for Ares to function as a symbol for war, carnage and devastation must always remain dear to him. As long as they are so, he promises to remain a convenient scapegoat for human war and conflict. Oeming's Ares, however, resists such a convenient assignation of blame. Instead, he seeks to redress this tradition and shift the responsibility back onto the human beings who perpetuate reckless violence.

---

58. Ibid., 5, 15.

59. On ambivalent attitudes surrounding Ares, aggression, and war see Doty (1993, 143) and Hillman (1987, 118–35).

9

"Seven Thunders Utter Their Voices"

Morality and Comics History in *Kingdom Come*

Benjamin Stevens

The study of Classics in comics, part of the study of Classics in popular culture, seeks to further debates about "high" and "low" culture and about what "Classics" are or may be.[1] A parallel is provided by the study of Classics in another modern art form, cinema: "[A] fundamental purpose of . . . comparative investigations of classics and cinema is to challenge the conventional definitions of classics and classicism that have received so much support since the late 1980s," from conservative critics like Allan Bloom.[2] To achieve this purpose and to avoid suggesting that modern receptions of ancient material are important "regardless of their artistic merit,"[3] studies of the Classics in popular culture must take account of the fact that most of popular culture does not engage with the Classics and, correspondingly, has "classics" of its own. In particular, most comics do not draw on the Classics.[4] The study of those that do is thus necessarily enriched by more general consideration of the art form's formal

---

1. See, for example, Storey (1993).

2. Wyke (1997, 7–8), as against, for example, Bloom (1987). Once "hindered by the notion of a divide between high culture, where most classicists traditionally situated the objects of their study, and low, a label that many academics, at least in the past, would assign to filmic production," Classics in cinema is a subject that is increasingly studied; see *Arethusa* 41.1 (2008), introduced by K. Day (1–9, quoted material from 2); Nisbet (2006), Cyrino (2005), Wyke (1997), and Winkler (1991). One hopes Classics in comics will be similarly productive.

3. Day sees too much "value [in] exploring the reception of classical antiquity in cinema *regardless of artistic merit*" (2–3; emphasis added). It must make a difference for reception when, for example, a biopic of Alexander the Great, *Alexander* (O. Stone 2004) is savaged by critics and fails to recoup its costs (grossing $167,297,191 worldwide, having cost $201,200,000).

4. Comics include adaptations of Greco-Roman stories, historical fictions with elaborated or invented stories in classical settings, atmospheric references to myth, and, arguably, some dependence on ancient storytelling styles via the intermediaries of modern theater and film (which, however, postdates sequential art); see Kovacs to this volume. Perhaps most famously in comics, the tagline to Alan Moore (w.) and Dave Gibbons (a.), *Watchmen* (DC, Sept. 1986–Oct. 1987), "Who Watches the Watchmen?," quotes Juvenal 6.347–48 indirectly through the Tower Commission Report, taking its place among other "classic," including Nietzsche, Elvis Costello, and Bob Dylan (the only source quoted more than once); the tagline is quoted in *Kingdom Come* as a graffito "[Who W]atches [T]he [Wat]chmen" (17.2), making *Watchmen* visually and literally part of the work's background.

properties and historical traditions, including important genres and "classics" intertextually defined.[5] Thus contextualized, comparative study stands to reveal truly meaningful comics reception of the Classics, as well as important differences that may themselves be suggestive for future work, both "critical" and "creative." If modern graphic literature and ancient Greco-Roman literatures are constructed similarly—simultaneously critiqued and "created" by their readerships—then the construction occurs literally and actively in comics, more figuratively and somewhat passively in the Classics. Exploration of this difference may perhaps suggest ways in which the Classics, a closed set of texts read mainly by scholars and students, might be made to reach a larger audience by drawing on models from comics, a set open to a much wider range of engagement.

To explore these issues, I examine one example of an important genre in comics: the superheroic *Kingdom Come*.[6] As its title suggests, *Kingdom Come* draws on a traditional interpretation of the "Lord's Prayer" ("thy kingdom come, thy will be done"; Mt. 6:9–13, Lk. 11:2–4), linking the apocalyptic fulfillment of Hebrew prophecy to the eschatology of Revelation.[7] The work's biblical intertext is mediated, first, by the cadence of an Americanized King James Version and its transformations relative to a 20th-century American understanding of ministry.[8] Second and more important, the apocalypse is set in the DC Universe: Although the ancient intertext is suggestive of overall plot, most of the parts are played by comics characters—some traditional, others invented for the story—and crucial plot points are both fulfillment of biblical prophecy and the consequence of superhero comics history. *Kingdom Come* thus depends on and helps define "classic" stories from

5. I write "comics" without assuming answers to definitional questions about comics, "comix," and/or "underground comics" (attributed to B. Stewart), "comic strips," "comic books" (S. Lee), "graphic novels" (W. Eisner, esp. his (w./a.) *A Contract with God, and Other Tenement Stories* (Baronet Books, 1978)), and "graphic literature," not to mention others like Franco-Belgian *bande dessinée* and Japanese *manga*.

On the study of comics, see Groensteen (2007, 1–2), who identifies "four successive layers in the critical discourse" about comics. His examples tendentiously imply, as his translators put it, that "[q]uestions of comics form have received relatively little attention in English-language scholarship" (vii). Anglophone scholarship has been interested in historical and cultural questions (e.g., Wright 2003; Bongco 2000) in surveys (e.g., the essential Sabin 2001), and in thematic studies (e.g., McLaughlin 2005), but it has also researched comics "aesthetics" (e.g., Carrier 2000; Harvey 1996), including "form" (e.g., Hatfield 2005, 32–67; Varnum and Gibbons 2001; see also Gordon, Janovich, and McAllister 2007). The most visible examples of attention to form have, however, been by creators like S. McCloud (esp. 1993) and W. Eisner (1985) and thus have been artistic or creative rather than academic or critical. See further the Preface to this volume and chapter 1.

A bibliography of scholarly materials for comics research is maintained by M. Rhode and J. Bullough (http://www.rpi.edu/~bulloj/comxbib.html); also helpful is G. Kannenberg Jr.'s more wide-ranging site (http://www.comicsresearch.org/).

6. Mark Waid (w.) and Alex Ross (a.) (DC, May–August 1996). *Kingdom Come* is annotated by Jess Nevins at http://www.geocities.com/athens/olympus/7160/annos.html. See Tallon and Walls (2005); see also Reynolds (1992).

7. On the Lord's Prayer see Charlesworth, Harding, and Kiley (1994, 186–201). For "Matthew," "Luke," and "Revelation" generally, see the respective volumes in *The Anchor Bible Commentary*: Albright and Mann (1971); Fitzmyer (1981); Ford (1975).

8. Also fatherhood: Pastor Norman McKay is named and modeled after the artist's father, Pastor Clark Norman Ross. (Against names like Super-Man and Bat-Man, does the narrator's name suggest "*nor*mal *man*," i.e., human?) Ross describes the work as his "tribute to his [father's] profession and good character" (230), and the character Norman says, "[I]t's flattering to be remembered somehow" (212.4.10: citation is page.panel.word-balloon).

comics history.[9] Those classics, with consequences for character, add drama to the work's loosely Biblical progression by deepening its human dimension.

Kingdom Come is thus highly intertextual, referring to and rewriting stories within its genre and across generic boundaries and constantly inviting its "model reader" to explore how familiar characters and stories are furthered or changed.[10] Like other works by Ross and his collaborators, it may be read as contrasting comics' Golden and Silver Ages with more recent work, especially its contemporary 1990s and the late 1980s (the "Modern Age").[11] By enacting this contrast in the conflict between older and newer superheroes and their values, the work figures Biblical revelation as superhuman revolution and thus imagines moral decision making depending on mediation between, and ultimately on the identification of, human and superhuman or divine.

These central themes may be sketched by a summary of the work's plot and visual and verbal strategies. *Kingdom Come* is hand-painted in a photorealistic style; there is no gutter, and the paneling is varied. The work is in four parts, each titled with reference to Superman history and introduced by at least one splash page combining shadowy images with quotations from Revelation as calligraphy on fragmentary parchment; the splash pages represent the narrator's visions, set the tone, and announce the work's overlap of Biblical and comics intertexts.

The first part, "Strange Visitor" (as in "from a distant planet"),[12] introduces Norman and his guide, the supernatural Spectre, who invisibly observe a near future from which familiar characters have retired and in which a new generation of superhumans, many of them visual variants (and/or descendants) of retired characters, run amok.[13] "Strange Visitor" ends with Superman's return in response to the destruction of Kansas, his adopted home, by the Justice Battalion (a militant, contemporary update of the Silver Age Justice League),[14] and with Norman's vision that "[t]he threat of Armageddon . . . | [has] just begun" (55.3.2–3).

9. *Kingdom Come* illustrates the role played by editors and publishers, at times against creators, in defining "continuity," the official set of stories; one mechanism is "retroactive continuity" or "retconning," in which the "canon" of stories is revised to reflect innovation. *Kingdom Come* is "outside of continuity," representing a possible future for the 1996 DC universe or, in line with DC's "multiverse" of Earths, whose conflicting storylines require occasional retconning (see esp. Marv Wolfman [w.] and George Pérez [a.], *Crisis on Infinite Earths* [April 1985–March 1986], and Geoff Johns [w.] and Phil Jimenez et al. [a.], *Infinite Crisis* [Dec. 2005–June 2006]), Earth-22, not that of most DC comics. Thus, the work is under DC's "Elseworlds" imprint.

10. On the "model reader" see Eco (1979, 3–46; 1990, 44–63).

11. To exemplify this, I note a program of allusion to Frank Miller (w./a.) and Lynn Varley (a.), *The Dark Knight Returns* (DC, Feb.–June 1986, henceforth *DKR*), seminal, despite its satire, for the "grim and gritty" turn of superhero comics through the mid-1990s. For Ross's comics-historical interests, see Kurt Busiek (w.) and Alex Ross (w./a.), *Marvels* (Marvel, Jan.–April 1994), retelling classic stories from a reporter's perspective, and Busiek (w.) and Brent Eric Anderson (a.), *Astro City* (first Image, then Homage, 1995–present), similar but with new characters, both written by Busiek.

12. From *The Adventures of Superman* radio show, first broadcast on February 12, 1940. For this and other Superman information I am grateful to an anonymous reader. Variations include "from the planet Krypton," from later episodes of the radio show, and "from another planet," from the television show.

13. *Kingdom Come*'s "retirements" (mainly 40–48: Flash, Hawkman, Green Lantern, Aquaman, Wonder Woman, the Legion, Batman) are similar to *DKR*'s (mainly vol. 3:16, Superman thinking of "Diana," i.e., Wonder Woman, and "Hal," i.e., Green Lantern, and himself). The allusion to *DKR* seems confirmed by the second half of *Kingdom Come*'s description (45–48), which is focused on Batman, corresponding to his position in *DKR*'s list (3:16.3.6–7).

14. The Justice League first appeared in Gardner Fox (w.) and Mike Sekowsky (a.), *The Brave and the Bold* 28 (DC, Feb.–Mar. 1960). Further exemplifying *Kingdom Come*'s interest in comics history, the battalion, led by the modern age-esque Magog, features versions of silver age characters acquired by DC from Charlton Comics in 1983.

The second part, "Truth and Justice" (a second reference to Superman, without the usual third element in the tricolon: "and the American way"),[15] specifies the factions, each representing a different kind of being: Superman and his league of superheroes; the United Nations (i.e., human government); Batman and other "antifascist" superheroes, later called the "legion" (169.1.1; possibly a take on the Silver Age Legion of Superheroes);[16] Superman archenemy Lex Luthor and fellow supervillains in the Mankind Liberation Front; and others. "Truth and Justice" ends with the Justice League's building a prison for recalcitrant superhumans and with Batman and Luthor joining forces.

In the third part, "Up in the Sky" (a third reference to Superman: "Look, up in the sky, a bird, a plane," from the Fleischer cartoons, quoted at Superman's reappearance in part one [53.3.4–5]), the prison has been filled, and important relationships are specified (Superman and Wonder Woman; Luthor and his enforcer, the brainwashed Captain Marvel).[17] Norman is revealed to the League and shares his visions. The prisoners riot, the UN hints at a human solution to the superhuman problem, and Luthor attempts to further chaos (ordering Marvel to "tumble down the walls of Jericho"; 139.5.17) but is double-crossed by Batman. The third part ends with Superman's attempt at containing the battle, which is stopped "by a single bolt of lightning" (i.e. Marvel, 155.1.1). As this happens, Norman announces that "Armageddon has arrived" (155.1.2).

The fourth part, "Never-ending Battle" (a fourth reference to Superman, also from the Fleischer cartoon and quoted by the Spectre at 40.3.5, perhaps also suggesting the struggle for morality or the soul), depicts Norman's visions, which have become reality. The battle culminates in the UN's launching of three nuclear weapons; Marvel, having been deprogrammed by Superman, sacrifices himself such that Superman and some others are saved from the weapon that detonates. Superman seeks revenge on the UN but is talked out of it by Norman. "Never-ending Battle" ends with a series of turns for the better, including Norman's preaching to a packed church whose congregation includes his guide, now in human form. An epilogue ("One Year Later") sees Superman and Wonder Woman name Batman godfather of their unborn child.[18]

15. The phrase seems to have originated in the Fleischer cartoons in 1941, predating its use on the radio series from 1942 to 1944. Variants include "truth and justice" (original comics series), "truth, tolerance, and justice" (movie, 1948), and "truth, justice, and freedom" (Saturday morning cartoon, 1966).

16. Batman's "legion" features Green Arrow, who advertises it as "the democratic response" to Superman's league (87.6.12); this echoes *DKR*, vol. 4, in which a caustically antifascist Arrow (33.9–34.7) helps Batman fight Superman (41–42). In *Kingdom Come*, the members of the Legion of Superheroes (first appearance in Otto Binder [w.] and Al Plastino [a.], *Adventure Comics* 247 [DC, April 1958]) have "lost themselves . . . in future times" (44.3.2); Batman's "legion" may evoke that utopian future, but, given biblical intertextuality, it also recalls the demon of Mk. 5:9 and Lk. 8:30.

17. Captain Marvel's insanity, connected to his dual identity, may allude to another superhero's famous insanity: that of Kid Miracleman (aka Kid Marvelman, sidekick of Miracleman [aka Marvelman, in imitation of Captain Marvel]), whose violent rampage destroys most of London (Alan Moore [w.] and John Totleben [a.] *Miracleman* 15 [Eclipse, Nov. 1988]).

18. The naming recalls the series of children raised to fight alongside him as Robin (noted by Batman at 210.6.16: "My record as a parent isn't spotless"). With heavy irony, the heroes' waitress at Planet Krypton restaurant is clearly modeled on the female Robin of *DKR* (208.1–4 and 209.1–2, including "[WAITRESS] Hi. I'm Robin. [BATMAN] Of course you are"). There is also light humor in this happy coda: For example, the heroes' drinks are served by a busboy dressed as Aquaman (206.5 and 207.4–5).

A visual and verbal frame emphasizes the story's central themes. It begins with Biblical quotation and imagery, colored immediately by comics history: Excerpts from Revelation 8:5–10:3 are read aloud as "visions" (14.3.7) by a dying Golden Age hero, Sandman,[19] whose bedside visitor, Norman, holds a Bible (11–14). The ending is closely parallel in form and themes: The loose trinity of Superman, Batman, and Wonder Woman "dream about the future," including "truth . . . justice . . . and a new American way" (212.6.16–18) while framed by two nostalgic comics images.[20] On their left are the hat, gloves, mask, and sleeping-gas gun used by Sandman (also alluded to by the word *dream*), and on their right are two Golden Age comics covers: *New Fun: The Big Comic Magazine* 1 (National Allied Publications, February 1935) and, more important, *Whiz Comics* 2 (Fawcett, February 1940), the first appearance of Captain Marvel, with cover art by C. C. Beck recalling *Action Comics* 1, the first appearance of Superman.[21] This first frame is emphasized by another: the epilogue's setting at Planet Krypton restaurant (also featured on 18–19) invokes Superman's destroyed homeworld and so echoes the destruction of Kansas, his adopted home, just before the story proper.

The ending also emphasizes what is revealed by prophecy come true: The trinity is overshadowed by Marvel, "the world's mightiest mortal" (132.3.7; cf. Superman's "powers and abilities far beyond those of mortal men," 32.1.1). Unlike the trinity, Marvel is by nature a combination human and superhuman;[22] that nature combines with his uncertain sanity (indirectly emphasized by the Spectre's saying that Norman's "sanity may be paramount to mankind's survival"; 29.1.3) to produce his unique role in deciding the outcome of the war (181–184). Marvel's struggles may be read as embodying *both* the superiority of Golden or Silver to Modern Age comics *and* the human struggle for morality in a superhuman world.

"Seven Thunders Utter Their Voices": Captain Marvel and Revelation 10:3

These themes are expressed in the work's climactic passage, the final phase of the war (174–186), which culminates in the self-sacrifice of Marvel (183–184, see figure 9.1). The passage offers a double reading of Rev. 10:3, "seven thunders utter their voices" (184.1.1; quoted also at

19. This is the Sandman, Wesley Dodds, created by Gardner Fox (w.) and Bert Christman (a.) (first appearance in *Adventure Comics* 40 (DC, July 1939). On comics "Sandmen" see Marshall in this volume.

20. The trinity is "loose" in that any theological implications are unsystematic. Although Superman is Christlike (first pictured as a carpenter shouldering a crossbeam, with three nails in one pocket [31.2 and .3]; at another point, 71.5, "walking on water"), he is also Godlike (implicitly in power, explicitly at points in the text, e.g., 192.5.14 and 191.2.9: His "wrath . . . would cower Satan himself"), while Wonder Woman is, as an Amazonian, incidentally the product of "virgin birth." This looseness illustrates the degree to which comics are able to redefine traditional and even Classical or ancient concepts via their own "classics."

21. Jerry Siegel (w.) and Joe Shuster (a.) (National Allied Publications, June 1938); the cover is quoted also at 76.2, alongside Bill Finger (w.) and Bob Kane (a.), *Detective Comics* 27 (National Allied Publications, May 1939), the first appearance of Batman. *New Fun* 1 is the first publication by the company that became DC.

22. Captain Marvel is human and superhuman at separate times: The human Billy Batson becomes the superhuman Marvel by saying the magic word, *Shazam* (an acronym standing for gods and heroes whose attributes Marvel possesses: Solomon's wisdom, Hercules' strength, Atlas' stamina, Zeus' power, Achilles' courage, and Mercury's speed). Marvel's dual nature, part cause of his importance to the plot, is analogous to the Christian concept of hypostatic union, the combination of human and divine in Jesus as Christ; I am grateful to an anonymous reader for this analogy.

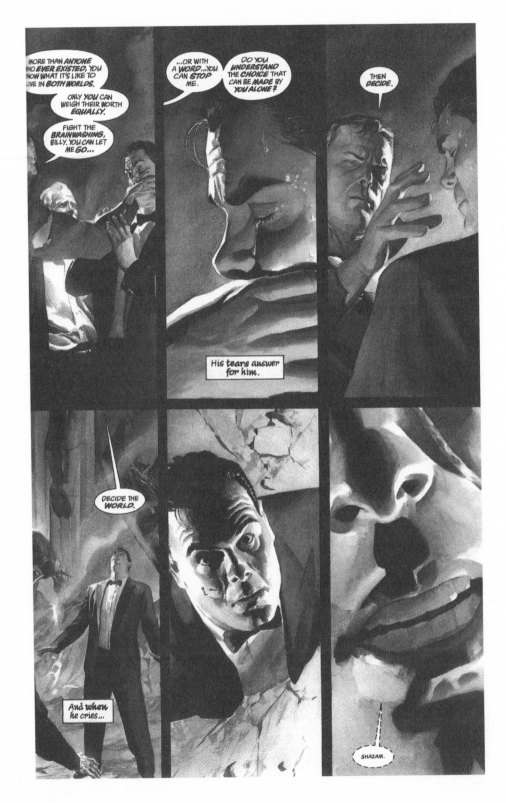

FIGURE 9.1 AND FIGURE 9.2 The language of Revelation in *Kingdom Come* as Captain Marvel decides the fate of the world. Art by Alex Ross. *Kingdom Come* 4 "Never-Ending Battle" (DC, August 1996) 183-84.

111.1.3, a splash page of Marvel as a mushroom cloud shot through with lightning and alluded to on the first page, 11.1.1–2: "There were voices . . . | and thunderings, and lightnings . . .," through 13.1.3), as denoting the comics notion of Marvel's powers depending on magical lightning and as suggesting, via his dual nature and psychological struggles, how moral decision making depends on identification of human and superhuman or divine.

As noted, Marvel's importance comes in part from contrast with the trinity: None can end the war individually, nor are they aligned to do so together. First, Superman, "the pinnacle of otherworldly power" (76.2.6, with visual quotation of *Action Comics* 1), is mocked by Batman while attempting to recruit him to the Justice League ("I bow to your superior wisdom"; 71.5.4);[23] he is also "prevent[ed] from containing the battle" (164.3.9) by Marvel, at that point "a soldier of chaos—the one who can counter Superman's every move" (164.3.8). Second, Batman, "the zenith of human fortitude and ambition" (76.2.5, with visual quotation of *Detective Comics* 27), is criticized in turn and in similar terms by Wonder Woman ("you . . . expect everyone to bow before your precious wisdom" 172.6.4), and despite "the sheer force of [his] presence" (169.4.5), Batman would not be powerful enough to end the war: A mere mortal, he has weakened with age and requires a supportive exo-skeleton.[24] Finally, Wonder Woman's inability hinges on her willingness to kill: Her attitude is criticized by Superman throughout, first implicitly (e.g., 79.2–3, where he cautions against excessive force and she responds (text 7): "If they want to act like warriors . . . I'll show them war"; cf. 125.5.11), then explicitly as war erupts (e.g., 145–146, where he "will not sanction lethal force" and is "uneasy" (145.5.11) with her sword), and then by Batman ("'Force peace.' The Amazon Tenet"; 171.1.4) after she has indeed killed an enemy with her sword (170.2).

The inefficacy of the trinity raises the question of how resolution is possible: Whose will, in ready words, be done?[25] After a fight in which Marvel's lightning (and its allusive "sound of distant thunder," 178.1.1, linking Marvel's introduction as "the captain of the lightning and the thunder" (83.6.14) to Rev. 10:3's "seven thunders") has stymied Superman (174–175), Superman forces Marvel to return to human form.[26] In quick succession, then, and with breathless overlap of characters and actions, Superman notices the third bomb falling (179.4–5); the Spectre declares that "[i]t is time" (179.6.7) for Norman to "[j]udge" (180.4.11) "who shall be held

23. Superman discovers Batman (and notices Green Arrow) in the Batcave, Wayne Manor having been destroyed "once [Batman's] identity got exposed" (72.2.6); this recalls the end of *DKR*: After Batman is revealed as Bruce Wayne, "Wayne Manor was leveled by a series of explosions" (45.7) so that Batman, having staged his death, could train an army including Green Arrow (47).

24. The exoskeleton seems modeled on Batman's arm brace at *DKR*, vol. 2:37.10.

25. "Whose will be done?" featured on a promotional poster for *Kingdom Come*, is not quoted in the comic but seems invoked by a stained-glass window depicting Jesus' "agony in the garden" (27.2 and 28.1: The Spectre first appears to Norman through the window) when he prays for the strength to accept God's will (Mt. 26:39, "not as I will but as you will").

26. Fights between the two characters are a staple of comics history: For example, Marvel's use of his magic lightning as a weapon is repeated in the *Justice League Unlimited* episode "Clash" (D. Riba [dir.], J. M. DeMatteis [w.], D. McDuffie [story], airdate June 11, 2005). They may also reflect the long legal battle (from 1941 to 1952) between National Comics (later DC) and Fawcett over the question of the latter's Marvel infringing on the former's Superman; Fawcett's final out-of-court settlement and the resultant shutdown of its comics division constitute one marker of the end of comics' golden age.

accountable" (180.4.9), and neither Superman, who "do[es]n't know what to do" (181.3.7), nor Norman, who sees "no 'evil' here" but only "tragedy and bedlam" (181.1.2–3), feels able to act.

These overlapping inabilities to act culminate in overlapping dialogue (182.5.7–9):

[SUPERMAN]   [T]hat decision . . . |

[NORMAN]   . . . is not for me to make. I'm not a god . . . |

[SUPERMAN]   . . . I'm not a man.

(This overlapping structure is echoed at 183.2.5–184.1.1 with which it frames Marvel's decision.) Instead of either speaking character, it is Marvel (silenced now by Superman's hand throughout the battle and saying only "Shazam") who must decide because he can, being both human like Norman and superhuman like Superman. As Superman has it, with some hyperbole about Marvel's hypostasy, "more than anyone who ever existed, you know what it's like to live in both worlds. | Only you can weigh their worth equally" (183.1.1–2). In the work's loosely Biblical scheme, Marvel is thus imagined as a second Christ figure, perhaps more naturally than the extraterrestrial Superman and indeed more purposefully since choosing self-sacrifice over exile.[27]

From this culmination the passage ascends to further clarity that is, if not strictly unprecedented, then striking in the immediate contexts of, first, the visual representation of war and, second, the interpretation of the Biblical intertext. First, the war is primarily represented with irregular panels: With only two exceptions, each page is different, and panels overlap and slant. Some are jagged edged, and others are shaped to accommodate superhuman powers, including Superman's horizontal heat vision (174.1–2) and then, as Marvel gains the upper hand, the latter's vertical lightning (174.4, 175.1, 175.6, 178.1; the panels return to horizontal for Superman's successful strike, 178.4–7).[28] The two exceptions are, precisely, the two pages depicting Superman's suggestion that only Marvel may decide (183) and Marvel's decision to stop the bomb (through 184): Like only two other pages (30, 121) out of the work's two hundred, 183 and 184 are paneled regularly, with two rows of three panels, each panel distinguished by a gray-black gutter.[29] On 183, the paneling emphasizes the stepwise logic of Superman's suggestion leading to Marvel's decision as the "camera" focuses on Marvel's face; while 184 depicts deliberate upward motion, an image of mediation between Earth and heaven, as first Superman and then Marvel, throwing him down, ascends to stop the bomb.[30]

Second, the two pages are less chaotic verbally without the preceding overlaps and visual sound effects and thus more ordered in fulfillment of Biblical intertext. Superman asks, "Do

27. The dependence of this Christ figuration on Marvel's dual nature is echoed in a later action by the mediating Norman, discussed later, and to a lesser extent by the Spectre, who returns at the end of the work to human form.

28. The vertical panels, the lightning wounding Superman, and the threat of nuclear annihilation recall a similar combination in *DKR*, vol. 4:25.6 and 27.1, where Superman is debilitated by lightning caused by the electromagnetic pulse of an exploded nuclear weapon; cf. 111.

29. Page 30 shows Norman's decision to follow the Spectre, while 121 shows him recoiling from a conference of "galactic lords and immortals" (120.1.3): Regular paneling seems to represent human exposure to superhuman worlds.

30. At 184.6, the swiftly receding Marvel is represented as a red star, perhaps suggestive of the "star of Bethlehem."

you understand the choice that can be made by you alone?" (183.2.5). Marvel cries, and Norman comments literally and allusively that "his tears answer for him" (183.2.6). This comment leads directly into Biblical quotation interrupted and interpreted by comics history:

[NORMAN]   And when he cries ... [183.4.9] |

[MARVEL]   Shazam. [183.6.10] | ...

[NORMAN]   ... seven thunders utter their voices (184.1.1).

This interrupted quotation forms a closing frame around the moment of decision making by echoing the overlapping structure at 182.5.7–9. Here the "thunder" is both angelic, as in Revelation, and the kind that accompanies Marvel's lightning (83.6.14, already quoted), while the "cry" itself is on multiple levels: It is the angelic cry or shout, Marvel's human tears, and his superhuman utterance, here only a whisper. The image emphasizes that Marvel may decide because his dual nature identifies both human and superhuman or divine.

Once Marvel decides, all is regular paneling and silence—no dialogue, no sound effects—until he cries "Shazam" over and over to stop the bomb in dramatic diagonal panels interlacing his attempt with other characters' reactions (185). That desperate shatter leads to a simple, powerful "split": A splash page (186) shows an atomic mushroom cloud angled along the same diagonal as Marvel's motions and arced through with his lightning (recalling 111, Marvel as mushroom cloud surrounded by text from Rev. 10:3).[31] All of this is followed by the Spectre's seemingly definitive declaration of "Judgment" (187.3.1).

The simple fact that the story continues, however, complicates any definitive reading of the explosion as "kingdom come" and thus any simple transcendent answer to "whose will be done?" by emphasizing the moral importance of two human beings. First, Norman ignores his guide's declaration of judgment and insists on seeing the story to its end. Thus positioned, he draws on his experience as pastor to talk Superman down from murderous revenge by appealing to the man, "Clark," inside Superman. "I can reach behind [his anger]" (191.4.11) to the moral being who has:

instinctive knowledge ... | ... of right ... and wrong ... | ... a gift of your own humanity. | ... [T]he minute you made the super more important than the man, the day you decided to turn your back on mankind ... that completely cost you your instinct. | That took your judgment away. (193.1.4–8)

This dénouement is thus another image of the importance of union between human and superhuman or divine.[32]

31. This atomic blast at the prison, "rise[n] from the ashen fields of Kansas" (106.1.2; cf. 113.1.1), signals the work's dénouement by forming a ring with the first atomic destruction of Kansas by the death of Captain Atom (36–38). Marvel's struggle with the bomb recalls similar struggles by comics characters in the period immediately after the atomic bombings of Hiroshima and Nagasaki; cf. *Captain Marvel Adventures* 66: "Captain Marvel Battles the Dread Atomic War!" (Fawcett, October 1946).

32. Superman's nonhuman identity, as the Kryptonian Kal-el, is ignored by Norman, although long preferred by Superman himself. The work's late declaration that Superman blames himself "for ten years that ended today" (192.1.2) precisely inverts the opening and thus reverses the values of *DKR*, beginning on the "tenth anniversary of the last recorded sighting of the Batman" (vol. 1: 3.8; cf. the description of Batman as "a dead man, ten years dead," 4.8.18).

Second, in the epilogue Superman and Wonder Woman ask Batman to be godfather of their unborn child, who, Superman says, "more than any other, will need the leavening influence of a mortal man . . . a moral man" (211.3.10–11). Alongside Norman's suasion of Superman, the latter's punning of "mortal" and "moral" emphasizes the importance of humanity. Marvel, Norman, and Batman are all asked to act in their capacity to mediate between human and superhuman, with the final decisions drawing not on superhuman powers—on what humans cannot do—but on the ability to do what superhumans need not: take account of how, regardless of superhuman action or divine revelation, human history continues to play out.[33]

Kingdom Come may thus be read as combining Biblical and comics intertexts to explore the possibility of a renewed morality. With its dystopic future drawing on the bombastic violence and exaggerated art of comics' Modern Age, the work highlights the values, however nostalgically understood, and visual aesthetics of the Golden and Silver Ages. Of special importance here is the struggle for control—not to say for the soul—of Captain Marvel. Out of that effort, in line with his dual nature, in the end Marvel embodies the struggle to uphold a set of values idealistically unlike those of the hyperviolent antiheroes characteristic of the Modern Age. As Superman has it, in the end Marvel, who had been "asked . . . to choose between humans and superhumans . . . knew that was a false division . . . | . . . and made the only choice that ever truly matters. | He chose life" (198.6.6–8).

Intertexuality and Comics History

In comics-historical terms, *Kingdom Come*'s interest in humanity and morality suggests movement away from the "grim and gritty realism" of the Modern Age. As noted, the near-future setting is based in part on the "classics" of that Age; I have made special reference to the work's program of allusions to *The Dark Knight Returns*, while others could be multiplied. As shown, too, the initial marginalization and lasting inefficacy of Golden and Silver Age characters is preparatory for a renewed valuation of life. That renewal is expressed through Marvel's private redemption and public sacrifice.

Deepening the comics-historical echoes, Marvel is unlike the antihero Magog, figured twice as the near-future's proximate cause. First, as noted in the summary, Magog and his Battalion are responsible for the destruction of Kansas, interpreted by Norman as fulfilling Rev. 8:7 and 8:12 (49.3.8–10) and as the cause of greater abandon by the new generation: "[T] hey're following Magog's reckless lead—and they're out of control!" (50.2.3).[34] The undesirability of his Modern Age leadership is emphasized by two Biblical allusions: Magog's costume features golden ram's horns, recalling the false idol, the golden calf, established by the Hebrews under Aaron (Ex. 32), and his name recalls the Biblical character (Gen. 10:2) and especially the nation (Ezek. 38:2) thought to be ranged alongside Gog against God in the apocalypse (Rev. 20:7–9, where Satan will "gather them together to battle").

Second, Magog is responsible for Superman's exile. Ten years before the story proper, Magog killed the Joker for the latter's killing, by his trademark laughing gas, of "[MAGOG]

---

33. For the sardonic Dark Knight, this is not without irony: Having agreed to be godfather, he asks rhetorically, "You realize you've just handed me influence over the most powerful child in the world?" (212.1.12).

34. Cf. Wonder Woman's attempt to talk Superman out of exile: "Our generation takes its lead from you" (38.3.7).

ninety-two men . . . | [SUPERMAN] and one woman [sc. Superman's love, Lois Lane]"
(96.3.7–8).[35] Acquitted of murder despite Superman's evident testimony against him (96–97),
Magog won a sort of moral victory over Superman in the court of public opinion, becoming
"Metropolis's new number one" (98.1.2) and appropriating the mantle "man of tomorrow"
(98.6.10) as embodying the talionic justice of the times (96–99; cf. 73.2.5–10). Magog's displacement of Superman is allegorically the replacement of nostalgically perceived Golden and
Silver Age values by the violent superheroics of the Modern Age. This is emphasized by Magog's
resemblance to the Marvel Comics character Cable (a scarred eye, armored shoulders, and an
arm of segmented metal), a partial creation of Rob Liefeld, one of the creators whose work is
considered as characteristic of the age.[36] Magog's eventual capture and rehabilitation (199.1–2,
without his horns) thus represent the ultimate supremacy of old-fashioned values, embodied in
the struggles of and for Captain Marvel.

Comics and "Classics"

As a work of art, *Kingdom Come* is generous to its audience, offering an aesthetic experience
that does not require special competence: It may be enjoyed for its story—thematic, action
packed, and character driven—and for its remarkable visual and verbal strategies. However, the
work tells its story and employs those strategies in ways that reward a reader who is aware of
superhero comics history and, thus, who may appreciate the work's inventive intertextual engagement with it. In addition to making a generally wide range of references available to the
comics aficionado, the work may be read as especially interested, via its historically allusive,
near-future setting and the struggles of its central figure, Captain Marvel, in contrasting Golden
and Silver with the Modern Age. Likewise, although the story also does not demand knowledge of its Biblical intertext, a reader with such knowledge is better able to appreciate the work's
overall structure and themes. By presenting itself explicitly as a comics fulfillment of Biblical
prophecy, *Kingdom Come* explores the question of moral decision making in a way that is, it
seems, only loosely Biblical rather than expressly theological by focusing on the idea that morality depends on mediation between and, ultimately, identification of human and superhuman
or divine.

In this comics-imagistic exploration of morality drawing loosely on the Bible, *Kingdom
Come* does not demand but invites a learned reader, in part because that reader is able to appreciate more fully the work's complex engagements with its overlapping literary and visual-artistic
traditions. This sort of invitation to an imagined or "model" reader is the very definition of literary allusion. Although *Kingdom Come* is in ways especially sophisticated or insistent about
allusion, it nonetheless exemplifies the intertextualities that are possible, even normal, in comics

---

35. This echoes the brutality of *DKR*: After the Joker has killed 206 people with laughing gas (vol. 3:27.6.8),
Batman breaks his neck (46.6–7), having earlier said that "from the beginning I knew . . . | . . . that there's nothing
wrong with you . . . | . . . that I can't fix . . . | . . . with my hands" (38.1.5–8).

36. Cable first appeared in Louise Simonson (w.) and Rob Liefeld (a.), *The New Mutants* 87 (Marvel, March
1990). For Liefeld's work see, for example, *X-Force* (Marvel, Aug. 1991–April 1992), featuring Cable, and *Young-
blood* (Image, April 1992–June 1996), with characters based on DC's Teen Titans. Liefeld's and others' 1992 "de-
fection" from Marvel to found the "independent" (i.e., creator-owned) Image Comics is considered a milestone in
modern age comics; see Khoury (2007).

generally. The fact that even this work, modeled directly on an ancient intertext, emphasizes modern stories and concerns suggests that comics intertextuality is less interested in traditional classics, including the Greco-Roman Classics as such, than in the "classics" of comics history and in the contemporary issues that they may address.

All of this is to suggest that the particular study of Classics in comics, like that of other traditions marginal to popular cultural forms, benefits from more general knowledge of the art form and its own traditions. Comparison of the two may help to reveal ways in which the Classics could be made to draw on the more popular traditions of comics, clearly much more widely available to readers and for ongoing creative adaptation. If such study cannot, of course, guarantee renewed importance and vitality for Greco-Roman materials, at the least it helps further debates about what "classics" are or may be and thus whether the Classics as such are or could be "classics"—well-known or widely accessible intertexts—in popular traditions.[37]

37. This chapter has benefited greatly from, and I am very grateful to, this volume's editors, the anonymous readers of an early draft, and the participants in the Third Annual Symposium on Comics at Bard College, April 26, 2008, especially its student organizers, Arla J. Berman '09 and Jonathan Gorga '09. Errors or infelicities are my own.

PART THREE

Drawing (on) History

10

Hard-Boiled Hot Gates

Making the Classical Past Other in Frank Miller's *Sin City*

Vincent Tomasso

In 480 BCE the Spartan king Leonidas defended the pass of Thermopylae against an invading Persian force even though he faced staggering odds. Despite his hopeless situation he was apparently not disturbed by his impending death: Plutarch, a later biographer, has him say, ἢ κτάμεν τὼς βαρβάρως ἢ αὐτοὶ τεθνάμεν θέλομες [either we kill the barbarians, or we ourselves die willingly] (*Moralia* 225B).[1] By contrast, Dwight McCarthy, the protagonist of *The Big Fat Kill* story line of Frank Miller's *Sin City* series, is unstable and insecure. Left by his enemies to suffocate to death in a tar pit, he prays fervently, "Don't let me die knowing I'm nothing but a jerk, a failure, a loser, a complete and total asshole."[2] Though these men could not be more different from one another, Dwight, by explicitly invoking and then (successfully) using Leonidas' military strategy at Thermopylae, compares his struggle with that of the Spartan king. In this discussion I explore how and, more important, why Dwight makes this improbable connection, which collapses distinctions of character and context. I conclude that the link in reality creates a sharp juxtaposition that emphasizes the differences rather than the similarities between the battle of Thermopylae and Western modernity.[3]

 Comics are an inextricable union of image (the iconic register) and text (the linguistic register), and recent critics stress that we must be aware of this when we interpret the medium: "Only a descriptive reading—attentive, notably, to its graphic materiality—and an interpretive reading allows the image to deploy all of its significations and resonances" (Groensteen 2007, 127; see also Carrier 2000, 7, and Bongco 2000, xv). Although this is an important observation, we must also acknowledge that our approach to any medium is entirely dependent on the

---

1. Quotations of Greek text are taken from Nachstädt's 1935 edition of Plutarch's *Moralia* and Legrand's 1948 edition of Herodotus' *Histories*. All English translations are my own.

2. Frank Miller (w./a.), *Sin City: The Big Fat Kill* 3 (Dark Horse, Feb. 1994), 23.1. Collected in *Sin City*, vol. 3 (Milwaukie, Ore.: Dark Horse, 2005).

3. I take the term *modernity* from Cawelti's summation of the hard-boiled crime fiction genre, of which *Sin City* forms a subset: "[W]e find empty modernity, corruption, and death" (1976, 141). For my discussion "modernity" is preferable to "the present" since no specific date is given for the narratives of *Sin City*.

sorts of questions we are pursuing. While Groensteen is examining the multiplicity of ways in which comics can express meaning, my focus is on how one character in one comic book narrative, *The Big Fat Kill*, receives and produces meaning from an exclusively linguistic narrative, Herodotus' *Histories*. *The Big Fat Kill* conveys these meanings primarily through the linguistic rather than the iconic register because the iconic portrayal of Thermopylae is limited to a single image accompanied by a block of text (see figure 10.1). Consequently, the iconic-linguistic linkage figures into my analysis, but at the same time in this particular case I scrutinize the linguistic register in greater detail.

Critics have also been concerned about the lack of theoretical sophistication in criticism of comics (e.g., Bongco 2000, 14), though Klock's 2002 application of Harold Bloom to the superhero genre may be the first sign of a reversal of the trend. For my discussion the approaches developed by narratologists are extremely helpful in making sense of the text.[4] Despite the fact that the importation of terminology used to explain other media—most notably film—to describe comics has been criticized in recent years (e.g., by Miller himself in Eisner, Miller, and Brownstein 2005, 87), narratology has been successfully applied not only to the novel, for which it was initially formulated, but also to a wide variety of media because its foundational principle is the narrative, a phenomenon that can occur in any medium. Nevertheless, since narratology was developed to analyze the way in which narratives are represented linguistically, not visually, I also employ the theories and terminologies of various comics scholars and artists to complete my analysis.

Herodotus' *Histories* 7.201–233 is not the only Greek account of the battle of Thermopylae, but it is the best known.[5] The Persian king Xerxes, eager to conquer Greece and avenge his father's defeat at Marathon in 490 BCE, began moving toward the Mediterranean in 481. After much indecisive bickering among the Greeks, the Spartan king Leonidas took with him three hundred warriors, around a thousand *perioeci*, and a number of helots to the pass of Thermopylae to make a stand. Other Greek regions also contributed troops. Even though they were able to resist the much larger Persian forces in the natural bottleneck created by Thermopylae's geography, the Greeks were betrayed by a local named Ephialtes, who showed the Persians how to outflank the Greeks' position. When he realized that they had been compromised, Leonidas sent away many of the Spartans' allies, and he and the remaining hoplites perished in the ensuing struggle. The Persians, unhindered, continued their march south, though the Athenians and their allies put an end to their advance at Salamis.

After his early work with company-owned creations at Detective Comics and Marvel, in the 1990s Miller began to create his own characters and worlds, one of the most critically acclaimed of which has been *Sin City*. Miller created, scripted, and drew the

---

4. See Groensteen (2007, 159–60).

5. The poet Simonides (quoted at *Histories* 7.228), the historian Diodorus Siculus (*Diodori bibliotheca historica* 11.4–11, ed. Vogel and Fischer 1888–1965), and the biographer Plutarch (*Moralia* 225 and 240D–E) all offer different perspectives on the conflict, and Diodorus offers a few details that differ slightly from Herodotus. However, when I refer to Thermopylae in my discussion, I am referring solely to Herodotus' account since his version is nearly canonical after the fifth century BCE—and thus was the most influential on later Western receptions. Furthermore, the depiction of Thermopylae in *The Big Fat Kill* does not reproduce any of the unique features of the non-Herodotean versions.

FIGURE 10.1 In a single splash page opening the final issue of *The Big Fat Kill*, the protagonist Dwight gives a (selective) account of the battle of Thermopylae. Art by Frank Miller. *Sin City: The Big Fat Kill* (Dark Horse Comics, March 1995) 133.

entire series—thirty-nine regular issues collected into four larger story lines, a 128-page graphic novel, and several one-shots (short stories spanning a single comic book issue)— and had them published intermittently from 1992 to 2000. *Sin City*'s primary influences are the hard-boiled crime fiction novels of the twentieth century, particularly those by Dashiell Hammett, Raymond Chandler, and Mickey Spillane, as well as the mise-en-scène of early film noir, which inspired its black-and-white *chiaroscuro* imagery (Wolk 2007, 176–77; Scaggs 2005, 83). Miller claims that none of his story lines has a one-to-one cor- respondence with any individual hard-boiled narrative (George 2003, 83); nonetheless, he describes the central protagonist of *The Big Fat Kill* as "a modern-day version of [Philip] Marlowe [Chandler's protagonist]" (*Sin City Special Edition DVD*).[6] Like the hard-boiled genre, *Sin City*'s narratives focus on crime, and its protagonists participate in the vigilan- tism of generic superheroes. Yet unlike superheroes, they often perish in their struggles against corrupt figures.[7]

Published at the close of 1994 and the start of 1995, *The Big Fat Kill* is the third story line of the series and highlights a dilemma faced by the city's prostitutes. Historically they have been a formidable force in the area, maintaining law and order in their own district, Old Town, and upholding a tacit truce with the corrupt police force, which stipulates that neither side will interfere in the affairs of the other. The second issue of *The Big Fat Kill* details how the prosti- tutes murder Jack Rafferty, whom they do not realize is an undercover police officer. Informed of Rafferty's status, they realize that if the police discover the murder, there will be open war; they are therefore desperate to dispose of Rafferty's body. Meanwhile, the mob sends a group of henchmen to retrieve the corpse as evidence to lure the police into a war with the prostitutes. The mob desires conflict so that power in the region will be destabilized, allowing them to gain control of Old Town. Enter protagonist Dwight McCarthy, who helps the prostitutes because he was formerly in love with their leader, Gail, and owes the girls a favor for saving his life in the previous story line.

The heading for the fifth and final issue of *The Big Fat Kill* is written in an angular, stereo- typically "Greek" style, signifying that this installment will be somewhat different from those that preceded it. On the next page an armored warrior, his shield emblazoned with a lambda, peers through a narrow canyon directly at the reader, and the accompanying text summarizes the events of Thermopylae (see figure 10.1).[8] On the iconic register there are no panels dividing the page; a single image dominates it, engulfing the reader in its totality. The column of text that elaborates the significance of the image is not immediately attributed to a speaker or character, but on the following page the reader discerns that Dwight's inner thoughts are responsible. Dwight is both the narrator and the focalizer of this version of Thermopylae, and, as such, any observations I make about how and why the battle is presented in *The Big Fat Kill* must take into account the

---

6. It should be emphasized that Miller is stating that *Sin City* is an *update* of classic film noir characters. In other words, *Sin City* is not a nostalgic vision of the past as portrayed by the genre; rather, it brings the genre into the contemporary world.

7. Scaggs (2005, 63) connects the vigilantism of Miller's protagonists with the hard-boiled, rather than the super- hero, genre.

8. Lambda represents another name of Sparta, Lacedaemon. Miller was most likely inspired to add this detail by the 1962 film *The 300 Spartans* (for the influence of which, see George [2003, 65] and later). There is also histor- ical attestation of this practice during the Persian wars: Anderson (1970, 18).

fact that a particular character's viewpoint informs that presentation.[9] Surprisingly, the conclusion of this version is not the same as that of the *Histories'* version—or that of any other version for that matter. Whereas Herodotus' version concludes with the Spartans' total annihilation, Dwight's ends on a didactic note without mentioning their fate: It is possible to defeat a much larger and better armed foe if you choose the battleground wisely, which is exactly what Dwight does when he returns to Old Town by enticing the mob's henchmen into an alleyway, where he and the prostitutes slaughter them.

The function of this version within the frame narrative is paradigmatic—that is, Dwight narrates the story of Thermopylae because he intends to employ it as a model for his current situation, which is made clear by a parallelism in both the linguistic and the iconic registers. He concludes that the Greeks' initial success was due to "a careful choice of where to fight," and later he describes his alleyway stratagem in identical terms.[10] In the iconic register the Thermopylae page is occupied by a jagged well of light that represents the confines of the pass, and this natural outcropping is mirrored by the jutting bricks of the alley walls when Dwight confronts the mob (see figure 10.2). Both are splash pages (full-page spreads), and both represent the protagonist in a central, dominating position surrounded by inky darkness. There is thus a synonymy of foreground and background, a nearly total assimilation of meaning on both the linguistic and the iconic registers, which Groensteen identifies as a communicative gesture: "Images . . . at a distance . . . are suddenly revealed as communicating closely" (2007, 158).[11] This identification of Dwight's strategy with Leonidas' at Thermopylae invites us to read the entirety of the embedded narrative into the frame narrative, but Dwight's sarcastic commentary highlights more differences than similarities. To better understand the relationship that Dwight constructs between the Thermopylaean past and his own present, I scrutinize both the nature of the narrator and the continuities and discontinuities between Dwight's version of Thermopylae, Herodotus' account, and the frame narrative of *The Big Fat Kill*.

Before I turn to the mechanics of Dwight's commentary, I need to clarify this discussion's terms of engagement with the multiple levels of Thermopylae reception in *The Big Fat Kill*. Here I am interested in Dwight's reception of Thermopylae via his own version of the battle as given in figure 10.1, and to that end I will be analyzing Dwight's commentary, not addressing the underlying logic and rhetoric of his formulation per se.[12] Although aspects of Dwight's version, such as the equation of Thermopylae with the struggle for "democracy" and "civilization," are hotly debated, I

9. The term *narrator-focalizer* (*narrateur-focalisateur*) was coined by the narratologist Bal (1977, 39–40) to refer to an individual who both tells a story (a narrator) and whose perspective affects how that story is presented (a focalizer: "whenever somebody tells anything, he or she will of necessity and often unconsciously at the same time also give an interpretation of the thing told" [de Jong 1987, 33]). For brevity's sake I refer to Dwight simply as "narrator" [sc. of the narrative of Thermopylae in *The Big Fat Kill*] throughout my discussion.

It is important to note that Dwight is not always the narrator of *The Big Fat Kill*. In a number of scenes the characters' speech is represented directly with no mediation by a narrator.

I refer to the various narrations of Thermopylae as "versions" in accordance with Lorna Hardwick's terminology for Classical reception studies (2003, 10).

10. Miller (w./a.), *Sin City: The Big Fat Kill* 5 (Mar. 1995), 1 and 25.

11. Groensteen further elaborates on this common feature of comics, which he calls "braiding" (*tressage*, 1999, 27): "[T]he fact of presupposing that there is a meaning necessarily leads him [the reader] to search for the way that the panel . . . re-reads in light of the others" (2007, 113).

12. Often analyses that examine modern receptions of antiquity based solely on their structure and rhetoric "all too easily become dead ends, by positing 'accuracy' as the only appropriate criterion for representing the ancient world" (Gamel and Blondell 2005, 118).

FIGURE 10.2 Dwight prepares to fight the mob, in a visually similar setting to the earlier Thermopylae splash page. Art by Frank Miller. *Sin City: The Big Fat Kill* (Dark Horse Comics, March 1995) 157.

am not interested in such issues for this discussion; moreover, these connections have been *topoi* in Western writing and art for centuries: "The reception of the Persian Wars has proved politically seminal. It . . . is implicated in the origins of notions of western liberty and democracy" (Bridges 2007, 5).[13] In any case, whether or not Dwight "correctly" depicts the Classical past is not my focus here but rather how he puts the past and present that he constructs into dialogue.

Miller lists the sources he used for his 1998 comic book adaptation of Herodotus' version of Thermopylae, *300*, but it is not clear whether these same sources inform Dwight's version as well.[14] Since Miller mentions a period of research in preparation for *300* (George 2003, 65), he likely had not yet read any secondary works when he was producing *The Big Fat Kill*. Prior to this research, Rudolph Maté's 1962 film, *The 300 Spartans*, had had the most influence on his perception of Thermopylae: "[I]t was the first time that I'd been exposed to a story where the notion of heroic sacrifice had even been introduced" (George 2003, 65). Indeed, as I discuss later, this film was so influential for Miller's ideas about heroes in general that Dwight's interpretation of the link between the past and modernity is a direct response to Maté's vision.[15]

It is odd that Dwight uses the paradigm of Thermopylae since he is precisely the opposite of Leonidas: an antihero familiar from film noir, he has a criminal past from the previous story line, *A Dame to Kill For*, when he accidentally killed an innocent man. As such he tries to avoid trouble but still gets embroiled in conflicts with the pervasive criminal elements of the city. By contrast, his fellow protagonist, Marv, routinely provokes and attacks criminals to such an extent that Dwight characterizes him as the embodiment of the Classical ethos of violence and heroism: "He'd have been okay if he had been born a couple of thousand years ago. He'd be right at home on some ancient battlefield, swinging an ax into somebody's face. Or in a Roman arena, taking a sword to other gladiators like him."[16] There is an additional irony here, for Marv fits the heroic story of Thermopylae

---

13. Dwight's claim that Thermopylae represented a crucial moment for the future of reason and humanity is ridiculously over the top, but at the same time Paul Cartledge argues that the battle may well have been a deciding one for the existence of Western democracy (see Cartledge 2004, 168n16) and that Sparta's actions in Herodotus demonstrate a "willingness . . . to put the good of the community, the city, and even of some notion of 'Greece' above purely personal or individual advantage" (Cartledge 2006, 92; see also 2001, 8).

14. The "recommended reading" page of *300* (F. Miller [w./a.], issues 1–5 [May–Sept. 1998], collected in *300* [Dark Horse, 1998]) lists *The Hot Gates* (Golding 1966), Herodotus' *Histories*, *Thermopylae: The Battle for the West* (sic: the title was reversed in reprints; Bradford 1980), and *The Western Way of War* (Hanson 1989) (in that order).

15. As demonstrated by *The Big Fat Kill* and *300* Miller is obsessed with the story of Thermopylae. Aside from these two texts, however, Miller's work references Classical civilization cosmetically rather than dialectically—that is, he does not engage with the Classical past in any meaningful way outside of them. Of course this is not to imply that Miller does not use the Classics in clever ways.

   Sin City contains two other Classical allusions: The protagonist in *Hell and Back* hallucinates that his ally is a Spartan hoplite (Frank Miller [w./a.], *Sin City: Hell and Back* 7 [Jan. 2000], 14.1), and Dwight's employer, Agamemnon, wears a shirt with the logo ΚΟΠΡΟΣ ΦΑΝΕΤΑΙ [*sic*] ("shit happens") (Frank Miller [w./a.], *Sin City: A Dame to Kill For* 2 [Dec. 1993], 15.3). In 1981 Miller created the female Greek assassin Elektra Natchios for Marvel's ongoing *Daredevil* series. In the opening panels of the later *Elektra: Assassin* (Frank Miller [w.] and Bill Sienkiewicz [a.], *Elektra: Assassin* 1 [Marvel, Aug. 1986], 1.9) she recalls that her mother was named Clytemnestra and her father Aggamemnon [*sic*] (the misspelling is intentional on Miller's part).

16. Miller (w./a.), *Sin City: A Dame to Kill For* 3 (Jan. 1994), 16.1. Even though "[t]he gladiator was a hero because he embodied the courage that people believed to be essentially Roman and because he achieved fame although he was outside polite society" (Potter 2004, 83), he was never considered a democratic hero like the three hundred Spartans. American reception does, however, often equates gladiators with the struggle for liberty: See especially Kubrick's *Spartacus* (1960), which was released just two years before Maté's *300 Spartans*, and, more recently, Scott's *Gladiator* (2000); see Winkler (2007, 8–9).

even more closely than Dwight since, like Leonidas, he dies for his values. In *The Hard Goodbye* he avenges the murder of a prostitute and is subsequently put into prison, where he is executed on the final page, winning a moral victory at the cost of his own life. Dwight, on the other hand, does not perish in *The Big Fat Kill*. In fact, he is the narrator of Thermopylae precisely because he does *not* fit the paradigm: The hard-boiled genre's image of urban life actively denies that traditional Western models of heroism can coexist with the corruption of modern social systems.[17]

There are two main features of Thermopylae that Dwight sees reflected in his own situation: choosing the correct battle site and facing off against a larger enemy. According to Dwight, at Thermopylae "the Persians find their numbers useless," while in Old Town "[the mob's] numbers don't count for so much."[18] Yet just after he establishes this resonance, Dwight creates a subtle undercurrent of disjunction, a tone that will dominate the rest of his commentary, by describing the Persians in an over-the-top way as "the mightiest military force ever assembled," while he depicts the mob as a much smaller group of two-bit hoods: "Dozens of them. Armed to the teeth."[19] We never see the innumerable Persian forces (though we imagine them swarming out of the darkness that surrounds Leonidas), whereas we *do* see the mob's henchmen as they file into the alley to destroy Dwight.[20] They are portrayed from a bird's-eye perspective, which makes them seem small and inconsequential in contrast to the "hundred thousand" of Xerxes' army. This challenging of the paradigm is realized to a far greater extent in the pages that fall between Dwight's version and the alley massacre, where there is a structural parallel between the embedded and frame narratives, but its content matches only in a distorted and ironic sense.

As he drives to save Gail and the other prostitutes in Old Town, Dwight dryly observes: "My companions. . . . A hooker and her assassin pal. Nobody'd call them the last hope of civilization, but they're my friends and you've gotta stick up for your friends," which creates an explicit, ironic intratext with his narration of Thermopylae: "The hope of civilization is kept alive by Spartan courage."[21] Although Dwight's sarcastic commentary here undermines his own values—"saving civilization" has a much loftier tone than "helping friends"—it nonetheless transvalues modernity's enterprise with that of the past.[22] The ancient Spartan value of saving civilization must be replaced because the world is no longer structured in the same way as when the Spartans marched against the Persians.[23] Dwight's city, and by extension modernity, is so corrupt that the individual becomes the most important unit of meaning, and an individual

---

17. See Fontana on Chandler's *Big Sleep*: "[T]he ideal of chivalry that Marlowe has attempted to live by is no longer relevant to the exigencies of personal survival" (Fontana 1995, 164).

18. Miller (w./a.), *Sin City: The Big Fat Kill* 5 (March 1995), 1.1 and 25.1.

19. Ibid., 1.1 and 24.3. Dozens of well-equipped thugs versus one unarmed man approximates the odds at the battle of Thermopylae after a fashion, but Dwight is also supported by at least eleven prostitutes with automatic weapons holding the higher ground (30–33), which makes the parallel ludicrous.

20. Ibid., 25.1.

21. Ibid., 2.1 and 25.1.

22. I derive the term *transvalue* from narratologist Genette (1997, 367 et passim), who coins it in his discussion of Giono's *Naissance de l'Odyssée*. There is copious attestation in ancient Greek literature of the ideal of valuing interpersonal relationships over the state: See, for instance, Blundell (1989).

23. Of course, Dwight's version of Thermopylae sets up this dichotomy; it is only from a modern Western perspective that such values can be attributed to the Spartans since they did not know the ways in which subsequent history would interpret their stand. See note 13.

cannot possibly bring down an entire system that enables a host of criminals to succeed. The structure of this system is emphasized by the importance placed on interpersonal relationships throughout the series, and *The Big Fat Kill* manifests this through Dwight's perceived debt to the prostitutes for saving his life in *A Dame to Kill For*, as well as his on-again, off-again relationship with Gail. Higher notions of "democracy," "freedom," "civilization," and loyalty to the state are untenable; relationships between individuals are the only value worth defending. This is partially a conceit of the hard-boiled genre, in which the law provided by the state, and by metonymy the state itself, either cannot be trusted or is incompetent (Scaggs 2005, 58).[24]

This aesthetic is complemented further by Dwight's stated reasons for butchering the mob's henchmen. He coldly rationalizes that their lives must be ended quickly as a warning to their employers but "[n]ot for revenge. Not because they deserve it. Not because it'll make the world a better place. There's nothing righteous or noble about it."[25] This is a pointed contrast with Dwight's explanation of the rationale behind the Spartans' stand against the Persians, which he portrays as a heroic struggle for the concepts of liberty and democracy, which will be extremely important to ancient Greece's Western descendants. Dwight's disavowal of an idealized meaning denies that the significance of the West's past conflicts can be grafted wholesale onto its present ones, and this is reinforced by his gesture at the ultimate failure of the Spartans' stand: "Where to fight. It counts for a lot. But there's nothing like having your friends show up with lots of guns."[26] The Greek resistance at Thermopylae failed in part because the promised reinforcements never arrived.[27] In Dwight's reperformance of the conflict, the soldier's idealized, abstract loyalty to national identity and values is replaced by loyalty to individuals and reliance on modernized weaponry, and this new context is able to alter the bleak ending of the Thermopylae narrative.

Once Dwight explicitly highlights the disjunction between past paradigm and present reality, a number of implicit contrasts also become evident. After he recounts the events of the ancient battle, Dwight spends nearly a page obsessing over his current situation, his thoughts rambling out onto the page in quick, nervous succession in long, contorted phrases, which contrasts with the measured, staccato rhythm of his version of Thermopylae on the previous page. His own assessment of his nerve-wracked state increases the tension further: "I'm doing my best to keep my stomach from jumping out of my mouth" and "nursing a chunk of hot gravel at the base of my throat."[28] This is hardly the unemotional and unwavering determination that he attributes to the soldiers of the Classical past when they face the Persians ("[they] hold

---

24. The hard-boiled genre tends to devalue personal relationships. Romantic encounters usually end up badly or never occur in the first place because the female endangers or threatens to endanger the male; the genre "emphasizes and glorifies the loneliness and independence of the male protagonist" (Nyman 1997, 180). *Sin City*'s male protagonists, by contrast, struggle on behalf of women whose voices are not heard in society and with whom they have, have had, or wanted to have a romantic relationship.

25. *Sin City: The Big Fat Kill* 5 (March 1995), 34.

26. Ibid., 30.4.

27. Herodotus briefly mentions reinforcements, which he claims were delayed by the Spartans' observation of a festival: μετὰ δέ, Κάρνεια γάρ σφι ἦν ἐμποδών, ἔμελλον ὀρτάσαντες καὶ φύλακας λιπόντες ἐν τῇ Σπάρτῃ κατὰ τάχος βοηθέειν πανδημεί [But afterward—for the Carneia festival was impeding them—they were intending, after they had celebrated and left guards in Sparta, to provide assistance quickly en masse] (7.206).

28. *Sin City: The Big Fat Kill* 5 (March 1995), 2.1.

their ground").[29] Even his description of the surroundings evokes the discontinuity of past and present as he implicitly juxtaposes the austerity and nobility of the past with the despair of the present: The old car Dwight uses is "a beat-up bucket of bolts" that "rattl[es] around" as it "slips and slides . . . along the straight stretches of barely-there back roads that just about nobody's used since the days of Prohibition."[30] This commentary on the relationship of past and modernity brings us face to face with the instability and corruption of the latter as opposed to the constancy and clear-cut morality of the former.

In addition to the linguistic phenomena that I have just discussed, the iconic register plays an important role in accentuating the contrast between Dwight's version of Thermopylae and the frame narrative. The iconography of Thermopylae is limited to a static splash page as opposed to the dynamic sequentiality of the fever-dream *Sin City* narrative: A single Spartan hoplite, presumably Leonidas himself, is not marching or battling foes but gazing through the pass and out at the reader. Because this page contains no panel lines or word balloons, the passage of time is brought to a halt (Eisner 1985, 30).[31] The ancient world is encapsulated on one page that temporarily disengages the reader from the frame narrative and is quickly replaced by the high-speed velocity of the frame narrative on the following page—literally, since the first panel depicts Dwight's car barreling down a road, its wheels not touching the ground.[32] The respective depictions of Leonidas and Dwight also encapsulate this relationship since the former's face is hidden in the recesses of his helmet, his expression unreadable and impenetrable, whereas the latter's fatigue is accentuated by the large bags under his eyes and a smoldering cigarette dangling from a corner of his mouth.[33]

The differences between Thermopylae and *Sin City* are accentuated even further by the fact that in his version Dwight omits two events that are essential to Herodotus' version: the deaths of the Spartans and their betrayal by Ephialtes. Herodotus very clearly indicates that nearly all of the Spartans at Thermopylae were annihilated by the Persians (7.225), but Dwight is not clear on this point, concluding his version by stating that the Spartans defended "civilization" and were able to rouse the rest of Greece to fight Persia. He does imply that Leonidas and his troops did not defeat the Persians, but the text could be interpreted to mean that the Spartans either were killed or retreated. This silence is all the more remarkable since the Spartans' selfless deaths are integral to the meaning of Thermopylae in Western reception—especially for

29. Ibid., 1.1. This discontinuity is underscored further by one of the Irish mercenaries, who, as he tries to retrieve Rafferty's head from the tar pit, juxtaposes his own abilities with those of the most (in)famous Classical hero: "[I]t's not like I'm Hercules, now is it? We'd be needin' us a friggin' crane to pull the bastard outta this soup" (ibid. 4 [Feb. 1995], 20.1).

30. Ibid. 3 (Jan. 1995), 11.1; 5 (March 1995), 2.1.

31. In comics a splash page suggests boundless temporality since "[t]ime is no longer contained by the familiar icon of the closed panel, but instead hemorrhages and escapes into timeless space" (McCloud 1993, 103).

32. *Sin City: The Big Fat Kill* 5 (March 1995), 2.1. This is typical of *Sin City*'s style: "I enjoy evoking the kind of kinetic craziness that's the modern world" (Eisner, Miller, and Brownstein 2005, 88). Every issue of *The Big Fat Kill* is introduced by a splash page, but the Thermopylae page is unusual in that its iconic register is not connected to what immediately follows.

33. It is true that on the parallel splash page, which depicts Dwight in the alley, his face is in shadow (figure. 10.2). Nevertheless, his facial features are depicted in most of *The Big Fat Kill*.

Miller, because when he saw Maté's film at five years of age "[t]he story of the Spartans and their sacrifice made a very deep, life-long impression" (George 2003, 65) on him. Moreover, it is a conspicuous silence since at several points in the frame narrative Dwight seems to betray knowledge of the Herodotean ending. He realizes that he may die while disposing of Rafferty's corpse, which further highlights the disparity between Leonidas' death and Dwight's life ("If I have to die for you [Gail] tonight, I will"), and as he lures the mob's thugs into the alleyway, he muses that victory does not always result from choosing the appropriate place for battle ("*Sometimes* you can beat the odds"; emphasis mine).[34]

In Herodotus' opinion Ephialtes was the primary cause of the Spartans' deaths because he betrayed them to Xerxes: ἔφρασέ τε τὴν ἀτραπὸν τὴν διὰ τοῦ ὄρεος φέρουσαν ἐς Θερμοπύλας, καὶ διέφθειρε τοὺς ταύτῃ ὑπομείναντας Ἑλλήνων [he indicated the path that extended through the mountain into Thermopylae and destroyed those of the Greeks standing their ground there] (7.213). Without Ephialtes' assistance the Persians would have had considerable difficulty finding a way to outflank the Greek position, and the Spartans, Herodotus implies, would have successfully blocked the Persian advance. In spite of the climactic role of the traitor in the *Histories*, a ubiquitous feature in the reception of Thermopylae (Clough 2004, 377), Dwight's version makes absolutely no reference to betrayal, and because he strongly suspects that the prostitutes have a traitor in their midst, the absence is once again conspicuous.[35] His suspicions are confirmed when Becky, the youngest in Gail's employ, reveals that she is helping the mob because their success is ensured and that they have threatened to kill her mother.[36] Despite the fact that Becky is an almost identical counterpart to Ephialtes, Dwight does not mention the traitor to the Greek cause in his version.

To be able to realize that these two silences exist, a reader must have knowledge of an ancient Greek account of Thermopylae or a secondary source that conveys similar information: They are either informed by the Classical material, or they are uninformed and derive their interpretation of Dwight's version of Thermopylae from another source.[37] Yet it is largely irrelevant whether the reader is informed or uninformed prior to the conclusion since all of the interpretations I have made thus far could theoretically be adduced by a "model reader" purely on the basis of the text given in figure 10.1.[38] When the reader reaches the conclusion, however, the success or failure to recognize the silences is a case of "fragmented comprehension" (Goldhill 2007a, 264; see also McElduff's "fractured understandings" [2006]), in which audiences with different kinds of knowledge interpret the conclusion differently.

34. *Sin City: The Big Fat Kill* 3 (Jan. 1995), 7.2, and *Sin City: The Big Fat Kill* 5 (March 1995), 25.1. Ancient accounts and modern scholarship are divided as to whether or not Leonidas knew that Thermopylae would be a suicide mission. See Grant (1961), as well as Cartledge (2006, 126–31).

35. *Sin City: The Big Fat Kill* 4 (Feb. 1995), 25.2.

36. Ibid. 5 (March 1995), 16.1 and 17.1.

37. I use these two terms, taken from Stanley Fish's theories about interpretive communities (1980, 48) in a descriptive, not pejorative, sense: All readers interpret any given text with their own particular types of knowledge.

38. "The author establishes the competence of the Model Reader, that is, the author constructs the addressee and motivates the text in order to do so" (Conte 1986, 30).

For a reader informed both by Herodotus' *Histories* and basic narratological principles the silences are most reasonably attributed to Dwight's focalization of Thermopylae. Dwight ends his version before the Spartans are slaughtered because to give the full story would nullify the value of the battle as a paradigmatic blueprint for his ambush against the mob's henchmen. If Leonidas' courage and strategic planning led only to death, it would be unwise for the clever Dwight to follow his example. Whereas the Spartans' moral victory encouraged the rest of Greece to fight and ultimately win against Xerxes, Dwight's death would mean only that Old Town had lost its defender, and thus the Spartans' heroic self-sacrifice is not an appropriate model for him. As a result he alters Thermopylae's tragic conclusion.[39] In addition, Dwight's silences idealize Thermopylae by erasing the crucial flaw in Leonidas' heroism, his inability to discern a traitor, which in turn is a subtle indication that Dwight, despite the disparities between past and present, which he is careful to indicate, romanticizes the Spartans' stand.

On the other hand, readers who are not informed about Thermopylae's outcome by Herodotus or another authority would most likely turn to the superhero genre to make sense of Dwight's conclusion. The ubiquity of superhero titles in the comics community, as well as the fact that Miller has spent much of his career reworking several of them (e.g., his transformation of Batman into a gritty, almost psychotic figure in *The Dark Knight Returns*) by imparting a darker, more realistic tone, means that readers usually come to his work expecting that he will subvert the *topoi* of the genre.[40] This is especially the case for *Sin City*, which is in large part a commentary on the inability of traditional superheroes to exist in a hopelessly corrupt modern world; the series' protagonists are depicted as flawed human beings who nonetheless stand up for what they believe. Consequently, they are often depicted in linguistic or iconic terms that make explicit the fact that they are not superheroes. In *The Big Fat Kill*, for instance, Shellie describes Dwight as "Superman," who is ironically frightened of a drunk and abusive Rafferty, and in a number of panels Dwight's trench coat billows out, giving it the appearance of a cape.[41] Any presuppositions the reader might have about Dwight's heroic character are completely shattered when he "confronts" Rafferty by sneaking up behind him, threatening him with a razor, and dunking him in a toilet.[42] By contrast, *The Big Fat Kill*'s solitary Spartan is accoutered like a typical superhero with a cape and a mask (i.e., a helmet that obscures his face).[43] To readers familiar with the genre these iconic clues in the context of Miller's relationship with

39. Despite the fact that in his internal monologues Dwight seems ready to die to save others, he realizes that he must stay alive to continue protecting those he cares about. This reflects a modern Western aesthetic of heroism: "For most Westerners, the point of war is to win—and survive" (Cartledge 2006, 130).

40. See Nisbet, who points out various influences ("baggage") on *300* that are derived from Miller's earlier work in the field with superheroes (2006, 72–77). See also Bongco (2000, 145).

41. "Superman" comment: *Sin City: The Big Fat Kill* 1 (Nov. 1994) 7.1. Cape: for example, *Sin City: The Big Fat Kill* 1 (Nov. 1994), 25.1; 2 (Dec. 1994), 14.1; 3 (Jan. 1995), 3.1. Cf. Marv's trench coat in *Dark Horse Presents: Sin City* 53 (Aug. 1991), 6.1 and 12.1.

42. *Sin City: The Big Fat Kill* 1 (Nov. 1994), 12.3–13.3.

43. Nisbet (2006, 73) notes the cape parallel in *300* and also points out that the lambda depicted on the shields is reminiscent of the "X" insignia often emblazoned on the costumes of Marvel's X-Men. As I pointed out, there are solid historical precedents for depicting a Spartan shield in this way, but what matters here is how an uninformed reader steeped in superhero lore would interpret the symbol.

superhero comics suggest that Thermopylae is in fact a typical superhero narrative, in which the protagonists champion civilization against a monstrous foe.[44] By failing to mention that the Spartans perish, Dwight assimilates the Thermopylae narrative to generic superhero expectations since superheroes usually do not die—or at least not for very long (Bongco 2000, 94; Eco 1972, 155). The outdated, though noble, values of Thermopylae are thus associated with a nostalgia for the uncomplicated world of golden age superheroes, "who could link contemporary American ideals to the prestige and potency associated with the past" (Stanley 2005, 144). Unlike the idealized world of costumed crime fighters who use their superhuman abilities to save the (Western) world, Dwight lives in a time and place where such ideals cannot exist.

In his analysis of Alex Shakar's short-story collection, loosely based on Ovid's *Metamorphoses*, Stephen Hinds identifies a reference by one of the characters to *Violator*, a spin-off of Todd McFarlane's wildly successful *Spawn* comic book series, and he wonders whether "the hyper-epic and . . . the comic-strip codes compete with one another, and perhaps even coalesce" (2005, 77). In the case of *The Big Fat Kill* the latter situation is preferable, in which both the informed and the uninformed readings merge to provide a unified interpretation. Indeed, Miller's intense engagement both with Herodotus' version of Thermopylae and the superhero genre demands that the two readings *not* be mutually exclusive. Ultimately both interpretations suggest the same meaning: Spartan heroics cannot be translated wholesale into the modern world. Consequently, Dwight's silences are not presented just as a sly wink to informed readers but are an essential part of the meaning that Miller wishes to attribute to Thermopylae in *Sin City*.

Classicists have long held the belief that reception "involves the acknowledgement that the past and present are always implicated in each other" (Martindale 2006, 12). This is certainly true of receptions of Thermopylae in the Western tradition, which has typically cited the event as a stand for some of the most basic values of political and social thought in the West from fifth-century-BCE Greece onward.[45] Popular receptions of Thermopylae by the United States in the nineteenth and twentieth centuries are quite similar to other Western receptions in that they construct the battle as a uniformly positive model for democratic ideology, and, consequently, the battle is depicted as parallel to American ideology and history. It was used during the civil war as a pretext for bloodletting (Rebenich 2002, 323), it was equated with the Alamo by the popular press and politicians of the time (Levene 2007, 394–398), and *The 300 Spartans* (dir. Maté, 1962) has been linked to the anti-Communist ideology of the Cold War (Levene 2007; Clough 2004, 375).[46]

Initially, by virtue of the paradigmatic status of Thermopylae in Dwight's plan to save Old Town, it seems that the battle will once again be used to legitimate the struggles of a democratic hero fighting against autocracy. Yet Dwight dismantles the connection between his own context

44. Indeed, Klock seems to interpret Miller's *300* in this way: "The story of a small and noble force holding out and eventually triumphing against disastrous odds shares obvious affinities with the standard superhero narrative. . . . Miller seems to have hit upon an especially early tale of heroism, perhaps a kind of origin story for the whole genre" (2002, 196).

45. I stress that this is a typical, not an invariable, trend. See Morris (2004) for the skepticism of intellectuals in Enlightenment England and France about the value of Thermopylae and Sparta as political and social models. For similar views in German historiography of the sixteenth through the nineteenth century, see Rebenich (2002). See Rawson (1969) for European reception generally.

46. Nisbet (2006, 76–77) similarly claims that Miller's *300* adopts the anti-Communist agenda of Maté's film.

and that of ancient Greece almost as soon as he makes it. Though his version presents Thermopylae as a model for the defense of Western ideals of "freedom," "democracy," and "civilization," he ultimately denies that his own present can reflect this model in any but the most superficial of ways. The military tactics of Dwight and Leonidas may be identical, but everything else is different. This emphasis on difference means that although Thermopylae retains the usual significations given to it by the West, it cannot be linked in any useful way with the West's present situation. This is specifically a response to *The 300 Spartans*, which Miller cites as the definitive influence for his conception of Thermopylae and the heroic ideal (George 2003, 65) and whose narrator parallels the battle with contemporary American democracy: "300 Greek warriors fought here to hold with their lives their freedom and ours." This is the typical Western view of the significance of Leonidas and his men, but Dwight's version of the stand makes Thermopylae, as glorious and important as it was in the West's past, foreign to the modern West—a noble and heroic enterprise that can have no ideological resonance amid urban decay and societal corruption.[47] *The Big Fat Kill* thus dismantles the resonances with Thermopylae that the West constructs for itself, revealing through Dwight McCarthy's reappropriation of the story that narratives of the past cannot necessarily be used to justify the present.[48] Whereas previous receptions have seen themselves clearly in Thermopylae's reflection, *The Big Fat Kill*, by stripping away the paradigm's value system and replacing it with modern sensibilities, shows us a distorted glimmer of the past in the mirror of modernity.[49]

47. This phenomenon can be paralleled in the proliferation of a variety of symbols in *The Big Fat Kill*. For instance, one prostitute is adorned with the Nazi swastika, the Jewish Star of David, and the Christian crucifix (*Sin City: The Big Fat Kill* 1 [Nov. 1994], 20.1), an Irish mercenary wears a crucifix (*Sin City: The Big Fat Kill* 3 [Feb. 1995], 9.2), and Stuka, one of the mob's henchmen, has a Nazi swastika tattooed on his forehead (*Sin City: The Big Fat Kill* 5 [March 1995], 16.3). These symbols often contradict one other and do not necessarily encode the moral compass of the characters who bear them. The once-potent symbols of the past thus lose any (former) signification. Thermopylae's absence from the film version of *Sin City* (2005), which Miller wrote and codirected, may be the ultimate sign that the battle is an ideological intruder into *Sin City*'s world.

48. By contrast, *300* constructs the significance of the battle in ways that are far more typical of Western reception of the event. A comparison between *300* and *The Big Fat Kill* would be very illuminating in this regard—not to mention that *300* requires a close, critical reading of its own—but I cannot do so here.

49. Earlier drafts of this chapter greatly benefited from the comments of Jason Aftosmis, Alessandro Barchiesi, Ruby Blondell, and Susanna Braund. I also thank my fellow presenters and the audience at the Classics and Comics panel at the American Philological Association's January 2008 meeting in Chicago. In addition, C. W. Marshall and George Kovacs deserve the lion's share of gratitude for their roles in creating that excellent panel and preparing this volume; their comments have improved my contribution immensely. Finally, I would like to thank the anonymous reader for Oxford University Press. Any remaining infelicities are my own.

11

Persians in Frank Miller's *300* and Greek Vase Painting

EMILY FAIREY

The medium of Classical vase painting has elements in common with that of contemporary comics. Comics and vase painting share qualities such as mass production,[1] the combination of drawing and writing, repeated representation of familiar characters, and even a paneling of sorts. However, a central question of this chapter is whether vase painting conveys a narrative or an ideological statement the same way that comics do. Addressing this issue, I wish to examine one common motif of ancient vase painting and modern comics, one that tells us much about the functions of different art media, as well as the state of mind of artists in different cultures, both at war: the depiction of Greeks fighting Persians.

In his *300*, graphic artist Frank Miller's artistic rendering of the Persians is so extreme that many have accused him of creating a racist and warmongering allegory that reflects the present conflict of the United States in the Middle East (Kashani 2007). He presents the Achaemenid Persians as morally deviant and corrupt and as ethnically Africans and Arabs. His Persians range from the power mad, deviant Xerxes to the arrogant, pierced, and studded ministers ready to bribe and corrupt the Spartan oracle, to the spooky, depersonalized "Immortals," and finally to the hapless Persian soldiers who are no better than victims and slaves of their king's monomania and certainly no match for the Spartans.[2] Overall, they are a bizarre and frightening collection of characters, with a variegated appearance that contrasts with the simplicity

---

1. They are alike in that they are both assembly-line products that a central "artist" would design and then delegate to a workshop for execution and production. Although the scale of modern comics production is larger, the collaborative workshop process of comics publishing is quite similar to that of vase painting. See note 17.

2. Dark Horse Comics initially published *300* as a monthly five-issue comic book limited series, the first issue published in May 1998. The issues were titled "Honor," "Duty," "Glory," "Combat," and "Victory." Later these were combined into one graphic novel, but I refer to the page numbers of each individual issue throughout this chapter. The first image of a Persian in *300* is the emissary of Xerxes, who comes to Sparta. A full close-up of his face delineates his clearly African features ("Honor," 12). Persian arrogance is manifest in his demands to the Spartans for "earth and water" ("Honor," 13). He is accompanied by troops in Bedouin-like head coverings ("Honor," 13), and Persian foot soldiers throughout *300* (e.g., "Combat," 2, 4) appear in similar gear, reminiscent of "Arab" costume. Persian spies shown bribing the Spartan "oracle" are represented as black Africans, as is King Xerxes himself, along with his satraps ("Duty," 6). For the facial piercings of Miller's Persians as indicative of moral weakness, see "Duty," 6, and "Combat," 7. See later discussion. For Miller's Immortals see "Combat," 10.

of the Spartan costume. In contrast, in Greek vase painting after the Persian Wars, although gods and mythological characters commit their traditional atrocious crimes on many pelikes, kraters, and amphoras, Persians overall are portrayed in a neutral or even positive light. On vases, one sees Persians engaged in combat with Greek hoplites as worthy adversaries, bearing the trappings of Persian culture or even presiding over dignified processions.[3] Yet the Greeks compensate for positive visual treatment of Persians in their moral judgments against them in literature. Miller adopts this literary critique of the ancients but selects only part of their visual depiction. While he draws the image of his Spartans from the heroic nudity of Greek hoplites on ancient vase paintings, his Persians bear little resemblance to their black- and red-figure counterparts.[4]

Following the Persian Wars, Greek writers did much to disassociate their culture from that of Persia. Herodotus, Miller's primary source, shows the Persians displaying the vices that attend too much success on their expeditions in book 7.[5] In particular, the Athenian tragedians after the Persian Wars systematically put down the Persians, amassing a host of contrasts that have come to be collectively termed the "Hellene-Barbarian antithesis." For example, in Aeschylus' *Persians* (72–75, 388–423), the Persians are like a herd and lack tenacity, in contrast to the discipline and courage of the Greeks. In depicting them in this way, Aeschylus explains the Greek victory in absolutist cultural terms.[6] Another example of this view is the fragmentary *Persians* of Timotheos of Miletos, in which Persians suffer a cowardly defeat at the battle of Salamis, showing servility to their own king, as well as to their conquerors, and drowning in the water while the Greeks swim.[7] The negative stereotype against Persians persists into the time of Aristotle, who suggests in the *Politics* that it is their warm climate that makes them so cowardly, albeit clever.[8]

One wonders then, whether Miller's source is more literary in nature than visual since Greek authors tend to concur with Miller's negative depiction of Persians. The literary dimension of *300* goes beyond the narrative limits of vase painting since Miller is able to use writing whenever he needs to. Yet drawing, not writing, is his primary tale-telling vehicle. He greatly

---

3. I have included a list and description of the vases at the end of this chapter and in the text refer to them by "VL" (= vase list) and the numbers I reference them under there, as well as an "Achaemenid art list," or "AAL." Some examples of vases depicting Persians in this light include VL 2, 17, 18, 19.

4. "Mr. Miller said in a recent telephone interview . . . 'When you look at the ancient Greek vase paintings, you'll see that soldiers are drawn nude, for the same reason I did'" (R. Ito, *New York Times* (Nov. 26, 2006).

5. To name a few examples, see Herodotus, *Histories*, book 7: the greed of Xerxes for gain (7.5); the greed of Mardonius for political power and his willingness to manipulate (7.6); the gullibility of Darius (7.6; 7.10) and harshness of his subjection of Egypt (7.7); the bridge over Hellespont, hubris of Xerxes (7.8, 36); the waffling of Xerxes' intent (7.12–14); the canal at Athos (7.22–24); the lashing of the Hellespont (7.35); the refusal of Pythias' request and the murder of his son (7.38–39); Xerxes riding in a litter (7.41).

6. See Aeschylus, *Persae*, 50–60; 230–45; for barbarians lacking "*paideia*," see Isocrates, *Antidosis*, 293–94. Also, for depictions of Phrygians as cowardly, see Eur. *Orestes* 1367–1529, *Alkestis*, 675–76, and Aristoph. *Birds* 1244–34, 1326–29).

7. The papyrus of Timotheos of Miletos relates four episodes of the battle of Salamis. The Persians are described as dying with "barbarian" grief and lamentation (111–13, 151) and as servile (166) and prostrating themselves (157–58, 189). See Timotheos of Miletos, Fr. 790; see also Hall (1994).

8. Aristotle, *Politics* 7.1327b3–37. Later, Plutarch (*Lives of* Artaxerxes, Cimon, Themistocles, Alexander, and Lycurgus; *Apothegmata Laconica*) and Diodorus Siculus (*Bibliotheca* 11–14) added to the polarized depiction of the noble Spartans and the degenerate Persians.

simplifies and mythologizes his Herodotean material, using only the broad moral colors and loose plot structure of the tale, along with some of the good Spartiate lines, quoted almost directly from Herodotus. For example, the throwing of the Persian emissaries into the well to "dig" for earth and water ("Honor," 4; cf. Her. *Hist.* 7.133) and Dianetus' line, given to "Stelios": "We will fight in the shade" ("Glory," 7; cf. Her. *Hist.* 7.226). Miller shows consciousness of the Classical tradition of laconic wit. Witness the Arcadian's remark: "Damn Spartans always know what to say" ("Duty," 8). Although he does not cite Plutarch's *Apothegmata Laconica* and *Life of Lycurgus*, he includes his material, changing the context, wording, or speaker of a famous line; for example, the famous response of Leonidas to Xerxes' offer of safe conduct if he gave up his troops—*molon labe*—may have become "Persians, come and get it" ("Glory," 13; cf. Plutarch, *Apophthegmata Laconica*, 225c.11).[9]

Perhaps Miller wants to simplify the literary tradition of his theme because it is not his central focus. His *300* relies mostly on visual constructions and character-driven action. Because of this, his Leonidas and Xerxes act like typically exaggerated comics heroes and villains and dominate the action of *300* much more than in the *Histories*. The complex, extended events of the *Histories*, then, become in *300* a simple clash of good and bad ideals—a "good" war with a clear moral basis. To this end, his literary sources are scarce. Looking at the penultimate page of *300*, one sees that Miller has included not a bibliography but a short list of "recommended reading." Clearly, he is not hampered by the need to weigh the opinions and evidence of a range of scholars and ancient authors. Perhaps this list, from which so many ancient and modern texts are absent, is meant to purposely disassociate *300* from a tradition that is so heavy with evidence that it could weigh down the tale.[10]

Nevertheless, to compare the different cultural perspectives of Frank Miller and the Greek vase painters after the Persian Wars requires some historical contextualization. Under the perceived ascendancy of the Greeks over the Persians in the fifth century BCE, a time when the Athenian Empire and the epitome of Classical culture were at their height, a surge of popularity of things Persian is evidenced in vase painting.[11] Perhaps after driving back their

9. At least some of the Plutarchian lines are filtered through the 1962 film *The 300 Spartans*, dir. Rudolph Maté, which Miller himself has identified as an important influence on his conception of heroes and heroism.

10. For this reason, the inclusion of historian Victor Davis Hanson seems particularly significant. Hanson, citing the classical literary tradition that Miller glosses over, argues that *300* is based firmly upon it. See Hanson (2006). He also suggests that Eastern cultural constructs are ineffective in battle compared with Western ones not only in the Persian Wars but also throughout the history of this conceptual geographic division (see Hanson 2001).

11. See Rhodes (2007: 31–46). According to Rhodes, there was evidence of both positive and negative Greek views of Persia from 479–330 BCE, depending for the most part on needs of the political moment. The Greeks enjoyed Persian luxuries while condemning their cultural character. Pericles' Odeum, for example, was built as a replica of a Persian tent. Parasols were also popular (ex. Arist. *Birds* 1549–51), and Eros holds one for Aphrodite on the Parthenon frieze (see Miller 1992). Later, according to Rhodes, the elite fashion switched over to Spartan austerity, and "Persian fashion moved down the social scale" (Rhodes 2007: 37), becoming most prominent in vase painting. Yet when politicians needed it to be so, Persia could easily take on the role of traditional enemy. Throughout the fifth century the Athenians maintained a curse in the opening ritual of the Assembly on anyone making overtures of peace to the Persians (Plutarch, *Arist.* 10.6, Isocrates *Panegyr.* 4.157), and the Peace of Antalcidas, in which the Eastern Greeks were essentially sold out to Persia, was contrasted rhetorically with the anti-Persian Peace of Callias (Rhodes 2007, 40). Yet although they periodically played the alien enemy, never again were the Greeks and the Persians so polarized as they were during the Persian Wars. Also see Miller (1997).

traditional enemy, many Greeks were ready to see more of their positive qualities since they no longer felt so deeply threatened by them. At least they felt comfortable enough with them to paint them frequently on their tableware.

Frank Miller, on the other hand, first published *300* in 1998, in the years leading up to the destruction of the World Trade Center on September 11, 2001, when tension and unresolved hostility toward the Middle East already abounded. To a degree, the atmosphere of distrust and alienation with all things Arabic, under which Miller worked and his readers lived, could be responsible for his negative characterization of the Persians.[12] Their qualities recall the viciously caricatured portrayal of Japanese in prewar comics such as *Tintin*,[13] in contrast to the postwar absorption of Japanese culture we see in the popularizing of Akira Kurosawa's films or even the Godzilla movies. Another analogy involves the wartime anti-Nazi propaganda films of the Allies, as opposed to the comedic postwar treatment of Nazis in TV shows like *Hogans' Heroes*. Miller's *300* has gained its greatest popularity in the aftermath of 9/11, a time when Muslims appear regularly in the media as terrorists opposed to Western culture. Unlike the Greeks, Frank Miller and his readers still live in a miasma of grave paranoia and insecurity about the Middle East and a severe lack of confidence in the ability of the United States to cope with it. This atmosphere has only intensified since the original publication of *300* in 1998 and has greatly influenced the reception of the comic itself, as well as the media treatment of the film version. In interviews from this period concerning the 9/11 attacks and the themes of *300*, Miller evinces a terrible fear of the single-mindedness of the Arab terrorists, as well as contempt for their "sixth-century barbarism."[14] At the same time, he voices criticism of the apathy and weakness of the United States, suggesting we have behaved like a "collapsing empire" reminiscent of that of the Persians in *300*.[15] Might it be possible, then, to see the Arabic enemies of the United States represented by the single-minded yet brutish Spartans, who know exactly what they want and who they are? Yet looking at Miller's views on the Spartans themselves, this parallel is not sustainable:

> Sparta was a very peculiar culture. . . . The Spartans were free people, and defenders of freedom, facing an army of slaves . . . and it is ironic that a tribe that was as tyrannical to so many of their subjects was also a fountainhead of freedom, but those were times full of irony. Without Sparta there would never have been a flourishing of Athens, and without Athens we wouldn't have had Rome. So, while the Spartans were a very rough bunch, they were also necessary against a tyrant who had swallowed the rest of the world.[16]

12. See Lynch (2005, 250). Also see Zakaria (2004).

13. Specifically, for instance, *Tintin and the Blue Lotus*.

14. *Talk of the Nation*, Jan. 24, 2007.

15. "It seems to me quite obvious that our country and the entire Western world is up against an existential foe that knows exactly what it wants . . . and we're behaving like a collapsing empire. Mighty cultures are almost never conquered; they crumble from within. And frankly, I think that a lot of Americans are acting like spoiled brats because of everything that isn't working out perfectly every time" (ibid.). Also see Dean (2006) for Miller's plan to draw a comic featuring Captain America against Osama bin Laden.

16. http://www.moviehole.net/interviews/20070305_interview_frank_miller.html.

To Miller, the Spartans of *300* are brutal and violent, yet they are "free men," making the Greek world safe for the "necessary" democracy and remain firmly aligned with the manifest destiny of Western culture. Neither do the visually stereotypical Persians of *300* seem to reflect any real people but rather a projection of all that is negative in American values. Revealingly, in the following excerpt Miller describes his feelings about 9/11 as finally showing him the difference between his made-up world of comics villains versus the shocking revelation of real-life evil:

> Now, I draw and write comic books. One thing my job involves is making up bad guys. Imagining human villainy in all its forms. Now the real thing had shown up. . . . For the first time in my life, I know how it feels to face an existential menace. They want us to die.[17]

One must remember that these interviews, as well as the mass marketing of *300*, have taken place long after the composition of *300* itself. It seems as if Miller wrote the comic in his normal mode of fictional invention (the mental state of unreality he describes), but following 9/11, he and his readers have inevitably invested it with a new identity, that of a summons to war and a warning to the apathy of the United States after the fact. To me, this makes any strict political interpretation of *300* suspect. There are different reasons, then, that the Persians of *300* are so much more lurid and shocking than those of vase painting.

Another approach to explaining the question of Miller's Persians is to look at them less in political terms than as an outgrowth of the potential of different art forms. Miller follows his long experience as a comics artist in making his villains frightening and ominous. Like him, the Attic vase painters follow their own artistic traditions, yet overall they portray their long-term enemies, the Persians, much more neutrally than Greek writers do. Does this discrepancy suggest that comics and vase painting actually have little in common as art media after all?

Comics bring writing and drawing together, with the narrative of the action parallel to the graphics. Vase painting is the closest one comes in ancient Greece to this union of writing and drawing. The only preserved medium that combines even a minimal amount of writing with a pictorial element, it also has a lot in common with comics in its repetition and stylization, as well as its cheapness and mass production.[18] Even the marginalized images, such as we see in the Pygmy and Crane battle on the famous François vase, work to a degree in a similar way to paneling in comics.[19] Finally, comics artists, as well as vase painters, share a certain social stigma. Until recently, with the rise of the "graphic novel," comics have been associated with a

---

17. *Morning Edition*, Sept. 11, 2006.

18. For evidence on mass production of Greek pottery and the social status of potters and painters, see Onians (1991), 66, Richter (1958), and Sparkes (1996).

19. See VL 6: François Vase. Lissarague (1997) writes that the placement of the Pygmy story on the borders of the vase marginalizes it as a visual narrative. This is different from the use of paneling in comics in that the vase uses "panels" to mark off a completely separate myth. Nevertheless, the idea of narrative separation is basically the same. Hurwit (1977) discusses the enlivening of the backgrounds of vases during this period, when they change from the static, decorative fields of the geometric style to a dynamic space with which the painted figure can interact, introducing an element of narrative and action.

certain low-class pulpiness and a sense of inferiority to literature and painting. Likewise, Attic potters were not high on the social stratum of artisans.[20]

For all of these reasons, one would think comics and vases have much in common. Yet major differences between them must be kept in mind. Although mythological scenes on vase painting often do tell part of a story, without the use of multiple panels it is the story itself, existing apart from the image, which has impact.[21] A given scene on a vase is metonymic if you know the myth. Therefore, if there is no myth being told, stock scenes show figures in a vacuum, separate from any plot structure, with a decorative and formulaic rather than narrative effect. Scenes such as battles of Amazons and hoplites, heterosexual and homosexual love, dressing, soldiers playing dice, and so forth do not appear to be part of any unified narrative structure. The depiction of Persians is a prime example of this. Unlike the famous lost painting of the battle of Marathon by Polygnotus, depictions of Persians engaged in combat with Greeks are completely out of context, with no theater of battle mentioned.[22] Persians who are not fighting are even harder to place and appear to exist only to carry their fans and flywhisks and wear their multipatterned outfits in a decorative fashion. In addition, the main function of vase painting was to decorate a household tool, whereas comics exist primarily to tell a story, and often a frightening one. Therefore, it makes sense for vases to be more decorative than shocking or frightening, although there are plenty of examples of grotesques on vases.

One element the two media do have in common is their stylization of social types. Vase painting relies on the repetition of familiar, recognizable mythological and cultural characters. Individual artists, as well as workshop and group trends, show a consistency of types over time. Likewise, Miller's Persians reflect his personal artistic tendencies, as well as his roots in comics. He uses an eclectic mix of tropes to create his "bad guys." To make his villains as unlike his heroes as possible, he draws on his stored models of what is frightening, hidden, and dangerous

20. This is a relative assertion since painters of fine wares may have had a higher social status than those of rough, cheaper pots. Since specific ancient literary evidence on potters is lacking, we can turn to evidence on the generally low status of banausic crafts (See Aristotle, *Politics* 1275b: 35; Xenophon, *Oeconomicus* 4, 2–3). On the hierarchy of artists, see Isocrates' memorable comment: "Who would dare compare Phidias to a maker of terracottas, or Zeuxis and Parrhasios to a painter of votive offerings?" (Isocrates, *Antidosis* 2). Of modern scholars, Webster (1972) argued for the theory of a century of close personal and social contact between potters and patrons, and Burford has maintained the opposing view that, no matter how valued an art object may be, the "maker was in no way admirable" (Burford 1972, 220,n2). Also see Boardman (1989, 158) for opposition to Webster's theory. See Bailey on the 6th-century policy of Solon to attract foreign craftsmen to Attica with offers of citizenship. On the other hand, see Sparkes (1996, 230) for evidence on the foreign nationality and even servile status of vase painters. See Miller's introduction to her 1997 book for prolific evidence on the same theme. Finally, see Cavalier (1995) for an overview of several of these arguments.

21. It is interesting to compare comics such as "The Far Side" or the cartoons of the *New Yorker*, which, although they are only single panels, are able to evoke a narrative context that is essential to the joke. I argue that in such examples it is not the goal to encapsulate an extended tale into one picture but rather to evoke a familiar situation or story that can then be manipulated to give rise to the joke of the comic. In this way, these single-panel cartoons are not unlike vase paintings. Also see Marshall (2001) for an interpretation of an Apulian phylax vase as narrative. In my opinion, the unusual presence of written "dialogue" (55) on the vase increases the narrative ability of its pictures.

22. One interesting exception is the Eurymedon vase (VL 11). This unattributed vase, which refers to the battle of Eurymedon against Persia under Cimon in 468 BCE, is the only case in which a Persian is shown at a distinct moral disadvantage, but this is expressed as a parody of the erotic pursuits, which also form a stock theme of vases. For discussion of various theories about this vase, see Smith (1999) and Schauenberg (1975, 118).

and expresses this through costume and ornate, fetishistic disguise. Entrenched in thirty years of practice in creating ninjas, punks, mutants, and costumed weirdos, Miller presents us with the Persians, opponents of the heroic Spartans, as supervillains.[23]

Similarly, vase painting also uses an eclectic set of stored tropes—but with very different results. Looking at many vase depictions of Persians, Scythians, Amazons, and other "barbarians," one sees a general image beginning to emerge. Vase Persians are purposefully brought together to create a visual contrast with portrayals of Greeks, almost as if they create a set. For example, ornate, repeated patterns of dress are extremely familiar from Persians' costumes on vase paintings, as are their long shields, bows, and caps.[24] Persians are placed repeatedly next to the heroically nude Greek hoplites, who bear the proper arms of the citizen of the polis.

Miller does imitate this contrast between clothed Persians and nude Spartans and takes some details of his Persians' costume from Greek and Achaemenid Persian art, especially his depiction of the rank-and-file soldiers.[25] In the social code of *300*, dress is extremely important in conveying socioeconomic and military status. Most Persians go fully clothed, ranging from the common infantry to the resplendently ornate satraps and aristocrats ("Glory," 3). This is consonant with what we know of the Asians' disapproval of nudity, which the Greeks found so bizarre.[26] Yet if one examines Miller's past body of work, his Persian "henchmen" actually have much more in common with the minor, expendable villains he has created repeatedly in his past work. For instance, one of the recurrent elements in his drawings is that his bad guys have their heads and faces covered. Miller's ninja motif occurs notably in *The Dark Knight Returns*, when the Mutants go from one brand of gogglelike headgear to another after turning into the "Sons of Batman."[27] Also, in *Ronin*, Miller's fantasy of a medieval samurai transported to a futuristic New York City, the eponymous hero encounters a full-page-spread group of actual ninjas with basketlike helmets.[28] Similar Persian face coverings often recur in *300*, whereas they do not in Greek vase paintings, and they are rare in Achaemenid Persian art. This deviation is particularly extreme in the rendering of the "Immortals," of whom we have an artistic record from Darius' palace at Susa and whom, on the other hand, Miller depicts in his preferred Japanese vein, with iron kabuki-like masks.[29] Finally, even when Miller does show the faces of common soldiers, they are not wearing the "Persian cap" of vase painting or the crowns and hoods of the Achaemenids but Bedouin-like turbans.[30] In this way, he taps into a stereotypical image of a modern Arab, while relying primarily on his ninja model with Greek additions. The

23. Miller began writing and drawing comics in the 1970s. He has worked on characters created already, such as Daredevil and Batman, and has also created his own, such as Ronin (1983), Martha Washington (1994), and the many characters of *Sin City* (1993–2005).

24. See VL 2, 17, 18, 19.

25. Hoods and trousers appear repeatedly in Achaemenid portrayals of servants. See AAL 1, 2.

26. See Herodotus, *Histories*, 1.10.

27. Frank Miller (w./a.), Klaus Janson and Lynn Varley (colorist), *Batman: The Dark Knight: The Dark Knight Returns*, vol. 1 (DC, 1986), 7, 22.

28. Frank Miller (w./a.) and Lynn Varley (colorist), *Frank Miller's Ronin* (DC, 1987), 16–17.

29. See AAL, 7. Contrast with "Combat," 10.

30. "Glory," 11; "Combat," 4.

fact that the Persians, dressed as such, appear simply as unimportant spear fodder in *300* suggests that he designs them by formula, without the special creativity and deviancy that goes into the depiction of the Persian elite.

Stranger costumes are in store for these upper-class Persians. In particular, Miller diverges from the Persian dislike of nudity with his depiction of *300*'s supervillain, Xerxes (see figure 11.1). Unlike the dignified Achaemenid portrayals of great kings, Miller's Xerxes is scantily dressed.[31] Parading around nearly naked and festooned with sharp wiry jewelry, he—by his exhibitionism—stands out from his fellow Persians, as well as from the simple, heroic nudity of the Spartans. The same kind of contrast is true of many of Miller's costumed superhero comics, where the henchmen often operate at a lower pitch of deviancy than the main archenemy, who often sexualizes a tendency to violence in dress.[32]

One prominent visual detail of *300* is the Persian practice of piercing the face and body. This recalls the many punks and freaks of Miller's previous comics, who use facial and bodily piercing as an external symbol of their deviance from society, as well as of their status and commitment to a cause.[33] Xerxes, then, as ruler, has the most piercings, and his satraps have fewer.[34] Again, contrast is key since the Persians' glut of gaudy visual trappings starkly opposes the Spartans' egalitarian nudity and matching red cloaks. Less interest in dress is coded as "strong" in the story. The one Greek who goes bad, Ephialtes, betrays the Greeks for a uniform. Miller makes him a sad, deformed monster who only wishes to be accepted by his society.[35] He offers his military service to Leonidas, who refuses him as his deformed left arm cannot support a shield. This tool of the Spartan battle line, in which they lock together in a wall, represents their single-minded, unified identity. The physically deficient Ephialtes seeks the outward trappings of group identity, the clothing rather than the shield of war. When he fails to attain a Spartan uniform, he achieves a Persian one through his treachery. His obsessive wish for any uniform underscores the association of dependency on dress with moral weakness, alienation, and monstrosity.

On vases, although the contrast in dress is there, the Persians lack the lurid, ominous quality of their counterparts in *300*, as well as the rampant bestiality of Greek mythological characters, such as centaurs and satyrs.[36] In addition, on vases, Greeks and Persians generally appear the same in their ethnicity. Although their costumes and weapons are quite different, their physical features belong to the same ethnic strain of Caucasian Mediterraneans.[37] They are "other," certainly, but not extremely so; they are only a step or so removed from the starting point of the adult male citizen of the Greek *polis*, and their ethnic similarity supports this.

31. See AAL, 6. Contrast with "Combat," 7, depicting the full figure of Xerxes.

32. See the transvestite villain Bruno in Miller, *The Dark Knight Returns* 3: 2, as well as the Mutant Leader in *The Dark Knight Returns* 2: 17.

33. *Ronin* 2: 40–44; *The Dark Knight Returns* 4: 7.

34. "Honor," 12; "Combat," 7.

35. "Glory," 1; 9.

36. See VL 14.

37. For examples of ethnic resemblance between Greeks and Persians see VL 1, 2, 10, 13, 20, 22.

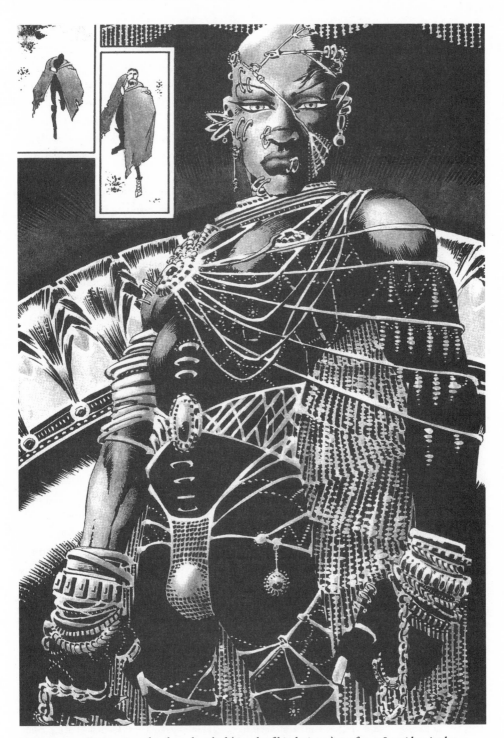

FIGURE 11.1 Xerxes, pierced and nearly naked (signals of his deviancy), confronts Leonidas. Art by Frank Miller. *300* "Duty" (Dark Horse Comics, June 1998).

Miller deviates glaringly from this in the blackness of his Persians. Yet this has precedent in his previous work. Take, for example, the polarized appearance of skinheads and panthers, whom he often depicts in his comics. In *Ronin*, these opposing groups govern the postapocalyptic nightmare of New York. In one particularly vivid panel, a black male panther and a white female skinhead snarl and try to stare each other down, startlingly different in appearance but united in their psychopathic extremism (see figure 11.2).[38]

In *300* Miller achieves the same contrast by making the Persians black so that they stand out from the white Greeks much more than their counterparts do in Classical vase painting. On the other hand, in classical art and literature, first, Persians are not black, and second, even though there is certainly a contrast between black Africans and white Greeks, there is little tendency to show "blackness" in a negative light. If anything, the Ethiopians are described in literary sources such as Homer and Herodotus as superior in many ways and beloved by the gods.[39] In vase painting, like the Persians, they are decorative rather than threatening.[40] Nor do Athenian artists represent either Persians or Ethiopians engaged in such bestial—one might say "barbaric"—behavior as the Greeks display in mythological depictions. Even doing battle, foreigners on vases do not have a horrific impact. That is reserved for mythological disasters such as the murder of Agamemnon or the sack of Troy.[41] Miller, on the other hand, mythologizes history in a horrifying way, drawing on a different cast of characters.

Stylistically, the Persians of *300* are cousins of the collection of rapacious cyberpunks, gangsters, ninjas, and deviant sexual freaks that have populated Miller's comic tales over the years. While Miller is a product of a cultural environment rife with stereotypes, the relationship of *300* to his past work is the determining factor in the character of his portrayal. The subliminal *result* of his making the Persians black Middle Easterners, however, is that readers connect the events of *300* to our current martial and cultural deadlock with Iran, Iraq, and Afghanistan.

Greek pottery, in contrast, seems disengaged from issues of racial prejudice as we understand them. Yet it does show strange developments in its cultural relationship with Persia over time. In the post-Persian war period, a marked tendency appears for Greek painters to abandon a great degree of racial and ethnic diversity in their depictions of foreigners in favor of gradually "Persianizing" all of them. Witness the story of Busiris, the hapless Egyptian king who tries to sacrifice Heracles. In an early fifth-century-BCE vase of the Pan Painter,[42] the priests and the king look like Egyptians, while in a later treatment of the myth by the Darius Painter, the king appears with a Persian hat, approached by a noble procession.[43] Likewise, Amazons who are dressed like hoplites in the sixth-century-BCE vases wear variegated colors and caps in those of

---

38. *Ronin* 3: 16.

39. *Iliad* 1.413; *Odyssey* 1.11; Herodotus, *Histories*, book 3.17–26, 94. Some scholarship dealing with ancient representations of black Africans includes Snowden (1970) and Hansbury (1977).

40. Claude Berard does make the case for class prejudice in the depiction of African royals on vases, for the servants are usually Negro and the princes Caucasian. Yet this occurs only in the context of mythological depictions rather than isolated images of Africans (see Berard 2000, 406).

41. See VL 9, 12.

42. See VL 15.

43. See VL 8. See Miller (2000) for further discussion.

FIGURE 11.2 Miller's deviants show great range, as seen in this panel from *Ronin* (DC, 1987). Art by Frank Miller.

the fifth.[44] Phrygian and Trojan kings, such as Midas and Priam, begin to be depicted in the Persian style as well.[45] The Athenians seem to have had Persians on their collective mind in reducing a variety of foreign types to their most familiar and decorative enemies.

The conclusions of scholars studying the postwar relations between Greece and Persia (after 479 BCE) generally show that these were more frequent and more positive than the literary sources might admit. Margaret Miller, for instance, discusses the fact that though classical Greek writers make much of the Greek-Barbarian contrast, in fact there was copious cultural interchange in post–Persian War period in the areas of art, dress, luxury, and cultural exchange. She offers extensive evidence that trade, as well as diffusion of spoils, plays large role in this.[46] David Castriota is another scholar who debunks the negative rhetoric about Achaemenid ideology before and after the Persian wars. He finds that the notions of statecraft that the Persians set forth on their monuments and documents are actually very similar to Greek conceptions of moral principle, justice, piety, and valor. Thus, Greek precepts were not actually much opposed to those of Persians.[47] Finally, Pierre Briant suggests that although the military incapacity of the Persians was one of the favorite topics of Greek authors in the Classical and Hellenistic periods, the idea of Persian "decadence" was not supported by the facts. Indeed, Briant believes that the repeated emphasis on decadence reflects the Greeks' fascination with the immense riches of Darius III, the Great King (Briant 1989).

44. See VL 16; VL 3.

45. See de Vries (2000, 338–64). De Vries describes the transmogrification of Phrygians in vase painting. In the early Classical period they appear in Hellenized dress, (344), whereas in the second half of the fifth century BCE they appear Persianized (345). See Athens Nat. Arch. Mus. Inv. no. 12257: 347, fig. 13.5.

46. Miller (1997) cites examples such as the adoption of Persian dress by Greeks (183), as well as extravagances like peacock raising (189–90), fans (198), parasols (193), and flywhisks (206). She points out that the possession of blacks, eunuchs, and other exotic slaves is attested in literary and epigraphic sources (212–15). She also makes the interesting analogy with Victorian "chinoiserie," which used an alien and subject culture as a source of decorative motifs (183). Finally, her use of Attic pottery as a marker of trade evidences the wide extent of Achaemenid-Greek trade relations.

47. Castriota (2000, 443–79). Castriota discusses the fact that the tomb of Dareios-Naqsh-i-Rustam, ca. 490 BCE represents more than thirty nations acknowledging Darius' divine right of kingship through his pious service of divinity and their collective support rather than subjection and slavery (449).

If the Greeks were in fact having much more positive contact with the Persians than their literature would like to admit, taking in Persian luxury items, trade goods, and even habits, the trappings of Persian life would have become increasingly familiar. Persians enabled Greece to enjoy the massive wealth that they had accumulated following the war. Persian culture, then, as "soft" as it was coded in the literary sources, had gained both popularity and familiarity among the Greeks. This could be a reason for the increasing "Persianization" of foreigners on vases: Soft culture was popular in real life, as much as it was decried in literature. Persia was popular.

Second, one must consider the relative accessibility of literature as opposed to vase painting. How many of the Athenians would have read Thucydides, Isocrates, Herodotus, or even remember Aeschylus' *Persae*? Only a small percentage of the body of citizens and metics was literate or could spend much time reading.[48] The attempt to justify Greek hegemony in writing was an act of the wealthy classes. On the other hand, everyone from aristocrats to slaves used clay vessels. Mythological tales were extremely familiar, transmitted orally and easily recognizable as "snapshots" of action in vase paintings. On the other hand, it could be difficult to portray the battle of Thermopylae on a vase. We must remember, too, that each vase painter had the model of actual Persians he may have seen himself, as well as the thousands of other Persians painted before that particular vase. Further, a large number of the vase makers were metic foreigners, including a number of Asians.[49] Thus, to an extent, the vase painter borrowed from real-life and very familiar tropes, in which it was not appropriate to see the Persians as the embodiments of monstrosity, bestiality, or weakness. Why should they, with such a wealth of mythological subjects possessing truly villainous qualities? Considering the strangeness of the monsters and homicidal maniacs that populate Greek mythology, it is not too surprising that the Persians should appear as relatively benevolent and mundane, familiar foreigners. The negative qualities attached to them in literature simply did not transfer to vase painting.

Miller's choice to make the Persians evil, corrupt, and black is based on conventional American villain making, which lacks relativism and complexity. The technical tropes of comics creation remain the driving force behind the political tenor of the work. The comic book "reflex," in which certain looks are associated with evil, as well as the reductive story line and moral coding, has made *300* into powerful propaganda, whether or not it was so intended, since its imagery cannot be read as neutral given the current political context. Therefore, when examining the construction of Miller's Persians, unreality, formula, and exaggeration are the most telling elements. Miller takes the boiled-down idea of Greek (and Western) cultural superiority and conveys this through a visual funnel, whereas the decorative Persians of vase painting, who never successfully made a connection to literature, do not perform the same role. Although the two media do share a visual immediacy and love of bizarre mythology, ultimately the Persians of vase painting are decorative and static, whereas Miller, with the help of the ideological impact of narrative, imbues his Persians with all of the terrifying evils of the supervillain.

48. For a discussion of this issue, see Harris (1989). Harris argues that the Athenian literacy rate in the 5th century BCE was at most 5%–10% of the entire population (114,327). Also see Robb (1994), who suggests that mimetic techniques like public recitation would have developed familiarity among the illiterate with works of drama, history and philosophy.

49. See note 17.

Appendix: Artworks Mentioned

Achaemenid Artworks List (AAL)

1. *Achaemenid Servant*. New York: Metropolitan Museum of Art, 34.158, fifth century BCE.
2. *Achaemenid Servants*. Boston: Museum of Fine Arts, 31.372, fifth century BCE.
3. *Persian Guard*. Boston: Museum of Fine Arts, 40.170, fifth century BCE, Archibald Cary Coolidge Fund.
4. *Achaemenid Spearman*. Fragmentary head of Achaemenid Spearman or Guard. Detroit Institute of Arts, Founders Society Purchase, Robert H. Tannahill Foundation, 78.47, fifth century BCE.
5. *Persian with Covered Bowl, Achaemenid*. Detroit Institute of Arts, Founders Society Purchase, Robert H. Tannahill Foundation Fund, 78.45, fifth century BC.
6. *Achaemenid Relief Depicting King Darius with Crown Prince Xerxes and Attendants behind Him*. Treasury, close-up of a relief in E Portico of a courtyard, depicting King Darius seated on a throne with his son Xerxes standing behind him. Oriental Institute of the University of Chicago, Photographic Archives P 56563, 520–500 BCE.
7. *The Frieze of Archers*. Glazed tile relief showing soldiers from the Ten Thousand Immortals. Tell of the Apadana, Palace of Darius I, Susa, Iran. Polychrome glazed siliceous brick. Height 4.75 m; width 3.75 m. Paris: Louvre, Near Eastern Antiquities, AOD 488. Achaemenid Persian Period, reign of Darius I, ca. 510 BC.

List of Greek Vases (VL)

1. Persian head rhyton. Athenian, red-figure, fig mug, figure vase mug, class w. London: British Museum, E791 (Beazley Archive 218694), fifth century BCE.
2. "Falling Persian." Decoration A: Archer (Persian) running with sword and bow. Decoration B: Fight, warrior with spear attacking archer (Persian) with sword and bow. Basel: Antikenmuseum und Sammlung Ludwig, BS480, 475–425 BCE (Beazley Archive 1287).
3. Attributed to Euphronios. "Amazons and Heracles." Komos volute krater, side A: Herakles and Amazons; side B: Amazons running up. Arezzo Museo Civico, 1465, 510 BCE.
4. Negro Alabastra Painter. Alabastron vase with Negro soldier. Boston: Museum of Fine Arts, fifth century BCE.
5. Black Head Rhyton Painter: mug in the shape of a man's head. Ceramic, black figure. Height 17.7 cm (61516 in.) Boston: Museum of Fine Arts, 500 BCE.
6. François Vase by Kleitias and Ergotimos. Size: 66 cm. (volute krater). Function: convivial. Technique: black-figure style. Miniature black-figure. Subjects: seven figure friezes on the body above one animal frieze; pygmies fighting cranes on the foot. Side A (top to bottom): Kalydonian boar hunt; Patroklos' funeral games; wedding procession moves toward the house; Achilles chases Troilos; Polyxena at the fountain house drops her water pot; animal frieze. Side B (top to bottom): Athenians arriving at Crete by boat and Theseus leading the group; Lapiths fighting centaurs; wedding procession; animal frieze.

Date: near mid-6th century: The unusual and finely made shape (first Athenian known in clay), wealth of small and finely executed mythological scenes, and proliferation of inscriptions, including the names of the painter Kleitias and the potter Ergotimos, indicate that this was a very special piece, exported to northern Italy in antiquity. Florence, Italy: Museo Archeologico, 4209, sixth century BCE.

7. Painter, Altamura. "Priam as a Persian King." Calyx krater (mixing bowl) with scenes from the fall of Troy. Boston: Museum of Fine Arts, 59.178, 465 BCE.

8. Painter, attributed to Darius. "Heracles and Busiris." Dinos, red figure, Greek, south Italian, Apulian. New York: Metropolitan Museum, formerly 1984.11.7 (now Nostoi no. 57; old no. 51), ca. 340–320 BCE.

9. Painter, Brygos. "Iliupersis Cup." Sack of Troy (side A). Paris: Louvre, G 152, 480–475 BCE.

10. Painter, Chicago. "Greek and Persian." Contrast of nude hoplite and archer Persian. Boston Museum of Fine Arts, 13.196 (Beazley Archive 207321), 460 BCE.

11. Painter, Circle of the Triptolemos. Eurymedon vase. Hamburg: Museum für Kunst und Gewerbe, 1981.173, ca. 460 BCE.

12. Painter, Dokimasia. "Death of Agamemnon." Calyx krater. Boston Museum Fine of Arts, 63.1246, 460 BC.

13. Painter, Eleusis. "Greek and Persian." Fragment (restored) of interior. Boston Museum of Fine Arts, 10.196, sixth century BCE.

14. Painter, Foundry. "Greek and Centaur." Tondo of an Attic red-figure kylix. Munich, Staatliche Antikensammlungen, Inv. no. 2640, ca. 480 BCE.

15. Painter, Pan. "Heracles and Busiris." Red-figure vase. Athens: National Archeological Museum, Inv. no. 9683, 470 BCE.

16. Unknown. "Amazons and Heracles." Amazons dressed as hoplites fight the Heracles. Fine Arts Museums of San Francisco, 1925.368, late sixth century BCE.

17. Leningrad Painter. Fragments of Persians playing pipes near an altar. Corinth, Archaeological Museum, T620 (Beazley Archive 206565), 500–450 BCE.

18. Meleager Painter. "Seated Persian King with Procession of Youths." Vienna, Kunsthistorisches Museum, 158 (Beazley Archive 217917), 400–300 BCE.

19. Mannheim Painter. "Persian King Presented with Cup by a Woman." Vatican City, Museo Gregoriano Etrusco Vaticano, 16536 (Beazley Archive 214363), 475–425 BCE.

20. Jena Painter. "Head of Persian." Bonn: Akademisches Kunstmuseum, 128 (Beazley Archive 231004), 400–300 BCE.

21. Follower of Douris. "Persian Seated on Rock, Walking Persian." Berlin: Antikensammlung, 3156 (Beazley Archive 209946), 475–425 BCE.

22. Brygos Painter. "Greeks and Persians Fighting." Oxford: Ashmolean Museum, 1911.615 (Richter 1958, 399), 500–450 BCE.

12

A Dream of Augustus

Neil Gaiman's *Sandman* and Comics Mythology

ANISE K. STRONG

Neil Gaiman's "August," the thirtieth issue of his comic series *The Sandman*, tells the tale of a fictional conversation between the historical Roman emperor Augustus and an unorthodox companion, the dwarf actor Lycius.[1] Gaiman inserts the supernatural character of the King of Dreams, the main protagonist of *The Sandman*, into an authentic historical setting and thus blends mythology and history. He creates a fantastic myth in order to explain Augustus' historical decision to restrict further Roman territorial expansion, a policy change that may have fundamentally changed the course of Western civilization. In his invocation of both individual psychological trauma and supernatural intervention to explain a larger historical turning point, Gaiman consciously follows in the tradition of ancient authors like the Roman historian Livy.

The Sandman marked a renaissance in comic books for traditional mythological tales. Earlier comics had featured heroes based on mythological figures such as Hercules and Thor, but they had generally focused on transplanted ancient heroes rather than on historical times and places. *The Sandman*, in contrast, offers fantastical tales in a wide variety of eras and geographic locations. Many issues seek to create new myths by providing fantastical explanations for historical or natural events: Issue nineteen, for example, presents Shakespeare's *Midsummer Night's Dream* as the result of a meeting between the Bard and real fairies.[2] Gaiman repeatedly uses Greek and Roman mythology and history as a source for his retellings; he thus gives his new fables the established authority of the classical canon.

Gaiman, who once summed up the theme of the series as "Change or die," repeatedly emphasizes that the myths and stories themselves are "tales written in the sand," which need to be rewritten for new audiences and new times ("Endless Nights," Prologue, 2003). Many issues reflect on the nature of stories and myths and the creation and shaping of tales; it is an extremely postmodern comic. Within this overarching theme, four issues focus specifically on emperors of various times and places. These four stories (issues 29–31 [August–October 1991]; 50 [June 1993]) are linked together as the "Distant Mirrors" series in reference to Barbara Tuchman's

---

1. Neil Gaiman (w.) and Bryan Talbot (a.), "August," *The Sandman* 30 (Vertigo, Sept. 1991).

2. Neil Gaiman (w.) and Charles Vess (w.), "A Midsummer Night's Dream," *The Sandman* 19 (Vertigo, Sept. 1990).

popular history book *A Distant Mirror: The Calamitous Fourteenth Century* (1978), which draws comparisons between medieval and modern Europe.[3] "Distant Mirrors" also focuses on themes of time and the calendar; titles include "Three Septembers and a January," a story about Emperor Norton in mid-19th-century San Francisco; "Thermidor," a tale about survival during the French Revolution; and "Ramadan," a fable about Haroun Al-Rashid's attempt to forever preserve the perfection of his Baghdad.

In "August," Gaiman creates a myth of personal trauma and revenge in answer to a complex historical question—why did Augustus order the establishment of permanent imperial borders in his will?[4] The setting of the story is historical, and Gaiman and the artist, Bryan Talbot, vividly evoke daily life in 1st-century-CE Rome. "August" weaves together three different moments in the life of Gaius Julius Caesar Octavianus Augustus. Gaiman begins with a set of three black-and-white panels that show only the terrified face of a sixteen-year-old boy lying in the darkness, refusing to cry (see figure 12.1). The "present" story is in color, while the scenes from Augustus' youth are predominantly black and white; these panels set that tone. This character is distinguished by negatives—what he will not do and who he is not: "[H]e is no barbarian, no Greek to give in to his feelings, to hide his fears" ("August" 1.1–3). We do not know who he is or what his name might be.

The bottom half of the first page is in color and frames a small dwarf against a background of a public Roman street, complete with columns, plaza, and temple pediment, which are instantly evocative of classical architecture (1.4). This dwarf is immediately identified, in contrast to the anonymous boy, as Lycius, a character based on a brief reference in Suetonius' *Life of Augustus* to a young actor named Lycius, who was "of respectable parentage, whom [Augustus] displayed as a wonder, for he was less than two feet tall and weighed only 17 pounds, but had a stentorian voice" (Suetonius, *Aug.* 43.3). Lycius' cheerful face and vertical posture immediately contrasts him with the horizontal, anxious, hidden gaze of the anonymous handsome boy; the misshapen, ugly man is here the happiest figure.

Like many of the *Sandman* comics, "August" also reflects on the nature of stories, myths, and truths. Lycius announces on the second page, "The things I write, I witnessed directly, or I was told, by our first emperor, who was a man, and is now a god" ("August" 2.1). Just as the Roman biographer Suetonius claimed authority as a historian through his access to the imperial archives and memoirs, so Lycius here places himself firmly in the tradition of a scholarly historian rather than a storyteller.[5] These claims of historicity cause the later introduction of supernatural figures like Morpheus and the appearance of mysterious prophecies to come as even more of a surprise to a modern reader. Augustus is himself portrayed as both mortal and immortal, simultaneously a real figure and a supernatural power, just as the story itself is represented as both history and myth.

3. The issues of the "Distant Mirrors" series were later collected and published together in the *Fables and Reflections* collection (*The Sandman* 6 [Vertigo, 1993]), although they were reordered for this volume by Gaiman and mixed with five other stories, three from the "Convergence" story arc, which focuses on the meeting of recurrent characters, and two other individual issues, including the longer "Song of Orpheus," first published as the *Sandman Special* (November 1991). "Ramadan," issue 50, was written contemporaneously with the other three tales in the "Distant Mirrors" series but published later due to artistic delays (introduction, *Fables and Reflections*).

4. Tacitus, *Ann.* 1.11.4; Dio LVI.33.6; Ober (1982, 306–307).

5. See, for example, Suetonius, *Augustus*, 51.2, 71.2–4, 76.1–2; *Tiberius* 21.4–7; Wallace-Hadrill (1983, 4–8); Baldwin (1983, 106).

FIGURE 12.1 The opening page of "August" shows two of the narrative strands: Augustus' childhood (in black and white) and the narrative "present." Art by Bryan Talbot. *The Sandman* 30 (DC/Vertigo Comics, Sept. 1991) 1.

Gaiman also plays with our expectations of truth and historical reality. The main framing narrative of the comic is presented as an excerpt from Lycius' memoirs. This emphasis on memoirs immediately places itself in the tradition of Robert Graves's *I, Claudius* novels and the BBC's late 1970s' *I, Claudius* television miniseries. Both the novel and the television show begin with an elderly man, Emperor Claudius, writing his autobiography and revealing hidden secrets.

On his way into the palace, Lycius meets Livia, Augustus' wife (2.4–5). Her face is directly based on that of Sian Phillips, the BBC actress who played Livia in the *I, Claudius* series for television rather than on the numerous statues of the historical Livia. A reader familiar with the television show can thus quickly identify the character. Gaiman and Talbot offer an explicitly fictional representation of a historical figure; we are given not the "real" Livia (although her statues depicted an idealized Roman matron) but rather a shadow of the ambitious, murderous Livia of television.[6]

In his notes for this scene, Gaiman explicitly instructs the artists to use *I, Claudius* as a model: "I have implicit trust in BBC researchers for things Roman" (Gaiman, script for "August," 2.3). Talbot's artistic vision of Augustus himself, the main protagonist, notably does not resemble Brian Blessed, the actor who played the character in the BBC series, perhaps because Blessed portrayed Augustus as a genial but weak old man with a foolish smile rather than the more complex and ambitious character in "August" or Suetonius' biography. The lines between history and myth are blurred as quickly as they have been established. Augustus' line "quicker than boiled asparagus" is also adopted frequently by Claudius in the BBC series (Suetonius, *Aug.* 87; "August" 4.4).

Augustus is simultaneously four different men—the young boy we have already met in the first panels; the brutal, oppressive triumvir Octavianus; the paternalistic emperor Augustus; and the future god, Divus Augustus. He is himself a symbol of change both in his transformation of the empire and in his assumption and shedding of names and roles. On this day, he plays "Caius the beggar" as well, a purely fictional and temporary part that allows him to escape his responsibilities. Ironically, although "Caius the beggar" is the one role for which Augustus dons a costume and uses another's lines, he assumes this guise precisely so as to avoid an audience, in this case the watchful eyes of the gods ("August" 18.4). Augustus himself is very aware of the roles he plays; toward the end of the issue, he comments wryly, "So today, I was the actor . . . or perhaps today, I did not have to act" ("August" 22.5). Only as "Caius," the beggar in the public Forum, ignored by most passersby, is Augustus truly and paradoxically offstage since at all other times he plays the emperor, as well as a private individual. Suetonius claims that Augustus' last public words directly invoked this sense of theatricality. The dying emperor quoted the standard last lines of Greek comedy to his friends: "I've played my part well; all clap your hands and dismiss me from the stage with applause" (Suetonius 99). Gaiman thus did not invent the conceit of Augustus as actor. However, while Suetonius (and perhaps the emperor himself) viewed

---

6. Tac. *Ann.*, I.3–6; but cf. Suet. *Aug.*, 62.2; Dio. LVII.12. Anthony Barrett begins his biography of Livia by admitting that, "if the general public has any impression of Livia, the wife of the first Roman Emperor, Augustus, it is that of the character created by Sian Phillips in the highly acclaimed BBC-TV production of *I, Claudius*" (Barrett 2002, ix). Apparently, the character of Tony Soprano's mother, Livia, from the later HBO series *The Sopranos*, was later named in honor of the character in *I, Claudius* (Fantham 2004, 3). For another take on the historical Livia and the Augustan construction of her image, see Bartman (1999).

Augustus' life as a triumphant comedy, Gaiman rewrites the same story as classical tragedy, complete with father issues and dire prophecies.

The central conceit of the main story thus focuses on an act of simultaneous deception and unmasking. Lycius helps Augustus disguise himself as a decrepit beggar, temporarily mutilating his face by means of makeup, so that Augustus can spend the day freely sitting on the public steps of the temple of Mars the Avenger. The story of the ruler wandering incognito is a traditional tale; indeed, it is referenced in two other stories in the "Distant Mirrors" series. Haroun al-Rashid, in "Ramadan," likes to disguise himself along with his vizier and wander through the bazaar of Baghdad in search of adventures. Meanwhile, in "Three Septembers and a January," Emperor Norton lives the opposite of this cliché; he is a homeless beggar who believes himself an emperor and eventually succeeds in persuading others to play along with his fantasy.

Augustus, however, has no interest in adventure or in discovering the true needs of the common people. He largely ignores the passersby who cross the foreground of most subsequent panels, choosing instead to talk to Lycius about his life and dreams. For most of the tale then, the reader is left with a riddle: Why does the most powerful man in the world want to be a beggar? Eventually, the Dream King himself answers the question: The gods watch emperors, but not beggars ("August" 20.25). Two mysteries remain: Why does Augustus fear the gods, and what does he wish to plan while away from their oversight?

Much of the comic takes place on the steps of the temple of Mars the Avenger, as Lycius and "Caius" while away the hours by begging and talking. Many if not most of Caius' lines are drawn directly from Suetonius. For example, Gaiman's "Caius" describes his abstemious diet as "dried dates, a few raisins, a glass of watered wine"; he also invokes both Augustus' own testament, the *Res Gestae*, and Suetonius' biography in claiming that Augustus has transformed Rome "from brick to the finest marble."[7] Gaiman commented that he wrote these scenes as "a sort of crossword puzzle game" based on Suetonius; it is very much a game that would be amusing to British public school students like Gaiman, who had read Suetonius as teenagers. He described his knowledge of the Augustan Age as coming from Suetonius and "lots of Roman reading that melted down into the back of my head" (personal correspondence, November 6, 2007). Such references invoke the classical canon and draw the educated reader into a sense of community with the author; these stories form part of the audience's common heritage and culture. There is an implicit assumption that at least some members of the audience know who Augustus is and vaguely remember his odd personal eating quirks and catchphrases, either directly from the ancient texts or filtered through *I, Claudius*.

At the same time, recognition of these subtle references of Suetonius is not key to comprehension of "August." Most American comic readers do not typically read the works of Suetonius and Tacitus in school and are also less likely to have watched *I, Claudius*. "August" functions both as a set of inside jokes for readers who share Gaiman's own background and simultaneously as an introduction to basic Roman history for those who do not. For an audience unversed in

7. Gaiman, "August" 4.4 and 5.4; cf. Suetonius, *Augustus* 76. See also "August" 5.3, *Res Gestae* 32, and Suet. *Aug.* 28–29 ("found it in brick, and have left it clad in finest marble"); "August" 6.1–2 on actors, and Suet. 43.3; "August" 6.3 on Pylades, and Suet. 45.4; "August" 8.6 on Augustus' children as "running sores," and Suet. 65.4; "August" 10.7, on Octavian's divine birth, and Suet. 94.4.

the classics, Augustus is as mysterious a figure as Emperor Norton or Haroun el-Rashid; in this case the "Distant Mirrors" series serves a didactic function, as well as an artistic one. In such a case, Gaiman's representation of Augustus and Rome is assumed to be a truthful history. For a more knowledgeable audience, Gaiman's version is more obviously an interpretation, one possible retelling or explanation of vaguely familiar historical events.

Bryan Talbot, the principal artist, illustrated a hundred panels of mostly static dialogue between the two protagonists by showcasing ordinary Roman individuals who walk in front of Lycius and Caius during their conversation, occasionally engaging them directly. In his script notes, Gaiman gave detailed descriptions of what sort of passersby he wished to see depicted and asked Talbot to show the passing of the hours by increasing and decreasing the number of figures (Gaiman, "Script for August" 6.1). Quite accurately, there are far larger crowds in the morning than during the heat of the afternoon, a time when urban Romans would have been napping or at the baths, if possible. Remarkably few passersby wear togas, a welcome if rare recognition of the toga's use in Roman society as formal business attire, not everyday shopping wear (Vout 1996, 210). In a set of panels, children chase balls similar to those seen in the Piazza Armerina mosaics (10.7); slaves in chain gangs slowly process across the panel (13.1), and a toga-clad nobleman casually urinates against the side of the temple (14.1–5). These vignettes visually highlight contrasts between ancient Rome and the modern world. The readers are reminded that while some aspects of society, like children's games, remain familiar constants, both economic institutions like slavery and alien habits like public urination mark Roman culture as fundamentally different from our own.

A variety of brief dialogues with passersby also illustrate Gaiman's view of both positive and negative aspects of ancient Roman society. Most of these figures have their heads cut off by the top of the panel; they serve as anonymous representations of certain viewpoints and stereotypes rather than as specific individual characters. In one case, Caius and Lycius overhear a miserly man, Marcus, who refuses to give money to them on the grounds that the gods will either provide for or punish beggars (9.1). Later, this figure is contrasted with a generous freedman who exemplifies "the Roman Dream":

> Once, I was a slave, but I was freed in my master's will, and I took what I had saved, and became a wine-seller. The gods smiled upon me, and now I own two ships, and have fifty slaves of my own. We know not what tomorrow brings, and but for the whim of the goddess Fortuna I myself might be sitting in the marketplace, begging for copper asses. No man knows the future. It behooves us all to walk with care. ("August" 15.2)

In this speech Gaiman invokes another common classical trope, the mutability of fate. As the wise Athenian Solon tells Croesus, no man's fate should be judged until he has died (Herodotus 1.28–33). This common ancient theme is also one of the central motifs of the *Sandman* series, where characters' fates are repeatedly overturned and even Destiny, Dream's eldest sibling, does not have absolute power.

"Caius" eventually reveals that he has come to the Forum because of a visit from the King of Dreams in the guise of his nighttime storyteller ("August" 17–20). Dream, who here appears as a mysterious, white-skinned figure in a black toga, tells Augustus a story from his own youth. We switch back into the horizontal, sketchlike black-and-white panels, and eventually it is revealed that Julius Caesar brutally raped Octavian when Octavian was sixteen and promised him power and plans for imperial domination in return for submissive silence ("August" 23.5). The memory of these rapes causes the elderly Augustus to wake up in terror and to have a story-teller always ready to comfort him with fantastic tales of childhood. Suetonius mentions that Augustus had frequent insomnia and demanded the nighttime companionship of a storyteller. Within the context of the ancient imperial biography, this detail comes across as the minor personal quirk of a domineering tyrant, able to force others to share his own restlessness (Suetonius *Aug.* 78). Gaiman, however, uses this detail from Suetonius to create a nightmare of childhood trauma and link Augustus to *The Sandman*'s central hero, the Dream King.

What is the source of this tale of rape and child abuse? Suetonius does mention Marc Antony's allegation that Octavian had earned his adoption through *stuprum*, or disgraceful sex, with Julius Caesar. Supposedly, Antony's brother, Lucius Antonius, further claimed that, after losing his virginity to Julius Caesar, Octavian subsequently sold sexual favors to Caesar's legate, Aulus Hirtius, for the extravagant sum of three hundred thousand sestertii (Suetonius *Aug.* 68). There seems little reason to take these insults any more seriously than Octavian's own slanders of Cleopatra or Antony's earlier wife, Fulvia; they formed part of the propaganda war of invective between the two triumvirs in the late 30s BCE (Volkmann [1958, 170–171]; Reinhold [1981, 97]).

However, they do suggest that the story of a sexual relationship between Caesar and Octavian was well known contemporaneously. In 43 BCE, Cicero seems to respond to such accusations by defending Octavian in the thirteenth Philippic as "a most innocent (*sanctissimum*) young man" of "unbelievable and divine manliness (*virtus*)."[8] Cicero then turns the slander back on Antony, claiming that Antony is drawing upon the memory of his own childhood debaucheries (Cicero, *Phil.* 13.9). Nevertheless, Suetonius never implies that Caesar forcibly raped Octavian or that the intercourse was anything but fully consensual.[9]

Indeed, an accusation of rape against the martyred and newly deified Julius Caesar would not have served the interests of Antony and his faction. The purpose of Antony's claim was to suggest that Octavian was an effeminate, mercenary young man who would sell his body—and, by implication, his honor—in return for power and money. It falls into a common category of Roman accusations of male sexual passivity; men who were passive partners in sex with other men were often thought to be unfit for public service and incapable of moral integrity.[10] Indeed, only a few years earlier the orator Cicero had publicly accused Antony himself of such behavior and of acting as "a wife" to another Roman nobleman. Cicero both condemned Antony's flagrant defiance of social norms and cast doubt on his fitness for public office (Cicero, *Phil.*

8. See also Cic. *Phil.* 3.15, where Cicero praises Octavian's chastity and modesty.

9. Hallett (1977, 152); Williams (1999, 129); Richlin (1993, 538). HBO's *Rome* series also played with the idea of a sexual relationship between Julius Caesar and Octavian, although the network ultimately represented it as a false scandal stemming from misinterpretation of an incident in which Octavian helped Caesar conceal an epileptic fit. This version of the story emphasizes the dominant straight masculinity of both season's protagonists, Caesar in season 1 and Octavian in season 2, which the writers contrast with Antony's eventual effeminization. In *Rome*, Octavian could never be an innocent sexual victim as in the Gaiman narrative; he is the consummate manipulator and a callous, ambitious power seeker: "Stealing from Saturn," *Rome* 1.4 (HBO 2005).

10. See, for example, Livy 39.15.12–4; Juvenal 2.42–44; Williams (1999, 110–22).

2.44.) Suetonius claims that Julius Caesar was similarly accused of having served as a passive sexual partner for King Nicomedes of Bithynia (Suetonius, *Jul.* 49).

On the other hand, little stain attached to men who were the active partners in same-sex intercourse.[11] By accusing Octavian of having gained Caesar' and Hirtius' favor through sexual intercourse, Antony laid all the blame on Octavian as the corrupt and venial agent (see Skinner 1982, 203). In this tale, Caesar' and Hirtius' desire for intercourse with an attractive youth like Octavian is entirely justifiable. It is Octavian's acceptance of their offer and, allegedly, his self-prostitution that endanger his masculinity and thus his political and military authority.

In "August" Gaiman tells not Antony's story about the sly, ambitious, seductive youth Octavian but rather a tale about the brutal, aggressive rapist Julius Caesar and his innocent, traumatized victim Caius. Why does Gaiman invent this myth of rape and forcible intercourse rather than following his ancient sources? To answer this question, I turn to Livy, who himself served as Augustus' official historian and storyteller. Livy chose to dramatize many moments of political change in early Rome with stories of rape or attempted rape.[12] These stories follow a standard pattern, suggesting that the details may have been adapted or fictionalized to empha-size the similarity. Tyrannical figures grow abusive of their powers and forget the rule of law; they rape a free person; the victims or their families speak out against the injustice; the Roman people rebel; and a new, more just order is restored. For instance, Tarquin, an Etruscan prince, raped the Roman noblewoman Lucretia in the late sixth century BCE. She denounced him to her relations and killed herself to protect her virtue; her action inspired both direct retaliation against Tarquin and the foundation of the Roman Republic (Livy 1.57–60). In another case, Appius Claudius, the tyrannical leader of the mid-fifth-century BCE Roman council of ten, attempted to possess and rape a centurion's daughter, Verginia; her father killed her rather than let her be dishonored. In anger at Appius Claudius, the Roman populace rose up and restored power to the Senate and the Assembly (Livy 3.44–58). In a third instance, Gaius Publilius, a young and handsome debt slave, complained publicly of his master's attempted rape and assault upon him; as a result, the senate and people ended debt slavery altogether (Livy 8.28).

Even prostitutes were supposedly allowed to protect themselves from rape by senators (Gellius, *Attic Nights* 4.14). According to Suetonius, Augustus himself, shortly after assuming power, gained notoriety by dragging a married noblewoman off into a bedroom in the middle of her husband's dinner party and returning her later with her "hair mussed and ears blushing" (Suet. *Aug.* 69). While the anonymous woman in question may have been a willing, if embar-rassed, partner, the incident serves as another means by which Suetonius demonstrates Augus-tus' complete control over the Roman aristocracy. Even former consuls are not able to protect the honor of their family members, a key component of the power and responsibility of the Roman *paterfamilias*. Gaiman omits any mention of this sort of incident from his story, refigur-ing Augustus as the helpless victim of rape rather than its perpetrator.

Rape, in the Roman context, becomes a signifier of tyranny. Sandra Joshel notes that rape in the Roman imagination is also inextricably linked to imperialism and mass slavery (Joshel 1992, 123). Freedom to rape is a power that Romans claim over both foreign and domestic

---

11. Williams (1999, 109); Richlin (1993, 524); Parker (1997, 55).

12. Joshel (1992, 113); Dunkle (1971, 16); Arieti (1997, 216–17).

enemies; Amy Richlin notes that Roman literature and graffiti frequently invoke rape as a threat against burglars (Richlin 1992, 79). In the Roman imagination, rape was simply the most visceral means of taking possession of a conquered people—Romanization in its harshest form. This glorification of rape in war has a necessary counterpart: Freedom from rape defines the most basic right of the Roman citizen (cf. Richlin 1992, xvi, 224; Arieti 1997, 219). Powerful men step outside permissible legal and social boundaries when they abuse their authority to rape fellow Romans. When such an abuse of power occurs, the inevitable response is riot and revolution. While we should not ignore the objectification of the victims in these stories, the survivors or their kin effect meaningful change and destroy the political futures of their rapists.

Caesar's rape of the young Octavian in "August" fits neatly into the larger Roman mythological pattern established by Livy and other Roman authors. Caesar, the tyrant, already conceiving of himself as a god, abuses a helpless victim, young Caius. Caius survives the experience, although he is traumatized, and duly leads the "Roman revolution," creating an autocratic empire. The adult Augustus tells Lycius, "When I am a god, I will no longer be scared" (10.8). He desires the security of becoming a god himself—someone who, in the Roman paradigm, will forever be dominant both ideologically and sexually and who can never again be abused (Parker 1997, 55–56).

Caius tells Lycius that he knows of two possible futures of Rome. One fulfills Caesar's ambition: The empire continues to expand and conquer every corner of the world from the Americas to India, creating a vast and wealthy empire that lasts for ten thousand years ("August" 15.6–7). In this future, the victim becomes the abuser, assuming his abuser's name. We see this persona of Caesar Augustus calmly describe the many people he has executed or murdered; he demonstrates his strength by killing a rat, whose blood smashes across the panel ("August" 16.3–6). In the other future, "the Romans sputter and flare like Greek fire, last a few hundred years and then are gone, eaten from outside by barbarians, from inside by strange gods" (15.5). Gaiman instructed Talbot to depict Augustus unconsciously making the sign of the cross in this panel, a detail that the artist ultimately omitted but which nevertheless suggests compassionate Christianity as an alternative to Roman imperialism (script notes for 15.5). Surprisingly, Caius seeks to create this second, apparently less desirable future and thereby thwart Caesar's vision for Rome.

It is easy to see this choice as an act of revenge, dooming Rome to insane emperors and chaos because of the suffering of one boy. However, it also echoes the larger themes of *The Sandman*. Change is good; death is necessary. Stagnation and stories without endings cause the only true death. Rome may be the Eternal City, but the only way to remain forever great is to be preserved in a bubble in Dream, a fate to which al-Rashid ultimately dooms Baghdad in the final "Distant Mirrors" tale, "Ramadan." Augustus chooses change for his city even if that means its eventual destruction.

Terminus, god of boundaries, initially aids Augustus and sends Dream to him. Just as rape in the Roman context is always an invasion of boundaries (Joshel 122)—Tarquinius enters both Lucretia's room and her body, and Livy and Ovid both focus lavishly on the knives as they pierce Lucretia's and Verginia's flesh (Richlin 1992, 172)—here the paradigmatic Roman act of war and imperialism also defies natural and national boundaries. By setting borders for the empire and preventing further expansion, an act that supposedly dooms Rome, Augustus is also symbolically resisting his own rape. Boundaries are important, both in space and time. By ending the policy expansion, he limits and protects Rome from becoming either abuser or victim, at least in the short term. Rome itself is the object of Augustus' love and potential abuse, his only true child (Bender 1999, 140). He chooses to be a responsible father figure, unlike Julius Caesar, and to allow Rome to evolve and choose its own new identity (Bender 1999, 132).

Gaiman turns the policy decisions of a paternalistic *princeps* into a desperate rape survivor's resistance against an abusive father figure. This theme echoes earlier *Sandman* issues that also focus on rape and rape survivors. Issue 17, "Calliope" (from the "Dream Country" sequence), tells the story of a writer's abduction and repeated rape of the Greek Muse Calliope in order to gain divine inspiration for his novels.[13] The undeclared question Caius faces is whether himself to be a rapist or a survivor. Augustus makes it clear to Lycius that he learned well the lessons Caesar taught him; he knows how to be cruel and merciless and how to impose his will on others. He chooses to limit the empire not because he wants to maintain his own glory but because he wants to escape the vicious cycle of imperialist abuse. He begins the day justifying his violent acts as necessary for the preservation of the empire; by evening, he has realized the Dream King's lesson: Empires, like stories, must be allowed to change and evolve into ever new stories.

---

13. Neil Gaiman (w.) and Kelley Jones (a.), "Calliope," *The Sandman* 17 (Vertigo, July 1990).

13

Francophone Romes
Antiquity in *Les Bandes Dessinées*

MARTIN T. DINTER

Derived from the expression "drawn strips," the designation *bandes dessinées* (BDs) does not imply a subject matter unlike its Anglo-American counterpart, *comics*. Indeed, both comics and graphic novels find their home under the umbrella term of *bandes dessinées*, and the ambitions of the genre manifest themselves in its standing as *le neuvième art* (the ninth art)[1] and in the prestige the authors, artists, and their creations enjoy in the francophone world.[2] The importance of *bandes dessinées* for the francophone book trade can hardly be overestimated: Every third book sold in France at present falls into the BD category, and *bandes dessinées* constitute an important percentage of global publishing in the French language.[3] According to the *Association des critiques et journalistes de bande dessinée* (ACBD), "the production of this sector again expanded by 4.4% in 2007. There were 4313 BD titles published that year, 3312 of which were new albums, 712 reprints, 204 art books and the remaining 85 essays related to BDs."[4]

In what follows I briefly discuss the development of postwar *bandes dessinées* with classical themes and then concentrate on one particular series, *Murena*, by Jean Dufaux (writer) and Philippe Delaby (artist), of which six volumes (of eight planned) have appeared since 2001. In a final section I also take a closer look at a very recent series *Les aigles de Rome* [*The Eagles of Rome*], by Enrico Marini, the first two volumes of which have now been published.

---

1. There is some confusion about the previous eight arts, but the term *ninth art* is consistently used for BDs in France. The term:

   > places *bandes dessinées* with the seven liberal arts, the traditional branches of learning: grammar, logic, rhetoric, arithmetic, geometry, astronomy and music. In France and Belgium, three new arts were added to the list: cinema (somewhat confusingly known as the seventh art), photography, and *bandes dessinées* as the ninth." (Screech 2005, 1)

2. Here are two examples: In February 1965 France sent a satellite named Astérix into orbit; Asteroid 29401 has also been named in honor of the hero.

3. "Les ventes d'albums BD représentent en effet aujourd'hui environ 33% du marché du livre et 6,5% du chiffre d'affaires global de l'édition française." Cf. http://www.republique-des-lettres.fr/10230-bande-dessinee.php. In addition, there is a useful summary of the evolution of the BD market during the past ten years in France: http://www.auracan.com/Dossiers/dossier.php?item=101.

4. Excerpt from the ACBD report of 2007, translated from the French. http://www.acbd.fr/les-bilans-de-l-acbd.html.

Since 1948 Jacques Martin has produced twenty-six volumes of *Alix l'intrépide* (see figure 13.1), a series which took its initial inspiration from *Ben Hur*—replacing Judas Ben Hur with a young nobleman from Gaul, Alix, who finds himself enslaved following the death of his father while fighting for Crassus in Parthia in 53 BC (Aziza 2008, 129). This character then (not unlike Ben Hur) reclimbs the social ladder and ends up traveling the ancient world as special agent for Caesar. Aziza makes a convincing case that the topics tackled in this series provide some insight into French postwar mentality. Collaboration, resistance, colonization, independence, revenge, and the notion that the past was greater than the present—all leave their mark on the story lines of *Alix*. The hero meets rebellious Gauls, Etruscans, and Greeks who long for their ancient glory, Egyptians and Africans who grapple with the new reality of being a Roman colony, Carthaginians desiring revenge, and Iberians pursuing independence.[5]

The blonde Alix is given a sidekick in his young, dark-haired servant, Enak. Enak provides necessary assistance to his master and is vital for keeping sex out of these volumes. Thanks to him, Alix is never given an opportunity to exercise his seductive Gallic *charme* while alone (the one exception is Cleopatra in a bathtub, but who seduces whom in this particular instance is open to debate). We still are a far cry here from the libertine and graphic notions of sexuality and violence, which popular perception associates with antiquity nowadays and which have subsequently been depicted in *Murena* and *Les aigles de Rome*.

In the same way that politics, culture, and society of the present resound in Alix' past, the attentive reader will also find that other versions of the past have influenced Martin's ancient world. I am not inclined to quarrel over whether the author's depiction of the Parthenon is archaeologically accurate or mirrors the whitewashed image created by the Victorians, as personally I consider this to be of subordinate importance. There are nevertheless instances in which the reader feels reminded of passages in Suetonius or discovers scenes inspired by Fellini: According to Suetonius (*Tib.* 44.1), the elderly emperor Tiberius famously entertained himself in his villa retreat on the island of Capri by having young boys dive though his legs while bathing in his pool in the nude, an image that Martin transfers onto a corrupt Roman governor who bathes in the company of youngsters.[6] When compared to its younger brother, *Astérix*, the *Alix* series provides a less ironically distanced image of antiquity. In-jokes and overt references to contemporaneous events feature much less prominently than in *Astérix*, where modern-day events such as the Tour de France or the French fashion industry are frequently woven into the plot.

The multilayered approach of the latter series—its humor works equally for its young and its mature readers—also results in a different attitude toward women. While we see them through the eyes of boys in *Alix*, *Astérix* provides us with an adult and at times rather chauvinistic perspective toward the female half of the human species—ancient Rome remains a man's world (as is exemplified by many of the names given to female characters in the English translation of Bell and Hockridge, including Bacteria, Melodrama, Influenza, and Impedimenta).

Translated into more than one hundred languages, *Astérix*, by René Goscinny (writer) and Albert Uderzo (artist), is the most famous francophone BD export. It appeared initially in

---

5. Aziza (2008, 131) lists detailed examples with a contemporaneous ring to the French audience, reminding those readers of World War II collaboration or massacres during the Algerian war.

6. Aziza (2008, 131) provides further examples, such as the use of the slaves' hair as napkins.

FIGURE 13.1   Alix, a young Gallo-Roman boy, got into all kinds of adventures. Art by Jaques Martin.
Cover art for *Alix l'intrépide* (Dargaud, 1956).

the magazine *Pilote* in Autumn 1959 but subsequently proved so popular that thirty-three volumes of the series have appeared since 1961; eight animated and three live-action film adaptations have also been made; and an Astérix theme park has been created near Paris.[7] Indeed, *Astérix* is ingrained in French culture in a way comparable perhaps only to the status enjoyed by *The Simpsons* in parts of the United States. Set in 50 BCE, the French series introduces the inhabitants of a village in the province of Armorica, near the northwestern coast of France. Thanks to the magic potion of their druid, Panoramix, they are able to resist the forces of Roman colonization and of Caesar in particular. With *Astérix*, the authors have deliberately created two antiheroes: the former, quick witted but somewhat short, is paired with a friendly but dumb counterpart of Herculean strength, who comes as a package with his minute pet, Dogmatix.

The origins of *Astérix* in the 1950s and '60s coincide with the administration of Charles de Gaulle, a period in which France made efforts to (re-)establish itself as a force in global politics and enjoyed times of unprecedented economic growth. In this period France showed a strong self-consciousness in rebuffing both the Soviet Union and the United States. France nurtured prestigious industrial and infrastructural projects (expressways, the extension of Marseille harbor, the supersonic Concorde planes), and it became the world's fourth nuclear power. In this period a strong France generally aimed to drive back the *impérialisme américain* on both a political and a cultural level. Looking at the stoutly independent Gallic community depicted in *Astérix*, which is fighting an overbearing Roman empire, one is tempted to draw parallels to contemporaneous French politics.[8]

Rather than seeking explicit references, however, I think *Astérix* plays in a humorous way with (and often flatters) the French self-perception of being *the* cultural exception.[9] This becomes apparent whenever *Astérix* ventures abroad. Foreign tribes are usually represented as satirized prototypes of their modern counterparts.[10] The British are thus shown as polite and phlegmatic, drinking hot water with a drop of milk and driving their chariots on the left side of the road (*Asterix in Britain* 1966). Apart from offering necessary strategic support to their British "cousins," the Gauls bring tea to what will quickly become a nation of tea drinkers (battle technique is somewhat hampered by 5 PM "hot water with a drop of milk breaks"). Passages like this manifest an ancient world populated by modern stereotypes to whom the Gauls can measure up and even contribute. These national caricatures might also help to

---

7. Animated films: *Asterix the Gaul* (1967), *Asterix and Cleopatra* (1968), *The Twelve Tasks of Asterix* (1976), *Asterix versus Caesar* (1985), *Asterix in Britain* (1986), *Asterix and the Big Fight* (1989), *Asterix Conquers America* (1994), and *Asterix and the Vikings* (2006). Live-action films: *Asterix and Obelix Take On Caesar* (1999), *Asterix & Obelix: Mission Cleopatra* (2002), and *Asterix at the Olympic Games* (2008).

8. It is, of course, true that the Goths, who represent the Germans in the worldview of the series, are being depicted in a rather unflattering and militaristic way following anti-German sentiment after World War II (cf. *Asterix and the Goths* 1963), but this seems to fade away in later volumes in which Goths feature (*Asterix the Legionary* 1966 and *Asterix and Obelix All at Sea* 1996). The depiction of the Romans, on the other hand, seems to be free from Nazi connotations.

9. For this reason the German-speaking press usually refers to France as "*la grande nation*."

10. In the ethnic geography of Astérix, suffixes denote origin. Normans use *-af* (Toocleverbyhaf), Vikings use *-ssen* (Herendthelessen), Egyptians use *-is* (Edifis, Artifis), Greeks use *-es* or *-os* (Diabetes, Thermos), Britons use *-ax* (Hiphiphurrax, Valueaddedtax), Goths (i.e., Germans) use *-ric* (Rhetoric, Choleric, Metric), and Spaniards use Spanish-sounding names such as Huevos Y Bacon ("Eggs and Bacon").

explain its huge success with the French audience and the immense difficulties confronted when translating them.

In this ancient world minor characters often resemble famous French people, a technique of cameo appearances now common in the American television series *The Simpsons*, with the marked difference that in the French series these cameos need to be fitted into antiquity. In *Obelix and Co.* (1976) the figure of the Roman bureaucrat Preposterus, who attempts to introduce the Gauls to capitalism, is a caricature of a young Jacques Chirac. What is more, Goscinny and Uderzo frequently employ popular images of the ancient world prevalent in their own day. Cleopatra in *Asterix and Cleopatra* (1965), for instance, is very Elizabeth Taylor-esque; a cheese fondue orgy scene in *Asterix in Switzerland* (1970) recalls Fellini's *Satyricon*; and in *Asterix and Obelix All at Sea* (1996), the leader of the escaped slaves, named Spartakis, is based on Kirk Douglas's portrayal of Spartacus in the 1960 film.

A further facet of the humor in this series derives from the speaking names of the minor characters, which are rendered differently in translation. Used sparingly in the early volumes of the series, this source of humor soon became a characteristic fixture. Dogmatix, for example, is a double pun on dog/dogmatics and thus to some extent takes up the original French pun on *idée fixe* in the original French name of *Idéfix*. The druid's name, however, has undergone considerable metamorphoses: Originally Panoramix in French, English translations have dubbed him—less respectfully—Getafix, and Germans named him Miraculix (evoking a famous instant spaghetti sauce). Examples abound.[11]

Moreover, there are even some overt references to Latin. Caesar uses the third person to talk about himself, an allusion to his *De bello gallico*, in which he reports on his conquest of Gaul in the third person. He also frequently parades "*et tu, Brute?*" in various contexts, as well as his proverbial "*alea iacta est*" [the die has been cast]. The authors do not shy away from the frequent use of Latin (usually annotated with a translation in a note) and let the most unlikely character of all, a peg-legged, second-in-command pirate, quote Latin almost constantly, usually in response to yet another sinking of the pirates' ship ("*sic transit gloria mundi*"). We also find Latin quotations from the Vulgate and more modern historical figures such as "*Cogito ergo sum*" (René Descartes), which is used as a password in *Asterix the Legionary* (1967).[12] As so often, the knowing reader will derive considerable entertainment from detecting from what elements the Rome of *Astérix* is built.

While the *Astérix* series is not solely aimed at mature readers and works well as children's literature as well, other series aim solely at a more mature market. Thus, we find a science-fiction adaptation of Gustave Flaubert's famous Carthage novel, *Salammbô* (P. Druillet, 3 vols., 1981,

---

11. The chief of the village Vitalstatistix is named *Abraracourcix* ("*à bras raccourcis*" ["with arms up [and] ready to fight"]) in French and *Majestix* in German. In *Asterix the Gladiator* (1964; English, 1969) a Roman guard uses this line: "Open up, Sendervictorius! It's me, Appianglorius!" This is a pun on lines from the UK's national anthem "God Save the Queen": "Send her victorious, happy and glorious." In addition, the British chief, Mykingdomforanos, is named in reference to the line "A horse, a horse, my kingdom for a horse!" from Shakespeare's *Richard III*, act 5, scene 4.

12. Some new puns are introduced in translation, often to great effect. Obelix' favorite line, "These Romans are crazy," first used in *Asterix the Gladiator* (1964), has its Italian equivalent in "Sono pazzi questi romani," which, like the banner of the Roman Empire ("*Senatus Populusque Romanus*"), abbreviates as SPQR. The French does not make this pun: *Ils sont fous ces Romains!*

1982, and 1986), as well as versions of both Apuleius' *Golden Ass* and Petronius' *Satyricon*.[13] Then there are also those *bandes dessinées* that aim solely at the adult market: The series *Les amours de l'histoire—bandes dessinées pour adultes* (Jean Arpa, Sexbulles, ca. 1975–1980, nos. 4–7) introduces us rather graphically to the sex life of ancient Rome. First, in *Cléobis, jumelle de Cléopâtre*, the younger sister of Cleopatra makes the intimate acquaintance of Mark Anthony. Then *Messaline impératrice* details the excesses of the wife of the emperor Claudius. Third, *Domitia et Domitien* gives insights into the Flavian bedroom. Finally, *La prostitution à Rome* provides a useful survey of what one might expect when visiting a Roman prostitute. Here ancient Rome serves solely as an excuse to serve up pornography hidden under the cloak of history.

In addition to using Greek and Roman antiquity in its original setting with story lines relating (however remotely) to ancient history, there are also examples of a creative employment of antiquity mixed with elements of science fiction. Most notable among these is the series *Le dernier Troyen* [(*The Last of the Trojans*], by Valérie Mangin (writer) and Thierry Démarez (artist). Six volumes have appeared since 2004, which, taking inspiration from Homer and Virgil, tell the foundation story of a galactic Rome. After the planet Troy suffers ten years of siege and is finally destroyed, Aeneas, one of the survivors, is urged by Minerva to go after Odysseus, who is held responsible for the fall of Troy.[14] The titles of the volumes mirror famous episodes from the epics but are set in the context of a space odyssey. While *Le cheval de Troie* [*The Trojan Horse*] (January 2004) tells of the fall of planet Troy, in *La reine des Amazones* [*The Queen of the Amazons*] (November 2004), Aeneas helps the warrior women to save their planet from Minerva's curse. *Les Lotophages* [*The Lotus Eaters*] (September 2005), *Carthago* (August 2006), and *Au-delà du Styx* [*Beyond the Styx*] (September 2007) construct a journey of Aeneas and his last Trojans along the lines of famous stops in the *Odyssey* and the *Aeneid* (or indeed both) before the travelers finally arrive on their new planet, Rome, which is inhabited by dinosaurs and harbors a sunken city in its swamps. This series, obviously inspired by ancient epic and myth, intelligently recontextualizes characters and events in a way that makes them work in the world of science fiction and thus creates galactic myth out of Greek myth.[15]

The story line of *Murena* (Dufaux and Delaby, 2001–present) begins in 54 CE. The death of the Emperor Claudius and the accession of his stepson, Nero, feature in the first volume, combined with a subplot, which focuses on Murena, the son of Claudius' historically attested mistress, Lollia Paulina (*PIR*[2] L 308). Murena is a friend of the young Nero. He sees his mother murdered through one of the ploys of Nero's mother, Agrippina, in the wake of the change of regime and vows revenge (not knowing yet whom he is fighting). At the end of the second volume Britannicus has been murdered, and by the end of the third Nero is smitten with Acte, whom he has taken from Pallas (whom the authors have murdered somewhat prematurely), and signs the death warrant for his aunt Domitia Lepida. Agrippina is at the height of her powers. Volume four details her slow demise and sounds the death knell for the first five "good"

13. For Apuleius see *Les sorcières de Thessalie* (G. Pichard, 2 vols., 1985 and 1986) and *La métamorphose de Lucius* (M. Manara, 1999) and for Petronius, *Péplum* (Blutch, 1997). In addition, there is also a version of the *Odyssey* in *Heavy Metal*, *Ulysses* (Sept. 2007) by Homer, Lob, and G. Pichard (see Jenkins in this volume).

14. My discussion is indebted to Aziza (2008, 155).

15. The website *Chroniques de l'antiquité galactique* provides a mythological key to the personage of the series; cf. http://www.mangin.tv/chroniques/troyen.html.

years of Nero's reign. Seneca appeases the Senate, and Poppaea sets her designs on Nero. Volumes five and six focus on the personal quest of Murena, his love for Acte, Nero's decline into mental instability, and Poppaea's scheming and voracious sex life. Volume six ends with the death of Acte, an event that, one assumes, will trigger some form of revenge by Murena in future volumes. While the first four volumes orient themselves strongly on classical sources, volumes five and six cover a period for which the body of source material is thinner and thus allow for more artistic freedom to be applied.

Murena clearly is a series with high aspirations. On the one hand, each volume concludes with a brief glossary that provides additional information about some scenes. Ranging from historical dates and details, such as when exactly Agrippina died and by soldiers of which regiment she was murdered, it also provides the occasional reference to ancient sources. Thus, shortly after observing Agrippina's attempt to seduce her son Nero, Seneca is shown writing a letter brooding over man's enslavement to his desires, which is identified in the glossary as letter 104 *ad Lucilium*. In addition, some information that might disturb the eroticism of this seduction scene is relegated to the back of the volume: Here we are told that, at the time, Nero was twenty-one years old, while Agrippina was forty-three. Furthermore, the authors also make use of the opportunity to give pointers to episodes in previous volumes that relate to particular passages in which characters have been introduced or props acquired (as when Agrippina acquires various potions and poisons in volume 1). On the other hand, each volume (except for the fourth) contains a detailed bibliography listing not only primary sources such as Suetonius and Tacitus but also a mix of secondary scholarly literature and also previous takes on ancient Rome, which have inspired the authors of *Murena*.[16] What is more, the back cover of each volume is graced by a quotation of an ancient author (in translation), many of which are also series characters: the voices of Seneca from *de brevitate vitae* and his letters, of Suetonius' *Life of Claudius* and *Life of Nero*, Agrippina (as recorded in a letter to Seneca), and the second-century orator Calpurnius Flaccus.[17] Simultaneously the authors signal from the outset, even to the potential buyer who has not even opened the volume, that they have done their study of sources.

The fourth volume (*Murena: Ceux qui vont mourir* [*Murena: Those Who Are about to Die*] 2002), however, poses an exception as it seeks the dialogue with the readers in a novel way. Instead of a bibliography, the final page offers a letter of thanks by the author, Jean Dufaux, to a number of academics who have provided production advice and corrections of technical terms that had been used or spelled incorrectly.[18] In addition, Dufaux announces that the reader has arrived at an important structural divide in the *Murena* series. The fourth volume

16. One example is the bibliography of volume three, *Murena—La meilleure des mères* ("The Best of All Mothers," 2001) in the original format: *La Rome antique* (B. Andreae); *La vie dans les cités antiques* (Conolly and Dodge); *Fragments de la Rome antique* (Massimiliano David); *La vie quotidienne à Rome à l'apogée de l'empire* (Jérôme Carcopino); *Quo Vadis* (H. Sienkiewicz); *La littérature latine* (P. Grimal); *Les jeux des Grecs et des Romains* (Wilhelm Richter); and *Histoire de la vie privée de l'Empire romain à l'an mil* (P. Ariès and G. Duby).

17. A quote from his eighth declamation, *Demens ter triumphalis* [The Insane Man Who Had Celebrated Three Triumphs] graces the back of vol. 6: "Un homme qui a connu une longue période de prospérité est sujet à toutes les catastrophes. Le succès ne sait se fixer et toutes les fois que la prospérité ne peut aller de l'avant, elle fait marche arrière" [A man who has experienced prosperity for a long time is subject to all kinds of catastrophes. Success cannot last, and whenever prosperity cannot continue without hindrance, it has to reverse] (H.8.15, *Omnium calamitatum materia est homo diu felix. Nesciunt stare successus, et quotiens felicitas prodire non potest, redit*).

18. *Frigidarium* for *frigidum* and "la gens Claudia" or "la gens des Claudii" rather than "la gens des Claudia."

features the death of Agrippina and the rise of Poppaea Sabina. This marks the end of the first cycle of four volumes, called *Le cycle de la mère*, in which Agrippina plays a decisive role. The second cycle, again in four volumes, is titled *Le cycle de l'épouse*, and one may realistically expect that Poppaea takes over where Agrippina leaves off.[19] Indeed, Poppaea is introduced to the reader as the successor chosen by Agrippina: The latter, aware that her time is up, meets the former and passes on a love potion that will secure sexual power over Nero. The mother's revenge is to install another unscrupulous woman at the side of her son. The vengeance plot inserts energy into the narrative and secures its continuation. Volume 4 also begins with a letter by Michael Green (researcher and consultant for the movie *Gladiator*), praising the virtues and the creative force of the *Murena* series. Clearly the authors aim to have their labors acknowledged and are not shy about displaying their ambitions. Indeed, in response to the commercial success of the series, the publishing house Dargaud brought out a special edition of the *Murena* volumes in 2007, accompanied by a DVD showcasing Dufaux and Delaby at work.[20] Dufaux is shown in his study/library with piles of art books, researching visualizations and archaeological reconstructions of the ancient world. Delaby reveals what lies behind the erotic appeal of some of his characters.[21]

All of this might lead the reader to expect a rather scholarly, not to say schoolmasterly, approach to the times of Nero. On the contrary, the *Murena* series successfully creates a fictitious ancient Rome with only the varnish of historical authenticity. Aziza speaks of a small miracle that reconciles the fans of *Alix* with those of *Messaline impératrice* (Aziza 2008, 168). Indeed, up to a certain point it is the frankness with which the authors depict violence, sexuality, and slavery, which makes *Murena* a great read for those in search of sex and crime while still allowing for a multilayered story line. In fact, it might be the characters of the slaves that allow the most freedom of design to the authors of *Murena*. Several subplots involve slaves. The opening scene shows naked gladiators fighting in an arena (figure 13.2). Only through the intervention of young Britannicus is one Nubian slave, named Balba, spared. He will later dedicate himself to the lost cause of Britannicus (and Murena). Agrippina as well has a former gladiator, her bodyguard, Draxius, with whom she has an erotic relationship. Nero recognizes that he cannot rid himself of his mother as long as her bodyguard is alive. Nero, too, uses a former gladiator, Massam, to do the dirty work for him. As the plot evolves, Massam and Balba soon find themselves in opposing camps.

What is more, several key scenes illustrate the social position of a slave in the world of Nero. In volume 1, when Agrippina goes poison shopping at Locusta's, the latter demonstrates the effects of her potion on a slave who duly swallows it and dies. Later Agrippina has one of her bath attendants drowned, Massam feeds the flesh of a slave actor to his panther, and Nero hands a sword to a slave with the command to slit his own throat so as not to have any witnesses to his command to kill his mother.

19. So far only two volumes of the second cycle have appeared.

20. *Murena, Le sang des bêtes, la sueur des auteurs* [*The Blood of the Beasts, the Sweat of the Authors*), by Chantal Notté and Nicholas Lourosa (Dargaud 2007).

21. Delaby models some of the major characters of *Murena* on famous actors whose movements and body shapes he studies in detail. The world of Murena is thus anachronistically peopled by a young Sophia Loren and Gina Lollobrigida as Agrippina and Poppea and an old Christopher Lee as a Gallic druid.

FIGURE 13.2 The *bande dessinée Murena* presents a Rome for a more mature audience. Cover art by Philippe Delaby. *Murena* 1 (Dargaud, June 2001).

Rome is a brutal and ruthless society in the eyes of Dufaux and Delaby and a world in which sex is the ultimate weapon. In addition to slaves of both sexes frequently featuring as sex toys, we find Agrippina stepping out of the bathing pool and attempting to seduce Nero, Petronius lusting after Murena, and Agrippina and Poppaea having sex with numerous characters in exchange for political favors. All in all, Dufaux and Delaby's concept of mixing history with fiction is daring and gripping (and not dissimilar from that applied in the recent BBC/HBO series *Rome*, which covers the rise of Augustus). They have successfully brought Rome into the twenty-first century in *bandes dessinées* format.

An even sexier Rome is provided by Marini in his volume *Les aigles de Rome* [*The Eagles of Rome*] (Dargaud 2007; see figure 13.3). At the request of Augustus, a Roman family brings up a young noble Gallic hostage as their son together with their own children, a daughter and a son. The two boys go through military training and discover the joys of courtesans. At the end of the first volume the Roman Empire is their oyster, though a Gallic revolt might put their friendship to a test. The second volume has now been published (2009) and the setup will allow for many more volumes to come. The future of Rome in *bandes dessinées* seems certain.

Even though my survey is brief, the examples nonetheless illustrate that *bandes dessinées* that are set in antiquity do not exist in a vacuum that is uninfluenced by the politics and culture of their own times. Contemporaneous conflicts, as well as fashions and attitudes, find their mirror image in the ancient Rome of *bandes dessinées*, which becomes ever more violent, sexual, and sophisticated; in this way the ninth Muse follows in the footsteps of her older sisters and secures enduring success and a wide audience for its visionary antiquity.[22]

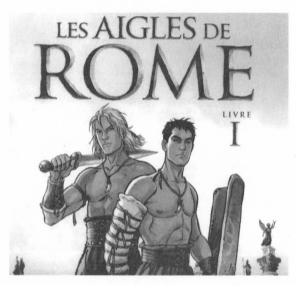

FIGURE 13.3 *Les aigles de Rome* is one of the most recent *bandes dessinées* to depict Rome. Art by Enrico Marini. *Les aigles de Rome* 1 (Dargaud, 2007).

22. I wish to thank Oliver Norris for his assistance with researching the material for this chapter.

PART FOUR

The Desires of Troy

EVEN THEN I KNEW SUCH A PROJECT WOULD BE A HUGE UNDERTAKING.

YEAH, RIGHT-- LIKE I'M NOT UP TO MY EYEBALLS IN WORK RIGHT NOW.

BUT THE IDEA WOULDN'T LET ME GO.

DOWN, BOY! *GO HOME!*

SO BEGAN *AGE OF BRONZE*, MY RETELLING OF THE TROJAN WAR IN THE MEDIUM OF COMICS.

AS A CHILD I'D BEEN THROUGH SEVERAL PERIODS OF ENTHUSIASM FOR GREEK MYTHOLOGY.

AFF-ROW-DIE-*TEE*?! YOU MEAN THE "E" ISN'T *SILENT*?

D'AULAIRE'S BOOK OF GREEK MYTHS

I'D GREATLY PREFERRED THE STORIES OF JASON, PERSEUS, AND THESEUS TO ANY KIDS' VERSION OF THE TROJAN WAR I'D READ.

AND OF COURSE I'D LOVED BOTH *JASON AND THE ARGONAUTS* AND *I, CLAUDIUS* ON TV.

EW, LOOK AT THE HAIRY BACK ON THE GUY PLAYING SEJANUS! WHO IS THAT?

SOME ACTOR NAMED -- UM -- PATRICK STEWART.

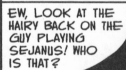

EXCEPT FOR SOPHOKLES'S **ANTIGONE** IN HIGH SCHOOL AND AN ABORTED ATTEMPT AT AESCHYLUS'S **AGAMEMNON**, I'D NEVER READ ANY GREEK OR ROMAN CLASSICAL LITERATURE. FOR THE FIRST TIME I CRACKED THE COVER OF HOMER'S **ILIAD**.

ACHILLES KILLING HEKTOR-- IT'S SO POWERFUL AND BRUTAL. I'M **ITCHING** TO DRAW IT.

UH, LET'S SEE, **HOW MANY** YEARS TILL I REACH THIS SCENE?

BACK THEN I HAD LITTLE CONCEPTION OF THE TRUE IMMENSITY OF MY TASK.

THE STORY OF THE TROJAN WAR IS AT LEAST 2800 YEARS OLD. THAT'S A LOT OF TIME TO ACCUMULATE VARIATIONS IN ALL SORTS OF MEDIA-- POETRY, PLAYS, PROSE, PAINTING, SCULPTURE, OPERA, POP MUSIC.

OKAY, I HAVE PLATO, COLLUTHUS, TRYPHIODORUS, LYCOPHRON, HYGINUS, OVID, PARTHENIUS, PINDAR...

GAAAH! THERE ARE **NO** ENGLISH TRANSLATIONS OF PHILOSTRATUS'S **HEROIKOS** AND JOHANNES TZETZES'S **HOMERICA!***

*THE **HEROIKOS** WAS FINALLY PUBLISHED IN ENGLISH IN 2001. STILL NO ENGLISH TZETZES AS FAR AS I KNOW.

THE STORY GROWS HEADS LIKE THE HYDRA. TROILUS, MENTIONED ONLY ONCE IN HOMER'S **ILIAD**, GAINED A DEATH DEVELOPED IN VASE PAINTINGS, GAINED A LOVER NAMED CRESSIDA IN THE MIDDLE AGES, WAS TAKEN OVER BY SHAKESPEARE IN THE RENAISSANCE, AND WAS GIVEN HIS OWN OPERA IN THE 20TH CENTURY.

...SO HENRYSON SAYS CRESSIDA BECAME A LEPER. DID LEPROSY **EXIST** IN THE AEGEAN LATE BRONZE AGE? OR IS IT A CODE WORD FOR VENEREAL DISEASE?

EVEN NOW, TEN YEARS AFTER **AGE OF BRONZE** BEGAN PUBLICATION, I'M STILL FINDING NEW MATERIAL. IT'S **ALL** GRIST FOR MY MILL.

THIS GUY SAYS THAT **DIOMEDES** WAS REINCARNATED AS **SADDAM HUSSEIN!**

THE STORY IS ONLY ONE ASPECT OF *AGE OF BRONZE*. COMICS HAVE DRAWINGS AS WELL AS WORDS.

THE CAST OF THE TROJAN WAR IS AS ENDLESS AS THE STORY'S SOURCES, SO I'VE GOT A LOT OF CHARACTERS TO DESIGN. MOST OFTEN I DEVELOP THEIR APPEARANCES THROUGH CASUAL SKETCHING.

ONCE IN A WHILE A PICTURE IN A BOOK OR MAGAZINE WILL STRIKE ME AS APPROPRIATE FOR A PARTICULAR CHARACTER.

I DON'T CARE IF HOMER MADE ACHILLES BLOND. I'VE *NEVER* SEEN A BLOND IN LATE BRONZE AGE AEGEAN ART.

I LIKED THE FACE OF THE CENTAUR CHEIRON IN THIS WALL PAINTING FROM FIRST CENTURY CE HERCULANEUM.

THAT'S WHAT *MY* CHEIRON LOOKS LIKE, TOO--EXCEPT THERE ARE NO OVERT SUPERNATURAL ELEMENTS IN *AGE OF BRONZE*. SO NO HORSE BODY FOR HIM.

WHEN IT CAME TO DESIGNING HELEN -- THE FACE THAT LAUNCHED A THOUSAND SHIPS -- I WAS A BIT INTIMIDATED. I STUDIED PAINTINGS AND SCULPTURES OF WOMEN FROM LATE BRONZE AGE GREECE -- THE MYCENAEAN PERIOD.

THIS WAS THE HEIGHT OF BEAUTY? HUH!

THEN I PERUSED LATER GREEK REPRESENTATIONS OF WOMEN... AND FOUND THE PEPLOS KORE, A STATUE FROM AROUND 530 BCE.

THAT EXPRESSION OF HAUGHTY HUMOR... *PERFECT* FOR HELEN.

I'VE INCORPORATED OTHER WORKS OF GREEK ART--FOR INSTANCE THIS ATTIC RED-FIGURE CUP OF ACHILLES AND PATROKLUS FROM AROUND 500 BCE.

YOUR ARM'S WOUNDED TWICE.

GOTTA CHANGE THAT CLASSICAL ARMOR TO *BRONZE AGE* GEAR, THOUGH.

IT'S IMPORTANT TO GET THE COSTUMES, THE HAIRSTYLES, THE ARCHITECTURE, AND THE LANDSCAPE RIGHT.

FORTUNATELY, THE MYCENAEANS-- HOMER'S ACHAEANS--LEFT MANY REPRESENTATIONS OF THEMSELVES.

SOME OF THEIR ARMOR AND WEAPONS STILL SURVIVE.

WILL YOU REQUIRE LINEN OR BRONZE GREAVES WITH THAT OUTFIT, SIR?

WE HAVE A GOOD IDEA WHAT THEIR CHARIOTS LOOKED LIKE...

...AND THEIR BOATS...

...AND THEIR PALACES.

WE HAVE GUESTS. THE SONS OF ATREUS—AGAMEMNON THE HIGH KING AT MYCENAE AND MENELAUS THE KING OF LAKEDAEMON. WELCOME.

OF COURSE, VARIOUS AMOUNTS OF RECONSTRUCTION ARE OFTEN NECESSARY.

I RESTORED THE DESIGN ABOVE THE LION GATE AT AGAMEMNON'S CAPITAL, MYCENAE, BY EXTRAPO-LATING FROM A BRONZE AGE GEM CARVING FOUND THERE.

THE BRONZE AGE LEVELS OF TROY IN NORTHWEST TURKEY CAN BE PLAUSIBLY RECONSTRUCTED.

BUT WHAT DID THE *TROJANS* LOOK LIKE? THEY LEFT NO PICTURES!

I LEARNED THAT MAJOR NEW EXCAVATIONS HAD OPENED AT TROY IN 1988. IN 1997 I WENT TO A SMITHSONIAN CONFERENCE TO ASK DR. MANFRED KORFMANN, THE EXCAVATION DIRECTOR:

WHAT WOULD THE LATE BRONZE AGE TROJAN PEOPLE HAVE LOOKED LIKE?

AND HE SAID:

LOOK AT THE HITTITES.

BUT WHAT WOULD MY CHARACTERS SOUND LIKE? I COULD HAVE FALLEN INTO THE TRAP OF ANACHRONISTIC, PSEUDO-SHAKESPEAREAN GOBBLEDY-GOOK.

MY LORD! WHAT HO, MY LORD! MEANEST THOU TO ATTACK TROY, MY LORD?

GOOD LORD!

AND ANY ATTEMPT TO SEEM CURRENT WOULD JUST DATE THE PROJECT FAST.

LET'S GET SHIZZY IN THE HIZZY!

WORD!

ABSURD!

I SETTLED ON PLAIN, UNADORNED ENGLISH--ALTHOUGH MANY OF MY SOURCES ARE ANYTHING *BUT*.

I CAN GET USED TO "V"S FOR "U"S AND "S"S THAT LOOK LIKE "F"S, BUT THIS MODERN ENGLISH TRANSLATION OF SOPHOKLES'S FRAGMENTARY PLAY *THE SHEPHERDS* IS *TOO MUCH*.

THERE'S ONLY *ONE* WAY TO TRANSLATE "STRIKING YOUR BUTTOCKS WITH THE FLAT OF MY FOOT"!

WITH HIS HELP I'LL KICK YOUR ASS!

RECONCILING CONTRADICTORY VERSIONS CAN BE TRICKY--LIKE THE ONE POPULARIZED BY THE 7TH-6TH CENTURY BCE POET STESICHORUS, WHERE HELEN NEVER WENT TO TROY BUT STAYED IN EGYPT DURING THE WAR.

I'LL HAVE HELEN GO TO TROY, BUT PARIS WILL EXPLAIN THAT DURING THEIR STOP IN EGYPT HE LEFT A WOMAN WHO **PASSED** FOR HELEN.

I WENT--I MEAN, I **SENT** BACK TO THE SHIPS TO GET ONE OF THE WOMEN I CAPTURED IN SIDON--ABOUT HELEN'S SIZE AND BUILD--

THEN THERE'S THE EPISODE IN WHICH AGAMEMNON SACRIFICES HIS DAUGHTER IPHIGENIA TO THE GODDESS ARTEMIS.

I USED EURIPIDES'S TRAGEDY **IPHIGENIA AT AULIS**, CIRCA 405 BCE, FOR MY STRUCTURE.

I WISH I COULD, MY DARLING. BUT I'M BOUND ON A LONG VOYAGE TO THE LAND OF THE TROJANS. YOU'LL BE TAKING A LONG VOYAGE, TOO-- AWAY FROM ME.

I INTEGRATED THE MANY OTHER WAYS IPHIGENIA'S STORY HAS BEEN TOLD OVER THE CENTURIES.

SUCH AS THE PORTENT OF TWO EAGLES KILLING A PREGNANT RABBIT RELATED BY THE CHORUS OF AESCHYLUS'S **AGAMEMNON**, HIS 458 BCE TRAGEDY.

BETWEEN 1929 AND 1931 EUGENE O'NEILL UPDATED THE SORDID STORY OF AGAMEMNON'S FAMILY IN HIS PLAY TRILOGY **MOURNING BECOMES ELECTRA**.

THIS SPEECH BY AGAMEMNON'S WIFE, KLYTEMNESTRA, WAS INSPIRED BY HER COUNTERPART'S DIALOG IN O'NEILL'S PLAY.

OTHER SOURCES PROVIDED A **VARIETY** OF DETAILS.

I FOUND THE NAME OF IPHIGENIA'S NURSE IN PINDAR'S ELEVENTH PYTHIAN ODE FROM 474 BCE--

--AND THE NAME OF ORESTES'S NURSE IN AESCHYLUS'S 458 BCE TRAGEDY **CHOEPHOROI**.

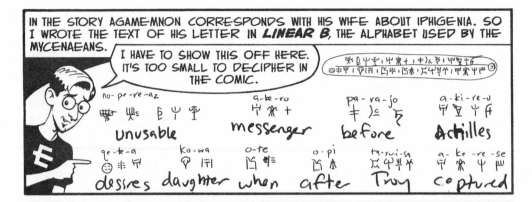

IN THE STORY AGAMEMNON CORRESPONDS WITH HIS WIFE ABOUT IPHIGENIA. SO I WROTE THE TEXT OF HIS LETTER IN *LINEAR B*, THE ALPHABET USED BY THE MYCENAEANS.

I HAVE TO SHOW THIS OFF HERE. IT'S TOO SMALL TO DECIPHER IN THE COMIC.

no-pe-re-a₂ — unusable
a-ke-ro — messenger
pa-ra-jo — before
a-ki-re-u — Achilles

qe-te-a — desires
ko-wa — daughter
o-te — when
o-pi — after
tu-rui-sa — Troy
a-ke-re-se — captured

WHEN I REACHED THE PART WHERE FOURTEEN-YEAR-OLD IPHIGENIA AGREES TO DIE SELFLESSLY FOR THE GREATER GLORY OF GREECE, I HAD A PROBLEM.

FATHER? I DON'T KNOW WHAT YOU NEED DONE, BUT I'D BE HAPPY TO DO IT FOR YOU--

WITH GREAT ACTORS AND A RECEPTIVE AUDIENCE, *MAYBE* THAT WORKS ON STAGE. BUT IN A COMIC BOOK? *NO WAY!*

FORTUNATELY I HAD OTHER SOURCES. JEAN RACINE'S PLAY *IPHIGENIA* DEBUTED IN 1674 AND GLUCK'S OPERA *IPHIGÉNIE EN AULIDE* ONE HUNDRED YEARS LATER.

RACINE MAKES IPHIGENIA AND ACHILLES LOVERS. GLUCK'S OPERA TAKES IT FURTHER AND ENDS WITH A CHORUS OF SOLDIER'S CELEBRATING THE LOVERS' WEDDING!

MON COEUR NE SAURAIT CONTENIR L'EXCÈS DE MON BONHEUR EXTRÊME...

THAT GAVE ME MY SOLUTION-- SHE DIES FOR LOVE! WHAT FOURTEEN-YEAR-OLD GIRL *WOULDN'T* WELCOME DEATH TO SAVE THE LIFE OF A SEVENTEEN-YEAR-OLD HUNK LIKE ACHILLES?

SON OF PELEUS, I WISH I REALLY *COULD* CALL YOU MY HUSBAND. YOU'D GIVE YOUR LIFE FOR ME-- LET ME GIVE MINE FOR *YOU*.

OF COURSE, SHE DOESN'T KNOW THAT HE'S ALSO CARRYING ON HOT AND HEAVY WITH *PATROKLUS!*

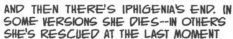

AND THEN THERE'S IPHIGENIA'S END. IN SOME VERSIONS SHE DIES--IN OTHERS SHE'S RESCUED AT THE LAST MOMENT BY THE GODS.

I'M ELIMINATING THE SUPER-NATURAL, SO I CAN'T SHOW IPHIGENIA FLOATING OFF ON A CLOUD. BUT THAT PART'S TOO WELL KNOWN TO IGNORE.

I FOUND A SOLUTION IN THE SPURIOUS ENDING TO EURIPIDES'S TRAGEDY. A MESSENGER RELATES THE RESCUED-BY-THE-GODS STORY TO KLYTEMNESTRA.

IF I GIVE THAT SPEECH TO ODYSSEUS, THERE'S *NO CHANCE* SHE'LL BELIEVE HIM. THAT COVERS BOTH VERSIONS *AND* BOLSTERS MY ANTI-SUPERNATURAL THEME! *PERFECT!*

A DOE... THEN WHERE'S MY DAUGHTER?

AS WE WATCHED A CLOUD CAME DOWN AND GATHERED HER UP. KALCHAS SAYS THE GODDESS SWEPT HER AWAY TO LIVE IN JOY WITH THE GODS.

IN THE MID-1990S I BEGAN TO LOOK FOR A PUBLISHER FOR *AGE OF BRONZE*.

IT'LL NEVER SELL!

IT'S THE *TROJAN WAR* FOR *&%$ SAKE! IF I CAN REACH AN AUDIENCE *OUTSIDE* THE SUPERHERO CROWD, IT *CAN'T* FAIL.

REJECTION NOTICE
Dear Mr. Shan
We received
regret to i

IN 1998, IMAGE COMICS--AT THE TIME KNOWN FOR BIG GUNS, BIG TITS, AND LITTLE SUBSTANCE--OFFERED ME A CONTRACT.

I'LL PUBLISH THAT!

WH-WHAT?

OF COURSE, I SEIZED THE OPPORTUNITY.

SINCE THEN, MAINSTREAM ACCEPTANCE OF COMICS IN THE FORM OF GRAPHIC NOVELS HAS BURGEONED. *AGE OF BRONZE* HAS DONE WELL. PARTICULARLY GRATIFYING IS THE ACCEPTANCE BY CLASSICISTS AND ARCHAEOLOGISTS.

WOULD YOU CONSIDER SPEAKING AT THE JOINT USC-UCLA GREEK SEMINAR?

MANFRED KORFMANN SENT ME HIS LATEST BOOK! AND MY AMAZON RANKING IS BETTER THAN IT WAS THIS MORNING!

Eric,
Just read the terrific article in Archaeology Magazine about Age

15

Eros Conquers All

Sex and Love in Eric Shanower's *Age of Bronze*

CHIARA SULPRIZIO

The graphic novel series *Age of Bronze* is the ongoing project of cartoonist Eric Shanower, whose professed goal is to "present the complete story of the world-famous War at Troy, freshly retold for the 21st century," by consulting and assimilating as many versions of the story as he can find. His source material includes ancient texts and modern adaptations, as well as media that fall in between both temporally and generically, such as Renaissance paintings, Romantic operas, and early twentieth-century excavation reports. Since 1998, twenty-eight issues have been published, and all except the most recent two have been collected into three volumes—*A Thousand Ships*, *Sacrifice*, and *Betrayal, Part One*.[1]

My first encounter with *Age of Bronze* (hereafter *AOB*) occurred in 2001, when a colleague informed me that a comic book about the Trojan War was being written that could perhaps be used as an undergraduate teaching tool. Epic and mythological subject matter features frequently in mainstream comic books and supplies them with a wealth of ancient figures, names, and places—one need only glance at an issue of *The Mighty Thor* or *Wonder Woman* to confirm this fact. However, these attributes are often subject to a standardizing process of comic "superheroization," which employs them in a way that bears little, if at all, upon their original contexts and renders them less than suitable for pedagogical purposes. It seemed probable that *AOB* would also fall into this category, but the striking image of two cartoon men labeled "Achilles" and "Patroklus" kissing in a passionate embrace and emblazoned on a red *AOB* T-shirt, which I encountered shortly after the exchange described, compelled me to rethink this assumption (figure 15.1). It rapidly became clear, after reading the official website and the first volume, that both the content and the intent of this comic were quite different from typical superhero-style renditions of the ancient Greek past. In his version of the Trojan War, not only is Shanower extremely attentive to detail and accuracy, drawing upon an exhaustive array of both literary sources and archaeological evidence in order to shape the narrative

---

1. The quote comes from the *Age of Bronze* website: http://age-of-bronze.com/aob/index.shtml. The three trade volumes were published by Image Comics, one each in 2001, 2005, and 2007, and each volume includes an extensive bibliography. All page numbers cited herein are keyed to these texts. In an interview, Shanower has stated that eight more volumes are planned, which he estimates may take twelve to fifteen years to complete; see Saunders (2007).

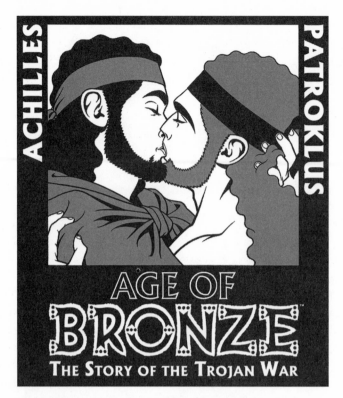

FIGURE 15.1   An image advertising *Age of Bronze* on a shirt signals
the importance of the erotic in the comic. Art by Eric Shanower.

and visual aspects of the story, but he is also exceptionally thoughtful and honest in his representations of the many distinct facets of human existence.

One might easily presume, given the focus on belligerence in the work, that this observation pertains especially to his depictions of the vagaries of war. This presumption is not so much
untrue as untried, however, since, at this point in the series, little actual fighting has occurred,
and scenes of sustained warfare between the Achaeans and the Trojans have yet to take place.[2]
This is a somewhat surprising absence, though, with eight more volumes to go, there is still
plenty of space for fighting in the future. What Shanower has chosen to foreground and elabo-
rate in the initial volumes are the personal relationships, in particular, the sexual and romantic
relationships, that both major and minor characters engage in. As the iconic image on the
T-shirt makes clear, the Trojan War that is depicted in *AOB* is, among other things, a remarkably sexy one, in which love and romance occupy a prominent place.[3] The cover art for each
issue currently in existence also bears out this claim. At least five of the covers, including the
first one, feature overtly erotic or amorous representations, while another five show female

2. A recent issue at the time of writing (*Age of Bronze* 27, July 2008) finally featured the first Achaean attack on the
Trojans during Hektor and Andromache's marriage ceremony.

3. There is one other *Age of Bronze* T-shirt, which shows Helen and Paris together, though they are not posed in
quite as racy or romantic a fashion.

characters who are largely defined by their roles as lovers, wives, and mothers in the epic in conspicuous, if slightly more ambiguous, positions vis-à-vis the male characters.[4]

In this chapter I investigate the broader significance of this artistic and authorial decision. Why have the themes of sex and love been given such extended treatment in *AOB*, at least up to this point? Is it a simple matter of being inclusive with regard to past versions of the story or something more? Also, how do Shanower's depictions of sexual and romantic relationships both shape and delimit his version of the Trojan War, and how are these depictions themselves defined by the serialized, comic medium in which they are presented? Finally, how has the decision to emphasize the amorous aspects of this story affected the composition of *Age of Bronze*'s audience?

The first of these questions has an obvious and seemingly simple answer. The themes of sex and love figure so prominently at the outset of the story precisely because they are foundational to it. As Shanower himself has pointed out, "The Trojan war began with sex and it ended in violence." Elsewhere he affirms, "You can't get away from the sex in the Trojan War. I mean, *that's why the war happened*. It's because of sex. I had to show that."[5] In nearly all ancient accounts, it is Paris' abduction of Helen that sets the narrative into motion, and without this turn of events—whether it was inspired by the goddess Eris' apple of discord and the infamous judgment it provoked or just by a vivid dream Paris claimed to have had of this incident, as is the case in *AOB*—there would be no war to recount.[6] Shanower accordingly gives their romance the attention it is due, and he does so in a way that consistently underscores the impulsive, lustful, and excessively physical nature of their attraction to one another (figure 15.2). The effects of this characterization, along with Helen's portrayal as a willing, if at times equivocal, participant in the relationship, are discussed later in the chapter. For now, however, it is safe to say that the level of attention Helen and Paris receive in *AOB* reflects the importance of their relationship and its prominence in the source material in a manner that is consistent with Shanower's goals of completeness, accuracy, and realism. But this raises the question: What about the other amorous liaisons that are presented throughout the course of the graphic novels? How should we account for their conspicuity?

A good number of these liaisons may be considered more tangential with regard to the larger narrative or less "traditional" (i.e., Homeric) than that of Helen and Paris, though they have been explored by Shanower with equal interest. These include the relationships between Paris and Oenone, Achilles and Deidamia, Troilus and Cressida, and Akamas and Laodike. There is also the troubling figure of Kassandra, who is represented along with her brother, Helenus, as a childhood

4. The first group of covers includes issues 1, 5, 10, 26, and the special issue, which reviewed the sordid family history of the Atreidae. The second group includes issues 7, 14, 16, 19, and 25. By way of comparison, the covers of eight issues depict combat scenes: issues 2, 6, 8, 12, 20, 22, 24, and 27. All can be viewed on the *Age of Bronze* website.

5. The quotes are from Romey (2004) and Keller (2000) (emphasis in the original), respectively.

6. Shanower's rendering of the judgment as a dream comes from an illustration in a late fifteenth-century manuscript of Raoul Le Fèvre's *Recueil des histoires de Troie* (1464). Like so many other medieval accounts of the Trojan War, Le Fèvre's version relied upon the fictitious eyewitness accounts of Dictys Cretensis and Dares Phrygius, titled "Chronicle of the Trojan War" (*Ephemeridos belli Troiani*) and "History of the Destruction of Troy" (*De excidio Troiae historia*), respectively. These Latin "translations" of purported Greek originals date to the fourth or fifth century CE and have typically been printed together. Frazer (1966) is the first modern English translation of the two works.

FIGURE 15.2   For Shanower, the physical element is important in explaining the motivations of Helen
and Paris. Art by Eric Shanower. *Age of Bronze* 23 (Image, May 2006).

victim of sexual molestation at the hands of the Trojan priest of Apollo (see figure 15.3). Finally,
the romance that receives the most detailed elaboration in *AOB*, apart from that of Helen and
Paris—is that of Achilles and Patroklus.

These relationships all share a similar structure, with young characters taking part in illegitimate and therefore ill fated affairs. Interestingly, they are all similarly represented by Shanower in
eroticized episodes that take on a graphic and sometimes violent quality in their physical depiction.[7] This standout aspect of the comic has been commented on by several reviewers, including
critic Douglas Wolk: "Many of the Trojan War's legends are about love so intense that it destroys
everything around it, and when Shanower draws lovers in each other's presence, the force of their
erotic attraction crackles from the page" (Wolk 2008, 2). Within the first twenty pages of the
work, for example, we encounter Paris surprising his bare-breasted lover, the mountain nymph
Oenone, with the news that he is leaving for Troy to participate in the games there. After some
discussion of his ill-omened decision, they are shown having what will be their last playful roll in
the hay, unaware that it will have serious consequences for both of them in the distant future.[8]

The presentation of this lesser-known story serves to introduce the reader in eye-opening fashion to Paris in his primary guise, that of impetuous lover (and big talker). However, it also sets a
certain tone for *AOB*, revealing it to be an erotically charged drama with some provocative content
and not just a heroic "guts and glory" war story. The theme of young lust is further developed in

7. Of course, other relationships contribute substantially to the narrative, such as that of Agamemnon and Klytemnestra, but, due to space constraints, I limit my discussion to those that fit my earlier description. I also exclude
from consideration the two young couples engaged in legitimate affairs, who have been only briefly introduced to
the story as of now: Aeneas and Kreusa, and Hektor and Andromache. It will be interesting to see how future issues
will portray the amorous aspects of these relationships.

8. See vol. 1, p. 27. The story of Oenone and Paris, in particular its tragic conclusion, in which she refuses to heal
him as he is dying, then regretfully throws herself on his pyre, is preserved in Quintus of Smyrna's *Posthomerica*
(10.259–489), a text that dates to the third century CE. According to his bibliography, Shanower relied on this
work (specifically, Combellack's 1968 translation), as well as Ovid's *Heroides*, Parthenius' *Erotica Pathemata*, Tennyson's poem "Oenone" (1833), and Thomas Heywood's Elizabethan *epillyon*, "Oenone and Paris" (1594), in constructing this episode.

FIGURE 15.3 As part of Shanower's rationalizing agenda, many divine "visitations" are given more sordid causes. Here Kassandra and Helenus recall their early apprenticeship in the temple of Apollo. Art by Eric Shanower. *Age of Bronze* 11 (Image, July 2001).

volume 1, as Paris goes on to seduce Helen and as Achilles becomes involved with Deidamia while living in hiding on Skyros as a daughter of King Lykomedes. This curious relationship, which has quasi-incestuous overtones (the two are ostensibly sisters) and places Achilles in the untenable position of being both a transvestite and a father, gives the reader insight into the hero's unusual prewar life. His own impulsive and violent tendencies are laid bare through the depiction of his rape of Deidamia, who fully believes him to be a girl despite one "pointed" episode to the contrary. Her rape is followed immediately by the birth of his son, Neoptolemus or Pyrrhus, and the intensity of this moment, as well as Achilles' frustration with it, is likewise captured through its explicit rendering in the text (figure 15.4).[9]

The gender trouble that Achilles finds himself in on Skyros is cut short for a brief time by his outing as a male at the hands of Odysseus and Diomedes, who then take him to join the assembling

9. Shanower's story of Deidamia and Achilles derives mainly from Statius' fragmentary work, *Achilleid* (first century CE), though the relationship also receives mention in Ovid's *Metamorphoses* (13.162ff.) and Apollodorus' *Library* (3.13.8). Note that the child's second name is a secret patronymic, which attests to Achilles' second identity as the girl Pyrrha.

FIGURE 15.4   Sexuality and its consequences are openly considered in *Age of Bronze* 7 (Image, April 2000). Art by Eric Shanower.

Achaean forces. However, his temporary return to Skyros in volume 2 (issue 14) brings his relationship with Deidamia back to the fore in a manner that again emphasizes its sexual aspect, only this time it serves to expose the limits of their impossible romance. Achilles' dissatisfaction in this episode brings him to yet another turning point with regard to his sexuality and compels him to express his hidden love for Patroklus in clear physical terms for the first time. Before turning to examine Shanower's portrayal of this exceptional affair, however, we should take note of two other romances that are given vivid treatment in *AOB*, namely, those of Troilus and Cressida, as well as Akamas and Laodike.

FIGURE 15.5   Menelaus recalls his wedding to Helen. Art by Eric Shanower. *Age of Bronze* 26 (Image, Sept 2007).

These two tales of tragic love are the furthest removed from the tradition that drives the main narrative, but each is given its own unique place in the graphic novel.[10] So far, the story of Troilus and Cressida has unfolded slowly. The two were introduced briefly in volume 1: she as the widowed daughter of the traitorous priest Kalchas, and he as the Trojan prince who secretly longs for her. Troilus' love grows throughout volume 2 but goes unrequited by Cressida, who laughs off his advances. Finally, in issue 24 he becomes lovesick and is overwhelmed by sexual fantasies of her. This brief episode is represented in rather explicit terms, although nothing has actually transpired between the two as of yet. Conversely, the story of Laodike and Akamas is introduced relatively late, near the end of volume 3 (issues 25 and 26). Their forbidden yet passionate encounter is given a few pages of elaboration (it also graces the cover of issue 26) and serves as a dramatic counterpoint to Menelaus' sad, drunken musings about his salad days with Helen (figure 15.5). How Shanower will

10. Troilus and Cressida's romance is a medieval creation made famous by Shakespeare, though it was also treated by literary greats such as Boccaccio, Chaucer, and Dryden. The story of Laodike and Akamas is alluded to only in passing by a few ancient sources, such as Tzetzes (*Schol. on Lycophron*, 495) and Parthenius (*Erot.* 16).

develop these two relationships remains to be seen, of course, but, for the purposes of this chapter, their significance lies in the contribution they make to *AOB*'s overall amatory atmosphere.

At first glance, the decision to depict these youthful romances in this way seems to conform to the interests and fantasies of the comic book genre's historically masculine, adolescent readership.[11] The racy sex scenes and the aggressive subtext underlying some of them may be viewed as providing the series with the elements of shock and scandal required by superhero-themed comics—elements that might otherwise be provided (at least in part) by battle and death scenes. Yet, when fuller consideration is given to both Shanower's authorial objectives and his inclusive approach to recounting the epic, it seems that his romantic depictions instead work to undermine many of the male-defined tropes and conventions that dictate how sexuality and violence are represented in comic books and graphic novels. Let us now examine the ways in which this unexpected result is brought about.

To begin with, Shanower's commitment to including as many variants and tangents of the story as possible reveals to (or recalls for) his readers, through sheer quantity alone, the preeminent place that love and sexual desire occupy in the literary and artistic tradition of the Trojan War. More important though, his distinctive method of "weaving all the versions into one smoothly flowing story" (Keller 2000) brings the issue of eros to the fore in a collective or integrated way—and in a vividly compelling way, given the medium—that no other adaptation does.[12] This effect may have been unintentional; as Shanower himself has noted, he did not set out to highlight these particular relationships over others.[13] Nevertheless, the romantic configuration of *AOB*, whether intended or not, foregrounds eros as a force that is as powerful and influential upon human life as war itself. In this Troy, love still serves to fan the flames of war, but just as often it offsets and overcomes them.

The critical role that sex and love are given in determining human action and structuring human interaction in *AOB* is part of Shanower's larger authorial goal of presenting a wide range of emotions and behaviors in a plausible fashion: "I want to tell the *entire* story of the Trojan War and make it look as close as possible to what it might have looked like if it were a true story. . . . It's a drama with as much of the texture of life and humanity as I'm capable of depicting" (Adler 2007; emphasis in the original). The variety of romantic liaisons he portrays contributes to this goal, as does the fact that all of these liaisons, however minor they may appear, have ongoing consequences both for the characters involved in them and for the bigger picture, even if these consequences are not yet wholly clear in some cases.[14] In short, these romances should not be seen simply as isolated or one-dimensional dalliances meant only to titillate and

11. On Western comic books and graphic novels' strong orientation toward a younger (heterosexual) male audience, see Carlson (2008), Wright (2003), and Pustz (1999, 66–109).

12. In a forthcoming paper, "Mythic Totality in Eric Shanower's *Age of Bronze*," George Kovacs (coeditor of this volume) examines Shanower's "general policy of inclusion over selection of narrative traditions" and the textual effects this policy produces by analyzing his depiction of the sacrifice of Iphigenia (issues 17–19). He concludes that Shanower's decision to incorporate multiple elements of causation found within the tradition (the killing of Artemis' sacred deer, Atreus' failure to sacrifice the golden lamb, the omen of the twin eagles, and Agamemnon's vow to sacrifice the most beautiful creature born on his estate) contributes to an ethos not simply of catalogical totality or completion but of creative repetition and reworking within *AOB*, which, I argue, underlies the romantic and sexual scenes as well.

13. Personal communication, September 9, 2008.

14. Shanower addresses this issue while discussing his compositional technique more generally in the interview cited in note 1: "There are seeds of events to come that I've had to sow all along the way, and I'm not sure how smoothly that works. I often imagine readers wondering why in the world I've presented something. For instance, Oenone's appearance at the end of issue #3 probably seems completely unnecessary. But it's actually a set-up for events still to come."

amuse, though that may be part of their appeal. Each contributes in its own way to a realistic portrait of love's complexity and power, and all are intimately implicated in the broader network of personal relationships that underpins this retelling.

Ultimately, what Shanower seeks to stress through his depiction of so many lives and loves intertwined is the need for individual responsibility with respect to one's own actions: "I'm trying to show human nature, why people did all these horrible things, what they were motivated to do, and, in the horrible situations they're put in, how they deal with the decisions they've made" (Romey 2004). "I'm hoping that readers will go, 'Oh, OK. This is how this story applies in my life. I'm responsible for my acts and I can choose what to do.'"[15] Obviously, this pertains in large part to the choices and actions that govern the practice of warfare and other forms of violence, but it is equally relevant to the issue of love and the practice of sexuality, which, as already noted, have received more attention than fighting has up to this point.[16] And it is in the latter area that Shanower has been most successful at conveying this message and achieving his authorial goals thus far. His candid portrayal of eros in all its terrible and wonderful variety has enabled him to play with and problematize dominant notions of sex and romance in the ancient world. Perhaps more important, though, by bringing to light the timeless, common aspect of the problems his characters face, he has promoted a reassessment of modern assumptions not just about what ancient people were like but also about what we are capable of ourselves, both in love and in war.[17]

Shanower's characterization of Achilles provides the most illuminating example of this process at work. Achilles' centrality to the story is well known: He is the Homeric über-hero whose prowess in war not only ensured victory for the Greeks at Troy but a short life and glorious death for himself as well. What Achilles is not as well known for, however, is the multifaceted love life in which he participates throughout the course of his brief existence. He is, as it turns out, the embodiment of erotic variety, having engaged in affairs with Deidamia, Iphigenia, Briseis, Penthesilea, and Polyxena, as well as with Troilus, Antilochus, and, most significantly, with Patroklus, his closest companion. This quality makes him an especially rich subject of representation for Shanower, whose inclusive and intimate approach greatly illuminates this obscured side of Achilles' personality.[18]

We have already seen some of the effects that this approach achieves in the episodes featuring Achilles' complicated relationship with Deidamia (see figure 15.4). For Shanower, the juxtaposition of the rape and birth scenes was the most expedient, dramatic means of conveying Deidamia's "hurried and hidden" pregnancy, as well as Achilles' angst over his "increasingly intolerable situation"

---

15. Deppey (2005). Consider as well Shanower's comment from Del Grande (2006) (translated from Italian): "One of my principal intentions is to show that refusing to take responsibility for one's own actions and decisions is wrong."

16. As Shanower mentions in the afterword to *A Thousand Ships* (2001), he was originally inspired to undertake the project by Barbara W. Tuchman's chapter on Troy in *The March of Folly: From Troy to Vietnam* (1985).

17. "The basic texture of civilization hasn't changed. Changes in science and philosophy aren't progress on a greater scale; they're simply new ways for us to talk [about] and look at the same questions we've been asking ourselves over and over again since prehistoric times. I don't think that morality progresses. It just swirls around and when it's swirling around you, you think that it's progressing" (Shanower, quoted in Adler 2007).

18. Shanower discusses the dramatic appeal of Achilles' "layered personality" in Katirtzigianoglou (2007).

(Keller 2000). The graphic quality of these scenes places rape and its consequences before the eyes of the reader in an immediate fashion and, at the same time, underscores Achilles' unwillingness to accept responsibility for his or Deidamia's "plight" (i.e., their illegitimate son). The same dramatic and immediate style of presentation also guides the narrative when Achilles returns to Skyros along with Patroklus in volume 2. He rebuffs Deidamia's sexual advances and, at that same moment, sees Patroklus from afar and rushes off to join him. When Patroklus tells him he intends to leave Skyros, Achilles finally acts upon his long pent-up feelings. He kisses Patroklus passionately and, in the heat of the moment, agrees to leave with him.[19] They are then shown running down a hill to a place where, Patroklus informs him, they can be alone for the night. The next day, Achilles declares his intentions to Deidamia and her father, much to their dismay. Achilles and Patroklus are next shown sailing away together, smitten and happy, as abandoned mother and son wave goodbye from the shore.

The relationship between Achilles and Patroklus is, like all the other relationships presented in *AOB*, attested in the sources, and Shanower therefore includes it in his retelling.[20] However, its uniqueness as a romantic relationship involving two men sets it apart from all the others, and Shanower capitalizes on the opportunity it presents for exploring another, less familiar facet of human experience by developing their story extensively throughout all three volumes. His decision to give this romance such prominence and to depict it in strongly erotic terms may be informed in part by his own status as a gay man, which he acknowledges gives him some "affinity" for it even though he was unaware of the tradition before beginning the project (Saunders 2007). Nonetheless, in actuality, his expanded representation of their affair serves a much greater purpose—it ties Achilles' decision to participate in the war and to fulfill his destiny directly to his love for Patroklus and his desire to be with him, no matter what. This connection is made clear when Achilles explains to King Lykomedes why he is leaving Skyros: He admits that it is *both* Patroklus and the war that have prompted him to depart.[21] By presenting these two aspects of Achilles' life as inextricably linked to one another, Shanower not only makes Achilles' choice to go to Troy, and to live fast and die young there, that much more understandable, especially to modern audiences, since it is this choice that enables him to be with his lover. He also succeeds on a broader level in humanizing the epic war hero, revealing him to be a man not just driven by rage (as he is so commonly depicted) but inspired by eros as well.[22]

The elaboration of Achilles' and Patroklus' affair as a heartfelt relationship with profound implications for *AOB*'s overall plot invests this lesser-known story with a new importance and works to subvert stereotypical representations of homosexuality, both ancient and modern. It also injects elements of human choice and responsibility into the story in a manner that renders the characters, the actions they take, and the decisions they make more accessible and sympathetic to

19. This kiss is depicted in figure 15.1.

20. In Homer, the nature of their relationship is not made wholly clear. Much of the post-Homeric source material concerning the pair suggests that their relationship was a sexual or romantic one (cf. Aeschylus, frags. 135, 136 (Radt); Plato, *Symposium* 179e–180b; Aeschines, *Against Timarchus* 133, 141–50). Although the debate continues up to the present day, it is nonetheless clear that the two characters have a very deep and special connection.

21. Vol. 2, p. 111.

22. In his review of *AOB*, Hodgman (2008, 2) remarks that "it was always Achilles' choice that made the story seem as remote as the moon." He goes on to praise Shanower's humanizing transformation of this story among others and to observe in conclusion that "Shanower's world never feels more convincing than when it reminds us that these humans—who died millenniums ago, if they ever lived at all—still feel painfully close" (3).

the reader. This is equally the case in the shorter vignettes that involve Kassandra, Troilus, and Laodike, and it is to these stories that we now turn.

Kassandra's complete lack of choice and the intolerable, madness-inducing lack of voice that results from it are both demonstrated and explicated through the evocative portrayal of her sexual assault as a child in volume 2 (figure 15.3; issue 11). Shanower's representation of this incident turns Kassandra into a character clearly worthy of pity despite her hideous appearance and her disruptive prophetic outbursts, which are embarrassing and perplexing to the Trojan nobility. In addition, it forces the reader to confront the uncomfortable issue of child molestation more generally and to consider its deleterious effect on the mental health of its victims.[23] In a similar, though slightly less serious, vein, Troilus is depicted masturbating and languishing in his bed, wracked with shame and misery over his long-standing love for Cressida. The intimate pathos of the scene calls into question the ideals of toughness, self-reliance, and impassivity, which define masculine identity, while the illustration of Troilus' pain in corporeal and therefore universally human terms reminds the reader of the overpowering influence that romantic rejection and emotional manipulation can have on individuals' lives and well-being.

Finally, in the case of Laodike, the reader is introduced to a surprising female character who goes after what she wants and gets it even though it is dangerous and totally inappropriate. She, a betrothed Trojan maiden, pursues the Achaean Akamas and, with the help of a female friend, executes the secret plan that brings them together. In fulfilling her desire, Laodike challenges the dominant image of ancient women as silent and submissive sex objects and makes evident the potential inherent in women's sexual agency to irrevocably alter the lives of men for better or for worse. In this regard, she recalls Helen and her own momentous decision to leave Menelaus and to pursue a recklessly lustful affair with Paris. This parallel is driven home by the intertwined images of Laodike and Akamas in the heat of passion and Menelaus' sad memories of his and Helen's wedding day (see figure 15.5). Although it is unclear as of yet what Laodike and Akamas' forbidden tryst will lead to, its dramatic contextualization suggests that this is no casual fling—it, too, will have consequences both for the couple and for the larger world of *AOB*.

All in all, Shanower's explicit eroticization of these romances and of the other relationships we have considered contributes significantly to his goal of presenting a variety of human experiences in a realistic way. Interestingly, this same goal also governed his decision not to include or represent the gods as characters whose will or actions determine the course of the narrative—a decision that has received much critical attention.[24] What this seems to suggest is that, in *AOB*, the force of eros is ultimately what guides the epic and compels the human actors

23. Aeschylus' *Agamemnon* is the best-known ancient source for the story of Kassandra's rape by Apollo (cf. lines 1202–12), though it is also mentioned by Apollodorus (3.12.5), Hyginus (*Fab.* 93), and Servius (Verg. *Aen.* 2.247), who mentions that the god spat in the girl's mouth to deprive her of her prophetic powers. Of course, Shanower alters the tale by making the priest of Apollo responsible for the crime; he also incorporates a lesser-known tradition, found in a Homeric scholion (*Il.* 7.44), in which her brother Helenus suffered with her. (In this version, snakes are found ominously licking the children' "organs of sense" as they sleep in the temple.) Shanower explains that he was most worried about depicting the episode in this way because of its potential to offend but that he received only one response—from fellow cartoonist Carla Speed McNeil, who complemented him on his depiction, saying that "that was the only way she would be able to think of Cassandra from then on" (Deppey 2005).

24. Nearly every review or interview cited thus far discusses this decision and the various reactions it has prompted; see especially Adler (2007), Cooper (2007), and Deppey (2005).

to do what they do—*in place of* the gods and, at least for now, *instead of* the war.[25] This force is divested of its traditional association with the divine realm in Shanower's passionately rendered relationships and instead manifests itself solely through human agents and vehicles, though all remain equally subject to its life-altering power. In the end, this characterization of love ensures that the themes of personal choice and responsibility, which are central to both the structure and meaning of *AOB*, stay continually at its forefront.

It is only appropriate that the character whose choices and actions best reflect this representation of eros and the message it seeks to convey is Helen, though, of course, they do so in a contrary fashion. From the first moment we see her, praying at an altar, and at several convenient points thereafter, she blames her "half-abduction, half-seduction" on the power of the goddess of love and claims to be helplessly walking her path.[26] Yet the ease with which she reconciles herself to the will of the goddess is suspect, and her persistent refrain of "the devil made me do it" becomes less persuasive at each hearing. What under-cuts Helen's words the most, however, are Shanower's many representations of her behavior toward her lover. Through them, he makes it clear that it was her and Paris' very earthly sexual attraction to one another and not divine will that made her decide to leave with him. He explains as much in an interview and relates it directly to the issue of "keeping the gods out of the story":

> Why would Helen run off with Paris [without the gods]? Why in the world? So I had to figure out, how am I going to present this story so that people would buy that? Well, you make it as erotic as you can and you sort of present it already decided. That's why I sort of started that issue [4] while Helen's having second thoughts about it. "Oh, I don't know if I want to do this! Well, I'll go." She [had] already decided to go.
>
> (Deppey 2005)

Helen's continued insistence on the goddess's control of her life only makes her look weaker, more selfish, and more irresponsible as the story goes on. This false front is instantly apparent to the newcomer, Andromache, who confronts her sister-in-law while she is having her hair and makeup done in anticipation of the Achaean embassy in volume 3. To Helen's claim that it was "hard" to sail away from all she knew and follow Paris but that "something inside" wouldn't let her stay behind, Andromache retorts, "If war comes to Troy, men will die. One of them might be Hektor. I love Hektor. It wasn't hard for me to leave all I knew and follow him to Troy. I would die for him. Can't you see? Vanity brought you here to Troy, not love. I don't want to lose my husband—my happiness—because of something as worthless to me as your vanity" (113; issue 24). In the end, it is her professed overdependence on the gods and its irrelevance to her actions

---

25. In a personal communication (see note 13), Shanower explains that "while there will be much more fighting in *Age of Bronze* than there has been up till now, the love and sex element isn't going to go away." He goes on to address the criticism that battle scenes present a "looming problem" because they are "visually all alike, and there's endlessly more to come" (LeGuin 2006) by acknowledging, "It's the interpersonal relationships that have to carry the story anyway. Battle upon battle would soon grow boring."

26. Hodgman (2008) refers to her capture in these terms. Note that when she pleads her case for staying in Troy she firmly says to Priam, "By my own choice I fled Sparta with your son" (vol. 2, p. 27).

that truly illuminate Helen's superficiality and heedlessness.[27] In addition, it is this contradiction that renders her not just an unsympathetic character but also the negative example par excellence of *AOB*, who illustrates through her hypocrisy the terrible things that happen—from individual feelings of pain and loss, to the violence and destruction of nations at war—when people accept no responsibility for their desire.

As his sophisticated portrait of Helen makes clear, Shanower has cultivated a distinctive style of representation that takes his work far beyond the realm of the average superhero comic. His honesty, his variety, his humanity, and, in particular, his privileging of eros and its power in the many relationships he delineates—all of these qualities make his account of the Trojan War appealing and accessible to other, nontraditional comic book audiences, which include adult, gay, and female readers.[28] Its amorous and erotic scenes most clearly reveal the ethos of intimacy and inclusivity that guides Shanower's artistic practice and which lies at the heart of his message of peace and personal responsibility. In sum, it is by making love and not war in his own skillfully crafted epic that Shanower ultimately inspires his audience to try to do the same.[29]

27. Shanower's characterization of Helen contrasts greatly with her portrayal as repentant and self-abusing in Homer's *Iliad* (3.172–80, 6.344–58). On this topic see Roisman (2006).

28. On the intended audience of *AOB*, see Romey (2004) and Beckett (2008).

29. I would like to thank the editors of this volume for the opportunity to be a part of this project. I would also like to thank Ric Rader, Jody Valentine, and Barbara Gold for the advice and support they provided me at various stages of the writing and editing process. Finally, many thanks to Eric Shanower for sharing his insights and his images with me—both proved indispensable.

16

Heavy Metal Homer

Countercultural Appropriations of the *Odyssey* in Graphic Novels

Thomas E. Jenkins

The "adult fantasy" magazine *Heavy Metal* might seem to be an unlikely source for involved meditations on the classical world; a recent collection titled "The Muse" raises suspicions when the muse in question turns out to be Veronika Kotlajic, a *Playboy* centerfold with a liberal attitude toward *déshabillement* (Kotlajic 2006). Other issues feature graphic novellas and photo essays generally celebrating female cleavage; in fact, a buxom female is de rigueur for the magazine's cover art. In addition, while its website warns that *Heavy Metal* is intended only for those over eighteen, one might suspect that its themes appeal, in the main, to teenage boys of a certain hormonal intensity.[1]

Nonetheless, *Heavy Metal*, the American version of France's *Métal Hurlant* [Howling Steel], has nothing to do with the head-banging Dionysian excesses of, say, Metallica and everything to do with the burgeoning industry of Continental comics, transmogrified for American consumption. A blend of American countercultural impulses—and the French academic revolt of the '60s—*Heavy Metal* is known primarily for its cheesecake depictions of the curvaceous female body in various states of undress.[2] However, it's also recognized for its potpourri of styles and sensibilities, including montages, interviews, photos, and—more to the point—serialized graphic novels or comics, including the occasional adaptation of preexisting narratives. As Prentis Rollins points out in his *Making of a Graphic Novel*, half the battle of creating a compelling graphic novel is crafting a coherent script even before preproduction; furthermore, while originality is obviously desirable, an existing novel or film at least promises a coherent and ready-made plot.[3] For a magazine dedicated to artsy explorations of the libido, Homer's *Odyssey*, then, must seem a tempting choice: A judicious excerpting of the plot allows for an odyssey not just of the mind but of (and in and generally around) the body as well.

---

1. For an overview of underground comics-reading communities, see Pustz (1999, 63).

2. Sabin (1996, 151–52). See also Hatfield (2005, 26–27), which traces *Heavy Metal*'s influence on later underground comics, such as *American Flagg!* (1983–1989) and *Mister X* (1984–1988).

3. Rollins (2006, 13–19). For Douglas Wolk, however, graphic novel adaptations of prose novels and epics are "almost uniformly terrible" (Wolk 2007, 13) since they are compelled to gut the original of a lot of significant content.

In fact, *Heavy Metal* lent its imprimatur to the *Odyssey* not once but twice—and it is worth exploring how two entirely separate comic-book adaptations of Homer's sprawling epic managed to arrive at a similar, *Heavy Metal*–friendly ethos. George Pichard and Jacques Lob's version, titled *Ulysses*, witnessed various incarnations. It first appeared in 1968 in the serialized Italian magazine *Linus* and was reissued in France (by Dargaud) first as two volumes in 1974–1975 and finally as one volume in 1981 by Editions Glénat. In the meantime, an English version was produced for *Heavy Metal* in 1978 (trans. Sean Kelly and Valerie Marchant) with some light (and to my mind not altogether felicitous) coloring; unfortunately, a recent reissue includes only the first volume. A retranslated version of both volumes (trans. Michael Koch and lettered by Monisha Sheth and Rachael Rodrigo) was produced for the series *Eurotica* in 1991; it retains the original black-and-white images, and, since it is available in both volumes, it is the version I cite in this chapter (the first number indicates the volume number). Franco Navarro and José María Martín Saurí's *Odyssey* was inked in Spain from 1979 to 1982 and published in *Heavy Metal* in 1983; the comic was reissued by *Heavy Metal* in 2005. Though both adaptations hit American shores about the time of a conservative shift in American politics and mores, they reflect a Zeitgeist much nearer to that of the Beatles, including an emphasis on personal discovery through sex and a political ideology heavily influenced by the countercultural impulses of the '60s and early '70s.[4] Intriguingly, both adaptations must negotiate the same interpretive stumbling block: the return of Odysseus to his faithful wife, Penelope. If the *Odyssey* à la *Heavy Metal* is to be read as a fantastically erotic voyage through a midlife crisis, any wife is at best a dead end, and Penelope—as spouse par excellence—even more so. Thus, both comic receptions of the *Odyssey* must negotiate one of the most vexing interpretative issues of the past forty years—the agency and subjectivity of Penelope—while remaining true (in whatever sense) to the *Odyssey*'s own sense of return and completion.[5]

The *Odyssey* of Navarro and Saurí is, in some senses, the more traditional of the two adaptations, though it is not without its surprises and certainly not without its birthing pains. A native Barcelonan (b. 1949), Saurí admits that his artsy adaptation of Homer was at first a hard sell; after Navarro (b. 1953) managed to wrestle the *Odyssey* into a script in 1979 (through "brute force," Saurí recalls), Navarro and Saurí spent three agonizing years, off and on, preparing the final project ("The whole world suffered my personal Odyssey.").[6] Originally turned down by Spanish presses, Navarro and Saurí next approached the publishers of *Heavy Metal* in their New York offices, only to be given a Spanish contract at nearly the same time. To this day, Saurí considers the *Odyssey* to be Navarro's "masterpiece," a judgment that seems confirmed by the graphic novel's recent twenty-fifth-anniversary reprinting (by the press Norma Editorial).[7] Considered in itself, Saurí's art is clearly a cut above that of an average *bande dessinée*: Saurí's

---

4. For a famous analysis of the interplay of ideology and comics, see Dorfman and Mattelart (1975, 33–40), especially on Disney's suppression of reproduction within a strictly patriarchal structure, which thereby normalizes the stasis of the underclass.

5. For two book-length examinations of Penelope's role in the *Odyssey* see Katz (1991) and Felson (1994). See also note 18.

6. From an interview with Benjamín Reyes, *El Dia* (May 8, 2008). http://www.eldia.es/2008–05–08/cultura/cultura7.htm.

7. So, for instance, as blogged by Javier Meso in something of a rhapsody: "Homer's *Odyssey*, in the hands of Navarro and Saurí, is a clear example of a mighty *opus* which even after twenty-five years retains all its splendor. The beauty of its images, its narrative force, its special literary properties: all these leave on the reader an indelible mark." http://www.zonalibre.org/blog/elcoleccionistadtbos/archives/105562.html.

careful attention to detail includes myriad "classical" touches, from ancient amphorae and urns (6.4) to statuary (23.1–2) to architecture (20.1).[8]

In terms of *narrative*, however, something of Navarro and Saurí's modus operandi can be glimpsed in their treatment of the famous "Song of the Sirens" episode from Odysseus' wanderings. As Peraino has elucidated, this is among the most self-referential and important songs in the Homeric poems, one that taps into Odysseus' sense of personal (even sexual) identity even when the hero is metaphorically and literally at sea (Peraino 2006, 355). In Homer's *Odyssey*, Circe warns Odysseus that the Sirens—half-avian female songstresses of the deep—entice sailors to their doom with the alluring sound of their voices (*Od.* 12.40). Circe—or, rather, Homer—cannily omits, however, the *content* of the song. That is a surprise for the listener as the Sirens serenade Odysseus, tied to the mast: "Come hither, far-famed Odysseus, and leave your ship ... [T]hose who listen to us sail away delighted, knowing so much more. For we know all that the Greeks and Trojans suffered, by the will of the gods, by wide Troy; we know whatever happens on this fertile earth" (*Od.* 12.184–90). In the worldview of the *Odyssey*, the thing most seductive to Odysseus is *knowledge*: knowledge not just of a synchronic present but also of a diachronic past, including Odysseus' own journey through war, accruing *kleos* ("fame") and sorrow in equal measure. In essence, the Sirens are singing the *Iliad*—exactly the poem that Odysseus is so desperate to escape.[9]

As envisioned by Navarro and Saurí, the curvaceous Sirens skip the war and go straight for the groin, as Odysseus explains: "They beckoned me, begging that I stop, that I listen to them, that I go with them, and I ... I desired with all my soul to please them" (34.3). Readers who wonder what could be so attractive are then directed visually to a spread of four callipygian Sirens, at least one of whom writhes in the throes of erotic ecstasy, in contradistinction to any actual singing.[10] Saurí navigates the difficulty of sexing up the Sirens by minimizing the corporal distortion—just the talons and wings are avian—and maximizing the curves. The depiction of Odysseus here (35.1) owes something to Baroque portraiture: Odysseus' pose has more than a touch of St. Sebastian's iconography (particularly with the sail whirling behind him like a baroque ornament; Rubens's experiment in Sebastian's pose dates from 1618). At least since the Renaissance, St. Sebastian has been something of a gay icon: a muscled, naked hero who meets his death through the penetration of multiple arrows.[11] It is intriguing that at the moment of Odysseus' greatest vulnerability—at the moment of women's greatest strength—Odysseus is figured as naked, powerless, and bound.

8. In this chapter, citations refer to the glossy, collected reprint of 2005 (Rockville Centre, N.Y.: Heavy Metal Press), which is unfortunately unpaginated. (It also misspells Saurí's name as "Salari" on the copyright page; *caveat lector*). It seems easiest, then, to keep the page:panel format, with the eight original issues comprising eight pages each of the final graphic novel.

9. Pucci (1998, 4). "The Sirens' conspicuous use of Iliadic traditional phrases can hardly be an accident; on the contrary, it forces upon the listener the realization that they mean to define Odysseus as the Odysseus of the *Iliad*." In similar vein, Homer's Lotus-Eaters—strangers who offer Odysseus' men the flower of forgetfulness (*Od.*9. 63–104)—are here figured by Navarro and Saurí as (beautiful) women (9.1): The metonymy between pleasurable oblivion and possessive women is explicit. The greatest danger to Odysseus is that he may forget his own epic.

10. It is worth noting in this context that in Kirk Douglas's 1955 film adaptation, the Sirens' "song" consists of the intertwined voices of Penelope and her son, Telemachus, beckoning Odysseus homeward. In the film, the most desirable thing in the world is family; in the comic, it is derrieres.

11. Kaye (1996, 89) explores the psychosexual ramifications of this particular pose in the West, including its isomorphism with "turn-of-the-century scientific, medical, and anthropological representation[s] of the individual," particularly of homosexuals.

It is not an image that recurs again in Navarro and Saurí's vision of the Homeric world; in a sense, Odysseus' vulnerability while confronting the Sirens only emphasizes his abundant virility and derring-do elsewhere in the comic. Inked in a detailed and often realistic black-and-white style, this *Odyssey* keeps only the rudiments of the original's structure: The first four books—which center on Telemachus' search for his father—are excised, and Navarro's creation begins with the rescue of Odysseus by Nausikaa, daughter of the Phaeacian king Alkinoos. The first six issues thus correspond roughly to *Odyssey* 5–12—the wanderings and shipwreck of Odysseus—while issues 7 and 8 compress *Odyssey* 13–23 (the return to Ithaka) into just sixteen pages. (As we shall see, *Odyssey* 24 is a problem for both *Heavy Metal* adaptations.) Our first glimpse of Odysseus is delayed by the introduction of the sensuous Nausikaa, playing with her fellow maidens; one particularly campy panel features Nausikaa pointing to an errant ball, hand perplexingly if seductively held behind her head, all the while cooing, "I think it's over here" (2.4). Odysseus, meanwhile, is drawn as a fantastically burly and eminently attractive object of desire; panel 3.6 shows Odysseus ogled by Nausikaa from afar—but in a sense also by us, from close up. To put it another way, the framing of the scene figures the (presumably male?) reader as an erotic interloper—just like Nausikaa or just like a protagonist in numerous tales from Ovid's *Metamorphoses*.[12] This is not to say that the scene is calculated to be homoerotic per se but that we are supposed to recognize Odysseus as particularly desirable: an appropriate hero for an erotic *Odyssey*.

Saurí's work abounds in ingenuity, from the use of charcoal shading for a flashback to Troy (8.1) to the shattered panel border for the Cyclops' gigantic rage (16.1); to a tongue-in-cheek phallic sword (most prominently at 17.2, 26.6, and 38.1, though it is rather hard to miss throughout). He even manages for Odysseus a farewell in the style of art nouveau as the hero departs Calypso's island (48.7). Throughout the novel's many pages, however, the emphasis on Odysseus' sexuality and sexually charged adventures remains unabated. Odysseus' trip to Circe's island, for instance, is played—as in Homer's *Odyssey*—as a battle between the sexes: femme fatale vs. the muscle-bound hero of epic. (Navarro even plays with contrast as he juxtaposes the effete, full-lipped god Hermes (22.2) with the rippling, helmeted Odysseus.) After Odysseus forces Circe into obeisance, the witch turns the situation to her own advantage, coaxing Odysseus into a year's stay on her island. Saurí's lush artwork—abloom with gardens and trees—reinforces the decadence of the island, as Odysseus narrates: "We remained for one entire year, day after day, with plenty of meat and sweet wine." The eye is then led to the center of the page—to Circe and Odysseus locking lips—and finally to the lower panel, "and love!" Here, Odysseus and Circe share an intimate, apparently postcoital moment (23.5; figure 16.1). A turn of the page, however, turns the tables on the reader: The moment is reconfigured as a precoital moment, as Odysseus, gloriously naked, takes matters to the next level, though the actual coupling is tastefully

---

12. Ovid's *Metamorphoses* abound in examples of such water-based interloping: Diana and Actaeon (*Met.* 3.165–205); Arethusa and Alpheus (*Met.* 5.572–641); Salmacis and Hermaphroditus (*Met.* 4.317–88). Cook (1999, 158) explores the larger metaphorical reversals of this particular bathing scene, as Nausicaa is compared to the hunter-goddess Artemis (Diana) and Odysseus implicitly to Actaeon: "Thus, in our story, it is the wild animal [i.e., Odysseus] who takes a bath, and is then transformed by the goddess into a handsome Aktaion."

FIGURE 16.1 **In Odysseus' erotic journeys, he and Circe get to know each other very well. Art by José María Martín Saurí.** *The Odyssey* (Heavy Metal Press, 2005) 23.5.

obscured by some dark inking (24.1). It is a quintessentially *Heavy Metal* illustration, erotic without being pornographic, revealing without being obscene. After Odysseus' return from the underworld, Circe bids the hero adieu but not without first revealing her ample bosom prior to one last fling in a pond (33.1 and 33.2); it is a wonder that Odysseus can tear himself away at all.[13]

But onward Odysseus goes: And the closer he draws to Penelope, the more ambivalent the hero—and the comic—becomes concerning the allure of such domesticity. Besides the hypersexualized Sirens, Odysseus encounters Calypso, who rescues him from shipwreck. Navarro's two pages on Calypso are a strange amalgam of erotic adventure and domestic banality, with an extra-Homeric twist. On 46 we are introduced to Calypso and her (entirely naked) handmaidens in a scene of surprising decadence, including a sponge bath, and lurid, centerfold poses (46.1). As the affair progresses, even Odysseus is puzzled at his own narrative: "Why did Calypso, the daughter of Atlas, treat me with civility and preference? Why did she seem to be in love with me, and very possessive at that?" (Partly, Navarro is playing on the etymology of Calypso from the Greek verb meaning "to hide or cover"; Calypso's raison d'être is, in fact, to smother.) Odysseus continues to relate his confusion: "I wasn't sure at the time, but this is what happened" (47). The answer, we discover in a narrative twist, is that Calypso wants to get pregnant; indeed, she manages it twice before Odysseus manages to escape. This is an extra-Homeric detail, culled from Hesiod's *Theogony*

13. Amusingly, panel 33.1 is reproduced on the cover of the 2005 reprint but with Circe's breasts now tastefully concealed.

(ll. 1017–1018), in which Calypso gives birth to two boys, Nausithoos and Nausinoos.[14] It is also the first episode that Navarro almost entirely rewrites: The question is, why?

The answer, I argue, is that the Calypso episode prefigures the other altered episode from the *Odyssey*, the reunion with Penelope; given *Heavy Metal*'s celebration of extramarital liaisons, it is little wonder that Navarro's *Odyssey* grows more slippery as it nears the end of the novel. After the death of the suitors—in a spectacular double-page spread on 60–61—Odysseus finally achieves his long-awaited return to his wife, Penelope, after twenty years. Though much of Penelope's story has been excised—including her deceptive weaving of the death shroud for Odysseus' father, Laertes—Penelope still implements the contest of the axes as a way of solving her own domestic predicament: her suitors' incessant wooing (55.6). Penelope continues to test Odysseus—as in Homer—with the trick of the marital bed, which she orders to be transferred from its current spot (*Od.* 23.174–180). (Odysseus, however, built the bed from live wood: It cannot be moved.) In Navarro's version, Odysseus responds (as in Homer) with a briefly kindled anger: "This is my mark. Now I don't know if my bed is safe. Who can be trusted now?" (63.4). Penelope apologizes as she and Odysseus cleave to each other in a detailed, bourgeois foyer; troublingly, perhaps, the centrally positioned panel of the kiss (63.5) mirrors that of Odysseus and Circe (23.4).

Regular *Heavy Metal* readers, already primed on a diet of shapely feminine flesh, would know that page 63 of an eight-issue version of the *Odyssey* can mean only one thing for page 64: that Odysseus goes out with a bang. Indeed, in Homer's epic, Odysseus' reunion with Penelope ends with the two in bed (or as Homer circumspectly puts it: "The two took pleasure in the joys of love"; *Od.* 23.300) even before Odysseus gets around to explaining his whereabouts for the past two decades (*Od.* 23.310–341). Navarro and Saurí certainly have not shied from sexy montages previously—62.1, for instance, features some wholly immodest handmaidens, as well as a glimpse of Penelope's backside through what must be an uncomfortably sheer garment. So it is with quickened pulse that the ideal *Heavy Metal* reader turns the page to discover the climax of the epic, the result of Odysseus' fantastic martial/erotic adventures, and discovers . . .

. . . a disconcertingly pensive scene, one in which Odysseus and Penelope stare at each other silently, banished to the background, as the camera zooms away from the garden (64; figure 16.2). It is a powerful, defamiliarizing ending: a single panel page in a comic that normally resists them (only the storm on page 25 is similarly full sized). Moreover, the heavy black backgrounds that once defined the affair with Circe are gone (e.g., 23.5), replaced by vast open spaces both of air and of patio. As Virgil does in his own *Aeneid*, Navarro and Saurí have thrown at the reader a literally "open" ending: one that admits of myriad interpretative possibilities. This includes the intimation that Penelope and Odysseus are not actually to be reunited or at least not happily reunited. There is a melancholy to the composition: in the smallness of the humans, in the autumnal array of the falling leaves, in the stillness of motion, and, above all, in the quiet. And—it goes without saying—there is none of the sex of the Homeric version or the flesh of Navarro and Saurí's previous sixty-three pages. What is any reader—Heavily Metallic or otherwise—to make of this?

---

14. Though the *Odyssey*'s Odysseus is the most famous literary treatment of this hero, his character was surprisingly malleable even in antiquity; besides the Hesiodic version of Odysseus' tryst with Calypso, there is also a product of Odysseus' year with Circe, Telegonus, destined to slay his father (this story is most fully realized in Proclus' summary of the epic cycle; see Gantz 1993, 710–11). Penelope, too, exists in multiple narrative threads; in an especially salacious version, Duris of Samos records (*FGrHist* 76 F21) that Penelope bears a child jointly conceived with the semen of every suitor and therefore named Pan ("from everything").

FIGURE 16.2 The view "zooms" away from Odysseus and Penelope at the conclusion of Navarro and Saurí's *Heavy Metal* adaptation of the *Odyssey*. Art by José María Martín Saurí. *The Odyssey* (Heavy Metal Press, 2005) 64.

In the first place, I think this "open ending" of Navarro and Saurí's *Odyssey* invites us to reread and reinterpret the crucial Calypso episode of pages 46–47, in which Odysseus bristles at Calypso's "possessiveness." Though Odysseus appears to be enjoying the opportunities for sex (47.1), he views

Calypso's pregnancy much more ambivalently; even Calypso notices the change: "Aren't you happy Odysseus? Soon you will be a father again!" Indeed, the next three panels seem to chart Odysseus' emotional journey on Calypso's island—first as a doting, happy father to a new son; next as hard-working, less happy *paterfamilias* to his family of four; and finally as genuinely unhappy outcast, physically estranged from his family but unable to execute a final severance (47.3–5). Odysseus' narrative voice captures his deep disquiet: "I cannot say that the seven years that I remained in Ogygia were totally unhappy, but not even the promise of immortality succeeded in calming my soul." The litotes is striking—"not totally unhappy" is not exactly an exuberant endorsement—and the voiceover's juxtaposition with the children indicates that family is at the root of the problem. By including these two children from Hesiod's *Theogony*, Navarro and Saurí have created a disquieting parallel—and precedent—for Odysseus' behavior in Ithaka. Would a man who happily leaves behind a "wife" and two sons on one island remain content with a wife and a son on another?

I sense that the answer is no: that in this *Odyssey*'s worldview, erotic satisfaction and marriage are, at best, fleeting acquaintances. The end of Saurí's *Odyssey* ends on a note of disquiet because the authors have so hypersexualized Odysseus' journey that mere marriage—and mere monogamy—now seem alien to the theme of Homer's *Odyssey*. Having flirted with monogamy with Calypso, Odysseus must now make a similar decision with Penelope, and the quiet, brooding ending makes it clear that Odysseus' choice will be an anguishing one.

For many readers, the arc of Navarro and Saurí's *Odyssey* may seem uncomfortably male centered. At least among scholars, a common reading of the *Odyssey* in the last forty years has been as an exploration of *female* agency and power within the frame of a traditional "return" narrative. Indeed, even in 1978, John Finley was moved to write that the end of the *Odyssey*—with its promise of a fair song for Penelope (24.192–202) "comes near [to] making our *Odysseia* a *Penelopeia*."[15] Marilyn Katz's *Penelope's Renown* and Nancy Felson-Rubin's *Regarding Penelope* squarely locate Penelope as the core about which the poem revolves: She is the shifting signifier/signified of marital harmony or marital infidelity. Her agency—as a wife and even seducer—is constantly renegotiated as additional men intersect her orbit, including her adolescent son, the boisterous suitors, and, finally, a mysterious beggar.[16] Even in antiquity, the reunion of Penelope with Odysseus was regarded as a *telos*, a "goal" or an "endpoint" of the poem, at least by the poem's Hellenistic editors.[17] Compared to the rather more martial material of the *Iliad*, the *Odyssey*, at least on one reading, offers the possibility of a text that meditates on the role and psychology of Penelope as a counterweight to the wanderings—sexual and otherwise—of her husband.

15. Finley (1978, 2). Margaret Atwood has made good that suggestion with her own recent *Penelopiad*, a retelling from the dead wife's point of view (Atwood 2005). On the *Odyssey* as a return song, see Foley (1999, 117): "[T]he *Odyssey* follows a narrative path well known throughout central and eastern Europe over many thousands of years—the track of the so-called Return Song."

16. For instance, Felson (1994, 19): "Cunning and calculating, [Penelope] blends her needs for survival, propriety, and pleasure within the constraints placed upon her by her husband, her society, and the gods." A more grim assessment of the epic's emphasis on the *oikos* [household] and property is offered by Wohl (1993, 27): "The Circe and Calypso scenes, then, show in its [*sic*] most basic and mythically transparent form the necessity and means for the subordination of women."

17. The Hellenistic editors Aristophanes and Aristarchus marked line 23.296—Odysseus and Penelope's approach to the bed—as a *telos*, an "endpoint," to the *Odyssey*, though the exact import of that designation is unclear. Certainly the reunion of Odysseus and Laertes in book 24 ties together several narrative arcs, including an emphasis on patrilineal inheritance and continuity. (Both comics ignore Laertes entirely; the only thing less erotic than a wife, it seems, is one's father.)

As I hope to make (perhaps too abundantly) clear, the *Ulysses* of Pichard and Lob has little to do with this particular school of Homeric reception; indeed, Pichard and Lob's adaptation is even more androcentric than Navarro and Saurí's. Banished are sensitive readings of Penelope and Telemachus as a desperate dyad awaiting the return of the hero; in their place is an unabashedly sexual odyssey: Odysseus as randy swinger on a particularly psychedelic trip. Odysseus' wanderings are thus figured as an erotic sci-fi voyage, replete with exaggerated sexual overtones and a surprising amount of gratuitous, even campy, nudity. After its share of climaxes—narrative and otherwise—*Ulysses* does, it is true, depict our hero arriving at Ithaca to reunite with Penelope. However, the changes to *Odyssey* 23 are even more striking than in Navarro's version: Odysseus' awkward "decision" about his marriage is less a crisis than an inevitability.

As published in the *Eurotica* series, *Ulysses* rubs shoulders with Pichard and Lob's *Illustrated Kama-Sutra*. That particular factoid is telling: This version of the *Odyssey* is literally just a bibliographical item away from a sex manual. However, *Ulysses* is more than just an excuse for an erotic parody of Homer; whereas Navarro's adaptation was classical in design and ethos (except, of course, for its sexual politics), Pichard and Lob's adaptation is unabashedly over the top, even satirical, as it mixes together elements of sci-fi, fantasy, and druggie porn.[18] This is firmly in keeping with *Métal Hurlant*'s initial focus on stories that combined "prehistory, mythology, medievalism, and futurism" (Screech 2005, 117).

For instance, the depiction of Zeus (1.7.2) is partly archaizing—a burly, bearded elder statesman on a throne—and partly pure comics: a superhero's leotard emblazoned with a big *Z* for a logo. Apollo's powers earn him a uniform with a large, radial sun (1.8.1), while Poseidon's cartoonish scuba gear (1.10.8) glances at the aquatic equipment of Pichard and Lob's previous *Submerman* series. But for Athena? Her uniform—what little there is—is skin tight, with a shiny metal brassiere that does little to support her breasts (see especially 2.53.5). Her helmet—a round ring penetrated by a sharp point—seems incongruous for a goddess of virginity, and her provocative poses have not quite the austerity of, say, Phidias' fifth-century representation in the Parthenon. Even within the sci-fi/super-hero *mise-en-scène* of Olympus, Athena, though powerful, is figured as erotic eye candy: the first of many physical idealizations of women in the comic.

As in Navarro's *Odyssey*, *Ulysses* drops most of the domestic scenes of the epic—including the opening books, which are centered on Telemachus—and leaps directly into Ulysses' return from Troy, a tale filled with obvious opportunities for mayhem and booty of every stripe. The novel starts with a full-blooded Cyclops scene—a creature here variously referred to as Polyphemus (as in Homer) or "the Sentinel." The scene proceeds along generally Homeric lines: Ulysses and his men trespass in a cave; they are discovered by a one-eyed giant; and after a gruesome

---

18. In his brief biographical sketch of George Pichard, Patrick Gaumer also warns against seeing the artist as a "simple hedonist and pleasing rascal" (Gaumer 2004, 626); Alessandrini notes Pichard's general air of parody and mockery but notes, too, that some complain of his unstinting vulgarity and fetishistic touches (Alessandrini 1986, 204). Knigge's more extensive appraisal (Knigge 1985, 186–93) surveys Pichard's full corpus, while Maurice Horn (Horn 1999, 614) concentrates on Pichard's notoriety, particularly his later *Marie-Gabrielle*, "a horrendous tale of a buxom, dark-haired beauty subjected to every conceivable torture and torment . . . perhaps as a take on one of Marquis de Sade's most famous anthology pieces." (On the rather less objectionable *Ulysses*, Horn notes that it is "highly intriguing.") Gaumer's sketch of Jacques Lob—the *scénariste* for *Ulysses*—surveys that artist's surprisingly varied and original career (488).

scene involving human *flambés*, the giant is blinded as the men scramble to escape. It is telling that in this first, entirely "male" episode, Ulysses' mind is still on Penelope; even as he is being attacked by Polyphemus' laser vision, Ulysses shouts "Ah! We'll never regain our homeland! I'll never see Penelope again" (1.15.4). As long as Ulysses is surrounded by mere men—or monsters—his thoughts turn easily and naturally to Penelope.

The subsequent episode, however, complicates matters, as Pichard and Lob reformulate the episode of King Aeolus and his bag of winds. In Homer, this is a comparatively brief encounter (*Od.* 10.1–55), as Homer reintroduces the theme of *xenia* ("host/guest relationship") into an epic for which the host/guest relationship is an overriding concern (particularly for Penelope and the rambunctious suitors, but also for King Alkinoos' generosity at his royal court).[19] In this sci-fi reenvisioning, Aeolus' randy daughters (who are, as in Homer, erotically linked to their brothers; 1.33.3) literally catch Ulysses' men during a fishing expedition and persuade their father to allow the men a bit of relaxation or, as one of them puts it: "Let's frolic in the atrium!" (1.28.4). The subsequent half-page panel (1.29.1) bursts with late '60s' whimsy: Naked, buoyant lasses float above a wind machine, ricocheting between blossoms even more evocative than Georgia O'Keefe's. This zero-g bacchanal is obviously trippy and psychedelic, and while the fun lasts, it is not unlike a pharmaceutically inflected bikini beach party. Alas, the "brutish" and "savage" (1.32.1–2) impulses of Ulysses' men culminate in an attempted assault. In disgust, Aeolus ejects the men from his island, granting them only a treacherous V-16 nuclear reactor (the sci-fi counterpart to Homer's bag of winds; *Od.* 10.19–20). Nonetheless, the seeds of Ulysses' subsequent adventures have been planted: When among men and monsters, there is violence; when among women, there is sex—and thoughts of Penelope are far, far away.

Part of Pichard and Lob's project, then, is to demonstrate how Ulysses' adventures cause a real severance between himself and Penelope: that Ulysses' initial proclamation of "Penelope, my angel, my dove! . . . How long it's been since I've seen you!" (1.5.1) will be tested by trials not just of geography but also of the spirit. (Ulysses is aided, of course, by appropriately countercultural instruments of soul searching.) Having bested Circe's efforts at bewitching his men, Ulysses agrees to spend one night in Circe's palace. He is awakened, however, by Circe's drug-induced moaning, as she gets high on some manner of intravenous hookah while inviting Ulysses to her bed (1.50.5). Curiously, Ulysses agrees to stay on the island, in part so that he can accept, paradoxically, an invitation to travel: "In a few moments, you and I are going for a long and marvelous voyage," Circe coos as she attaches the drug "paraphernalia" to Ulysses' veins (1.51.8). Ulysses' trip, ushered in by drugs, incense, and the opening staves to Beethoven's *Appassionata* sonata (*Opus* 57), is first a voyage back in time, as Penelope's face rises out of the ocean: austere, classical, and inscrutable (1.52.4). Ulysses screams "Penelope!" in despair as her features shatter with a "CRACK": the past turned to rubble. Penelope's face is replaced, however, by Circe's enticing visage, rising from the water with an evocative "AAAM-MMM"; this incantation slowly surrounds Ulysses until the witch and Ulysses make love while superimposed on the words "YOU ME YOU ME ME YOU ME YOU." The implications are pellucid: Sex—at least psychedelic sex—is the ultimate union of two bodies (just a me and a you, dissolving into one) until that union explodes in a human supernova (1.53.5) and Ulysses' orgasmic shout of "AAAAAAAAAA" literally spirals its way throughout the sun-spangled galaxy (1.53; figure 16.3).

---

19. See Katz (1991, 134–37) for the ways in which *xenia* constantly resurfaces in the *Odyssey* as an important leitmotif.

FIGURE 16.3 An example of the psychedelic sex experienced by Ulysses in Picard and Lob's adaptation of the *Odyssey*. Art by Jaques Lob. *Ulysses*, vol 1 (Heavy Metal Press, 2006) 53.

No wonder Penelope shattered; she could hardly compete.

Still, the year-long erotic hallucination so freaks out Ulysses that he decides to leave the island, managing, at least this once, to escape "the trap of love and the trap of drugs" (1.58.1). As in Navarro and Saurí's *Odyssey*, Ulysses' encounters in even the "minor" episodes of the *Odyssey* are figured as erotic lessons and opportunities. Pichard and Lob cleverly tie the Sirens' episode back to Circe: Ulysses is bound to the mast not because he is (initially) attracted to the Sirens but because he is having withdrawal symptoms from Circe's drugs, and his men are administering tough love. However, soon enough he hears the Sirens, who helpfully describe themselves: "O Ulysses, imagine two ravishing young girls with long blonde hair . . . pleasing facial features, big blue eyes, small delicate mouths, pearly white teeth . . . imagine slim, graceful necks . . . perfectly proportioned shoulders . . . and pretty sculpted breasts, neither too full nor too thin" (1.62.3–4). In truth, the Sirens are scaly monsters, feasting on a mountain of skulls, but in Ulysses' hallucinatory state, his mind imagines the most bewitching enticement of all: beautiful, *Heavy Metal* women. Even a trip to the underworld has its sexy moments as vampy vampiresses attack Ulysses' men (2.4–5). Ulysses' re-ascent—and reunion with Circe—is figured as a bittersweet moment as Ulysses prepares to leave her for good. As Ulysses' ship sets sail, the two pensive figures silently articulate "Good-bye, Ulysses . . . Goodbye, Circe" as the ever-roving Ulysses discovers new erotic adventures.

As in Navarro and Saurí's version of the *Odyssey*, the Calypso episode demonstrates the most striking structural changes—changes that help inform our reading of the Penelope reunion scene and therefore the end of the comic. On Calypso's island, Ulysses once again launches into an orgy of love making with a large-breasted and apparently unscrupulous goddess, and while not as overtly trippy as the Circe episode, the Calypso sequence still features plenty of groovy imagery. The panels on page 43, for instance, feature Calypso at her most lustful, with a billowing, practically disco coiffure and similarly billowing speech ("Oh, Ulysses! I'm crazy about you!"). Her hair and heavy breathing inevitably segue to a magnificently composed orgasm scene (2.43.4), in which the novel's floral imagery—present since at least the Aeolus episode, in various manifestations—here blossoms into obvious metaphor, as Ulysses and Calypso's genitals, hidden by overlarge petals, merge to moans of "OOOOH . . . AAAAAAAA" (2.43.5). Still, Ulysses feels disquiet about the relationship: He admits that, though his body can no longer resist Calypso (2.45.5), his mind is more agitated: "[I]n truth you've given me everything but the right not to depend on you" (2.45.3).

No small part of Ulysses' uneasiness stems from the innovated figure of Andros, Calypso's neutered manservant and, in a sense, a doppelgänger for Odysseus himself. Indeed, Andros' name seems calculated to recall the first Greek word of the *Odyssey*, *andra*: the heroic "man" of the story (that is to say, Ulysses). At first, Ulysses is bothered by Calypso's cavalier treatment of her slave—until the goddess explains that Andros is no man at all but a congener of the word Andros: an android. In a curious demonstration that is meant to allay Ulysses' fears, Calypso and Ulysses tour Andros' bachelor pad: a cubist fantasia on manliness, including a Picasso-esque monkey wrench, a surreal trash 'bot, and what appears to be, at left, an enormous spermatozoon (2.42.3). But Andros' quarters contain one more surprise: a shelf of removable, fungible heads (2.42.4). As Calypso explains, "Andros can change heads at will, according to the situation! It's very practical. I wish sometimes I could do the same." A visibly distraught Ulysses exits the room with a backward glance at Andros screwing on a new, blond head.

In a sense, the tables have been turned on Ulysses. In a comic in which female bodies have been largely interchangeable—only the heads are different, and even that aspect hardly matters—Ulysses must now confront the uneasy prospect of a male body that epitomizes (and even celebrates) conformity and mass manufacture. In effect, Ulysses discovers the male body subjected to the same dissecting, consumerist gaze that he has employed on women since the beginning of the comic. He doesn't like it. In his attempt to escape the island by raft, Ulysses enlists the aid of Andros, who, having been retrofitted with a Swiss-army knife for a forearm, handily crafts a raft for Ulysses (2.47.3). Still, this assistance is of no avail: Andros betrays Ulysses (says Calypso to Ulysses: "Did you think for a minute that Andros would leave me in the dark about your activities?" 2.48.2), and Calypso torches the raft. The implications are clear: Though Andros may be the perfect man in form, it is a woman—his creator and director—who controls his appearance, labor, and volition. He is the prototype of Ulysses himself, and Ulysses knows it. The more Ulysses protests his lack of agency ("You've given me everything but the right not to depend on you . . . Calypso, your love ensnares me like a golden yolk [*sic*] and weighs me down"; 2.45.5), the more he becomes just another mechanical slave for Calypso, the smother goddess.

Fortunately for Ulysses, Athena has, on Zeus' orders, manufactured an escape from the island, and Calypso—as in Homer—yields to the inevitable. It is striking that after Ulysses' final tryst with Calypso (2.51.2), his concluding farewell scene is with Andros, who watches silently (perhaps poignantly so) as Ulysses sails away. Even as Ulysses nears Ithaka, Pichard and Lob intimate that a narrative twist is sure to follow: "We'll soon be reunited with our loved ones. I should be thrilled, but I'm not . . . could this long awaited homecoming be coming too late?" (2.51.4).

Ulysses' return to Ithaka is a marvel of compression, with nearly half of the *Odyssey* crammed into six pages. The famous slaughter of the suitors is notably cartoony (the perforation-by-arrow of Antinous could easily be ripped from the pages of *MAD* magazine; 2.57.4), and the novel quickly reaches its Homerically inspired dénouement with Penelope's famous recognition scene. The recognition scene, however, now features some distinctly modern twists: As Ulysses embraces Penelope—for the first time in twenty years—she brushes him off at her loom, complaining "Please dear, not now. You can see I'm busy" (2.59.3); having "gotten in the habit" of weaving, the obsessive-compulsive Penelope simply cannot stop (2.59.4). A surprising jump cut in time finds Penelope and Ulysses in bed, thereby providing a perfect example of what Scott McCloud terms "closure": the necessary deduction on the part of the reader to supplement a fragmented narrative sequence (McCloud 1993, 70–72). "What's wrong, Ulysses? You don't want me any more?" (2.59.5) Penelope complains. Her question thus forces the reader to supply what must have happened in the gutter between panels: that Ulysses was unable to maintain an erection. Limply, he can only offer the following excuse: "Forgive me." Penelope's reply does not exactly represent the vanguard of feminist thought: "It's not your fault. I don't know how to excite you any more . . . It's been so long. We've both changed. You've been with other women" (2.59; figure 16.4). That is to say, Penelope blames herself for not being able to live up to the expectations of Ulysses' own erotic odyssey: She understands that his philandering has exposed him to a world of sexual experiences that she can never hope to replicate. Nonetheless, the reader of the whole comic knows more than that: that Ulysses' liaisons with Circe and in particular with Calypso have also made him wary of the prospect of domesticity and concomitant domestication. Having previously escaped a metamorphosis into a household slave (à la Andros), Ulysses can no longer be satisfied with a monogamous relationship, not even with his wife and not even on Ithaka. Though Penelope replicates certain features of the goddesses—her breasts, for instance,

FIGURE 16.4 Penelope does not know how to cope with her worldly husband in Picard and Lob's adaptation of the *Odyssey*. Art by Jaques Lob. *Ulysses*, vol 2 (Heavy Metal Press, 2006) 59.

are as ample as any in the novel—Ulysses now seeks satisfaction only through novelty. Sans drugs, sans lasers, sans danger, and sans polyamory, Ulysses has but one choice. As the reader turns to the final page of the novel, we discover a Ulysses haunted by dreams of the past, by the "memory of Calypso" and Circe, and by his quondam closeness to the gods. The final panel, therefore, shows Ulysses taking his leave of home (2.60.4), not because he is fulfilling Teiresias' enigmatic oracle about a winnowing fan (*Od.* 11.121–137) but because his marital lust has turned rather to wanderlust.[20] In Ulysses' erotic world, home is emphatically *not* where the heart is.

20. A position not so different from Tennyson's famous take in *Ulysses*: "I cannot rest from travel: I will drink/ life to the lees."

In their desire to exaggerate the psychosexual element of Ulysses' journey, Pichard and Lob—like Navarro and Saurí—realized that a traditional ending and thus a traditional marriage would never do. In the novel's final panel, therefore, Ulysses leaves Ithaca not to die but to seek and conquer new erotic worlds, both Homeric and Aquarian. Though published earlier, it is, in a sense, the more radical of the comic book versions of Homer, as it posits a *Heavy Metal* world in which marital fidelity and domestic happiness constitute the oddest *Odyssey* of all.[21]

21. I gratefully acknowledge the comments and suggestions of Richard Armstrong, Erwin Cook, Timothy O'Sullivan, and the editors and anonymous readers of this volume.

A Reading List of Classics in Comics

This reading list is presented in four sections.

First are those comics titles that we identify as important points of contact with the ancient world. This is a selective list and, in its way, a personal one. Key creators are listed, with frequent collaborations noted. All of these are discussed either briefly or at length in this volume, and references to the relevant chapter are indicated except where the survey chapter (1) is the only discussion.

Second, the superhero genre features in many of the contributions to this volume, as it did to the formative years of its two editors. As such, we include a short reading list of comics that have made important contributions to the medium and would serve as entry points for an inexperienced reader. With these we have included some important independent comics. These do not have classical content explicitly, but in different ways they show what is happening in North American comics in recent decades and point to some (but certainly not all) influential creators.

The last two lists identify useful resources, in print and online, including dependable catalogs, some fundamental works in comics-based theory, and a few works that have already begun the study of Classics and comics.

Not all of these are currently in print, nor are all available in English. Out of print does not necessarily mean inaccessible. Market websites such as Amazon, eBay, and AbeBooks are all useful. Dedicated comics shops often keep out-of-print titles in stock or have means of obtaining them. Information listed here is accurate as of August 2010 (this includes all URLs, which were confirmed active at this time).

"Classical" Comics

Action Philosophers!

Evil Twin Comics: nineteen issues (Apr. 2005–July 2007): Fred van Lente (w.) and Ryan Dunlavey (a.)

An often humorous but engaged and informative presentation of "history's A-list brain trust." This comic provides biographical information and synopses of the intellectual contributions of thirty-seven influential thinkers, from the pre-Socratics to Joseph Campbell (three in each of the first eight issues, plus a "lightning round" in the ninth issue). The complete series was bound in 2009 as *The More Than Complete Action Philosophers!* Entries are reordered, so Ancient philosophy (Classical and Chinese) and Augustine occupy pages 3–72.

Age of Bronze

Image Comics: thirty issues to date (Nov. 1998–): Eric Shanower (w./a.)

A retelling of the Trojan War focusing on human events rather than divine motivations and featuring a thorough synthesis of a staggering number of sources, both ancient and modern. Shanower keeps a detailed website with links to related material and readings: http://age-of-bronze.com/, and the trade paperbacks include complete bibliographies, genealogies, and other notes on Shanower's research (see Shanower, Sulprizio, Kovacs).

Alix

Casterman: twenty-eight volumes to date (1948–): Jacques Martin (w./a.) et al.

French-language comic about the adventures of a young Gallo-Roman in the late Roman Republic. Originally the comic appeared as a feature in *Tintin*, though since 1956 it has been published under its own title (see Dinter).

Apollo's Song

Vertical, Inc. (English translation): Manga (1970), Osamu Tezuka (w./a.)

Written by one of the most popular creators of manga, Osamu Tezuka (perhaps best known in the West for *Astro Boy*), this Japanese comic tells the story of young Shogo as he overcomes the psychological trauma that stems from his troubled relationship with his mother. After a dream encounter with Athena, Shogo lives a series of very different lives, all permeated with *Oresteia*-inspired imagery and all featuring incarnations of the girl he loves. An English translation is available, arranged from left to right, a reversal of the original Japanese production (see Thiesen).

Ares

Marvel: Five-issue miniseries (March–July 2006), Mike Oeming (w.) and Travel Foreman (a.)

Ares has retired to live with his human wife and son, but events on Olympus and beyond draw him back to his role as the Olympian god of war. Integrated with Marvel continuity (see Simms). The full series was bound as a trade paperback in 2006.

Astérix

Hodder and Stouton/Orion (English translation): thirty-three volumes to date (1961–), René Goscinny (w.) and Albert Uderzo (a.; since 1977 w./a.); English translations by Anthea Bell and Derek Hockridge.

Perhaps the best-known French-language comic in the world, thanks to widespread translation. Features the adventures of a band of intrepid Gauls keeping Julius Caesar and his Roman legions at bay in 50 BCE with the help of a magic potion. Visual gags, verbal puns, and slapstick comedy characterize the work (see Dinter, Kovacs).

Bacchus

Various publishers (1987–1995); Eddie Campbell Comics: sixty issues (May 1995–May 2001), Eddie Campbell (w./a.) et al.

Though most of the major Olympian gods are dead and gone, the wily Bacchus still turns up in taverns around the world. Though the stories were originally published as features in other comics, along with some miniseries and single issues, Campbell later collected and published them serially as *Eddie Campbell's Bacchus*. Many stories are short mythological yarns, while longer ones have the descendants of the Olympians competing for Zeus' lost powers. Two volumes comprising the entire series are promised by Top Shelf Productions in 2011.

The Cartoon History of the Universe

Rip-Off Comics: nineteen issues (1977–), Larry Gonick (w./a.)

A pedagogical series narrated by a cartoon professor who is surveying human history. Told (and drawn) with a sharp wit, filled with humorous historical anecdotes and lots of puns and visual jokes, the history of the universe is told in the first nineteen issues (bound in three volumes), and then Gonick begins applying new, more specific titles, such as *The Cartoon Guide to Statistics* or *The Cartoon Guide to Sex*.

Classics Illustrated

Gilberton: 167 issues (July 1941–March 1962) Various writers/artists

Started by immigrant Albert Lewis Kanter to interest children in "serious" (mainly European) literature. Titles ranged from early Classical works to near contemporary fiction. Kanter employed a wide array of young artists and attributed the scripts to the original author, hence issue 35, "The Last Days of Pompeii," Edward Bulwer-Lytton (w.) and Jack Kirby (a.). Of interest for this volume: 68 "Shakespeare's Julius Caesar"; 77 "The Iliad"; 81 "The Odyssey"; 130 "Caesar's Conquests"; 161 "Cleopatra." Ownership of the title has frequently changed hands, but in 2007 Jack Lake Productions produced *Classics Illustrated* 170 "The Aeneid," Virgil (w.) and Reed Crandall (a.).

Epicurus the Sage

Piranha Press: two volumes (1989, 1991), William Messner-Loebs (w.) and Sam Keith (a.)

A humorous pastiche of Greek culture, myth, and especially philosophy. Epicurus, accompanied by his best friend, Plato, and a young Alexander the Great wander the landscape of Greek myth, meeting numerous notable historical and mythological characters from Homer to Diogenes. Accessible to any reader and sometimes annotated internally by the characters themselves, the work is still particularly rewarding to the informed reader. DC collected the full series into a single volume in 2003.

Eternals

Marvel: Various series (July 1976–Jan. 1978; Oct. 1985–Sept. 1986; Aug. 2006–Mar. 2007; Aug. 2008–Mar. 2009). Created by Jack Kirby (w./a. of the first series)

In the 1970s, Jack Kirby was the premiere creative influence in comics, and his reputation was such that both DC and Marvel allowed him to create whatever titles he wished, with independent continuity. For DC he produced the *New Gods*, an epic story told across multiple titles that incorporated high concepts of mythology and science fiction. For Marvel, he produced *The Eternals*, which employed many of the same conceits. *The Eternals*, however, is more implicitly associated with Greco-Roman myth. The Eternals are immortal, designed from protohuman DNA by the ancient, godlike Celestials, and possess many superhuman powers. Each Eternal possesses specific skills, often derived from common superhero tropes and/or the Classical figures from whom many get their names (e.g., Zuras [Zeus], Thena [Athena], Makkari [Mercury], Ikaris [Icarus], Sersi [Circe]). Makkari, for instance, is a speedster, like earlier Marvel heroes Mercury and Hurricane (both characters were initially developed by Kirby; later retconning established all three as the same figure).

Fables

Vertigo: ninety-seven issues to date (July 2002–), Bill Willingham (w.) and Mark Buckingham et al. (a.)

Many of the characters of fairy tale and folklore now live in New York, driven from their Homelands by a dark and mysterious Adversary. Although no characters from Greco-Roman myth or folktale have appeared to date, this series demonstrates how traditional characters can be reimagined in new contexts. So far the characters have been derived from European and Arabian folktales, but Willingham limits himself only to characters in the public domain. Willingham frequently experiments with genre, telling different types of stories in his narrative arcs and employing comic book tropes from other genres.

The Golden Vine

Shoto Press: Manga (2003), Jai Sen (w.) et al. (a.)

An alternate history from New York–based Japanese writer Jai Sen, telling the story of the Alexander IV, heir to a successful Alexander the Great. This volume is currently out of print, though the website of Shoto Press promises reprinting and even a trilogy (http://www.shotopress.com/titles/golden_vine.php). The website also has several features on the research and creative process behind *The Golden Vine*.

Heavy Metal

Ulysses: two volumes (1968), George Pichard (w.) and Jacques Lob (a.)
Odyssey: one volume (1983), Franco Navarro (w.) and José María Martín Saurí (a.)

Two versions of the *Odyssey* published by French magazine *Métal Hurlant* a decade apart. Both versions are for mature readers, depicting Odysseus' journey home to his wife in an erotic and psychedelic mode. Pichard and Lob recast Ulysses' journey as science fiction, while Navarro and Saurí retain the more traditional fantastic narrative of *Odyssey* 9–12 (see Jenkins). A caveat for the potential buyer, however: *Heavy Metal* reprinted the first volume of *Ulysses*, lightly colored, but did not produce a second volume.

The Infinite Horizon

Image Comics: six issues (four to date, Dec. 2007–), Gerry Dugan (w.) and Phil Noto (a.)

A reimagining of the *Odyssey* as an unnamed army Captain must make his way home from the Middle East after a global communications blackout plunges the world into anarchy. Along the way, the Captain meets analogs of the Cyclops, Calypso, and the Sirens, while his wife, unknowing of his fate, struggles to protect the family homestead in upstate New York. Dugan and Noto use the narrative to explore the role of military and family in the modern militarized world.

Kingdom Come

DC: four-issue miniseries (1996), Mark Waid (w.) and Alex Ross (w./a.)

In the future, the superhumans of Earth have become estranged from the regular humans they have sworn to protect. They do battle with each other with little sense of morality or accountability. Superman is in self-imposed exile, and the other members of the Justice League pursue their own, often conflicting, agendas. As a showdown develops, the story is mapped out against the language of the biblical Apocalypse, as witnessed by Pastor Norman McKay, the point-of-view character. This comic combines biblical imagery and comics intertexts to produce a particularly thoughtful superhero comic (see Stevens).

Marvel Illustrated

Iliad: eight issues (Feb.–Sept. 2008), Roy Thomas (w.) and Miguel Angel Sepulveda (a.)
Odyssey: eight issues (Nov. 2008–June 2009), Roy Thomas (w.) and Greg Tocchini (a.)
The Trojan War: five issues (July 2009–Nov. 2009), Roy Thomas (w.) and Miguel Angel Sepulveda (a.)

These retellings of the *Iliad* and the *Odyssey*, written by comics veteran Roy Thomas, are surprisingly faithful to their literary models. The third series, *The Trojan War*, is the epic cycle to Thomas's Homeric epics, covering events before and after the *Iliad*. Fast paced and mostly unannotated, with characters speaking a pseudo-Shakespearean English that might alienate some readers.

Murena

Dargaud Benelux: eight volumes (six to date, Jan. 1997–), Jean Dufaux (w.) and Phillipe Delaby (a.)

French-language comic that follows the machinations of the imperial family after the death of Claudius in 54 CE. The two story arcs focus first on Agrippina and then on Poppaea. Volume 1 has been translated into English as *Swords of Rome*, vol. 1: *The Conquerors* (IBooks, 2005).

The Sandman

Vertigo/DC: seventy-five issues, plus miniseries and one-shots (Jan. 1989–Mar. 1996), Neil Gaiman (w.) and various artists

One of the most popular and influential comics of recent history. The title character is Morpheus or Dream, one of the Endless, embodiments of the basic foundations of the universe. Many issues tell self-contained stories (see Strong), while other story arcs span several volumes, but the entire series has a macronarrative tied specifically to the Greek Furies (see Marshall). Gaiman draws on the mythologies and histories of countless major cultures in human history, though Norse and Greco-Roman myths are consistent favorites.

300

Dark Horse Comics: five-issue miniseries (May–Sept. 1998), Frank Miller (w./a.), with Lynn Varley (a.)

Frank Miller's imaginative retelling of the battle of Thermopylae in 480 BCE. Historical accuracy is not on the agenda, though Miller does cite Herodotus as one of his sources. Miller uses the figure of Leonidas and his Spartans to explore models of heroism (as he has elsewhere; see Tomasso). Thanks to the film version of 2007 (dir. Zack Snyder, Warner Bros.), the comic is well known and controversial post-9/11 (see Fairey). Available in a single, oversize volume published by Dark Horse in 2001.

Thor

Marvel: various titles and series since *Journey into Mystery* 83 (Aug. 1962). Created by Stan Lee, Larry Leiber, and Jack Kirby.

Originally sent to Earth by his father, Odin, to learn humility as a human, Thor has had many careers, from solo superhero to founding member of the Avengers to Lord of Asgard. Though not a Greek or Roman god, Thor is a model for how a divinity appropriated from a known mythological tradition interacts both with his established pantheon and the modern world (as it exists in Marvel continuity, at least), as well as with the Olympians on a regular basis. Thor represents another moment in Kirby's lifelong (if unsophisticated) interest in mythological divinities and themes. Introduced as a feature of *Journey into Mystery*, Thor almost immediately dominated the series, which was retitled *Thor* with issue 126 (in which he battles Hercules).

Wonder Woman

DC: various titles and series since *All Star Comics* 8 (Dec. 1941). Created by William Moulton Marston

The long history of Wonder Woman has seen a labyrinthine series of retcons and reinventions since she first ventured from Paradise Island (later Themiscyra, after Herodotus 4.86) to bring justice to the world of man. Originally conceived by psychologist William Moulton Marston (under the pseudonym Charles Moulton) as a foil to the masculine heroes appearing in comics, Wonder Woman has at times been a symbol of women's liberation, though after Marston's death, editors frequently softened the character. Periods of note (for this volume) include Marston's original run (1941–1949), George Pérez's supervision of the series (which begins to exploit Wonder Woman's Amazonian heritage more meaningfully, 1987-1992), and the 2002 one-shot, *The Hiketeia* (Greg Rucka [w.] and J. G. Jones [a.]; see Marshall).

Some Non-Classical Hero Comics

Alan Moore, *Watchmen*

Watchmen rewrites the history of hero comics by reimaging new generations of heroes arising in the wake of World War II. Along with *V for Vendetta* and the out-of-print *Miracleman*, *Watchmen* provides a detailed and complex examination of the hero's role in society. Also of interest is Moore's earlier run on *Swamp Thing*, which reinvigorated horror comics.

Frank Miller, *Batman: The Dark Knight Returns*

Set in a dystopic future, this short series presents Batman single-mindedly maintaining justice in Gotham City against increasingly psychotic villains and a government that appears compromised. Using totalitarian force, the human Batman works alone and independently of the street gangs that emulate him and the government authorities, which are using Superman.

The Justice League

There are many team comics, but, in its various incarnations, DC's Justice League sets a standard. Particularly well-written runs include Grant Morrison's *JLA* series (1997–2000, issues 1–41) and *Identity Crisis* 1–7 (2004–2005; Brad Meltzer [w.] and Rags Morales [a.]).

Dave Sim, *Cerebus*

The three-hundred issues of this independently published, black-and-white comic trace the adventures of the aardvark Cerebus as he moves from barbarian (cut from the cloth of Conan) to prime minister to pope to (for the second half of the series) an ineffectual life in retirement. Sim employs detailed literary intertexts throughout, introducing characters from other sources and patterning stories using the prose styles of Wilde, Fitzgerald, and Hemmingway.

Jeff Smith, *Bone*

The Walt Kelly–inspired Bone and his two cousins travel through the Valley after losing their way in a desert storm of locusts. Another single-creator comic, *Bone* begins simply but quickly reveals a dark fantasy world that permeates the fictional universe. Appropriate for children but of interest to all, the series was originally black and white but is available in color editions targeted at the schools market.

Terry Moore, *Strangers in Paradise*

Terry Moore's independent comic concerns a group of more or less ordinary friends and their relationships. While a covert agency and government conspiracies exist in the background, this is a grounded story that has a particular appeal to people who think they do not enjoy comics.

Marvel Comics

All of the preceding works are from the past few decades, but there are reasons to want to go even further back, and a fun starting point for some will be with the classic stories from Marvel Comics in the 1960s, '70s, and '80s. Personal favorites of the editors (all available in reprint volumes) include the following: *The Fantastic Four* 38–61 and especially 48–51 (featuring the world-eating Galactus); *Spider-Man* 96–98 and 121–22 (the latter is discussed by Rogers in this volume); *Iron Man* 123–33 (in which the hero battles alcoholism); *X-Men* 97–101 and 129–37 (the Dark Phoenix Saga); and *Daredevil* 227-33 ("Born Again").

Print Resources

Plowright, Frank, ed. 2003. *The Slings and Arrows Comics Guide*, 2nd ed. Great Britain: Slings and Arrows, Inc.

> This is neither a price guide nor a catalog but rather a critical assessment of more than twenty-five hundred titles. Arranged alphabetically, the entries offer a brief description and analysis of the subject, including recommended issues and periods in publication histories. Length of entries is proportional to the title's run and impact on comics culture. This work is astonishingly thorough, with entries on some very obscure comics (less reliable for the *obscura* of Europe and Japan). Readers will not agree with every judgment, but every opinion is carefully considered and provides a starting point for the critical analysis of almost any series.

Eisner, Will. 1985. *Comics and Sequential Art* (extended edition, 1990) Paramus, N.J.: Poorhouse Press.

———. 1996. *Graphic Storytelling and Visual Narrative*. Paramus, N.J.: Poorhouse Press.

> Eisner's career in comics spanned five decades. He is best known as the creator of *The Spirit*, itself stylistically varied and experimental, and his *Contract with God* is widely considered to be the first "graphic novel." These books are not how-to manuals but considerations of the medium itself. *Comics and Sequential Art* represents the first systematic attempt to understand the medium in structural and theoretical terms. Each chapter is effectively a short essay on an element of the medium, illustrated with pages from Eisner's own extensive oeuvre.

McCloud, Scott. 1993. *Understanding Comics: The Invisible Art*. Northampton, Mass.: Kitchen Sink Press.

———. 2000. *Reinventing Comics: How Imagination and Technology Are Revolutionizing an Art Form*. Northampton, Mass.: Kitchen Sink Press.

———. 2005. *Making Comics: Storytelling Secrets of Comics, Manga, and Graphic Novels*. Northampton, Mass.: Kitchen Sink Press.

> *Understanding Comics* is perhaps the single most influential work on the comics medium in the West. Written in a comics format, *Understanding Comics* popularized comics theory and has generated endless debate among comics practitioners and fans. More thorough and systematic than Eisner before him (McCloud frequently acknowledges his debt to Eisner), McCloud dedicates chapters to iconography and vocabulary (often the same thing), panel transition, time and motion, and the artistic process. His conclusions have often been challenged, but this is merely evidence of healthy debate, and this work has ramifications beyond the comics medium. McCloud followed up his groundbreaking work with *Reinventing Comics*, which anticipated the position of comics within the rapidly developing digital age. *Making Comics* is still not quite a how-to manual but closely examines the process by which creators are able to turn their ideas into reproducible comics pages.

Groenstein, Thierry. 1999. *Système de la bande dessinée*. Paris: Presses Universitaires de France. 2007, trans. Nick Nguyen as *The System of Comics*. Jackson: University Press of Mississippi.

Just as comics developed separately in continental Europe, so, too, did comics theory. Groenstein's is one of the few works of European comics theory currently available in English. Though he and McCloud often cover similar topics, the latter's *Understanding Comics* is acknowledged only once—in a footnote. Groenstein's work is characteristic of continental intellectualism, dense in thought and language, and sometimes feels disengaged from its subject matter. Nevertheless, Groenstein has much to say about how the reader understands comics (see Johnson).

Bender, Hy. 1999. *The Sandman Companion*. New York, DC Comics.

An authorized companion to Neil Gaiman's *Sandman* series. Chapters on each of the series' collected volumes feature plot summaries, analysis of sources, and production notes. These are supported by interviews with Gaiman himself.

Levine, Daniel. 1994. "Classica Americana Troglodytica: V. T. Hamlin's *Alley Oop* (Apr. 1939–Feb. 1940); the Epics Meet the Comics," *Classical and Modern Literature* 14: 365–86.

van Royen, René, and Sunnyva van der Vegt. 2000. *Asterix en de wijde wereld*. Amsterdam: Prometheus.

Stanley, Kelli E. 2005. "'Suffering Sappho!': Wonder Woman and the (Re)Invention of the Feminine Ideal," *Helios* 32: 143–71.

MacEwen, Sally. 2006. *Superheroes and Greek Tragedy: Comparing Cultural Icons*. Lewiston, N.Y.: Mellen.

Pitcher, Luke. 2009. "Saying 'Shazam': The Magic of Antiquity in Superhero Comics," *New Voices in Classical Reception Studies* 4: 27–33. http://www2.open.ac.uk/ClassicalStudies/GreekPlays/newvoices/issue%204/issue4index.htm.

These are works that have begun to examine the intersection of Classics and comics, each using a different touchstone. Levine examines the demands that writer V. T. Hamlin placed on his audience when he brought his caveman hero to a classical setting. Dutch scholars van Royen and van der Vegt consider the historical accuracy of favorite moments in *Asterix*. Stanley traces the evolution of the Wonder Woman character and how that development has been affected by contemporary sociopolitical contexts. MacEwen examines modern hero constructs to better understand them in the ancient world, particularly within Greek tragedy. Pitcher zooms in on a specific motif found in many comics, the use of magic, and considers how and why the use of magic is distorted when derived from Classical models.

Digital Resources

Grand Comics Database (GCD)—http://www.comics.org

The Comic Book Database (CBD)—http://comicbookdb.com

Two online catalogs of comics. Both are very thorough but slightly different in the way they present their information: The *GCD* is more thorough, particularly with older titles, but the *CBD* is slightly more user friendly. Both provide writer and artist information, publication history (often linking to reprints), and cover scans. Both sites depend on online communities for accuracy and completeness, so it is a good idea to consult both.

ComicsResearch.org—http://www.comicsresearch.org
   An online bibliography of comics-based research arranged by category. The site is dedicated mainly to book-length studies but also includes links to journals and web resources. Bibliographic entries often include links to tables of contents.

The Comic Page—http://www.dereksantos.com/comicpage/comicpage.html
   A history of American superhero comics. Easily navigable by subject or year, with cover images of important titles in the development of American comics.

The Sandman Annotations—http://www.arschkrebs.de/sandman
   Provides thorough annotations for the seventy-five issues of the regular series (not for the later one-shots). Particularly useful for understanding the comics intertext in which Gaiman operates (and develops) and for suggesting possible inspirations for the ideas and imagery in *Sandman*. New readers should beware, however: Spoilers are common.

The Asterix Annotations—http://www.asterix.openscroll.com
   Provides annotative notes for the thirty-three volumes of Asterix, with information on geography, ancient terminology employed in the comic, and puns that appear in the English translations. Includes lists of names found in all of the volumes.

Appendix to the Handbook of the Marvel Universe—http://www.marvunapp.com/list/appprebc.htm
   Provides profiles of minor characters in Marvel Comics, with various methods of arrangement (by creator, by nationality, etc.). The link given here is an alphabetical listing of all Marvel characters originating between 8000 BCE and 0 CE. A corresponding list for the first ten centuries CE contains no classical figures.

Contributors

Craig Dethloff currently works for the administration of Indiana University. He received his PhD in Classics from Johns Hopkins University in 2003. His research interest lies in the field of Greek religion and epigraphy. His favorite superhero is his father, and his favorite team is the Invaders.

Martin T. Dinter is lecturer in Latin Literature and Language at King's College London. His main research interests are Latin epic, especially Virgil and Lucan, Latin epigram, and Latin drama, as well as Classics and popular culture. He is currently looking forward to the second volume of *Les aigles de Rome*.

Emily Fairey received her doctorate in Classics from CUNY in 2006, and her thesis was titled "Slavery in the Classical Utopia." She was Research Assistant and Acting Director of the Database of Classical Bibliography from 2000 to 2008. She was an editor for the Oxford University Press Bibliography of Classics (2009) and is currently adapting her thesis into a book, and writing an article on ancient Roman brass bands.

Thomas E. Jenkins is Associate Professor and Chair of Classical Studies at Trinity University and the author of *Intercepted Letters: Epistolarity and Narrative in Greek and Roman Literature* (2006). His recent publications have concentrated on contemporary ideological appropriations of classical myth and culture; he also received the inaugural Paul Rehak award for his work on the reception of Lucian in the Harlem Renaissance.

Kyle P. Johnson is currently a PhD candidate at New York University, where he is writing a dissertation on communication in Julius Caesar's *Commentaries*. His research interests also include Archaic Greek epic, ancient botany, and the Greek novel. He is a cofounder of *Hephaistos Text*, an online platform for free, open, and collaborative research in the discipline of classics. His favorite comic book character is Mr. Natural.

George Kovacs has poor combat skills, enjoys a healthy relationship with his living parents, and accordingly pursues his second career choice as Assistant Professor in Ancient History and Classics at Trent University. He recently completed his doctoral dissertation on the performance and reception of Euripides' *Iphigenia at Aulis* at the University of Toronto.

C. W. Marshall is Associate Professor of Greek and Roman Theatre at the University of British Columbia. He is the author of *The Stagecraft and Performance of Roman Comedy* (Cambridge University Press, 2006), among other things. He has been conducting research for this volume since he was eleven.

Gideon Nisbet, Lecturer in Classics at the University of Birmingham and formerly a researcher on the Oxyrhynchus Papyri Project, is the author of *Greek Epigram in the Roman Empire: Martial's Forgotten Rivals* (2003) and *Ancient Greece in Film and Popular Culture* (second edition, 2008). Forthcoming publications include an introduction to epigram for Greece and Rome New Surveys and an edited collection on Rome in film.

Brett M. Rogers is Assistant Professor of Classics and Women, Gender, and Sexuality Studies at Gettysburg College. He has written on Greek and Roman drama, Socrates and Athenian democracy, and *Buffy the Vampire Slayer*. He is writing a monograph about why tyrants talk like teachers in Greek tragedy. Inspired by the greatest story ever told—"The Joker's Utility Belt" (*Batman* 73)—he also plans to write on, then himself undergo, the Villain's Journey.

Eric Shanower is the Eisner Award–winning cartoonist of *Age of Bronze*, a retelling of the Trojan War. His past work includes the *Oz* graphic novel series, many comic books, and children's book illustrations. Examples can be found at www.age-of-bronze.com. His favorite comics include *Blueberry*, *Cerebus*, and *Love and Rockets*.

R. Clinton Simms is visiting Assistant Professor in the Department of English Language and Literature at the University of Nizwa (Sultanate of Oman), after completing his doctoral thesis on Statius' *Thebaid* at the University of Otago (New Zealand). His research interests include Flavian epic and classical reception in early modern English literature.

Benjamin Stevens has published on Latin literature, linguistic thought, sensorial anthropology, and religious art; he has also published poetry. Since 2005 he has advised an annual symposium on comics featuring undergraduate research and art. In 2009 he was awarded a grant to design and teach "Reading Comics: An Introduction to Comics as Literature" at the University of Colorado–Boulder. He is Assistant Professor of Classical Studies at Bard College.

Chiara Sulprizio is Visiting Scholar at the UCLA Center for the Study of Women, where she is pursuing research on the urbanization of the feminine in Aristophanes' early plays. She is also interested in the geopolitics of the ancient world, especially as they are represented in Herodotus. Her favorite comic book character is Electra, the Greek ninja assassin and lover of Daredevil.

Anise K. Strong is a Roman social historian specializing in the study of gender and sexuality, as well as reception studies. She is currently teaching at Stanford University and finishing a book on Roman prostitutes. As a child, she discovered that Asterix comic books inspired in her a love of both Roman history and comics.

Nicholas A. Theisen is Lecturer in Classical Studies at the University of Michigan, where he received his PhD in comparative literature. He works on comparative poetics, in particular the relationship between poetry and popular music, as well as multimedia translation and adaptation. He is an incurable admirer of Dave Sim's *Cerebus*.

Vincent Tomasso is the ACM postdoctoral fellow in Classics at Ripon College. He received his PhD from Stanford University with a dissertation on the reception of Homer by Quintus of Smyrna. His professional interests include Greek literature, particularly of the archaic and imperial periods, mythology, and reception studies. He does not follow specific comic book properties as much as authors—Neil Gaiman, Frank Miller, and Alan Moore are foremost among them.

Bibliography

Abel, Jessica, and Matt Madden. 2008. *Drawing Words and Writing Pictures: Making Comics: Manga, Graphic Novels, and Beyond*. New York: First Second.

Adler, Matt. 2007. "Age of Humanity: Shanower Talks *Age of Bronze*." *Comic Book Resources*. http://www.comicbookresources.com/?page=article&id=10829.

Aihara, Kōji, and Kentarō Takekuma. 2002. *Even a Monkey Can Draw Manga*. San Francisco: Viz Communications.

Albright, W. F. and C. S. Mann. 1971. *Matthew: Introduction, Translation, and Notes*. Anchor Bible vol. 26. Garden City, NY: Doubleday.

Alessandrini, Marjorie. 1986. *Encyclopédie des bandes dessinées*. Nouv. éd. Paris: A. Michel.

Allen, Thomas W. 1931. *Homeri Ilias*, vols. 1–3. Oxford: Clarendon.

Anderson, John Kinloch. 1970. *Military Theory and Practice in the Age of Xenophon*. Berkeley: University of California Press.

"Are Comics Fascist?" *Time Magazine* (Oct. 22, 1945). http://www.time.com/time/magazine/article/0,9171,778464–1,00.html.

Arieti, James A. 1997. "Rape and Livy's View of Roman History." In *Rape in Antiquity: Sexual Violence in the Greek and Roman Worlds*, ed. Susan Deacy and Karen F. Pierce, 209–29. London: Duckworth.

Atchity, K. J. 1978. *Homer's Iliad: The Shield of Memory*. Carbondale: Southern Illinois University Press.

Atwood, Margaret. 2005. *The Penelopiad: The Myth of Penelope and Odysseus*. New York: Canongate.

Auerbach, Erich. 1968. *Mimesis: The Representation of Reality in Western Literature*, trans. Willard R. Trask. Princeton: Princeton University Press.

Aziza, Claude. 2008. *Guide de l'Antiquité imaginaire: Roman, cinéma, bande dessinée*. Paris: Les Belles Lettres.

Bakker, Egbert J. 1993. "Discourse and Performance: Involvement, Visualization, and 'Presence' in Homeric Poetry." *Classical Antiquity* 12: 1–29.

———. 1997. *Poetry in Speech: Orality and Homeric Discourse*. Ithaca: Cornell University Press.

Bal, Mieke. 1977. *Narratologie: Essais sur la signification narrative dans quatre romans modernes*. Paris: Klinksieck.

Baldwin, Barry. 1983. *Suetonius*. Amsterdam: Hakkert.

Barrett, Anthony. 2002. *Livia: First Lady of Imperial Rome*. New Haven: Yale University Press.

Barthes, Roland. 1967. *Elements of Semiology*. trans. Annette Lavers and Colin Smith. London: Cape.

———. 1972a. "Literature and Discontinuity." In *Critical Essays*, trans. Richard Howard, 171–83. Evanston: Northwestern University Press.

———. 1972b. "The Structuralist Activity." In *Critical Essays*, trans. Richard Howard, 213–20. Evanston: Northwestern University Press.

Bartman, Elizabeth. 1999. *Portraits of Livia: Imaging the Imperial Woman in Augustan Rome*. New York: Cambridge University Press.

Bates, Bob. 2005. "Into the Woods: A Practical Guide to the Hero's Journey." *Gamasutra*. http://www.gamasutra.com/view/feature/2330/into_the_woods_a_practical_guide_.php.

Beard, Mary. 1999. "The Erotics of Rape: Livy, Ovid, and the Sabine Women." In *Female Networks and the Public Sphere in Roman Society*, ed. Päivi Setälä and Liisa Savunen, 1–10. Rome: Institutum Romanum Finlandiae.

Beazley, J. D. 1946. *Potter and Painter in Ancient Athens*. London: Cumberledge.

Becker, Andrew. 1990. "The Shield of Achilles and the Poetics of Homeric Description." *American Journal of Philology* 111.2: 139–53.

———. 1992. "Reading Poetry through a Distant Lens: Ecphrasis, Ancient Greek Rhetoricians, and the Pseudo-Hesiodic 'Shield of Herakles.'" *American Journal of Philology* 113.1: 5–24.

———. 1995. *The Shield of Achilles and the Poetics of Ekphrasis*. Lanham, Md.: Rowman and Littlefield.

Beckett, Chris. 2008. "For Your Consideration: *Age of Bronze*: Betrayal, Part One." *Comicon—Pulse: Comic Book News, Opinion, and Insight*.http://www.comicon.com/cgi-bin/ultimatebb.cgi?ubb=get_topic;f=39;t=000364.

Bender, Hy. 1999. *The Sandman Companion*. London: Titan.

Berard, Claude. 2000. "The Image of the Other and the Foreign Hero." In *Not the Classical Ideal: Athens and the Construction of the Other in Greek Art*, ed. Beth Cohen, 390–411. Leiden: Brill.

Blanshard, Alastair. 2007. "The Problems with Honouring Samos: An Athenian Document Relief and Its Interpretation." In *Art and Inscriptions in the Ancient World*, ed. Zahra Newby and Ruth Leader-Newby, 19–37. New York: Cambridge University Press.

Bloom, Allen. 1987. *The Closing of the American Mind*. New York: Simon and Schuster.

Blundell, Mary Whitlock. 1989. *Helping Friends and Harming Enemies: A Study in Sophocles and Greek Ethics*. New York: Cambridge University Press.

Boardman, John. 1975. *Athenian Red-figure Vases: The Archaic Period*. London: Thames and Hudson.

———. 1989. "Herakles, Peisistratos, and the Unconvinced." *Journal of Hellenic Studies* 109: 158–59.

Boivin de Villeneuve, Jean. 1715. *Apologie d'Homère et du bouclier d'Achille*. Paris: François Jouenne.

Bolen, Jean Shinoda. 1989. *Gods in Everyman: A New Psychology of Men's Lives and Loves*. San Franciso: Harper and Row.

Bongco, Mila. 2000. *Reading Comics: Language, Culture, and the Concept of the Superhero in Comic Books*. New York: Garland.

Bowermaster, Phil, and Stephen Gordon. 2007. "Seinfeld, Superman, and the Singularity." *The Speculist*. http://www.blog.speculist.com/archives/001336.html.

Bradford, Ernle. 1980. *The Battle for the West: Thermopylae*. New York: McGraw-Hill.

Briant, Pierre. 1989. "Histoire et idéologie: Les Grecs et la 'décadence perse.'" Reprinted as 2002. "History and Ideology: The Greeks and 'Persian Decadence.'" Trans. Antonia Neville in *Greeks and Barbarians*, ed. Thomas Harrison, 193–210. New York: Routledge.

Bridges, Emma. 2007. "Introduction." In *Cultural Responses to the Persian Wars*, ed. Emma Bridges, Edith Hall, and P. J. Rhodes, 3–29. New York: Oxford University Press.

Bukatman, Scott. 2003. *Matters of Gravity: Special Effects and Supermen in the 20th Century*. Durham: Duke University Press.

Burford, Alison. 1972. *Craftsmen in Greek and Roman Society*. London: Thames and Hudson.

Burgess, Jonathan. 2008. "Recent Reception of Homer: A Review Article." *Phoenix* 62: 184–95.

Burroughs, Edgar Rice. 1963. *Princess of Mars*. New York: Ballantine. First published in serial form as "Under the Moons of Mars" in *All-Story* (Feb. 1912).

Burton, Diana. 2001. "The Death of Gods in Greek Succession Myths." In *Homer, Tragedy and Beyond: Essays in Honour of P. E. Easterling*, ed. Felix Budelmann and Pantelis Michelakis, 43–56. London: Society for the Promotion of Hellenic Studies.

Burton, Philip. 1995. "The Values of a Classical Education: Satirical Elements in Robert Graves's Claudius Novels." *Review of English Studies* 46.182: 191–218.

Busiek, Kurt. 1996. Introduction to *Astro City: Life in the Big City*. La Jolla: Homage Comics.

Butrica, James L. 2005. "Some Myths and Anomalies in the Study of Roman Sexuality." In *Same-sex Desire and Love in Greco-Roman Antiquity and in the Classical Tradition of the West*, ed. Beert Verstraete and Vernon Provencal, 209–70. Copublished simultaneously in *Journal of Homosexuality* 49.3–4: 209–70.

Byre, Calvin. 1992. "Narration, Description, and Theme in the Shield of Achilles." *Classical Journal* 88.1: 33–42.

Camille, Michael. 1992. *Image on the Edge: The Margins of Mediaeval Art*. London: Reaktion.

Campbell, Joseph. 1949. *The Hero with a Thousand Faces*. Princeton: Princeton University Press.

———. 1991. *The Power of Myth*. With Bill Moyers. New York: Anchor.

Canfora, Luciano. 2008. *The True Story of the So-called Artemidorus Papyrus*. Bari: Edizioni di Pagina.

Cantarella, Eva. 1994. *Bisexuality in the Ancient World*. New Haven: Yale University Press.

Carlson, Johanna Draper. 2008. "Superhero Comic Readers Still Mostly Male." *Comics Worth Reading*. http://comicsworthreading.com/2008/01/24/superhero-comic-readers-still-mostly-male.

Carrier, David. 2000. *The Aesthetics of Comics*. University Park: Pennsylvania State University Press.

Cartledge, Paul. 2001. *Spartan Reflections*. Berkeley: University of California Press.

———. 2004. "What Have the Spartans Done for Us?: Sparta's Contribution to Western Civilization." *Greece and Rome* 51.2: 164–79.

———. 2006. *Thermopylae: The Battle That Changed the World*. London: Macmillan.

Castriota, David. 2000. "Justice, Kingship, and Imperialism: Rhetoric and Reality in Fifth-century B.C. Representations following the Persian Wars." In *Not the Classical Ideal*, ed. Beth Cohen, 443–80. Leiden: Brill.

Cavalier, K. 1995. "Did Not Potters Portray Peisistratos Posthumously as Herakles?" *Electronic Antiquity* 2.5. http://scholar.lib.vt.edu/ejournals/ElAnt/V2N5/cavalier.html

Cawelti, John. 1976. *Adventure, Mystery, and Romance*. Chicago: University of Chicago Press.

Cech, John. 1997. *A Rush of Dreamers: Being the Remarkable Story of Norton I, Emperor of the United States and Protector of Mexico*. New York: Marlowe.

Chabon, Michael. 2000. *The Amazing Adventures of Kavalier and Clay*. New York: Picador.

Charlesworth, James, Mark Harding, and Mark Kiley, eds. 1994. *The Lord's Prayer and Other Prayer Texts from the Greco-Roman Era*. Valley Forge: Trinity Press International.

Clarke, Michael. 1999. *Flesh and Spirit in the Songs of Homer: A Study of Words and Myths*. New York: Oxford University Press.

Clauss, James J. 1996. "A Course on Classical Mythology in Film." *Classical Journal* 91: 287–95.

Clough, Emma. 2004. "Loyalty and Liberty: Thermopylae in the Western Imagination." In *Spartan Society*, ed. Thomas J. Figueira, 363–84. Swansea: Classical Press of Wales.

Cole, Thomas. 1998. "Venus and Mars (*De Rerum Natura* 1.31–40)." In *Style and Tradition: Studies in Honor of Wendell Clausen*, ed. Peter Knox and Clive Foss, 3–15. Stuttgart: Teubner.

Coleman, John E., and Clark A. Walz. 1997. *Greeks and Barbarians: Essays on the Interactions between Greeks and non-Greeks in Antiquity and the Consequences for Eurocentrism*. Bethesda, Md.: CDL.

Conte, Gian Biagio. 1986. *The Rhetoric of Imitation: Genre and Poetic Memory in Virgil and Other Latin Poets*, ed. Charles Segal. Ithaca: Cornell University Press.

Conway, Gerry. 2006. "Introduction: Turning Point." In *Webslinger: Unauthorized Essays on Your Friendly Neighborhood Spider-Man*, ed. Gerry Conway and Leah Wilson, 1–4. Dallas: Benbella.

Coogan, Peter. 2006. *Superhero: The Secret Origin of a Genre*. Austin: Monkey Brain.

Cook, Erwin. 1999. " 'Active' and 'Passive' Heroics in the *Odyssey*." *Classical World* 93: 149–67.

Cooper, Guy L. 2002. *Greek Syntax: Early Greek Poetic and Herodotean Syntax*, vols. 3–4. Ann Arbor: University of Michigan Press.

Cooper, Park. 2007. "Olympus-mature: Suggested for Mature Readers (The Eric Shanower Interview)." *Comics Bulletin* 14. http://www.comicsbulletin.com/pb/118978816249187.htm.

Cribiore, Raffaella. 2001. *Gymnastics of the Mind: Greek Education in Hellenistic and Roman Egypt*. Princeton: Princeton University Press.

Crotty, Kevin. 1994. *The Poetics of Supplication: Homer's* Iliad *and* Odyssey. Ithaca: Cornell University Press.

Csapo, Eric. 2005. *Theories of Mythology*. Malden: Blackwell.

Cyrino, Monica S. 2005. *Big Screen Rome*. Malden: Blackwell.

Dale, Amy M. 1968. *The Lyric Metres of Greek Drama*, 2nd ed. New York: Cambridge University Press.

D'Angelo, M., and L. Cantoni. 2006. "Comics: Semiotic Approaches." In *Encyclopedia of Language and Linguistics*, 2nd ed., ed. Keith Brown, 627–35. Oxford: Elsevier.

Daniels, Les. 2000. *Wonder Woman: The Complete History*. San Francisco: Chronicle.

Darmon, Jean-Pierre. 1991. "The Powers of War: Ares and Athena in Greek Mythology." In *Mythologies*, ed. Yves Bonnefoy, 414–15. Chicago: University of Chicago Press.

Davison, J. A. 1962. "Literature and Literacy in Ancient Greece: II. Caging the Muses." *Phoenix* 16.4: 219–33.

Deacy, Susan. 2000. "Athena and Ares: War, Violence, and Warlike Deities." In *War and Violence in Ancient Greece*, ed. Hans Van Wees, 285–98. London: Duckworth.

———, and Karen F. Pierce, eds. 1997. *Rape in Antiquity: Sexual Violence in the Greek and Roman Worlds*. London: Duckworth.

Dean, Michael. 2006. "The New Patriotism: Comics and the War in Iraq, Part II." *Comics Journal* 276. http://www.tcj.com/index.php?option=com_content&task=view&id=362&Itemid=48.

DeFalco, Tom. 2004. *Comics Creators on Spider-Man*. London: Titan.

de Jong, Irene J. F. 1987. *Narrators and Focalizers: The Presentation of the Story in the* Iliad. Amsterdam: Grüner.

de Vries, Keith. 2000. "The Nearly Other: The Attic Vision of Phrygians and Lydians." In *Not the Classical Ideal: Athens and the Construction of the Other in Greek Art*, ed. Beth Cohen, 338–64. Boston: Brill.

Del Grande, Carlo. 2006. "Intervista a Eric Shanower." *Comicus*. http://www.comicus.it/view.php?section=interv iste&id=106.

De Man, Paul. 1989. "The Rhetoric of Temporality." In *Blindness and Insight: Essays in the Rhetoric of Contemporary Criticism*, Second Edition. 187–228. Minneapolis: University of Minnesota Press.

Denniston, John Dewar. 1959. *The Greek Particles*, 2nd ed. Oxford: Clarendon.

Deppey, Dirk. 2005. "Eric Shanower: Interviewed by Dirk Deppey." *Comics Journal* 265. http://www.tcj.com/index.php?option=com_content&task=view&id=329&Itemid=48.

Diggle, James. 1981. *Studies on the Text of Euripides*. New York: Oxford University Press.

Doherty, Thomas Patrick. 2007. *Hollywood's Censor: Joseph I. Breen and the Production Code Administration*. New York: Columbia University Press.

Doran, Michael. 2008. "Diamond's September 2008 Comics Sales Charts and Market Share." *Newsarama*. http://www.newsarama.com/comics/081020-diamond-sales-charts.html.

Dorfman, Ariel, and Armand Mattelart. 1975. *How to Read Donald Duck: Imperialist Ideology in the Disney Comic*, trans. David Kunzle. New York: International General.

Doty, William G. 1993. *Myths of Masculinity*. New York: Crossroad.

Dougherty, Carol. 1998. "Sowing the Seeds of Violence: Rape, Women, and the Land." In *Parchments of Gender*, ed. Maria Wyke, 267–84. New York: Oxford University Press.

Doyle, Thomas F. 1943. "What's Wrong with the 'Comics'?" *Catholic World* 156: 548–57.

Dunkle, J. Roger. 1971. "The Rhetorical Tyrant in Roman Historiography: Sallust, Livy, and Tacitus." *Classical World* 65.1: 12–20.

Dunniway, Troy. 2000. "Using the Hero's Journey in Games." *Gamasutra*. http://www.gamasutra.com/view/feature/3118/using_the_heros_journey_in_games.php.

Eco, Umberto. 1972. "The Myth of Superman," *Diacritics* 2, 14–21. Reprinted In *Arguing Comics*, ed. Jeet Heer and Kent Worchester (2004), 146–64. Trans. N. Chilton. Jackson: University Press of Mississippi.

———. 1979. *The Role of the Reader: Explorations in the Semiotics of Texts*. Bloomington: Indiana University Press.

———. 1990. *The Limits of Interpretation*. Bloomington: Indiana University Press.

Edmunds, Lowell. 2002. "Mars as Hellenistic Lover: Lucretius, *De rerum natura* 1.29–40 and Its Hellenistic Subtexts." *International Journal of Classical Tradition* 8.3: 343–58.

Edwards, Mark W. 1991. *The Iliad: A Commentary. Books 17–20*, vol. 5. New York: Cambridge University Press.

Eisner, Will. 1985. *Comics and Sequential Art: Principles and Practice of the World's Most Popular Art Form*, expanded ed. Tamarac, Fla.: Poorhouse Press.

———. 1996. *Graphic Storytelling and Visual Narrative*. Tamarac, Fla.: Poorhouse Press.

———, Frank Miller, and Charles Brownstein. 2005. *Eisner/Miller*. Milwaukee: Dark Horse.

Ellis, Mark, and Melissa Martin-Ellis. 2008. *The Everything Guide to Writing Graphic Novels*. Avon, Mass.: Adams Media.

Fantham, Elaine. 2004. Review of A. Barrett, *Livia: First Lady of Imperial Rome*. *Amphora* 3.1: 1–5.

Farkas, Ann. 1974. *Achaemenid Sculpture*. Istanbul: Nederlands Historisch-archaeologisch Instituut in het Nabije Oosten.

Felson, Nancy. 1994. *Regarding Penelope: From Character to Poetics*. Princeton: Princeton University Press.

Field, Syd. 1979. *Screenplay: The Foundations of Screenwriting*, expanded ed. New York: Dell.

———. 1998. *The Screenwriter's Problem Solver: How to Recognize, Identify, and Define Screenwriting Problems*. New York: Dell.

Fingeroth, Danny. 2004. *Superman on the Couch: What Superheroes Really Tell Us about Ourselves and Our Society*. New York: Continuum.

———. 2007. *Disguised as Clark Kent: Jews, Comics, and the Creation of the Superhero*. New York: Continuum.

———. 2008. "Interview with Brian Michael Bendis." In *The Best of Write Now!* ed. Danny Fingeroth, 6–19. Raleigh: TwoMorrows.

Finley, John H. 1978. *Homer's Odyssey*. Cambridge, Mass.: Harvard University Press.

Fish, Stanley. 1980. "Interpreting the Variorum." In *Is There a Text in This Class?: The Authority of Interpretative Communities*, 147–73. Cambridge, Mass.: Harvard University Press.

Fischer, Curt Theodor, and Friedrich Vogel, eds. 1964. *Diodori bibliotheca historica*, vol. 1. Leipzig: Teubner.

Fitzmyer, Joseph. 1981. *Luke: Introduction, Translation, and Notes*. Anchor Bible vol. 28. Garden City, NY: Doubleday.

Foley, John Miles. 1999. *Homer's Traditional Art*. University Park: Pennsylvania State University Press.

Fontana, Ernest. 1995. "Chivalry and Modernity in Raymond Chandler's *The Big Sleep*." In *The Critical Response to Raymond Chandler*. ed. J.K. Van Dover, 159–166. Westport: Greenwood Press.

Ford, J. Massyngberde. 1975. *Revelation: Introduction, Translation, and Commentary*. Anchor Bible vol. 38. Garden City, NY: Doubleday.

Fowler, Don P. 1991. "Narrate and Describe: The Problem of Ekphrasis." *Journal of Roman Studies* 81: 22–35.

———. 1995. "From Epos to Cosmos: Lucretius, Ovid, and the Poetics of Segmentation." In *Ethics and Rhetoric: Classical Essays for Donald Russell on His Seventy-fifth Birthday*, ed. Doreen C. Innes, Harry Hine, and Christopher Pelling, 3–18. Oxford: Clarendon.

Francis, E. D. 1990. *Image and Idea in Fifth-century Greece: Art and Literature after the Persian Wars*, ed. Michael Vickers. New York: Routledge.

Frazer, Richard M., Jr. 1966. *The Trojan War: The Chronicles of Dictys of Crete and Dares the Phrygian*. Bloomington: Indiana University Press.

Furley, David. 1970. "Variations on Themes from Empedocles in Lucretius' Proem." *Bulletin of the Institute of Classical Studies* 17: 55–64.

Fusanosuke, Natsume. 2003. "Japanese Manga: Its Expression and Polarity," trans. Ueki Kaori. *Asian/Pacific Book Development* 34.1: 3–5. http://www.accu.or.jp/appreb/09/pdf34-1/34-1P003–005.pdf.

Gallazzi, Claudio, Bärbel Kramer, and Salvatore Settis. 2008. *Il papiro di Artemidoro*. Milan: LED.

Gamel, Mary Kay, and Ruby Blondell. 2005. "Introduction." *Ancient Mediterranean Women in Modern Mass Media*. *Helios* 32.2: 111–26.

Gantz, Timothy. 1993. *Early Greek Myth: A Guide to Literary and Artistic Sources*. Baltimore: Johns Hopkins University Press.

Gaumer, Patrick. 2004. *Larousse de la bande dessinée*. France: Larousse.

Genette, Gérard. 1997. *Palimpsests: Literature in the Second Degree*, trans. Channa Newman and Claude Doubinsky. Lincoln: University of Nebraska Press.

George, Milo, ed. 2003. *The Comics Journal Library*. Vol. 2, *Frank Miller*. Seattle: Fantagraphics.

Gertler, Nat, and Steve Lieber. 2004. *The Complete Idiot's Guide to Creating a Graphic Novel*. Indianapolis: Alpha.

Goldhill, Simon. 2002. "Battle Narrative and Politics in Aeschylus' *Persae*." In *Greeks and Barbarians*, ed. Thomas Harrison, 50–61. New York: Routledge.

———. 2007a. "*Naked* and *O Brother, Where Art Thou?* The Politics and Poetics of Epic Cinema." In *Homer in the Twentieth Century*, ed. Barbara Graziosi and Emily Greenwood, 245–67. New York: Oxford University Press.

———. 2007b. "What Is Ekphrasis For?" *Classical Philology* 102.1: 1–19.

Golding, William. 1966. *The Hot Gates*. New York: Harcourt, Brace, and World.

Gordon, Ian, Mark Janovich, and Matthew P. McAllister, eds. 2007. *Film and Comic Books*. Jackson: University of Mississippi Press.

Gould, John. 1973. "Hiketeia." *Journal of Hellenic Studies* 93: 74–103.

Grant, John R. 1961. "Leonidas' Last Stand." *Phoenix* 15.1: 14–27.

Groensteen, Thierry. 2007. *The System of Comics*, trans. Bart Beaty and Nick Nguyen. Jackson: University Press of Mississippi.

Hajdu, David. 2008. *The Ten-cent Plague: The Great Comic-book Scare and How It Changed America*. New York: Farrar, Straus, and Giroux.

Hall, Edith. 1989. *Inventing the Barbarian: Greek Self-definition through Tragedy*. Oxford: Clarendon.

———. 1994. "Drowning by Nomes: The Greeks, Swimming, and Timotheus' *Persians*." In *The Birth of the European Identity: The Europe-Asia Contrast in Greek Thought 490–322 B.C.*, ed. H. A. Khan, 44–80. Nottingham: University of Nottingham.

———. 1996. *Aeschylus: Persians*. Warminster, England: Aris and Phillips.

———. 2008. *The Return of Ulysses: A Cultural History of Homer's* Odyssey. Baltimore: Johns Hopkins University Press.

Hallett, J. P. 1977. "Perusinae Glandes and the Changing Image of Augustus." *American Journal of Ancient History* 2: 151–71.

Hammerstaedt, Jürgen. 2000. "Gryllos: Die antike Bedeutung eines modernen archäologischen Begriffs." *Zeitschrift für Papyrologie und Epigraphik* 29: 29–46.

Hamon, Philippe. 1981. "Rhetorical Status of the Descriptive," trans. Patricia Baudoin. *Yale French Studies* 61: 1–26.

Hanfmann, George M. A. 1957. "Narration in Greek Art." *American Journal of Archaeology* 61.1: 71–78.

Hansbury, William L. 1977. *The William Leo Hansbury African History Notebook: Africa and Africans as Seen by Classical Writers*, ed. Joseph E. Harris. Washington, D.C.: Howard University Press.

Hanson, Victor Davis. 1989. *The Western Way of War*. New York: Knopf.

———. 2001. *Why the West Has Won: Carnage and Culture from Salamis to Vietnam*. London: Faber and Faber.

———. 2006. "History and the Movie '300.' " *Private Papers*. http://www.victorhanson.com/articles/hanson101106.html.

Hardie, Phillip R. 1985. "Imago Mundi: Cosmological and Theological Aspects of the Shield of Achilles." *Journal of Hellenic Studies* 105: 11–31.

Hardwick, Lorna. 2003. *Reception Studies: New Surveys in Classics*. New York: Oxford University Press.

———, and Christopher Stray, eds. 2008. *A Companion to Classical Receptions*. Malden, Mass.: Blackwell.

Harris, William V. 1989. *Ancient Literacy*. Cambridge, Mass.: Harvard University Press.

Harvey, Robert C. 1996. *The Art of the Comic Book: An Aesthetic History*. Jackson: University of Mississippi Press.

Hatfield, Charles. 2005. *Alternative Comics: An Emerging Literature*. Jackson: University Press of Mississippi.

Heer, Jaret. 2006. "Little Nemo in Comicsland." *Virginia Quarterly Review* 82: 104–21.

Henderson, John. 2007. "The 'Euripides Reds' Series: Best-laid Plans at OUP." In *Classical Books, Scholarship, and Publishing in Britain since 1800*, *BICS* suppl. 101, ed. Christopher Stray, 143–75. London: Institute of Classical Studies.

Henry, Freeman G., ed. 1994. *Discontinuity and Fragmentation in French Literature*, vol. 21. French Literature Series. Atlanta: Editions Rodopi.

"Heroes of the California Rebels." 1965. *Esquire* (September).

Heubeck, Alfred, Stephanie West, and J. B. Hainsworth. 1988. *A Commentary on Homer's* Odyssey: *Introduction and Books I–VIII*, vol. 1. Oxford: Clarendon.

Hillman, James. 1987. "Wars, Arms, Rams, Mars: On the Love of War." In *Facing Apocalypse*, ed. Valerie Andrews, Walter Bosnak, and Karen Goodwin, 118–36. Dallas: Spring.

Hinds, Stephen. 2005. "Defamiliarizing Latin Literature, from Petrarch to Pulp Fiction." *Transactions of the American Philological Association* 135.1: 49–81.

Hodgman, John. 2008. "Comics." *New York Times: Sunday Book Review* (June 1): 2–3.

Hordern, James H. 2002. *The Fragments of Timotheus of Miletus*. Oxford classical monographs. New York: Oxford University Press.

Horn, Maurice. 1999. *The World Encyclopedia of Comics*, 2nd ed. Philadelphia: Chelsea.

Hughley, John R. 2005. "IU's Red-hot Superfriends. Exhibit Explores Comics as Modern Mythology." *IU Home Pages*. http://homepages.indiana.edu/2005/09–30/story.php?id=65.

Hurwit, Jeffrey. 1977. "Image and Frame in Greek Art." *American Journal of Archaeology* 81.1: 1–30.

Iser, Wolfgang. 1978. *The Act of Reading: A Theory of Aesthetic Response*, trans. David Henry Wilson. Baltimore: Johns Hopkins University Press.

Ito, Kinko. 2008. "Manga in Japanese History." In *Japanese Visual Culture: Explorations in the World of Manga and Anime*, ed. Mark W. MacWilliams, 26–47. Armonk, N.Y.: Sharpe.

Ito, Robert. 2006. "The Gore of Greece, Torn from a Comic." *New York Times*. http://www.nytimes.com/2006/11/26/movies/26ito.html.

Jones, William B. 2002. *Classics Illustrated: A Cultural History, with Illustrations*. New York: Basic Books.

Joshel, Sandra R. 1992. "The Body Female and the Body Politic: Livy's Lucretia and Verginia." In *Pornography and Representation in Greece and Rome*, ed. Amy Richlin, 112–30. New York: Oxford University Press.

Kahane, Ahuvia. 1994. *The Interpretation of Order: A Study in the Poetics of Homeric Reception*. New York: Oxford University Press.

Kakalios, James. 2005. *The Physics of Superheroes*. New York: Gotham.

Kallendorf, Craig W., ed. 2007. *A Companion to the Classical Tradition*. Malden, Mass.: Blackwell.

Kaplan, Arie. 2006. *Masters of the Comic Book Universe Revealed! Will Eisner, Stan Lee, Neil Gaiman, and More!* Chicago: Chicago Review Press.

———. 2008. *From Krakow to Krypton: Jews and Comic Books*. Philadelphia: Jewish Publication Society.

Kashani, Tony. 2007. "*300:* Proto-Fascism and the Manufacturing of Complicity." http://dissidentvoice.org/Apr07/Kashani05.htm.

Katirtzigianoglou, Elias. 2007. "Eric Shanower: An Epic in Progress." *Comicdom*. http://www.comicdom.gr/interviews.php?id=23&lang=en.

Katz, Marylin A. 1991. *Penelope's Renown: Meaning and Indeterminacy in the Odyssey*. Princeton: Princeton University Press.

Kaveney, Roz. 2008. *Superheroes! Capes and Crusaders in Comics and Films*. New York: Tauris.

Kaye, Richard A. 1996. "Losing His Religion: Saint Sebastian as Contemporary Gay Martyr." In *Outlooks: Lesbian and Gay Sexualities and Visual Cultures*, ed. Peter Horne and Reina Lewis, 86–105. London: Routledge.

Keller, Katherine. 2000. "The Wizard of Bronze: An Epic Interview with Eric Shanower." *Sequential Tart* 3.7. http://www.sequentialtart.com/archive/july00/shanower.shtml.

Kelly, Tadhg. 2005a. "The Hero's Journey." *Gamasutra*. http://www.gamasutra.com/php-bin/letter_display.php?letter_id=888.

———. 2005b. "The Hero's Journey: The Saga Continues." *Gamasutra*. http://www.gamasutra.com/php-bin/letter_display.php?letter_id=895.

Kennedy, Duncan F. 2002. "Recent Receptions of Ovid." In *The Cambridge Companion to Ovid*, ed. Phillip Hardie, 320–35. New York: Cambridge University Press.

Kern, Adam. 2006. *Manga from the Floating World: Comicbook Culture and the Kibyōshi of Edo Japan*. Cambridge, Mass.: Harvard Asia Center.

Kessler, Peter. 1995. *The Complete Guide to Asterix*. London: Hodder Children's Books.

Khoury, George. 2007. *Image Comics: The Road to Independence*. Raleigh: TwoMorrows.

King, Anthony. 2001. "Vercingetorix, Asterix, and the Gauls: Gallic Symbols in French Politics and Culture." In *Images of Rome: Perceptions of Ancient Rome in Europe and the United States in the Modern Age*, *JRA* suppl. 44, ed. R. Hingley, 113–23. Portsmouth, R.I.: Journal of Roman Archaeology.

Kinsella, Sharon. 2000. *Adult Manga*. Honolulu: University of Hawaii Press.

Kirby, Jack. 2004. *Marvel Visionaries*, vol. 1. New York: Marvel Comics.

Kirk, Geoffrey Steven and John Earle Raven. 1957. *The Presocratic Philosophers: A Critical History with a Selection of Texts*. New York: Cambridge University Press.

Klock, Geoff. 2002. *How to Read Superhero Comics and Why*. New York: Continuum.

Knigge, Andreas C. 1985. *Sex im Comic*. Frankfurt am Main: Ullstein.

Kotlajic, Veronica. 2006. *The Muse: A Pictorial Journey of Fantasy and Pin-up*. New York: Heavy Metal Magazine.

Kovacs, David. 1995. *Euripides: Children of Heracles, Hippolytus, Andromache, Hecuba*. Cambridge, Mass.: Harvard University Press.

Koyama-Richard, Brigitte. 2007. *One Thousand Years of Manga*, trans. David Radzinowicz. Paris: Flammarion.

Kramer, Bärbel. 2001. "Urkundenreferat 2000." *Archiv für Papyrusforschung und verwandte Gebiete* 47 : 284–367.

Krieger, Murray. 1992. *Ekphrasis: The Illusion of the Natural Sign*. Baltimore: Johns Hopkins University Press.

Krukowski, Samantha. 1990. "Pots on Pots: Images of Pottery-making Processes on Ancient Greek Vases." http://www.rasa.net/writings/pots.html.

Lamberton, Robert. 1986. *Homer the Theologian: Neoplatonist Allegorical Reading and the Growth of the Epic Tradition*. Berkeley: University of California Press.

Langlands, Rebecca. 2006. *Sexual Morality in Ancient Rome*. New York: Cambridge University Press.

Leaf, Walter, and M. A. Bayfield. 1962. *The Iliad of Homer*. London: Macmillan.

Lee, Stan, and George Mair. 2002. *Excelsior!: The Amazing Life of Stan Lee*. New York: Simon and Schuster.

Legrand, Phillipe Ernest. 1948. *Hérodote: Histoires, Livres 1–9*. Paris: Belles Lettres.

LeGuin, Ursula. 2006. "Some Books I've Liked." Home page. http://www.ursulakleguin.com/Note-Books-061210.html.

Lent, John A., ed. 1999. *Pulp Demons: International Dimensions of the Postwar Anti-comics Campaign.* London: Associated University Presses.

Lessing, Gotthold Ephraim. 1766/1853. *Laocoon: An Essay on the Limits of Painting and Poetry,* trans. E. C. Beasley. London: Longman, Brown, Green, and Longmans.

Levene, David. 2007. "Xerxes Goes to Hollywood." In *Cultural Responses to the Persian Wars,* ed. Emma Bridges, Edith Hall, and P. J. Rhodes, 383–403. New York: Oxford University Press.

Levine, Daniel. 1994. "Classica Americana Troglodytica: V. T. Hamlin's *Alley Oop,* April 1939–February 1940; The Epics Meet the Comics." *Classical and Modern Literature* 14: 365–86.

Lissarrague, François. 1997. "The Athenian Image of the Foreigner." In *Greeks and Barbarians,* ed. Thomas Harrison, 101–24. New York: Routledge.

Lloyd-Jones, Hugh. 1982. *Blood for the Ghosts: Classical Influences in the Nineteenth and Twentieth Centuries.* Baltimore: Johns Hopkins University Press.

Lynch, Marc. 2005. *Voices of the New Arab Public: Iraq, al-Jazeera, and Middle East Politics Today.* New York: Columbia University Press.

Lynn-George, Michael. 1988. *Epos, Word, Narrative, and the Iliad.* Atlantic Highlands, N.J.: Humanities Press International.

Maas, Paul. 1958. "The ΓΡΥΛΛΟΣ Papyrus." *Greece and Rome* 27: 171–73.

MacCary, Thomas. 1972. "Menander's Soldiers: Their Names, Roles, and Masks." *American Journal of Philology* 93: 279–98.

Mackie, Chris J. 1992. "Vergil's Dirae, South Italy, and Etruria." *Phoenix* 46: 352–61.

MacKinnon, Kenneth. 1986. *Greek Tragedy into Film.* London: Croom Helm.

Marshall, C. W. 1999. "Some Fifth-century Masking Conventions." *Greece and Rome,* 2nd ser. 46: 188–202.

———. 2001. "A Gander at the Goose Play." *Theatre Journal* 53: 53–71.

Martindale, Charles, and Richard F. Thomas, eds. 2006. *Classics and the Uses of Reception.* Malden, Mass.: Blackwell.

McCloud, Scott. 1993. *Understanding Comics: The Invisible Art.* Northampton: Kitchen Sink.

———. 2000. *Reinventing Comics: How Imagination and Technology Are Revolutionizing an Art Form.* Northampton: Kitchen Sink.

———. 2005. *Making Comics: Storytelling Secrets of Comics, Manga, and Graphic Novels.* Northampton: Kitchen Sink.

McElduff, Siobhán. 2006. "Fractured Understandings: Towards a History of Classical Reception among Non-Elite Groups." In *Classics and the Uses of Reception,* ed. C. Martindale and R. Thomas, 180–91. Malden, MA: Blackwell.

McDonald, Marianne. 1983. *Euripides in Cinema: The Heart Made Visible.* Philadelphia: Centrum Philadelphia.

———. 2002. "Moving Icons: Teaching Euripides in Film." In *Approaches to Teaching the Dramas of Euripides,* ed. Robin Mitchell-Boyask, 60–69. New York: MLA.

McLaughlin, Jeff, ed. 2005. *Comics as Philosophy.* Jackson: University of Mississippi.

———, ed. 2007. *Stan Lee Conversations.* Jackson: University Press of Mississippi.

Miller, Margaret. 1992. "The Parasol: An Oriental Status-symbol in Late Archaic and Classical Athens." *Journal of Hellenic Studies* 112: 91–105.

———. 1997. *Athens and Persia in the Fifth Century B.C.: A Study in Cultural Receptivity.* New York: Cambridge University Press.

———. 2000. "The Myth of Bousiris: Ethnicity and Art." In *Not the Classical Ideal: Athens and the Construction of the Other in Greek Art,* ed. Beth Cohen, 413–42. Leiden: Brill.

Minchin, Elizabeth. 2001. *Homer and the Resources of Memory: Some Applications of Cognitive Theory to the Iliad and the Odyssey.* New York: Oxford University Press.

Monro, David Binning. 1891. *A Grammar of the Homeric Dialect,* 2nd ed. Oxford: Clarendon.

Moore, Fabienne. 2000. "Homer Revisited: Anne Le Fevre Dacier's Preface to Her Prose Translation of the *Iliad* in Early Eighteenth-century France." *Studies in the Literary Imagination* 33.2: 87–107.

Morris, Ian MacGregor. 2004. "The Paradigm of Democracy: Sparta in Enlightenment Thought." In *Spartan Society,* ed. Thomas J. Figueira, 339–62. Swansea: Classical Press of Wales.

Murphy, B. Keith. 2006. "The Origin of the Sandman." In *The Sandman Papers,* ed. Joe Sanders, 3–24. Seattle: Fantagraphics.

Muellner, L. 1976. *The Meaning of* Euxomai *through Its Formulas*. Innsbruck: Innsbrucker Beiträge zur Sprachwissenschaft.

Nachstädt, Wilhelm. 1935. *Plutarchi Moralia*, vol. 2.1. Leipzig: Teubner.

Nisbet, Gideon. 2002. " 'Barbarous Verses': A Mixed-media Narrative from Greco-Roman Egypt." *Apollo* 156.485: 15–19.

———. 2006. *Ancient Greece in Film and Popular Culture*. Exeter: Bristol Phoenix.

Nolan, Christopher, dir. 2008. *The Dark Knight*. Warner Brothers Pictures.

Nolan, Michelle. 1996. "Beauty and the Marvel Beasts. Venus Was Several Comic Books in One!" *Comic Book Marketplace Monthly* 2.39: 19–22.

Nyberg, Amy K. 1998. *Seal of Approval: The History of the Comics Code*. Jackson: University Press of Mississippi.

Nyman, Jopi. 1997. *Men Alone: Masculinity, Individualism, and Hard-boiled Fiction*. Atlanta: Rodopi.

Ober, Josiah. 1982. "Tiberius and the Political Testament of Augustus." *Historia* 31: 306–28.

O'Connor, Thomas F. 1995. "The National Organization for Decent Literature: A Phase in American Catholic Censorship." *Library Quarterly* 65.4: 386–414.

O'Neil, Dennis. 2001. *The DC Comics Guide to Writing Comics*. New York: Watson-Guptill.

———. 2005. "The Crimson Viper vs. the Maniacal Morphing Meme." *Superheroes and Philosophy: Truth, Justice, and the Socratic Way*, ed. Tom Morris and Matt Morris, 21–28. Peru, Ill.: Open Court.

Ong, Walter. 1945. "The Comics and the Super State: Glimpses down the Back Alley of the Mind." *Arizona Quarterly* 1.3: 34–48.

Onians, John. 1991. "Idea and Product: Potter and Philosopher in Classical Athens." *Journal of Design History* 4.2: 65–73.

O'Rourke, Dan, and Pravin A. Rodrigues. 2007. "The 'Transcreation' of a Mediated Myth: Spider-man in India." In *The Amazing Transforming Superhero! Essays on the Revision of Characters in Comic Books, Film, and Television*, ed. Terrence R. Wandtke, 112–28. Jefferson, N.C.: McFarland.

Otto, Walter Friedrich. 1954. *The Homeric Gods: The Spiritual Significance of Greek Religion*, trans. Moses Hadas. New York: Pantheon.

Pack, Roger Ambrose. 1965. *The Greek and Latin Literary Texts from Greco-Roman Egypt*, 2nd rev. and enlarged ed. Ann Arbor: University of Michigan Press.

Page, Denys L. 1957. "P.Oxy. 2331 and Others." *Classical Review* 7: 189–92.

———. 1981. *Further Greek Epigrams*. rev. R. D. Dawe and James Diggle. New York: Cambridge University Press.

Parker, Holt. 1997. "The Teratogenic Grid." In *Roman Sexualities*, ed. Judith P. Hallett and Marilyn B. Skinner, 47–65. Princeton: Princeton University Press.

Peraino, Judith Ann. 2006. *Listening to the Sirens: Musical Technologies of Queer Identity from Homer to Hedwig*. Berkeley: University of California Press.

Pinney, Gloria Ferrari. 1984. "For the Heroes Are at Hand." *Journal of Hellenic Studies* 104: 181–83.

Pope, Alexander. 1715–1720. *The Iliad of Homer*. 6 vols. London: Lintot.

Potter, David S. 2004. "Gladiators and Blood Sport." In *Gladiator: Film and History*, ed. Martin Winkler, 73–86. Malden MA: Blackwell.

Pucci, Pietro. 1998. "The Song of the Sirens." In *The Song of the Sirens: Essays on Homer*, 1–9. Lanham: Rowman and Littlefield.

Pustz, Matthew. 1999. *Comic Book Culture: Fanboys and True Believers*. Jackson: University Press of Mississippi.

Raimi, Sam, dir. 2002. *Spider-Man*. Columbia Pictures.

Raven, D. S. 1962. *Greek Metre: An Introduction*. London: Faber and Faber.

Rawson, Elizabeth. 1969. *The Spartan Tradition in European Thought*. Oxford: Clarendon.

Raysor, Thomas, ed. 1936. *Coleridge's Miscellaneous Criticism*. Cambridge, Mass.: Harvard University Press.

Rebenich, Stefan. 2002. "From Thermopylae to Stalingrad: The Myth of Leonidas in German Historiography." In *Sparta: Beyond the Mirage*, ed. Anton Powell and Stephen Hodkinson, 323–49. Swansea: Classical Press of Wales.

Reinhold, Meyer. 1981. "The Declaration of War against Cleopatra." *Classical Journal* 77.2: 97–103.

Revermann, Martin. 2008. "Some Recent Work in Reception Studies of Greek Drama." *Journal of Hellenic Studies* 128: 175–78.

Reynolds, Richard. 1992. *Superheroes: A Modern Mythology*. London: Batsford.

Rhodes, P. J. 2007. "The Impact of the Persian Wars on Classical Greece." In *Cultural Responses to the Persian Wars*, ed. Emma Bridges, Edith Hall, and P. J. Rhodes, 31–46. New York: Oxford University Press.

Rice, Prudence M. 1984. *Pots and Potters: Current Approaches in Ceramic Archaeology*. Los Angeles: Institute of Archaeology University of California Los Angeles.

———. 1987. *Pottery Analysis: A Sourcebook*. Chicago: University of Chicago Press.

Richard, Olive. 1942. "Our Women Are Our Future." *Family Circle*. http://www.wonderwoman-online.com/articles/fc-marston.html.

Richlin, Amy. 1992. "Reading Ovid's Rapes." In *Pornography and Representation in Greece and Rome*, ed. Amy Richlin, 158–79. New York: Oxford University Press.

———. 1993. "Not before Homosexuality: The Materiality of the Cinaedus and the Roman Law against Love between Men." *Journal of the History of Sexuality* 3: 523–73.

Richter, Gisela Marie Augusta. 1958. *Attic Red-figured Vases*, rev. ed. New Haven: Yale University Press.

Robb, Kevin. 1994. *Literacy and Paideia in Ancient Greece*. New York: Oxford University Press.

Roberts, Colin H. 1954. "2331: Verses on the Labours of Heracles." In *Oxyrhynchus Papyri 22*, ed. Edgar Lobel and Colin H. Roberts, 84–88. London: Egypt Exploration Society.

Roisman, Hanna M. 2006. "Helen in the *Iliad*; *Causa Belli* and Victim of War: From Silent Weaver to Public Speaker." *American Journal of Philology* 127.1: 1–36.

Rollins, Prentis. 2006. *The Making of a Graphic Novel Double-sided Flip Book*. New York: Watson-Guptill.

Romey, Kristin. 2004. "Achilles at the Gates!" *Archaeology* 57.3. http://www.archaeology.org/online/interviews/shanower.html.

Rozakis, Bob. 2003. "The Furies." *Silver Bullet Comics*. http://www.silverbulletcomicbooks.com/bobro/105878867911875.htm.

Sabin, Roger. 1996. *Comics, Comix, and Graphic Novels: A History of Graphic Art*. London: Phaidon.

Sanders, Joe, ed. 2006. *The Sandman Papers*. Seattle: Fantagraphics.

Saunders, Stephen G. 2007. "Rise of the Aegean: Eric Shanower." *Comics Bulletin*. http://www.comicsbulletin.com/features/117305441030066.htm.

Sawyer, Michael. 1987. "Albert Lewis Kanter and the Classics: The Man behind the Gilbert Company." *Journal of Popular Culture* 20.4: 1–18.

Scaggs, John. 2005. *Crime Fiction*. London: Routledge.

Schauenberg, K. 1975. "Εὐρυμέδον εἰμί." *Mitteilungen des deutschen archäologischen Instituts, Athenische Abteilung* 90: 118.

Schmidt, Victoria. 2005. *Story Structure Architect*. Cincinnati: Writer's Digest Books.

Scodel, Ruth, and Anja Bettenworth. 2008. *Whither Quo Vadis?* Malden, Mass.: Blackwell.

Screech, Matthew. 2005. *Masters of the Ninth Art: Bandes dessinées and Franco-Belgian Identity*. Liverpool: Liverpool University Press.

Seabrook, John. 1999. "Letter from Skywalker Ranch: Why Is the Force Still with Us?" In *George Lucas: Interviews*, ed. S. Kline, 190–215. Jackson: University Press of Mississippi.

Segal, Charles. 1986. *Interpreting Greek Tragedy: Myth, Poetry, Text*. Ithaca: Cornell University Press.

Segal, Robert. 1987. *Joseph Campbell: An Introduction*. New York: Garland.

Sekunda, Nick, and Simon Chew. 1992. *The Persian Army, 560–330 BC*. Elite series 42. London: Osprey.

Skinner, Marilyn. 1982. "Pretty Lesbius." *Transactions of the American Philological Association* 112: 197–208.

Smith, Amy C. 1999. "Eurymedon and the Evolution of Political Personifications in the Early Classical Period." *Journal of Hellenic Studies* 119: 128–41.

Snowden, Frank. 1970. *Blacks in Antiquity: Ethiopians in the Greco-Roman Experience*. Cambridge, Mass.: Belknap.

Solomon, Jon. 2001. *The Ancient World in the Cinema*. New Haven: Yale University Press.

Sommerstein, Alan, ed. 2008. *Aeschylus*, 3 vols. Cambridge, Mass.: Harvard University Press.

Sparkes, Brian A. 1996. *The Red and the Black: Studies in Greek Pottery*. New York: Routledge.

Spurgeon, Tom, ed. 2006. *The Comics Journal Library 6: The Writers*. Seattle: Fantagraphics.

Stanley, Kelli E. 2005. " 'Suffering Sappho!': Wonder Woman and the (Re)Invention of the Feminine Ideal." *Helios* 32: 143–71.

Steranko, Jim. 1972. *The Steranko History of Comics*, vol. 2. Supergraphics. Reading, Penn.

Stone, Oliver, dir. 2004. *Alexander*. Warner Bros.

Storey, John. 1993. *An Introductory Guide to Cultural Theory and Popular Culture*. London: Harvester-Wheatsheaf.

Takeuchi, Osamu, Yoshihiro Yonezawa, and Tomoko Yamada, eds. 2006. *Gendai Manga Hakubutsukan* [*Encyclopedia of Contemporary Manga*], *1945–2005*. Tokyo: Shōgakukan.

Tallon, Felix, and Jerry Walls. 2000. "Superman and Kingdom Come: The Surprise of Philosophical Theology." In *Superheroes and Philosophy: Truth, Justice, and the Socratic Way*, ed. Tom Morris and Matt Morris, 207–20. Chicago: Open Court.

Tezuka, Osamu. 1977. *Tezuka Osamu manga zenshū 35–37: Aporo no uta*, vols. 1–3. Tokyo: Kōdansha.

Thomas, Roy, and Peter Sanderson. 2007. *The Marvel Vault*. Philadelphia: Running Press.

Tuchman, Barbara. *A Distant Mirror: The Calamitous Fourteenth Century*. Franklin Center, Penn.: Franklin Library, 1978.

———. 1985. *The March of Folly: From Troy to Vietnam*. New York: Random House.

Ullman, B. L. 1915. Editor's letter in *Classical Weekly* 8: 201–202.

van Gennep, Arnold. 1909. *Les rites de passage*. Chicago: University of Chicago Press.

Varnum, Robin, and Christina T. Gibbons. 2001. *The Language of Comics: Word and Image*. Jackson: University of Mississippi Press.

Versaci, Rocco. 2007. *This Book Contains Graphic Language: Comics as Literature*. New York: Continuum.

Veugen, Jil. 2005. "Response to Tadhg Kelly on the Hero's Journey." *Gamasutra*. http://www.gamasutra.com/php-bin/letter_display.php?letter_id=894.

Vogler, Christopher. 2007. *The Writer's Journey: Mythic Structure for Writers*, 3rd ed. Studio City, Calif.: Michael Wiese Productions.

Volkmann, Hans. 1958. *Cleopatra: A Study in Politics and Propaganda*, trans. T. J. Cadoux. New York: Sagamore.

Vout, Caroline. 1996. "The Myth of the Toga: Understanding the History of Roman Dress." *Greece and Rome* 43.2: 204–20.

Voytilla, Stuart. 1999. *Myth and the Movies: Discovering the Mythic Structure of 50 Unforgettable Films*. Studio City, CA: Michael Wiese Productions.

Wagner, Pamela, dir. 1999. *The Mythology of Star Wars with George Lucas and Bill Moyers*. Films for the Humanities.

Wallace-Hadrill, Andrew. 1983. *Suetonius: The Scholar and His Caesars*. London: Duckworth.

Wasley, Aidan. 2005. "Star Wars: Episodes I–VI: The Greatest Postmodern Art Film Ever." *Slate*. http://www.slate.com/id/2129225.

Waugh, Eric-Jon. 2007. "GDC: Evan Skolnick Asks Game Writers to 'Make It Snappier.' " *Gamasutra*. http://www.gamasutra.com/php-bin/news_index.php?story=12999.

Webster, T. B. L. 1972. *Potter and Patron in Classical Athens*. London: Methuen.

Weinraub, Bernard. 1999. "Luke Skywalker Goes Home." In *George Lucas: Interviews*, ed. Sally Kline, 216–25. Jackson: University Press of Mississippi.

Weinstein, Simcha. 2006. *Up, Up, and Oy Vey!: How Jewish History, Culture, and Values Shaped the Comic Book Superhero*. Baltimore: Leviathan.

Weitzmann, Kurt. 1947. *Illustrations in Roll and Codex: A Study of the Origin and Method of Text Illustration*. Princeton: Princeton University Press.

———. 1959. *Ancient Book Illumination*. Cambridge, Mass.: Harvard University Press.

———. 1977. *Late Antique and Early Christian Book Illumination*. London: Chatto and Windus.

Wertham, Fredric. 1954. *Seduction of the Innocent*. New York: Rinehart.

West, Martin L. 1978. *Hesiod: Works and Days*. Oxford: Clarendon.

———. 1982. *Greek Metre*. New York: Oxford University Press.

Westbrook, Raymond. 1992. *The Trial Scene in the Iliad. Harvard Studies in Classical Philology* 94: 53–76.

Whitehouse, Helen. 2007. "Drawing a Fine Line in Oxyrhynchus." In *Oxyrhynchus: A City and Its Texts*, ed. Alan K. Bowman, Revel A. Coles, Nikolaos Gonis, Dirk Obbink, and Peter J. Parsons, 296–307. London: Egypt Exploration Society.

Willcock, Malcolm M. 1976. *A Companion to the Iliad*. Chicago: University of Chicago Press.

Williams, Craig A. 1995. "Greek Love at Rome." *Classical Quarterly*, n.s. 45.2: 517–39.

———. 1999. *Roman Homosexuality: Ideologies of Masculinity in Classical Antiquity*. New York: Oxford University Press.

Winkler, Martin M., ed. 1991. *Classics and the Cinema*. Lewisburg, Penn.: Bucknell University Press.

———, ed. 2001. *Classical Myth and Culture in the Cinema*. New York: Oxford University Press.

———, ed. 2005. *Gladiator: Film and History*. Malden, Mass.: Blackwell.

———, ed. 2006. *Spartacus: Film and History*. Malden, Mass.: Blackwell.

———, ed. 2007. *Troy: From Homer's Iliad to Hollywood Epic*. Malden, Mass.: Blackwell.

Wohl, Victoria. 1993. "Standing by the *Stathmos*: The Creation of Sexual Ideology in the *Odyssey*." *Arethusa* 26: 19–50.

Wolff, Jurgen, and Kerry Cox. 1988. *Successful Scriptwriting*. Cincinnati: Writer's Digest Books.

Wolk, Douglas. 2007. *Reading Comics: How Graphic Novels Work and What They Mean*. Cambridge, Mass.: Da Capo.

———. 2008. "War Goes Graphic." *Salon.com*. http://www.salon.com/books/review/2008/02/21/shanower.

Wright, Bradford W. 2003. *Comic Book Nation: The Transformation of Youth Culture in America*. Baltimore: Johns Hopkins University Press.

Wyke, Maria. 1997. *Projecting the Past: Ancient Rome, Cinema, and History*. New York: Routledge.

Zakaria, Fareed. 2004. "How We Could Have Done It Right. Like It's 1999." *New Republic*. http://www.fareedzakaria.com/ARTICLES/other/nr_2004.html.

Ziolkowski, Jan M., and Michael C. J. Putnam, eds. 2008. *The Virgilian Tradition: The First Fifteen Hundred Years*. New Haven: Yale University Press.

Index